Justice v. Law in Greek Political Thought

Politikos III

The other titles in the Politikos series are

Educating the Ambitious: Leadership and Political Rule in Greek Political Thought, edited by Leslie G. Rubin. Pittsburgh: Duquesne University Press, 1992.

Aristotle's Criticism of Socratic Political Unity in Plato's Republic, edited by Kent Moors. Pittsburgh: Duquesne University Press, 1989.

Justice v. Law in Greek Political Thought

Edited by
Leslie G. Rubin

ROWMAN & LITTLEFIELD PUBLISHERS, INC.
Lanham • New York • Boulder • Oxford

ROWMAN & LITTLEFIELD PUBLISHERS, INC.

Published in the United States of America
by Rowman & Littlefield Publishers, Inc.
4720 Boston Way, Lanham, Maryland 20706

12 Hid's Copse Road
Cummor Hill, Oxford OX2 9JJ, England

Chapter 1, "The Problematic Character of Socrates' Defense of Justice in Plato's Republic,"
originally appeared in *Interpretation*, 1996. Reprinted with permission.
Chapter 6, "The Roots of the Laws" originally appeared in *Metaphysics as Rhetoric: Alfarabi's
Summary of Plato's "Laws"* by Joshua Parens. Published by State University of New York Press,
Albany. Copyright © 1995 State University of New York. All rights reserved.
Chapter 7, "Hegel, the Author and Authority in Sophocles' *Antigone*" © 1996 by William E.
Conklin.
Chapter 8, "Aristotle on How to Preserve a Regime," is reprinted in slightly revised form from
Judith A. Swanson, *The Public and the Private in Aristotle's Political Philosophy.* Copyright ©
1992 by Cornell University. Used by permission of the publisher, Cornell University Press.
Chapter 9, "Aristotle and American Classical Republicanism," © 1996 by Fred D. Miller, Jr.

British Cataloging in Publication Information Available

Library of Congress Cataloging-in-Publication Data

Justice v. law in Greek political thought / edited by Leslie G. Rubin.
    p. cm.
    Includes bibliographical references and index.
    ISBN 0–8476–8422–9 (alk. paper). — ISBN 0–8476–8423–7 (pbk. : alk. paper)
    1. Justice. 2. Law, Greek. 3. Philosophy, Ancient. I. Rubin, Leslie G.
K246.J834   1997
340'.11—dc20   96–38949

Printed in the United States of America

⊖™ The paper used in this publication meets the minimum requirements of American
National Standard for Information Sciences—Permanence of Paper for Printed Library
Materials, ANSI Z39.48–1984.

Contents

Preface

Leslie G. Rubin

Especially during an election year, but, let's face it, every year is an election year, we are reminded that a large segment of the American populace believes that law and order is a top priority for its governments. Also during an election year, such a popular medium as *Parade* magazine asks in a cover story, "Is Justice Possible?" and points to popularly perceived miscarriages of justice in the court system. In the popular mind, we know both that humans are fallible and therefore need laws to support just relationships among them, and that humans are fallible and therefore laws will be either imperfectly written or imperfectly implemented. Right at the juncture of justice and law lies a perennial political problem—a problem that has grave political ramifications both for the lives of the individuals prosecuted by the laws and for the moral character and the morale of the people who regularly abide by the laws.

Do we believe the law good because it is just, or is it just because we think it is good? To what degree or under what circumstances should the law be judged by a standard external to the community that creates it? To what degree is our understanding of justice determined by the laws under which we live? Is there a body of laws, a way of life regulated by law, that is simply the most just? Are there certain universal requirements that any tolerably just law or constitution must fulfill? These questions are not by any means confined to liberal democracy. They are as old as political order itself. Yet they pose an acute problem for us because the more people are empowered to participate in the formulation of law, the more widespread the feeling of helplessness in the face of the dilemma.

The multifaceted and subtle arguments of the Greeks demonstrate the perennial nature of the problem and suggest some practical political teachings to ameliorate its effects, though a final solution seems impossible. This, the third, *Politikos* collection of essays addresses the relationship of justice to law through the works of Homer, Herodotus, Plato, Aristotle, Sophocles, and the medieval Islamic thinker, Alfarabi. The issues explored include the foundations of our understanding of justice; the foundations of the authority of the law; the relative merits of the rule of law versus the rule of a wise and just king; and the necessity of the rule of law to the goodness and success of a political order. Often the authors make explicit comparisons to modern situations and contemporary debates.

The main issues raised by each essay fall into two broad categories: those beginning with the notion of justice and proceeding to discuss law, and those beginning with the law and ascending to discuss justice more generally. In each of the two parts of the collection we begin with the more generally theoretical accounts and move to more specific examinations of legal problems.

Part One: Beginning from Justice

It is not surprising that one of the two key works examined in this part of the book is Plato's *Republic*. What may be more unusual is the attention paid to Homer's epics in connection with one of the most abstract yet crucial questions of political philosophy: What is justice? Perhaps it is a result of Plato's success in arguing that poetry cannot give the most satisfactory account of the deepest questions that we do not generally take Homer seriously as a political thinker, but Nick Janszen and Patrick J. Deneen argue persuasively for the abandonment of that prejudice.

First, however, we take up the search for justice from a vantage point outside the city of Athens and away from the stricter enforcement of laws, i.e., in the *Republic*. Looking at Socrates' defense of justice in that work, In Ha Jang focuses on three sections: Book II, in which Glaucon and Adeimantus demand such a defense, Book IV, in which Socrates seems to provide it, and Book VII, in which the discussion of the philosopher-king raises questions about the justice of Kallipolis' laws and, more fundamentally, about Socrates' definition of justice in the first place.

Demonstrating another way to approach Socrates' puzzling defense of justice, Katherine Philippakis' article examines the stories of Gyges told by Herodotus and by Glaucon in the *Republic*. When demanding a defense of the life of justice for its own sake, Glaucon uses Gyges' life as an example of committing unjust acts—adultery, murder, and usurpation—without suffering bad consequences. Can we say persuasively that Gyges' life was bad and that the life of justice should be chosen even if we could get away with murder? Or is it the case that the goodness of laws enforcing justice applies only to the powerless, but those who can make themselves invisible, in some sense, i.e., immune to the law, can commit injustice quite happily? Philippakis points to the Myth of Er and suggests that Socrates can give no philosophically satisfactory answer to Glaucon. He must tell a story of his own that makes justice look preferable to the life of pleasure ordinarily understood.

John T. Scott also examines the *Republic* from the perspective of Book II, in this case the very beginning of Socrates' answer to Glaucon's demand for a defense of justice. We look in detail at the "city of sows" that Socrates discusses first in pursuit of a city in which justice can be seen and analyzed. Scott argues that the criticism of Plato's *Republic* in Book II of the *Politics* far from exhausts Aristotle's analysis of that complex book, and yet provides a key both to Aristotle's understanding of the whole *Republic* and to Aristotle's own political theory. The problems that prompt Socrates and his interlocutors to add to and modify the "city of sows" remain central to the character of the kallipolis they eventually build—there is no justice there. Aristotle's criticism of his teacher and friend is, in Scott's view, an act of justice that teaches us that people in cities differ, not accidentally, but essentially. Justice is dealing with those differences, and justice so understood makes for politics. It is the refusal to deal with those differences, to do justice through laws, that makes the *Republic* apolitical.

In stark contrast to Socrates' explicit arguments, but perhaps deeply in tune with Socrates' actions in the *Republic*, Nick Janszen argues that poetry is more powerful and more persuasive than philosophy in defining and promulgating justice. Through what he calls "The Divine Comedy of Homer," Janszen sees a coherent and profound teaching about the "fundamental tension between the rational and irrational parts of the soul," which accounts for the difficulty of knowing and doing justice in the human world. Rather than subdue the irrational to the rational part, Homer seems to teach that the two must be reconciled to produce true justice.

In another look at the political implications of Homer's poetry, Patrick J. Deneen sees the Odyssey as something of an allegory of the voyage of political theory toward an understanding of the relationship of justice and the natural world. Odysseus' progress toward home and reestablishment of law in Ithaka, like the birth of political philosophy, contain the seed of a democracy only to grow and be defended much later.

Part Two: Beginning from Law

Approaching the relationship of justice to law from the point of view of the law, takes our authors into different texts. In this area, Plato's *Laws* comes to mind, as well as Aristotle's *Politics* and *Rhetoric*. These books take the specific arrangements of a city seriously and ask what they have to do with doing justice or creating a just way of life. This section of the collection also takes up the powerful challenge to human laws posed by Antigone's impassioned speeches in Sophocles' play. When discussing law made by human beings for human beings, the necessity for persuasion and force arises. Practical experience teaches that people do not obey laws simply because they are sensible, but often must be coerced in some way to do the right thing. When their refusal to obey turns on the rightness of the laws, the political question of order turns into the philosophical question of justice.

As in his book, *Metaphysics as Rhetoric*, Joshua Parens here uses Alfarabi's *Summary of Plato's "Laws"* to discuss the foundations of law. Unlike the medieval Christian commentators on Plato, Alfarabi was able to see that the legislation and argumentation in Plato's *Laws* were rooted not in theology or what came to be known as "natural law," but rather in natural right. Parens argues that both Alfarabi and Plato emphasize the philosophical and political defenses of law above the theological approach. There is a need for both a theoretically solid examination of the purpose of law in general and a rhetorically solid public defense of the particular laws under which a city lives.

Using Hegelian categories to analyze Antigone's situation, William E. Conklin distinguishes between the authority of divine law and that of human law. Like Parens, Conklin sees the differences between theological justification and political rhetoric as crucial, and he goes on to suggest that they are irreconcilable.

Once the justice of some particular laws has been questioned, it seems natural to ask: What fundamental laws *would* be best for human society? How *is* order to be maintained and justice done in practical life? Who among us are suited to take the lead in writing laws, and how are they to decide which punishments are appropriate to which crimes?

The contribution of Judith A. Swanson, which is reprinted in slightly revised form from her book, *The Public and the Private in Aristotle's Political Philosophy*, argues that Aristotle got the jump on modern constitutionalism by "identifying the rule of law as the foremost preserver of regimes." Aristotle's development of the characteristics of the rule of law, discovered through an account of his regime called polity, bring out three characteristics which render it effective in preserving a decent regime.

Also emphasizing the rule of law and the modern relevance of Aristotle's theories of the middling constitution, Fred D. Miller, Jr., looks carefully at the writings of various American founders, John Adams prominent among them, for the lessons they gleaned from wrestling with the writings of Aristotle.

Taking the issue from another angle, Clifford A. Bates, Jr., sees the roots of Aristotle's defense of the rule of law in his critique of Plato's philosopher-king, what Aristotle calls the *pambasileia*.

The rule of law, of course, entails the existence of lawmakers or legislators. Is the task of making laws subject to general principles or what may be called a "science"? Arguing that Aristotle views the lawgiver as, in part, a physician of the regime, Tim Collins tries to show that the *Politics* and the *Nicomachean Ethics* are lessons in Aristotelean "legislative science," that is, in conservative reform toward aristocracy in the process of preserving what is good about an existing regime.

Which people are best suited to the making of laws? Can they be distinguished from the general citizenry? Paul Bullen also considers the lawmakers in his article, and he examines Aristotle's *Politics*, in conjunction with the *Ethics* and a close examination of a passage in the *Rhetoric*, to get a profile of the lawmaker and the means by which he is to be distinguished from "ordinary people."

Practically speaking, the death penalty is the ultimate law. By looking closely at "The Death Penalty in Plato's *Laws*," Brian Calvert shows much about the theory behind its use and poses questions through which we can examine its justice. He also asks how much of Plato's view applies to contemporary debates over the death penalty.

All the papers in this collection were presented at panels sponsored by the Society for Greek Political Thought, North American Chapter, at meetings of the American Political Science Association, the Midwest Political Science Association, and the Southwest Social Sciences Association over the past four years. The Society attempts to encourage interdisciplinary discussion across the many schools of thought currently brought to bear upon issues in Greek political theory. I hope this collection illustrates some success in that attempt.

By way of doing justice on a small scale, I heartily acknowledge the help of all of the contributors and the patience of Rowman & Littlefield's Robin Adler and Julie Kuzneski during the preparation of the manuscript.

Thanks are also due to the previous publishers of three of the contributions: "Aristotle on How to Preserve a Regime: Maintaining Precedent,

Privacy, and Peace through the Rule of Law" is reprinted in slightly revised form from Judith A. Swanson: *The Public and the Private in Aristotle's Political Philosophy.* Copyright © 1992 by Cornell University. Used by permission of the publisher, Cornell University Press. In Ha Jang's "The Problematic Character of Socrates' Defense of Justice in Plato's *Republic*" is reprinted with permission from *Interpretation.* "The Foundations and Defense of Law" is reprinted from *Metaphysics as Rhetoric: Alfarabi's Summary of Plato's "Laws"* by Joshua Parens by permission of the State University of New York Press. Published by State University of New York Press, Albany. Copyright ©1995 State University of New York. All rights reserved.

Without the generous support, moral and technical, of my husband, this book would never have been completed. Indeed, without his confidence in my editing capabilities and in the power of WordPerfect, it might never have been begun. Thanks, Charlie.

PART ONE

Beginning from Justice

Chapter 1

The Problematic Character
of Socrates' Defense of Justice
in Plato's *Republic*

In Ha Jang

Of the many great scholarly controversies regarding Plato's *Republic*, two deserve especially to be noted for their interconnection.[1] The first controversy, started by Sachs several decades ago and kept alive by numerous responses since then, concerns this problem: although Glaucon and Adeimantus at the beginning of Book Two ask for a defense of justice as ordinarily understood, Socrates responds in Book Four by defending justice on the basis of a definition of the justice of the individual that appears to have little link with justice as ordinarily understood.[2] The other controversy—which is much older but is still a source of sharp debate today—deals with Socrates' argument in Book Seven that it would be just for the philosophers to rule in the best regime even if this entails their having to lead worse lives. How can Socrates hope to defend justice in thus pointing to a crucial instance where justice seems to be at odds with happiness?[3] It is obvious that the issues that gave rise to these heretofore separate controversies are linked in that they both bear on the question of the adequacy of Socrates' defense of justice in the *Republic*. But the connection between these issues, in this and other important respects, has not been sufficiently explored and emphasized by those who have participated in the controversies.[4] I here seek to remedy this situation in the course of considering the overarching theme of the problematic character of Socrates' defense of justice in the *Republic*.

In trying to understand Socrates' view of justice in the *Republic*, it is important for us to take account of the fact that he presents, throughout most of the work, a defense of justice. In Book One, for example, having heard Thrasymachus' assertion that justice is not good at all for the one who practices it (338c-339a, 343b-344c), Socrates defends justice by getting him to agree to the following: that justice is both virtue and wisdom; that it is stronger than injustice; and that it brings happiness (348a-354a). But it is not too hard to see that Socrates, in his discussion with Thrasymachus, is not above defending justice by hook or by crook. Thus Glaucon and Adeimantus are justified, at the beginning of Book Two, in forcing Socrates to provide a truly adequate defense of justice (357a-367e). That Socrates engages in a rhetorical defense of justice in Book One, however, serves as a clear warning to us. There is no guarantee that the defense of justice that Socrates provides in the rest of the *Republic* is not itself rhetorical. Just as Thrasymachus may be too easily charmed by Socrates' arguments—as Glaucon suggests (358b)—we must beware of suffering the same fate. I argue that Socrates' defense of justice in the rest of the *Republic*, designed to prove that justice is intrinsically good and that it is better than injustice, is in fact problematic. This paper delineates the key difficulties of this defense, to which one must pay the utmost attention in attempting to grasp Socrates' view of justice in the *Republic*.

Justice in the Socratic Sense

Responding to the request of Glaucon and Adeimantus for a true defense of the justice of the individual, Socrates first endeavors to bring to light the justice of the city. For, he says, since the justice of the city is bigger and easier to see than the justice of the individual, it is better for those who cannot see sharply to turn to the justice of the individual after examining the justice of the city (368c-369b). To facilitate the discovery of the justice of the city, Socrates outlines (through Book Four) a succession of cities: first, the city based on needs; next, the luxurious city; and, finally, the city purged of luxuries—a city that is characterized by the existence of a warrior class, the recipients of an extensive civic or moral education (369a-427c). After looking for justice in this last city, the good or virtuous city (in which justice is most likely to be found [420b-c, 434d-e]), Socrates declares that the justice of the city can be defined as each of the three classes of the city—whether it is the ruling, guarding, or wage-earning class—minding its own business (432d-434c). Then, on the premise that the justice of the city is parallel to the justice of the individual, Socrates defines the justice of the individual as each of the three parts of the soul—the rational, the spirited, and the appetitive—minding its own business (442d-e, 443c-e).[5] He also makes clear that the just individual is concerned not with affairs that are external to him but with the harmony of his own soul; and that such an individual calls "just" any action, whether political or otherwise, that helps produce this condition in the soul (443c-e). By arguing that the justice of the individual as defined in this way is analogous to the health of the body, moreover, Socrates ultimately leads us to draw the conclusion that justice is intrinsically good because it is a kind of health of the soul (444d-445b).

Unfortunately, however, there are difficulties with Socrates' definition of the justice of the individual, on which his argument in favor of the intrinsic goodness of justice relies. In the first place, while according to this definition the just man is concerned with the harmony of his own soul or with his own good, the just man is ordinarily thought of as being eminently devoted to others or to the common good.[6] Furthermore, according to this definition, the just man calls "just" any action that conduces to the harmony of his own soul. Hence this definition has the troubling implication that, at least in principle, an action that is ordinarily considered unjust could be just (and vice versa). It also has the surprising result that an action that is not even in the realm of justice and injustice—for instance, the act of engaging in mathematical studies—could, in principle, be just or unjust. These difficulties cast doubt on Socrates' assurance that the justice of the individual as embodied in his definition would be perfectly in keeping with the ordinary standards of justice—that is, his assurance that the just man who allows each of the parts of his soul to mind its own business would not steal, cheat, dishonor his parents, and so on (442e-443b).[7] Socrates' definition of the justice of the individual, for all these reasons, is paradoxical and has little relation to justice as ordinarily understood. It contrasts with the more commonsensical definitions of justice offered in Book One, e.g., justice as giving back what one takes and telling the truth (331b-c).[8] We have to wonder, then, whether Socrates' definition of the justice of the individual in Book Four is not arbitrary, a mere invention of his mind. If it is arbitrary, Socrates' defense of justice, to the extent that it relies on such an arbitrary definition, would not be adequate.[9]

As noted, this definition is based on the existence of a strict parallelism between the justice of the city and the justice of the individual (368e-369a, 434d-435a, 441d-e, 442d-443c). But the questionable character of this premise is ultimately acknowledged by Socrates himself: while he tries to support the existence of such a parallelism through making the lengthy argument that the soul, like the city, has three parts, Socrates reveals—precisely in the context of elaborating on the justice of the individual—that there may be more than three parts of the soul (435b-441c, 443d-e).[10] In opposition to the above premise, moreover, we can point out that justice sometimes demands much more from individuals than from cities. During times of war, for instance, individuals are often asked to sacrifice their lives on behalf of justice; but cities are seldom, if ever, asked to sacrifice their existence on behalf of justice. It is also worth observing that Socrates is not completely successful at giving definitions of justice that would lead one to believe firmly in the existence of a strict parallelism between the justice of the city and the justice of the individual. First, his definition of the justice of the city as each of the three classes of the city's minding its own business is consistent with rule by merit and absolute dedication to the city, which are ordinarily believed to be just (420b-421c). Hence it is not as paradoxical as his definition of the justice of the individual as each of the three parts of the soul's minding its own business.[11] Second, his definition of the justice of the city does not necessarily rule out the potential lack of happiness in any one of the three classes of the city (419a-421c; cf. 465e-466c, 519e-520a). But, by contrast, his definition of the justice of the individual is not indicated to entail the potential unhappiness of any one part of the soul.

Despite the questionable character of the argument that results in Socrates' definition of the justice of the individual, it is possible that this definition, taken by itself, could be correct. Yet, as noted, there are difficulties connected with this definition considered by itself—such as, that according to this definition the just man is exclusively concerned with his own good. This particular aspect of the definition, though, appears to receive some justification from Socrates' analysis of the justice of the city (as discovered in a good or virtuous city). While Socrates' definition of the justice of the city does not take account of foreign affairs, it is in keeping with the good or virtuous city's looking exclusively to its own advantage. Indeed, Socrates indicates that such a city takes care of its own good in a less than scrupulous way: in order to preserve itself, it promotes something like civil war in other cities (422a-423c). If even the good or virtuous city is guided only by its own good, the question arises whether there is not some justification for describing the just individual as one who is concerned solely with his own good. It can be retorted, however, that the fact that the good city is concerned merely with its own good is problematic from the point of view of justice. That is, one could excuse the good city for pursuing its own good—even to the detriment of other cities—insofar as it must preserve itself; but one could not, at the same time, call such a city positively just, at least with respect to other cities. (Of course, it would be difficult to excuse the good city if it had an expansionist foreign policy that is geared toward neither security nor inner harmony.) This means that the way in which the good or virtuous city behaves toward other cities can hardly be used to justify similar actions on the part of the individual at least if he is to be regarded as *positively* just in regard to other individuals.

The paradoxical character of the justice of the individual in the Socratic sense is underscored by the fact that the most important members of the good and just city, as described from Book Two through Book Four, do not necessarily possess such justice. Socrates does give the impression at one point that both the guardians and the rulers of this city would be able, through the sort of education they receive, to acquire the justice of the individual as harmony of the soul (441e-442a). Yet he delineates the following two ingredients of such justice, which neither the guardians nor the rulers would possess: the wisdom of the individual that consists in the knowledge of what is beneficial for each of the three parts of the soul as well as for the soul as a whole (442c, 443e-444a); and, the rule in the soul of the reasoning part that provides "speeches"—i.e., reasoned arguments—as to what is truly to be feared and is capable of making one wise as an individual (442c). Instead of being guided by the "speeches" about what is to be feared, the guardians rely on the "lawful opinion" as to what is terrible and what is not (429a-430c). The rulers, moreover, are wise in the sense of knowing how the city as a whole would best deal with itself and the other cities (428c-d). But, while they are thus the source of the city's being wise, they do not necessarily possess the wisdom of the individual as embodied in the knowledge of what is good for the individual soul. Indeed, they are chosen to be rulers only if they have love for the city as well as the accompanying conviction that one must do what is best for the city (412c-d). Yet Socrates reveals that this conviction is not simply true—at least insofar as it is meant to be in keeping with the assumption that a man would "love something most when he believed that the same things are advantageous to it and to himself, and when he supposed that if it did well, he too himself would do well along with it, and if it didn't, neither would he" (412d). For, in response to Adeimantus' objection that he is making those who govern the city unhappy, Socrates argues that what is best for the city need not be consistent in every case with the individual good (420b-c; cf. 465e-466c, 519e-520a).

While they are not just in the Socratic sense, however, the guardians and rulers would be regarded as just in the ordinary sense.[12] They certainly contribute to the justice of the city understood as each of the classes' doing its own job and are devoted otherwise to the good of the city. For they would send even their own children to a lower class to ensure rule by merit. And, in having no privacy and no more property than what is needed, they would remain guardians and rulers instead of becoming money-makers and hence would preserve the city (414d-417b). In being dedicated in these ways to the city and its justice, moreover, they would, from the perspective of ordinary justice, be considered to be just as individuals. But Socrates indicates that they are far from being just on purely rational grounds: their justice is dependent on the noble lie as well as on the institutional arrangements concerning privacy and property that are forced upon them (414d-417b). (So too, while defending the city would not only be an act of courage but also to some extent an act of justice [see 332e], the guardians would defend the city on the basis only of lawful opinion [429a-430c]. And, the rulers would do what is best for the city and hence be just in the ordinary sense as a result of a mere conviction, whose truth is not beyond dispute [412c-d].) Socrates, of course, never speaks thematically about justice in outlining the official discussion of the education for the rulers and guardians. For he does not want to speak about their education to justice prior to discovering what the truth about justice is—even if this means refraining from criticizing certain traditional views on justice that cast doubt on its goodness (392a-b). Thus, contrary to the expectation that he raises at the outset, his discussion of their education does not contribute, in any obvious fashion, to an understanding of justice (376c-d). But, after his discussion of their official education, he indicates, in various ways, that the sort of justice that they would acquire would be less than fully rational. The question that Socrates appears to pose therefore is this: can ordinary justice rest on a strictly rational foundation, just as justice in the Socratic sense surely does?

The definition of the justice of the individual in Book Four, as analyzed in the foregoing, must also be considered in the light of what occurs in the rest of the *Republic*. Having examined the virtues of both the city and the individual, Socrates attempts, at the end of Book Four, to turn to a discussion of the forms of vice (445c-e). Yet, at the beginning of Book Five, he is asked by Adeimantus to delve into the proposal for the community of women and children, a proposal that he had mentioned without any discussion in founding his good city (449c, 423e-424a). Hence he is induced, in the first place, to outline the arrangement concerning the equality of the sexes (which is in keeping with the community of women and men in education) and to show its possibility and goodness (451d-457c). He then is led to indicate the character of the community of women and children as well as its goodness (457c-466d). Asked to show, however, the possibility of the community of women and children, Socrates introduces the proposal for the philosopher-kings—the greatest of the three waves (471c-473e). This has the result, as Glaucon points out, that from Book Five through Book Seven Socrates brings to light a finer city and individual than he had earlier done (543c-544a). Now, Socrates and Glaucon agree, at the end of Book Seven, that it is plain who this finer individual is (541b). And it is safe to say that they have in mind the philosopher: the philosopher, after all, is the individual who is parallel to the city ruled by philosophers. Socrates confirms this when he turns to an analysis of the defective regimes and individuals in Book Eight. He there identifies the "good and just man" with the father of the timocratic man; and this man is almost a caricature of Socrates himself (544e, 549c-550b).[13] By calling the philosopher good and just, then, Socrates puts forward the equation of the just man and the philosopher. He makes this equation quite explicit in trying to prove that justice is better than injustice in Book Nine. For he employs the argument that tyranny, i.e., injustice *par excellence*, is inferior to justice because the pleasures of the philosopher are better and more real than the pleasures of the tyrant (580d-587e). This is a crucial development in Socrates' argument, especially since the equation of the just man and the philosopher is from the ordinary perspective rather suspect (see 473e-474a and 487b-d).

In the light of this development, we must ask, "What is the status of the definition of the justice of the individual as provided in Book Four?" The account of the soul on which this definition is based certainly goes through some revision by the end of Book Nine: while still maintaining the existence of the three parts of the soul, Socrates reveals that the rational and spirited parts of the soul have desires and pleasures of their own (580d-583a; cf. 435e-441c).[14] But the definition of the justice of the individual given in Book Four too undergoes some modification. Socrates, at the end of Book Nine, modifies that definition by making clear that the philosopher is just in the sense outlined in Book Four. Speaking of the just man who would rule in the best regime—that is, the philosopher—Socrates says, in terms that hark back to his statements regarding the just man in Book Four, that such a man is concerned with the harmony of his own soul and does everything with a view to bringing about such harmony (591c-592b; cf. 549c-550b, 496d).[15] This turn in the argument may not be wholly surprising. For the just man in Book Four is described as being ruled by reason and able to act on the basis of wisdom regarding what is best for his soul as a whole (443c-444a). Hence he is a harbinger of the philosopher, who seeks, if not possesses, the knowledge of the good (504a-521b).[16] But, insofar as the philosopher is just in the sense outlined in Book Four, the equation of the just man and the philosopher is problematic for the same reasons that the definition of justice in Book Four is problematic. To begin with, the philosopher does not act wholly in accordance with ordinary standards of justice—his activity of thinking, for instance, requires that he question the authority of law (consider in this regard Socrates' discussion of dialectics [537e-539a]). Furthermore, he spends a substantial amount of his time in activities that appear to have very little connection with justice (such as, investigating what nature is). But the main difficulty is that the philosopher would be concerned exclusively with his own good. For, in being just in the sense described in Book Four, he does everything for the sake of the harmony or health of his own soul.

From the point of view of ordinary justice, contributing to the good of others if and only if it is conducive to one's own good would be question-able. But the possible coincidence between what one does in pursuing one's own good and what is good for others is critical in terms of establishing at least some link between justice in the Socratic sense and justice as ordinarily understood. Socrates points to the existence of such a coincidence precisely in the context of making clear, at the end of Book Nine, that the philosopher is just in the Socratic sense. In response to Glaucon's statement that the man who is just in the sense of pursuing a healthy soul would not mind the political things, Socrates declares that such a man—i.e., the philosopher—would mind the political things at least in the best regime (592a-b).[17] Unfortunately, that the philosopher would rule in no other city suggests the remoteness, at least on the political level, of the possibility of a coincidence between the good of the individual who is just in the Socratic sense and the good of others. For, according to Socrates, it is very difficult, though not impossible, for the best regime to come into being (499b-d, 502c, 540d). It should be noted, moreover, that Socrates says that ultimately it does not matter whether the regime in which the philosophers rule is or will be somewhere (592b). For the best regime that exists in speeches can serve as a vehicle for individual reform by being a pattern "for the man who wants to see and found a city within himself on the basis of what he sees" (592b). At any rate, Socrates provides an extended argument in favor of the possibility of philosophic rule in his discussion from Book Five through Book Seven. Hence an examination of this discussion will help us to see whether there can really be any coincidence on the political level between the good of the individual who is just in the Socratic sense and the good of others. In another respect, too, this discussion will shed light on the precise relation between justice in the Socratic sense (as practiced by the philosopher) and justice as ordinarily understood: while being silent about the philosopher's being just in sense described in Book Four, Socrates there speaks explicitly of the way in which the philosophers can be said to be just in the ordinary sense.

The Philosopher-Kings and Justice in the Socratic Sense

In Book Five, Socrates puts forward the proposal for the philosopher-kings as the single necessary and sufficient condition for the transformation of an ordinary city into the best regime (473b-e).[18] In defending this proposal against Glaucon's vehement objection, Socrates tries to show, among other things, that "it is by nature fitting for [philosophers] both to engage in philosophy and to lead a city, and for the rest not to engage in philosophy and to follow the leader" (473e-474a, 474b-c). According to Socrates, the philosophers are fit to rule for the following reasons: they would be best able to guard, as well as to give, the laws of the city because they are superior intellectually (due to their being able alone to comprehend the *ideas*); and they are neither lacking in experience nor inferior in the rest of virtue (484b-c, 484d). After listing a number of the philosopher's virtues, moreover, Socrates makes clear that there is no way in which "the orderly man, who isn't a lover of money, or illiberal, or a boaster, or a coward, could become a hard-bargainer or unjust"; and hence that, starting from youth, a philosophic soul would be both just and gentle (486b). Thus, while he is more or less silent about the philosopher's being just in the sense described in Book Four, Socrates here argues that the philosopher is qualified to rule in part because he is just in the ordinary sense. It is worth noting, however, that Socrates hints at the fact that the philosopher would be just in this sense simply because he lacks interest in those things that ordinarily lead to injustice. As Socrates suggests, the philosopher is concerned not with the pleasures of the body but with those of the soul. And, "when someone's desires incline strongly to some one thing, they are therefore weaker with respect to the rest, like a stream that has been channeled off in that other direction" (485d).[19] At any rate, if the philosophers are fit to rule for the reasons that Socrates mentions, they would have the capacity to be just in the broad sense of being able to provide for the common good.

But, expressing a strong doubt as to the justice of the philosophers, Adeimantus objects to the proposal for the philosopher-kings on the grounds that the most decent of the philosophers are useless while the rest are all but vicious (487b-d). In response, Socrates first indicates through an image that the philosopher, who possesses the true political skill, is useless to the city because ordinary political life is so defective that it allows only those who are skillful merely at gaining political power to rule (488a-489b). He makes clear, moreover, that in this situation the blame for the uselessness of the philosophers must be placed on those who do not make use of them: "For it's not natural that a pilot beg sailors to be ruled by him nor that the wise go to the doors of the rich" (489b). As for Adeimantus' charge that the philosophers are vicious, Socrates offers the counter charge that potential philosophers are corrupted by the city itself, which is the true sophist (489d-495c). Having done so, he points out that the philosophers' reputation for viciousness is due merely to the pretenders to philosophy (495c-496a). Returning to the theme of the uselessness of the philosophers, he then makes the following argument: the philosopher cannot safely come to the aid of justice in ordinary cities—and be useful in this way—given the savageness present within those cities; hence he is forced to mind his own business instead of participating in politics in a substantial way (496a-e). To this, Glaucon replies that the philosopher would still leave his life here "having accomplished not the least of things" (497a). But Socrates remarks in turn that he would not accomplish "the greatest either if he didn't chance upon a suitable regime. For in a suitable one he himself will grow more and save the common things along with the private" (497a). To the extent that saving the common things along with the private is tantamount to justice, Socrates here asserts that justice is the greatest of things—something which, under the right circumstances, the philosophers would be able to come to the aid of. Furthermore, Socrates indicates that justice is beneficial for the philosophers themselves in implying that they would "grow more" in saving the common things along with the private.

Socrates' overall argument in defense of the proposal for the philosopher-kings, as outlined in the foregoing, is open to a number of questions. The first question has to do with Socrates' view as to the right conditions under which the philosophers would rule. In the passage where he speaks about the greatest of things, Socrates describes the philosophers' simply coming upon a suitable regime in which they would rule (497a; cf. 497b-c). But he first indicated that the rule of philosophers is the single necessary and sufficient condition for the transformation of an ordinary city into the best regime (473b-473e). Hence it is not clear that the right conditions under which the philosophers would rule will be present without any action on the part of the philosophers themselves. In this connection, it is worth calling attention to the fact that, while he initially points to the need for a coincidence of philosophy and political power (473c-d; cf. 592a), Socrates also asserts that some sort of necessity (together with chance) is required: "neither city nor regime will ever become perfect, nor yet will a man become perfect in the same way either, before some *necessity* chances to constrain those few philosophers who aren't vicious, those now called useless, to take charge of a city, whether they want to or not, and the city to obey" (499b-c, my emphasis; see also 499c-d and 500d). But it remains to be seen whether such necessity—which would have to overcome the great obstacles to the philosophers' being useful (and hence being positively just) in ordinary cities—would ever exist. We observe that, by saying here that there needs to be some sort of necessity for the philosophers to lead a city "whether they want to or not," Socrates raises the difficulty that the philosophers may not, for reasons yet to be made fully clear, willingly undertake the transformation of an ordinary city into the best regime. But he also leaves the impression that the philosophers would ultimately welcome such a transformation by pointing to the view that they will become "perfect" only by becoming rulers. Unless the best regime is possible, though, such perfection (not to mention the growth of the philosophers that Socrates mentions at 497a) would be imaginary.

Even if the best regime is possible—to this issue I will return a bit later—Socrates reveals that the willingness of the philosophers to rule (and hence also their willingness to come to the aid of justice in the ordinary sense) in an already existing best regime is not as certain as he first suggests. In Book Seven, Socrates says that the philosophers ought not to be allowed to pursue philosophy uninterruptedly to the end but that they must take turns in ruling the city (519b-521b). To this, Glaucon asks whether they are not doing an injustice to them in making them live a worse life when a better is possible for them (519b-d). While not contradicting Glaucon's assertion that the philosophers would lead worse lives,[20] Socrates first reminds him of the fact that the concern of law is not to bring about the well-being of any one class in the city but the well-being of the city as a whole (519e-520a). Socrates then states that they will not in fact be doing injustice to the philosophers and that they will say just things to them while compelling them in addition to rule and share in the labors of the city (520a). They will say that when philosophers come into being in ordinary cities it would be fitting for them not to share in the labors of those cities: "For they grow up spontaneously against the will of the regime in each; and a nature that grows by itself and doesn't owe its rearing to anyone has justice on its side when it is not eager to pay off the price of rearing to anyone" (520a-b). But Socrates asserts that they would owe something to the best regime, which is responsible for their receiving a superior education and rearing; and hence that it would be a matter of justice that they rule. Socrates still maintains, however, that they must be compelled to rule (520b-521b).[21] Therefore he points out that the simple appeal to justice is not enough to get the philosophers to act in accordance with justice. The philosophers, in Socrates' account, would indeed be unwillingly just. It is true that, when Socrates asks whether the philosophers would disobey the command to rule, Glaucon replies that this is impossible since they would be "laying just injunctions on just men" (520e). But, having noticed Socrates' stress on the need for compulsion in this case, Glaucon quickly adds that they would still regard ruling as a necessary thing (520e).

Now, Socrates says that the potential philosophers must also be compelled to pursue the study of the Idea of the Good (515c-516c, 519c-d). And, since the compulsion used in this case is something that is ultimately desirable—as it would lead to the greatest good for a human being (519c, 496c)—one might be tempted to believe that the compulsion for the philosophers to rule could also be desirable in the end.[22] But the compulsion to rule is not declared to lead to a positive good at all. Indeed Socrates' paradoxical argument is that the philosophers are fit to rule precisely because they, due to their belief that ruling is not some great good, are least eager to rule and have the most contempt for the political life (520d, 520e-521b, 500b-c; cf. 540d-e).[23] Thus, according to this argument, if the philosophers ever come to regard ruling as a positive good, as do all others who engage in politics, they would no longer be considered as fit to rule. It is significant that Socrates suggests that compulsion would be needed precisely by those who are guided by the study of the good—which he calls the greatest study (503e-506a)—rather than by those who are guided by some sort of conviction or by lawful opinions. The philosophers' keen sense of their own good as separate from the good of the city is responsible for their needing to be compelled to rule. (For the philosophers, ruling would be different from engaging in the greatest studies in that the latter, unlike the former, would ultimately lose its compulsory character. For once one becomes aware that something is good, one would automatically pursue it.) Socrates' reference, at the end of Book Seven, to the philosophers' acting on the basis of the view that justice is the "greatest and the most necessary" thing, then, has to be understood in a certain way (540e; cf. 497a). They would regard justice in this way only in connection with their ruling (540d-e). They would not consider it as the greatest and most necessary simply.[24]

As noted, if the philosophers must be compelled to rule because they do not regard ruling as a positive good, then they would be unwillingly just. They would surely be unwillingly just in regard to justice understood as giving what is owed. But they would be unwillingly just in a more fundamental way because ruling, at least when it is geared toward the common good, could encompass greater acts of justice than merely giving what is owed. This is all the more distressing because Socrates' argument is that the philosophers have the greatest capacity to be just (in the ordinary sense) through ruling. Indeed, they would be especially fit for rule because they possess the knowledge of what is good for human beings (503e-506a; cf. 520c). Still more disquieting is the fact that, for Socrates, the philosophers have the greatest latitude to be just in the best regime. There they no longer have the excuse of the obstacles of ordinary political life that prevent them from ruling and coming to the aid of justice. This suggests that it is politics as such (rather than merely unhealthy politics) that is questionable for them. Even the sort of politics as practiced by the best regime—which aims to be as rational as possible—is questionable for the philosophers. The philosophers thus can hardly be understood to be paragons of justice, at least understood in the ordinary sense. But there is no reason why they would not be just in the Socratic sense.[25] In fact, it is precisely their concern with justice in the Socratic sense that would lead them to be less than fully just in the ordinary sense. This, I believe, points powerfully to the problematic character of justice in the Socratic sense as practiced by the philosophers.

The tension between ruling and philosophy, we note, undercuts the following suggestions made by Socrates in the course of defending the proposal for the philosopher-kings: that it is natural for philosophers both to philosophize and to lead a city (474b-c); that the philosophers would "grow more" in the best regime (497a); and that they would become "perfect" in becoming rulers (499b-c).

At this point, we can return to the question of the possibility of the best regime. An answer to this question would decide, among other things, whether the philosophers would even have the opportunity to reveal that they would be unwillingly just when they have the greatest latitude to be just. According to Socrates, philosophic rule is the single necessary and sufficient condition for transformation of an ordinary city into the best regime (473b-e). But, evading the issue of what is really involved in such a transformation, Socrates at various times speaks as if the best regime already exists without explaining how this regime comes into being (497a, 502c-d, 519b-521b). He in fact implicitly indicates that the kind of transformation required for the best regime to come into being is impossible. To begin with, having heard Adeimantus' statement that perhaps the many will become less angry after hearing truthful arguments in favor of philosophic-rule, Socrates rests satisfied with the mere assertion that they would indeed be completely persuaded (502a). Furthermore, he reveals that, in order for the best regime to come into being, the philosophers will have to exile all those over the age of ten from an ordinary city that they want to transform (540e-541a). It would be difficult to find greater evidence of the impossibility of the best regime than this: there is obviously no possibility of persuading the many to leave the city; and no army loyal to the philosophers is available to carry out a forcible expulsion of them.[26] An equally massive obstacle, however, is that the philosophers would, in the final analysis, refrain from undertaking the transformation of an ordinary city into the best regime due to their lack of desire for ruling (519b-521b). Besides, if the philosophers do not owe anything to ordinary cities (520a-b), then they would even have justice (though in a narrow sense) on their side in not endeavoring to achieve such a transformation. There is, in short, no "necessity" that, according to Socrates, would lead to the transformation of an ordinary city into the best regime (499b-c, 499c-d, 500d). If the best regime is, for the above reasons, impossible, one could doubt the truth of Socrates' assertion that philosophic rule is natural (474b-c): for how can anything impossible be natural? Moreover, one can say that the philosophers are not required by justice (in a broader sense than merely repaying what one owes) to try to transform an ordinary city. For, just as nothing impossible can be natural, so nothing impossible can be just.

Now, Socrates speaks about the philosopher's desire to release some from the confines of the cave (515c-516a). And this raises the question whether the philosophers' interest in providing a philosophic education does not furnish them with an incentive to rule in the best regime.[27] For Socrates, of course, there is no possibility of providing the city as a whole with a philosophic education, as the truly philosophic natures to which such an education is properly directed are few (503b-d). In keeping with this, Socrates makes clear that political society as such is a kind of a cave; and hence that even the best regime as ruled by philosophers, in contrast to the best individual, cannot be fully rational (514a-521b). (It is worth noting here that, in his account of the virtues in Book Four, Socrates indicates that the education to civic virtue—as opposed to education to virtue simply, which is geared toward individuals as individuals—is not entirely rational [427e-434c, 441c-444a].) But there is a philosophic education provided for the rulers of the best regime. Socrates' proposal for the philosopher-kings, which is aimed partly at ameliorating the tension that ordinarily exists between philosophy and the city as a whole (490e-493d, 496a-e), dictates that the city itself should supply its potential rulers with an education to philosophy whose core is dialectics (502e-540e). The question, then, is whether this aspect of the best regime does not offer a sufficient incentive for the philosophers to rule willingly. By indicating that the philosophers must be compelled to rule in spite of this aspect of the best regime, Socrates gives a negative answer to this question. For the philosophers, the unwelcome burden of ruling—which, even in the best regime, is aimed at many things other than fostering a philosophic education (and hence for this reason, among others, has the character of a drudgery)—far outweighs whatever attraction the possibility of providing a philosophic education in the best regime has.

Socrates also indicates that the sort of education provided for the rulers in the best regime is problematic from the perspective of what is required for a strictly philosophic education. For he initially says that the kind of study that is suitable for the potential philosopher-kings must be good equally for turning the soul to being—i.e., for philosophy—as for war (521d). But, when, in regard to astronomy, Glaucon says that a better knowledge of seasons, months and years is appropriate not only for farming and navigation but also for generalship, Socrates rebukes him by saying that he seems like a man who is fearful of the many in not wishing to appear to demand useless studies. He then points out the great benefit of astronomy in the pursuit of the truth, of which the many are wholly unaware (527d-528a).[28] By thus revealing the existence of a great gulf between the sort of education required for philosophy and the sort required for ruling, Socrates points to the view that any attempt at an assimilation of the two ways of life is doomed to fail. In the light of all this, it may be reasonable to conclude that the philosophers would prefer to provide a philosophic education privately in ordinary cities, where they do not have to rule. This concern of the philosophers to provide a philosophic education, moreover, must be taken into account in determining whether justice in the Socratic sense, as practiced by the philosophers, has any connection with justice as ordinarily understood. For if the best regime is impossible, then a coincidence between the good of the one who is just in the Socratic sense and the good of others cannot exist on the political level. But the philosophers' interest in providing a philosophic education to potential philosophers in ordinary cities suggests the possibility of such a coincidence's existing at least among a small circle on the private level (cf. 496a-e). Certainly, there is room for optimism with respect to this possibility because knowledge is the kind of good that can be shared without the compromise of any person's own good. Still, it is far from clear whether this coincidence that takes place in private, and for the very few, is sufficient either to justify Socrates' identification of the just man and the philosopher or to provide a strong link between justice as ordinarily understood and justice in the Socratic sense.

In this connection, it is worth noting that, from the point of view of the requirements of a philosophic education, democracy may be more suitable than one is first led to believe. To be sure, Socrates argues that democracy is opposed to what he, along with the others, solemnly said in founding the best regime—"that unless a man has a transcendent nature he would never become good if from earliest childhood his play isn't noble and all his practices aren't such" (558b). But one cannot overlook his suggestion that the individual who has a "transcendent nature" need not be adversely affected by the lack of a good education in a democracy. And, since his reference to such an individual brings to mind his description of the philosopher as one who comes into being spontaneously against the will of bad regimes and who has a nature that grows by itself and does not owe its nurturing to anyone (520b), it is possible to argue that for Socrates those who possess truly philosophic natures would not regard democracy as a great impediment to their education. We observe that Socrates also implicitly indicates that philosophers may look favorably upon democracy at least to the extent that, unlike the best regime, it does not compel to rule even those who are fit to rule (557e).[29] Of course, Socrates also says that democracy is a regime that "dispenses a certain equality to equals and unequals alike" (558c, cf. 557a). This means, among other things, that democratic justice is defective because it does not take account of the differences among human beings that are relevant to the question of who ought to rule.[30] But, insofar as he does not wish to rule, the philosopher may not be too perturbed by this defect of democracy, at least as far as his own interest is concerned. This, however, would give us further reason to wonder about the truth of the equation of the just man and the philosopher.

The Rhetorical Advantages of Justice in the Socratic Sense

Given the problems connected with justice in the Socratic sense (as practiced by the philosophers), we are led to ask why Socrates introduces such justice at all. In order to answer this question, we must begin by reexamining the key passage concerning the philosophers' return to the cave. There Socrates, while being silent about justice in the Socratic sense, speaks of justice as ordinarily understood: first, by mentioning justice as paying back what one owes, which recalls Cephalus' definition of justice in Book One (cf. 520b and 331b-d); second, by making the argument (for the third time in the *Republic*) that it is not the concern of law to bring about the well-being of any one class but the well-being of the city as a whole, an argument which points to the ordinary understanding of justice as devotion to the common good (420b-421c, 465e-466c, 519e-520a). Socrates first introduced this argument in response to Adeimantus' question whether he is not making the guardians (who are to have no privacy and no more property than what is needed if they are to remain a part of the guardian class) unhappy (419a-421c). And this argument has the crucial implication that the definition of the justice of the city as each of the three classes' minding its own business is not necessarily in keeping with the good of every individual. Socrates is now suggesting that happiness conceived not in any childish way (the sort of happiness the guardians run the risk of pursuing [466b]) but genuine happiness as experienced by the philosophers must be sacrificed to the demands of such justice.[31] The call for some sort of sacrifice, of course, is in keeping with the ordinary understanding of justice. Yet the problem is that justice is also ordinarily identified with the good—something that puts the stamp of approval on the enterprise of the *Republic* as a whole, which is nothing so much as an attempt to show that justice is indeed good for oneself. There is, it appears, an inner difficulty with justice, a difficulty that is reflected in the curious fact that forcing the philosophers to rule is viewed by Socrates, on the one hand, as just and by Glaucon, on the other, as unjust.

It is true that Socrates attempts in the *Republic* to found a regime that is in keeping with a true or complete common good, which would encompass the individual good without difficulty. In particular, the proposal for the community of women and children is intended to eliminate the tension between the individual and the common good. The aim of this proposal, after all, is to create the greatest unity possible within a city, the sort of unity usually associated with an individual human being (in whom the pleasures and pains that are experienced by a part are also necessarily experienced by the whole) (462a-465c). Yet, Socrates implicitly suggests that this sort of unity—which would secure the greatest good for a city if it is possible (462a-b)—would not be possible. To be sure, he argues that the rule of philosophers, being the single necessary and sufficient condition for the transformation of an ordinary city into the best regime, would bring about such unity (473b-473e). But he tacitly indicates that the rule of philosophers itself is not possible (see especially 540e-541a).[32] And one of the reasons why it is not possible is the tension between the philosophers' own good and the good of the city: why would philosophers want to transform an ordinary city into the best regime in which they would be compelled to rule? Ironically, although the best regime ruled by philosophers is the only regime that is meant to bring about both a private and public happiness (472c-473e), it does not secure this in the highest case of the philosophers. Perhaps, then, Socrates' awareness of the problem within ordinary justice—the tension between the individual good and the common good—explains why he takes refuge in the *Republic* in what we have called justice in the Socratic sense. For, unlike justice in the ordinary understanding, this sort of justice is meant to be wholly in keeping with the individual good.

Now, we cannot know what justice in the ordinary understanding is unless we address, more adequately than we have done here, the difficulty regarding its goodness. It is true that Socrates, at the end of Book One, tries to separate the question of the goodness of justice and the question of what justice is (354a-c). But Socrates' serious view, expressed in the context of his elaboration of the Idea of the Good in Book Six, is that we cannot know what justice is unless we know the way in which it is good (506a). As for the criticism that the enterprise of the *Republic* as a whole—i.e., trying to defend justice in terms of its goodness—is wrong and that this leads us to raise falsely the issue of an inner difficulty of justice, we can say the following.[33] In the first place, Socrates' rather unambiguous thesis in Book Six is that *all* human beings strive for the good (505d-e). Hence, for Socrates, the demand that justice must be good if it is to be acceptable would not come as a surprise. Moreover, according to the *Republic*, the belief in the goodness of justice is part of the ordinary understanding of justice. This is especially made clear in Book One. There Cephalus and Polemarchus, who provide definitions of justice that are in keeping with the ordinary understanding of justice, assume that justice is good: the former rejects the justice of returning a weapon to a madman because he thinks that justice is good for all concerned, while the latter believes that justice is human virtue (331c-d, 335c). These two interlocutors apparently do not even feel the need to raise the question of the goodness of justice precisely because they assume that justice is something good. This leads one to wonder, however, whether those who want to see the goodness of justice defended are not somehow already beyond the ordinary perspective on justice. It is probably no accident, after all, that the first to raise the question of the goodness of justice in the *Republic* is Thrasymachus, who is a great critic of justice (338c-339a, 343b-344c). But this question is also raised by individuals like Glaucon and Adeimantus, who, perplexed by the claims made by Thrasymachus and others, want to see justice defended in terms of its goodness (357a-367e). And since it is not adequate simply to assume that justice is something good, Glaucon and Adeimantus appear to be in this respect superior to Polemarchus and Cephalus. Thus Socrates' attempt to defend justice in terms of its goodness is, according to the *Republic*, fully justified from the point of view of justice itself.

There is a further important reason why Socrates is induced to make the equation of the just man and the philosopher or to posit justice in the Socratic sense. At the beginning of Book Two, Glaucon and Adeimantus ask Socrates to show that justice is intrinsically good and hence to make it clear that men are capable of being just not merely for the external rewards that come from the reputation for justice. For they are aware that, if justice is good merely for its external rewards, then there is always the temptation to practice injustice: one could garner the rewards of justice by merely *appearing* to be just (357a-367e). Now, in Book Ten, Socrates says that since they have already shown that justice is intrinsically good, they should return the external wages and punishments for justice and injustice by allowing the just man to have the reputation for justice and the unjust man the reputation for injustice (612a-d). But Socrates was able to show that justice is intrinsically good only by referring to the justice of the individual as outlined at the end of Book Four—to justice as harmony of the soul, which is analogous to the health of the body—and ultimately to the philosopher's being just in this sense. Certainly, the pleasures of the philosophers, which Socrates cites in order to prove not only that justice is intrinsically good but also that it is superior to injustice in the form of tyranny, are intrinsically good and compatible with maximum self-sufficiency. The difficulty, however, is that Socrates had been asked to show that ordinary justice is intrinsically good. And, as far as I can tell, he nowhere shows this. If anything, he points to the obstacles that would prevent one from simply accepting such a view.

As for Socrates' turn to the external rewards and punishments for justice and injustice, it is clear that from the point of view of justice in the Socratic sense, which is intrinsically good, they would be more or less superfluous (see 588e-591b). (Socrates does allow for punishments that would improve the unjust [591a-b].)[34] Hence his desire to turn to them does not make much sense. But in fact Socrates gives back the external rewards and punishments not to justice in the Socratic sense but to justice in the ordinary sense, which, as I noted, had not been shown to be intrinsically good. This is confirmed by the fact that the external rewards and punishments for justice and injustice are linked with the reputation for justice and injustice among ordinary human beings (612a-614a). Here, the question may arise whether the just man in the ordinary sense would regard the external rewards as mere icing on the cake, as it were, rather than as absolutely necessary. Socrates implicitly indicates that the latter is closer to the truth. For, in Book Three, he argues that the decent man would not mourn the loss of loved ones due to his self-sufficiency as well as to his belief that death is not something terrible at least for the decent man (387d-388a). But, in Book Ten, Socrates consciously takes this argument back by suggesting that, despite the law forbidding mourning, it is impossible for the decent man not to mourn the loss of loved ones (603b-606b).[35] This points to the view that, for Socrates, the decent man would likely demand external rewards for justice—from gods and human beings, both in this life and the next—precisely because of his lack of self-sufficiency. From this, it would appear that Socrates identifies the just man with the philosopher or introduces justice in the Socratic sense in trying to prove at all costs that justice is good without reference to external rewards: perhaps only the philosopher, being the most self-sufficient of human beings, would not hope for external rewards for his justice.[36]

It is worth calling attention to the fact that, just as Socrates' argument aimed at showing that justice is intrinsically good appears to be rhetorical in certain respects, his argument in support of the view that justice is better than injustice (in the form of tyranny) has rhetorical elements. Socrates first tries to argue on the basis of the assumption, which he maintains throughout the *Republic*, that there is a parallelism between the city and the individual. One implication of this assumption, which Socrates delineates, is that "as city is to city with respect to virtue and happiness, so is man to man" (576c-d). Hence, if, as Socrates says, with respect to both virtue and happiness, the tyrannic city is the worst and the kingly city the best, then the tyrant himself must be deemed to be unhappy (576d-e). But, perhaps due to his awareness of the fact that the tyrant himself, as opposed to the city ruled by him, could plausibly be happy,[37] Socrates does not immediately draw this conclusion.

Instead he stops to point out the importance of judging the tyrant's happiness simply by observing him up close (576e-577b). Unfortunately, however, Socrates merely pretends that they are in the presence of someone who can provide a first-hand account of the tyrant's life (577b). And no sooner does he point to a truly adequate sort of investigation regarding the happiness of the tyrant than he returns to the less than adequate one based on the faulty assumption of a parallelism existing between the city and the individual. For he goes on to argue that if a man is like his city, it is also necessary that the same order that exists in his city will also be in him (577d; cf. 351d-352a). Thus, among other things, just as a city that is under a tyranny least does what it wishes, the soul as a whole that is under a tyranny least does what it wishes; and, just as a city under a tyranny is poor and full of fear, the tyrannic soul is poor and full of fear (577e-578a). By this questionable line of reasoning, Socrates is able ultimately to conclude that while the kingly man, who is the most just man, is happiest, the tyrant, who is the most unjust man, is most wretched (578b, 580b-c). The inadequacy of Socrates' argument becomes even clearer when one reflects on the fact that he did not establish that the kingly man—i.e., the philosopher who rules in the best regime—is as happy as the city that he rules (519e-520a).

While saying that the foregoing provides one proof against tyranny, moreover, Socrates offers two more proofs which, like the first proof, are based on the assumption that the just man is the philosopher (580c). According to these proofs, justice is superior to injustice because the pleasures of the philosopher are better and more real than the pleasures of the tyrant (580d-587e). Here one difficulty is that Socrates criticizes tyranny on the basis of the identification of the tyrant, whom he had earlier described as an erotic man, with the money-lover (cf. 573c and 580d-583a).[38] A more serious difficulty is that, for reasons mentioned, it is far from clear that the just man is the philosopher. Even if one grants Socrates' argument that philosophy is superior to tyranny in regard to pleasure, one could wonder whether this proves that justice is better than injustice.[39] Still, Socrates reveals the supreme importance of his equation of the just man and the philosopher to his defense of justice by pointing out, at the very end of the *Republic*, that only the philosopher is able truly to resist the temptation to tyranny. In his Myth of Er, Socrates relates how a man who "lived in an orderly regime in his former life, participating in virtue by habit, without philosophy" chose the greatest tyranny in having the opportunity to select a way of life (619b-d). Through this story, Socrates indicates that the only thing that separates the just man (in the ordinary sense) and the unjust man is habit (cf. 500d, 518d-e). He also indicates that only the philosopher's justice, being based on knowledge rather than on habit, would not be subject to corruption. Nor, according to Socrates, would it require any external supports. Indeed, unlike the man who is just merely due to living in an orderly regime that produces a certain habit of living, the philosopher is just even in a regime that is not good (see 549c-550b).

Even if Socrates' account of the justice of the individual is not entirely free from rhetoric or even arbitrariness, it can still educate us. While forcing us to seek clarity on our own regarding the question of the goodness of justice, it offers food for thought by pointing to what justice must be like if it is to be understood as leading to happiness. It certainly allows us to see the character of what Socrates calls "the best pursuit"—namely, philosophy (495b; cf. 407b-c). In calling attention to the philosophic life, moreover, Socrates sheds some light on the philosophic approach to justice. He points out that, from a strictly rational perspective, there is little place for moral indignation: if justice is good, it is due to ignorance that the unjust are unjust; and, since they are thus not willingly unjust, they should not be blamed (589b-591b; cf. 336e, 549c-550b). Moreover, he indicates that from the point of view of philosophy the unwilling lie—the lie in the soul that is due to ignorance—is more to be hated than the willing lie, which is ordinarily regarded as unjust (535d-e, 382a-383a, 389b-d, 331b). But as to the fundamental problem with which we are faced in the *Republic*—the adequacy of Socrates' definition of the justice of the individual in Book Four and his argument that the philosopher is just in this sense—a turn to a full-scale study of Book One may be of some help. For there Socrates takes up definitions of justice that are linked with certain commonly held views about justice—definitions that can serve as a fitting counterpoise to his rather paradoxical presentation of justice in the rest of the *Republic*. Of course, in keeping with what is required by dialectics understood as the core of philosophy (537e-539a), Socrates questions the adequacy of these definitions. Hence he inevitably leads us to ask whether the defects of the ordinary understanding of justice as presented in Book One fully justify his account of justice in the rest of the *Republic*.

Notes

1. All quotations from the *Republic* are from the translation of Allan Bloom (New York: Basic Books, 1968).

2. David Sachs, "A Fallacy in Plato's *Republic*," *Philosophical Review* 72 (1963): 141-58. For a selective bibliography of the many responses to Sachs, see Julia Annas, *An Introduction to Plato's "Republic"* (Oxford: Clarendon Press, 1981), 169.

3. See, for example, Ernest Barker, *Greek Political Theory: Plato and His Predecessors* (London: Methuen & Co., 1918), 234-36; M. B. Foster, "Some Implications of a Passage in Plato's *Republic*," *Philosophy* 11 (1936): 301-8; S. H. Aronson, "The Happy

Philosopher—A Counter to Plato's Proof," *Journal of the History of Philosophy* 10 (1972): 383-98; Allan Bloom, "Response to Hall," *Political Theory* 5 (1977): 316-23; Timothy A. Mahoney, "Do Plato's Philosopher-Rulers Sacrifice Self-Interest to Justice?" *Phronesis* 37 (1992): 265-82.

4. George Klosko (*The Development of Plato's Political Theory* [New York: Methuen, 1986], 113) merely notes that the two controversies have come to be associated with one another.

5. Just as the definition of the justice of the city is based on the sort of justice found in a good or virtuous city, the definition of the justice of the individual is based on the kind of justice possessed by the good or virtuous individual.

6. This difficulty is noted by R. Demos, "A Fallacy in Plato's *Republic*?" *Philosophical Review* 73 (1964): 396.

7. Cf. Sachs, "A Fallacy," 154.

8. Cf. Demos, "A Fallacy?" 395.

9. In "A Fallacy," Sachs distinguishes between two kinds of justice: the "Platonic conception of justice," which is tantamount to the sort of justice that Socrates describes at 443c-e; and the "vulgar conception of justice," which is equal to the sort of justice that he outlines at 442d-443b and is in keeping with "ordinary morality" (142-43, 152, 154). Sachs claims that, in order to satisfy the request of Glaucon and Adeimantus (who hold the "vulgar conception of justice" [143]), Plato must prove two things: (1) that Platonic justice would result in the sort of actions required by "vulgar justice" and (2) that the man who is just according to the "vulgar conception of justice" would also be Platonically just (152-53). But, according to Sachs, Plato proves neither of these things and hence commits "the fallacy of irrelevance" that "wrecks the *Republic*'s main argument" (141, 154-56). There have been many responses to Sachs's thesis over the years. All of them are, in one way or another, aimed against it. Nevertheless, some of these responses acknowledge the apparently paradoxical character of Socrates' definition of the justice of the individual. While there are significant differences between Sachs's formulation of the problematic character of Socrates' definition of justice and my own, I am sympathetic with his overall thesis. Consider also Leo Strauss, *The City and Man* (Chicago: Rand McNally, 1964), 115, on the "the two meanings of justice" in the *Republic*.

10. Cf. R. C. Cross and A. D. Woozley, *Plato's "Republic": A Philosophical Commentary* (New York: St. Martin's Press, 1964), 113.

11. Cf. Gregory Vlastos, *Platonic Studies*, 2d ed. (Princeton: Princeton University Press, 1981), 115-17, 119.

12. For the view that the citizens of the good or virtuous city would possess the justice of the individual, see M. B. Foster, *The Political Philosophies of Plato and Hegel* (1935; reprint, New York: Russell & Russell, 1965), 63; and R. Demos, "Paradoxes in Plato's Doctrine of the Ideal State," *Classical Quarterly* 51 (1957): 170-71. Cf. Barker, *Greek Political Theory*, 205-6. As to whether there is a tension between the justice of the individual and the justice of the city, see Robert W. Hall, "Justice and the Individual in the *Republic*," *Phronesis* 4 (1959): 158; Aronson, "Happy Philosopher," 387; and Mary Nichols, *Socrates and the Political Community* (Albany: State University of New York Press, 1987), 59, 78.

13. Cf. Richard Nettleship, *Lectures on the "Republic" of Plato*, 2d ed. (London: Macmillan, 1925), 305; and Bloom, "Interpretive Essay," in *Republic*, 420.

14. More precisely, Socrates now indicates that the spirited part of the soul contains the love of honor and the rational part contains the love of wisdom (580d-583a; see also 568d-e). It is also worth calling attention to the fact that, in speaking of the *eros* of the tyrant, Socrates points out that the account of the soul in Book Four is defective in that it is simply silent about *eros* as distinct from, or as a special part of, desire (572d-575a).

15. Nicholas P. White ("The Classification of Goods in Plato's *Republic*," *Journal of the History of Political Philosophy* 22 [1984]: 404) correctly notes the similarity between the arguments at the end of Book Four and at the end of Book Nine.

16. Cf. Strauss, *City and Man*, 109; and Richard Kraut, "Reason and Justice in Plato's *Republic*," in *Exegesis and Argument: Studies in Greek Philosophy Presented to Gregory Vlastos*, E. N. Lee, Alexander P. D. Mourelatos, and R. M. Rorty, eds. (Assen, Netherlands: van Gorcum & Co., 1973), 214.

17. Socrates does mention that some sort of "divine chance" could result in the philosopher's ruling in a different regime (592a), but he earlier indicated his unwillingness to engage in discussions that are like prayers (499c).

18. Cf. Strauss, *City and Man*, 118, 122, 126.

19. Cf. Kraut, "Reason and Justice," 214-15; Gerald Mara, "Politics and Action in Plato's *Republic*," *Western Political Quarterly* 36 (1983): 601.

20. Nicholas P. White, "The Ruler's Choice," *Archiv für Geschichte der Philosophie* 68 (1986): 27.

21. The problem of the philosophers' having to be compelled to rule is stressed by Strauss, *City and Man*, 123-25 and Bloom, "Interpretive Essay," 407-8. For a critique of their position, see Dale Hall, "The *Republic* and the 'Limits of Politics,'" *Political Theory* 5 (1977): 293-313 and George Klosko, "Implementing the Ideal State," *Journal of Politics* 43 (1981): 365-89.

22. Cf. Richard Kraut, "Egoism, Love and Political Office in Plato," *Philosophical Review* 82 (1973): 342; Hall, "The *Republic* and 'Limits,'" 302.

23. Cf. Aronson, "Happy Philosopher," 393.

24. There is, according to Socrates, a greater object of study than justice and the other virtues—namely, the Idea of the Good (504d-505b).

25. Cf. Foster, "Some Implications," 303-4; White, "Ruler's Choice," 27-31.

26. Cf. Strauss, *City and Man*, 126.

27. Cf. Kraut, "Reason and Justice," 223; John M. Cooper, "The Psychology of Justice in Plato," *American Philosophical Quarterly* 14 (1977): 156.

28. In keeping with all this, when Glaucon suggests that as much of geometry as is needed for war is necessary, Socrates argues that in fact only a small part of geometry—as of calculation—is necessary for war but that it must be determined "whether its greater and more advanced part tends to make it easier to make out the *idea* of the good" (526d-e). Both astronomy and geometry, of course, do not really turn the soul to being as dialectics does (531d-534e). Cf. Bloom, "Interpretive Essay," 408.

29. Strauss, *City and Man*, 131.

30. Cf. M. B. Foster, "On Plato's Conception of Justice in the *Republic*," *The Philosophical Quarterly* 1 (1950-51): 209.

31. Cf. Aronson, "Happy Philosopher," 393; Foster, "Some Implications," 301-4.

32. Because the possibility of the proposal for the women and children depends on the possibility of the proposal for the philosopher-kings, Socrates points to the impossibility of the former in implicitly indicating the impossibility of the latter. Accordingly, Socrates is far from proving the naturalness of the community of women and children.

33. For a Kantian critique of Socrates' attempt to defend justice in terms of its goodness, see H. A. Prichard, *Moral Obligation and Duty and Interest* (Oxford: Oxford University Press, 1968).

34. Any other kind of punishment for the unjust may not be appropriate, strictly speaking: if justice is better than injustice, then the unjust man must be dealt with gently, for he is not "willingly mistaken" (589c).

35. Cf. Bloom, "Interpretive Essay," 433; Nichols, *Socrates and Community*, 141-42.

36. Cf. Strauss, *City and Man*, 137.

37. Being aware of this difficulty, Socrates tells Glaucon to look to the tyrannic city as a whole, rather than only the tyrant and those around him, in determining its happiness (576d-e).

38. Cf. Annas, *Introduction to "Republic,"* 306.

39. Cf. Richard Kraut, "The Defense of Justice in Plato's *Republic*," in *The Cambridge Companion to Plato*, R. Kraut, ed. (Cambridge: Cambridge University Press, 1992), 323.

Chapter 2

See No Evil:
The Story of Gyges in Herodotus and Plato

Katherine Philippakis

Would you kill a king and take his wife and throne if you knew you wouldn't be caught? This question forms the basis of the story of Gyges as told by Glaucon in Book Two of Plato's *Republic*. Glaucon's story is an adaptation of Herodotus' account of Gyges in his *Histories*. In both stories Gyges becomes invisible and commits injustice: he kills the king, takes the king's wife, and becomes king himself. The similarities between the two stories are certainly apparent, but their differences are more significant. Why does Glaucon tell the story differently from Herodotus? What do his additions and exclusions imply about the teaching of the *Republic* as a whole? By looking at the concept of justice in each of the stories we can learn something about the meaning of justice and its relation to philosophy.[1]

The theme of the *Republic* is justice: what it is, whether it is possible, and whether it is desirable. The character of Glaucon plays a major role in the formulation of the arguments of the book, and so his discussion of justice merits particular attention.[2] It is Glaucon who accompanies Socrates down to the Piraeus to observe the festival in Book One; it is Glaucon who speaks for Socrates and agrees to stay with Polemarchus, Adeimantus, and the others; and it is to Glaucon that Socrates addresses his closing remarks at the end of Book Ten. Glaucon is responsible for much of the action of the *Republic*, and his contribution to the discussion sheds light on its true meaning.

Glaucon's speech about justice is given in Book Two, and its central feature is the story of Gyges, a shepherd who finds a ring which makes him invisible. Gyges uses the power of the ring to possess the king's wife and kill the king. Glaucon posits that we would all act like Gyges if we could, if we were invisible. Glaucon wants Socrates to prove that we would not, that justice is choiceworthy for its own sake and not because of rewards or punishments. Glaucon wants Socrates to discuss justice all alone by itself, or the idea of justice. Whether this can be done—whether justice can be separated from its consequences—is a question that can only be answered by examining in detail the components of both stories of Gyges.

The story of Gyges appears early in the *Histories*, where Herodotus tells tales gathered from his wanderings. Like some sections of the *Republic*, the *Histories* presents its arguments in the form of stories, or myths: the book is a narrative that teaches by providing anecdotes about the things Herodotus ostensibly has seen.[3] Herodotus tells us that the book was written "in order that the memory of the past may not be blotted out from among men by time, and that great and marvelous deeds done by Greeks and foreigners and especially the reason why they warred against each other may not lack renown." (I, 1)[4] Herodotus is writing something both universal and particular; he is telling the story of the war between the Greeks and the Persians, but he is telling it for men of the future, for all men. By recounting the reasons why some men warred, he teaches of the causes of war among men in general. Herodotus speaks of the customs of the Greeks and Persians which led to the war, but in so doing, he transcends custom, or *nomos*; he looks at the opinions of particular men from the vantage point of universal knowledge or truth. Herodotus, the storyteller, is not bound by his own tales but can look directly at the customs of other cities and reveal the nature underlying them.

Herodotus begins his account by telling the cause of the feud, which was the taking of Io, the daughter of the Greek Inachus, by the Phoenicians. This kidnapping caused a series of offenses which culminated in the Trojan war. (I, 1-5) Or rather, as the Persians tell the tale, the kidnapping of Io led to the feuds; according to the Phoenicians, however, it was done with her consent. By showing the disagreement among those involved, Herodotus demonstrates the differences in customs which contribute to wars among men. The words Herodotus attributes to the Persians exemplify these differences in men's opinions: "We think that it is wrong to carry women off: but to be zealous to avenge the rape is foolish: wise men take no account of such things . . ." (I, 4) This quote both establishes differences in men's conceptions of justice and also makes a distinction between justice and prudence: it is unjust to carry women off, but it is unwise to avenge the act. According to Herodotus, the Persians recognize that justice may vary according to the city, but they believe that wisdom is universal; they say that they "think" rape is wrong, but that vengeance "is" foolish. Although both statements are really no more than Persian opinion, this distinction between wisdom and justice resurfaces in the story of Gyges: what is wise is not necessarily just, and what is just is not necessarily wise.

Further, the Persians say that one should take no account of the rape of women, of taking what belongs to another. The Greeks, however, are willing to attack Troy over the rape of Helen and go to war. Herodotus, then, begins his inquiries with a discussion of "one's own" as a cause of war and conflict. In his *Herodotean Inquiries*, Seth Benardete writes: "What distinguishes barbarians from Greeks is the difference in their customs. Customs are the obstacle to understanding directly the nature of human things. Human beings disagree . . . about what is just and unjust."[5] One's own, whether it be customs or women, is essential to the Greeks, and yet it is precisely one's own which must be given up in order to found Socrates' republic: in the best city all must say "my own and not my own" together. (*Republic*, 462c)[6] Immediately, then, we begin to discern a tension between the teaching of the *Republic* and the opinions offered in the *Histories*.

After distinguishing between the Phoenician and Persian accounts of the rape, Herodotus declines to verify either version, but instead "goes forward" with his "argument" (*tou logou*, I, 5). Herodotus removes himself from the particular to the universal; he will not comment on which party was responsible for the injustice, but instead will speak of "small and great cities alike." He explains: "For cites that were in ancient times great have become small, and those great in my time were formerly small. Knowing, then, that human happiness never remains in the same place, I shall make mention of both alike." (I, 5) The feuds of the Persians and Phoenicians cannot impede the *logos* of Herodotus. Indeed, Herodotus' usage of the word *logos* (as reasoned speech or argument) does not seem accidental here, for he is intimating the existence of a plan in his book. That plan is the examination of cities, not Greek cities or Persian cities in particular, but cities in general.[7] Herodotus identifies the happiness of a city—a fleeting happiness—with its political greatness, and his book will show in what that greatness consists.

Herodotus then begins the story of Gyges, telling how the sovereign power of the Heraclid kings fell to the Mermnadae. Candaules is the last of the descendants of Heracles and is king of the Lydians. Gyges is his bodyguard and confidant, for Candaules "entrusted all his weightiest secrets to him." (I, 8) Candaules holds the beauty of his wife in high esteem and wishes for Gyges to gaze upon her naked body; he fears that Gyges doesn't believe the queen is truly beautiful, for "human ears are less to be trusted than eyes." (I, 8) Candaules wants to do away with convention and let Gyges see the nature of his wife; he does not realize that nature must be clothed by convention. As we shall see, Candaules does not consider that it may be politically unwise to bare human nature, however "beautiful" that nature may appear.

Gyges, however, exclaims loudly:

O master, what unhealthy words have you spoken, bidding me to behold my
mistress naked? When a woman removes her clothes she removes her shame as
well. Long ago the beautiful things (*ta kala*) were discovered by human beings,
from which you must learn; and among them is this one: let each man look at his
own. I am persuaded that she is the most beautiful of all women, and I beg you not
to demand unlawful things. (I, 8)

Gyges is concerned with preserving shame, for shame is a convention
necessary to man; shame clothes human nature and prevents men from
committing injustice.[8] Shame is one of the beautiful things discovered by the
men of long ago. Gyges defers to these men, his ancestors, who teach the
rules, or laws, which are called beautiful, and it is an "unlawful thing" to
disobey their teachings. The king thinks that nature is beautiful, but Gyges
calls convention beautiful, and convention dictates that each man look only
at his own. It can be unjust to let some men see the beauty of nature, for the
man who looks on the "naked truth" has no shame. A man without shame
will not hesitate to disobey the laws (*nomoi*), and so law must dictate that
man cannot look upon the beauty of nature. Beautiful laws hide beautiful,
but politically dangerous, natures from men's sight.

It does not matter that the queen is beautiful; because she belongs to
Candaules, it is unlawful for Gyges to see her. Gyges knows this and is
content to hear of the queen's beauty, but Candaules insists that he see it.
The king does not realize that it is dangerous to let his bodyguard see the
beauty of his own wife. A ruler cannot allow those beneath him to scrutinize
the "beautiful things," be they women or laws. One must trust the word of
the king, for to see beauty for oneself is somehow to take possession of it.
The king must keep the beauty of nature hidden from sight under the cover
of clothing or of the past; there is no need for him to show it to his subjects
and let them determine what is or is not beautiful. By permitting Gyges to
determine what is beautiful, Candaules induces him to undermine the power
both of the king and of the laws, for Candaules gives Gyges power to accept
or reject the word of the king. Gyges, the bodyguard, realizes this, and he
wishes to guard the laws just as he guards the king, to shield them from
harm.

The consequences of Candaules' actions are disastrous. At his bidding,
Gyges hides in the queen's bedroom to watch her undress. Candaules has
assured him that he can view the queen in such a way that "she shall never
know that you have seen her," i.e., invisibly. (I, 9) Candaules advocates
injustice because it can be committed invisibly; it is not shameful if no one
knows. In Herodotus' story, just as in Plato's, invisibility allows for
injustice. The queen, however, discovers Gyges and is thus dishonored. She
gives him a choice: kill the king or die himself. Gyges, after being compelled

to injustice by the king, is compelled to punish the instigator of injustice by the queen. Where the king was interested in the beauty of nature, the queen, like Gyges, is interested in the beauty of convention. Natural beauty demands that convention be observed. The beauty of nature is shameful when seen by the wrong man, and so it must be protected by the beauty of a convention, Lydian law.

If the queen were not Lydian, however, she would not demand vengeance, for she would not have been dishonored. We are reminded of the words of the Persians, who say that it is unjust to rape women (i.e., to shame them) but unwise to take revenge, and that a rape is not a cause for a war. The Persians think that it is foolish to avenge shameful acts, but the Lydian queen does not agree. According to her belief, one must protect the conventions one has created. To the queen, her actions are not unwise; rather, her husband behaved unwisely by ignoring Lydian custom. The queen, then, demonstrates the opposite of the Persians' belief: it is politically wise to protect one's own through the enforcement of the laws of shame.

The queen, like Candaules, equates justice with visibility and thus exonerates injustice if it is invisible. Waiting until morning to confront Gyges, she holds her peace during the night, when all is hidden, and acts in the light of day, making her actions seem just.[9] However, she orders Gyges to kill the king in his sleep (I, 11), when Gyges cannot be seen. The queen tells Gyges: "You must either kill Candaules and take me for your own and the throne of Lydia, or yourself be killed now without more ado; that will prevent you from obeying all Candaules' commands in the future and seeing what you should not see." (I, 11) The queen offers Gyges a choice—kill the king or die himself—but it is a hard choice. Herodotus tells us that when Gyges saw that "dire necessity" was upon him, "he chose his own life." (I, 11)

Given these conditions, it seems that Gyges wisely chooses to kill Candaules and take the queen and the throne for himself. The question arises, however, as to whether this is the *just* choice. After all, it would be easier for Gyges to run away from the city, to flee from the law. He does not do this, however; he lets himself be compelled to remain in the city, and he seizes political power. Like Socrates, Gyges lets the laws of the city dictate to him, but unlike Socrates, Gyges becomes king. Gyges' choice illustrates the radical tension between injustice and law: those who practice injustice must either die in the name of law or seize power, using the law to sanction their actions by calling them just.

Although Gyges recognizes the necessity of politics, of remaining in the city, just as Socrates does, Gyges is the opposite of Socrates: when he is forced to choose between the law of the city and himself, he chooses himself.

He is not willing to be put to death for the sake of the city's conventions, and instead he takes political power for himself and rules for thirty-eight years. And the gods sanction his actions, for Herodotus tells us that Gyges was confirmed by the oracle. (I, 13) Although Gyges is a Lydian who does not believe in the Greek gods, "he [is] the first foreigner of our knowledge to place offerings at Delphi after the king of Phrygia, Midas, son of Gorgias." (I, 14) Gyges can become king because he is willing to obey the demands of politics, to worship the city's gods and enforce the city's laws. After impiously gazing upon the naked beauty of nature, Gyges is willing to return to the clothed world of convention, and he chooses to rule, protecting the conventions of the city.

The story of Gyges implies that man may look upon what is not his own, and disregard the law of the city, only if he is willing to accept the consequences. And like Gyges, Herodotus also looks at what is not his own. Through his storytelling, he deliberately disobeys Gyges' injunction that one must look only on one's own, for he looks at the customs of other cities and reveals the nature beneath them. Herodotus shamelessly strips the clothing off of human conventions, and the story of Gyges shows what follows from such action. Herodotus is not concerned with the particular, with conventions that demand shame or vengeance; instead, he wishes to look to the universal, to the true nature of things. But Herodotus' actions, like Gyges', are subversive of politics: he is "killing the king" just as surely as Gyges is, for to throw off conventions is to throw them away. Herodotus is like the philosopher who wants to look at the beauty of the whole, who is not concerned with particulars such as one's own.

Political life, however, demands that nature be clothed in custom, that citizens gaze upon the robes of the queen and not her naked body. Herodotus appears to recognize this, for he cloaks the teaching of the *Histories* in the wrappings of myth. Herodotus does not claim to uncover the true and universal nature of things; rather, his stories offer a variety of particular customs, leaving it to the reader to determine for himself the naked truth hidden beneath the conventions of Greeks and Persians.

Glaucon's version of the story of Gyges appears in Book Two of the *Republic*, as the central feature of a beautiful and powerful speech where he demands a proof that justice be shown to be choiceworthy for its own sake. In Book One the first definition of justice is given by Cephalus, who says that justice is giving back what one owes. (331b) Cephalus believes he can get more thanks by giving back what he has taken than if he never took at all. Polemarchus then expands on this definition by saying that justice is helping one's friends and harming one's enemies. (332d) Socrates tells him, however, that "it is not the work of the just man to harm either a friend or anyone else, Polemarchus, but of his opposite, the unjust man." (335e) At this, Thrasymachus bursts in and demands that Socrates himself give a definition of justice. (336c-d) Thrasymachus asserts that justice is the advantage of the stronger, saying that "in every city the same thing is just, the advantage of the established ruling body." (339a) Socrates tell him, however, that rulers must look to the advantage of the ruled. (342e)[10]

Thrasymachus maintains that "injustice, when it comes into being on a sufficient scale, is mightier, freer, and more masterful than justice; and, as I have said from the beginning, the just is the advantage of the stronger, and the unjust is what is profitable and advantageous for oneself." (344c) Thrasymachus thinks that unjust men are both good and wise (348d), but Socrates turns the argument around and proves that they are both bad and unwise. (350c) At the end of Book One, Socrates demonstrates that the just man is blessed and happy and the unjust man wretched. (345a)

At the beginning of Book Two, Glaucon prefaces his story of Gyges by stepping in and asking Socrates if there is a kind of good which "we would choose to have not because we desire its consequences, but because we delight in it for its own sake." (357b) He then asks if there is a kind of good which "we like both for its own sake and for what comes out of it. . . ." (357c) Finally, he asks if there is not also a third kind which is "drudgery but beneficial to us." (357c) Socrates maintains that justice belongs to the central type of good; it is liked both for its own sake and for what comes out of it. (359a) Glaucon, however, disagrees, saying that the opinion of the many holds justice to be a form of drudgery which is practiced for wages and reputation. "All by itself," he says, "it should be fled from as something hard." (358a) Glaucon is not interested in the consequences of justice; he wants to separate it from its consequences and look at it "all alone by itself." (358b) Glaucon demands a proof of something other than what Socrates says is true. Socrates wants to prove that justice is choiceworthy both for its own sake and for its consequences. Glaucon, however, refuses to let him do this and demands instead that Socrates prove what he does not believe.

Glaucon begins his speech about justice by telling Socrates that he will accomplish three things: "First I'll tell what kind of thing they say justice is and where it came from; second, that all those who practice it do so unwillingly, as necessary but not good; third, that it is fitting that they do so, for the life of the unjust man is, after all, far better than that of the just man, as they say." (358c) And so, Glaucon begins his speech with his definition of justice. He says that injustice is natural and justice artificial, for it is good to practice injustice but bad to suffer it, and so men get together and contract for their protection. Injustice is overreaching, or taking more than one's share, and justice is the advantage of the weaker. The weak set down a compact to enforce justice against the strong who practice injustice. Justice is "a mean between what is best—doing injustice without paying the penalty—and what is worst—suffering injustice without being able to avenge oneself." (359a)

Glaucon argues that those who practice justice do so unwillingly. Justice is not a natural state, but one which comes about as a result of law, and in the absence of the restraint of law, "we would catch the just man red-handed going the same way as the unjust man out of a desire to get the better." (359c) To illustrate this belief, Glaucon tells the story of the ring of Gyges. Gyges, or rather the ancestor of Gyges, is a shepherd who finds a ring that makes him invisible. Significantly, Glaucon speaks not of Gyges, but of his ancestor, and this is the first reference in the story to the past. An ancestor is one who lived before, who provided the conventions that define the way we live. Glaucon is telling us that his story looks back to the origins of conventional justice: since justice is artificial, they are also the origins of the city, the compact among weak men.

Notably, Gyges finds his ring after an earthquake splits open the ground: the means of injustice are brought about by disorder and dissolution just as justice is brought about through order and contract. Injustice is also brought about by the power of an earthquake which can tear open the very ground on which Gyges is standing. In a very real sense, then, the origin of injustice is in nature itself, lurking beneath the ground of civilized society and awaiting an opportunity to erupt and disrupt the artificial order of justice which man attempts to impose on nature.

Gyges goes down into the earth, just as Socrates goes down to the Piraeus and the philosopher goes down to the cave, implying that, in order to discover the truth about justice, one must be willing to descend. Gyges goes down to the graves of his ancestors, where he finds a corpse with a ring which he takes. Gyges disturbs a burial, and in taking the ring he robs a grave, an act of impiety. Glaucon, like Herodotus, implies that one must be impious and shameless to investigate the origins of justice. Gyges is like the philosopher who, in his quest for knowledge, replaces piety and shame with curiosity.

Glaucon carries the theme of nakedness from Herodotus into his own story, for his Gyges also looks upon a naked body. In both stories, nakedness is equated with truth; to look upon something naked is to see it as it really is. But Glaucon's Gyges sees nothing beautiful in the truth; it is a corpse, a dead thing. This corpse is described as looking "larger than human size," (359d) and it is contained inside a hollow bronze horse. The horse contains the corpse of an ancestor, and this ancestor is heroic: he is larger than human size. In the earth Gyges finds the legacy of the heroic age, a ring which is a sign of rule and of the power of a king.[11] Glaucon's story leads us to the beginnings of political power in the heroic age when injustice was committed on the grandest scale. The horse is also a reference to the heroic age of Greece, for it is like the Trojan horse. In Herodotus' story the attack upon Troy begins the war, and in Glaucon's story the Trojan horse contains the means of injustice. Trojan horses may be unjust and deceptive, but they also bring political power. Glaucon's horse contains a naked body, representing the truth about the nature of things, but that truth is encased in a lie, a hollow horse. In Herodotus' story the truth is clothed in convention, and Plato tells us through Glaucon that convention may be a lie, a necessary—if not noble—lie.

The earthquake occurs at a time when Gyges is acting lawfully, when he is doing his job, herding sheep. Given the opportunity, however, Gyges commits an act of impiety and injustice and seizes the means of political power from his ancestors. He takes the ring and goes off to the monthly gathering of shepherds to make their report to the king about the flocks. Glaucon tells us: "now, while he was sitting with the others, he chanced to turn the collet of the ring to himself toward the inside of his hand; when he did this, he became invisible to those sitting by him, and they discussed him as though he were away." (359e) Gyges turns the collet inward, making it invisible, and this makes him invisible. With the power of the ring, he can escape the eyes of the law and the king's assembly, and he can observe unobserved. But it is not enough for Gyges to remain quietly invisible. He tests the power of the ring by turning the collet out again; he is curious to see what he can and cannot do. Gyges found the ring by chance, but he uses it by choice, and he uses it to take the king's wife and throne and to kill the king.

Political power rests on the ability to commit injustice; if one can become invisible, one can act unjustly and become king. Gyges begins a just reign as king with an unjust act. Justice, then, rests on injustice just as the glory of Greece rested on the injustices of the heroic age, and just as the feet of the shepherd tending his flock rest on the earth containing the ring of invisibility and power. The means of injustice always lie beneath the feet of the just man, and if he unearths these means, he might willingly use their power. The man who can act as Gyges did will become king; the man who cannot will spend his life herding sheep.

Glaucon maintains that "all men suppose injustice is far more to their private profit than justice." (360d) He goes on to set in opposition the lives of the just and unjust man, or rather, the life of the just man who is considered unjust and the life of the unjust man who is considered just. Glaucon tells Socrates that the unjust man is said to be happier: "Thus, they say, Socrates, with gods and with humans, a better life is provided for the unjust man than for the just man." (362c)

The rest of the *Republic* can be seen as Socrates' answer to Glaucon's speech. Socrates creates the city in speech in order to show Glaucon what justice is. Socrates presents two definitions of justice in the *Republic*: justice for the city and justice for the philosopher. These two definitions of justice appear in Book Four where Socrates distinguishes between doing one's job and doing one's job well. Doing one's job is the justice of the city; it requires adherence to the city's laws and conventions. But doing one's job well requires philosophy: it requires knowledge of the good, both for the city and for the philosopher. Accordingly, the philosopher is the truly just man because he has knowledge of the good. If justice is equated with knowledge, the philosopher's justice is choiceworthy for its own sake.

The city's justice is not choiceworthy for its own sake, but for its consequences; in fact, the perfectly just city is impossible, for it would require men to give up their own conventions, which, as Herodotus' stories imply, cannot be done. The arguments in Books Three through Seven detail Socrates' creation of the just city, a city in speech only. The just city would require the rule of philosopher-kings, but philosophers do not want to rule, for to rule is to be concerned with the particular and conventional, but philosophers desire the universal.[12] The city is necessary, but it is particular and not universal. It is necessary because it cares for the body, but it is particular because it neglects the soul. The city must create conventions to enforce its justice; it must cloak unjust human nature in just laws and customs. The city is dependent upon its laws and its gods, for they preserve its artificial justice which protects the weak.

Although Glaucon identifies injustice with natural strength, it seems that in the city, under the eyes of the law, strength is not sufficient to commit injustice. One must also be invisible in order to be unjust successfully. Law protects the weak, and one must escape the law in order to practice injustice. There are two ways to accomplish this: first one may become invisible. This, however, is difficult if one lives in the city under the eyes of the law. But there is another way to escape the law—to be above it. Who is above the law? Not the philosopher, for he obeys the law even if it opposes his quest for the truth, recognizing that law is necessary, if not sufficient. There is, however, one man who is above the law, and this man is the tyrant. Gyges is a tyrant, for his ring enables him to obtain the two things that a tyrant desires: pleasure and power, or the king's wife and the king's throne. Socrates must prove to Glaucon that this life of tyranny is not desirable, and he does this in Book Nine. The tyrant is not happy, according to Socrates, because he only gratifies his "unlawful desires." The tyrant satisfies his body, but he neglects his soul. He cannot see the good; he is supremely conventional.

In Book Ten Socrates tells Glaucon: "For the contest is great, my dear Glaucon, greater than it seems—this contest that concerns becoming good or bad—so we mustn't be tempted by honor or money or any ruling office or, for that matter, poetry, into thinking that it's worthwhile to neglect justice and the rest of virtue." (608b) The philosopher, Socrates implies, is greater than the tyrant because he is not bound by the city and its conventional desires. He can look beyond the city, beyond one's own, to the whole, and only in this sort of knowledge can one find happiness.[13]

Socrates, however, proves the superiority of philosophy to tyranny by looking to the consequences of justice, or rather injustice. He tells Glaucon:

> And in what way is it profitable to get away with doing injustice and not pay the penalty? Or doesn't the man who gets away with it become still worse; while, as for the man who doesn't get away with it and is punished, isn't the bestial part of him put to sleep and tamed, and the tame part freed, and doesn't his whole soul . . . gain a habit more worthy of honor than the one a body gains with strength and beauty accompanied by health, in proportion as soul is more honorable than body? (591a-b)

Glaucon wants to look at bare justice, but bare justice is bare injustice, and both the philosopher and the tyrant practice it by casting aside the city's laws. In order, then, to choose between philosophy and tyranny, one must look beyond justice all alone by itself to its consequences. The consequences of philosophy are the pure pleasures of the soul, and those of tyranny, the impure pleasures of the body. Socrates must prove to Glaucon that happiness lies in philosophy, not in political greatness, for otherwise Glaucon will have to believe that one should, in fact, act like Gyges. Socrates proves his point by looking to the consequences of justice, for justice is ultimately political in its concern with the city. Glaucon is searching for natural justice, but Socrates knows this is not possible in a political context.

The philosopher knows that he is bound to the city, for he cannot separate his soul from the needs of his body. The city is necessary because not all men can practice philosophy, and it is only in the city, which cares for the body, that the philosopher can be free to care for the soul. The name of Gyges resurfaces in Book Ten, where Socrates tells Glaucon: "But we found that justice by itself is best for soul itself, and that the soul must do the just things, whether it has Gyges' ring or not, and, in addition to such a ring, Hades' cap." (612b) The philosopher, however, must practice his justice, which is philosophy, in the city among men, and his philosophy subverts the city, for it questions the city's conventions. The philosopher wants to look beyond mere *nomos*, to see the naked truth, but he recognizes the need for the city's conventions which enforce its justice.

It is for this reason that Socrates tells the myth of Er, which demonstrates that justice is good because the soul is immortal. To practice justice for the immortality of the soul is to look to its consequences, to deny what Glaucon demanded. But this is the only kind of justice that is possible for the city. The city cannot practice philosophy, it cannot practice justice for its own sake, and so Socrates gives it a myth, a convention which makes its justice possible. Socrates' myth hides the truth about justice from the eyes of the city; it puts the clothing back on the queen. All men cannot see the truth; instead, they must see their myths and conventions which preserve the city's artificial justice. It is only Socrates, the philosopher, who can gaze upon the truth. Ultimately, however, this practice kills even Socrates. Unlike Gyges, who was willing to kill the city's ruler, Socrates is willing to let the city kill him. Both Socrates and Gyges demonstrate the price to be paid for disregarding the city's conventions, for looking beyond one's own. To disregard *nomos* successfully, one must be invisible; otherwise, one must be willing to hide the naked truth in the clothing of convention, as Gyges ultimately does, or to cloak *logos* in *mythos*, as Herodotus and Plato do.

In both Plato and Herodotus, the case for injustice becomes the case for philosophy. It is unjust by the city's standards to look on the true nature of things, and so the philosopher must keep his knowledge of truth to himself, or pay the penalty. In Herodotus' story the truth is beautiful, it is the naked body of a woman, and so looking on the truth is beautiful. But Glaucon's story questions the connection between beauty and truth. Glaucon's truth is ugly and unerotic; it is a naked corpse. For him, the unjust discovery of truth is not beautiful, but merely useful. Glaucon, the potential tyrant, needs Socrates to prove to him the beauty of truth.[14] He needs Socrates to prove that justice is choiceworthy for its own sake. Socrates cannot do this, however; he knows that truth must be sought within the walls of the city, and that, because of this, justice cannot be separated from its consequences.

Socrates knows that the pursuits of the philosopher and the pursuits of the city are irreconcilable; the city will always see the philosopher's justice as injustice. And so, he provides Glaucon with a myth, a myth which makes justice desirable, and which saves Glaucon from the lures of tyranny. Glaucon had asked if the just man would not act like the unjust man if he could. Socrates' answer seems to be yes, he would, unless he can be taught to prefer the philosophic life to the life of conventional pleasure. This is the final function of the *Republic*—it teaches Glaucon to live like Socrates, and not like Gyges.

Notes

1. See Mary Nichols, "Glaucon's Adaptation of the Story of Gyges and Its Implications for Plato's Political Teaching," *Polity* 17, no. 1 (1984): 31. Nichols also believes that Glaucon's story is a deliberate retelling of Herodotus' and, as such, provides insight into the philosophic teaching of both Plato and Herodotus. In addition to the benefits of Nichols' work, I must acknowledge a tremendous debt to Professor Harvey Mansfield who, for many years, has informed and enlightened my understanding of ancient thought and who originally brought the story of Gyges to my attention.

For a different interpretation of the story, see Kirby Flower Smith, "The Tale of Gyges and the King of Lydia," *American Journal of Philology* 23 (1902): 261. Smith argues that Herodotus deliberately left the magic ring out of the well-known tale of the Lydian king, in an attempt to rationalize the story. According to Smith, Plato recounts the story of Gyges' finding the ring, while Herodotus' story is a modified tale of Gyges' actions *after* finding the ring.

2. See Nichols, "Glaucon's Adaptation," 30-31; also Leo Strauss, *The City and Man* (Chicago: University of Chicago Press, 1978), 100.

3. If truth is the standard by which to judge history, Herodotus can hardly be called a historian, for his *Histories* is full of factual untruths. It is, in fact, so untruthful in its account that Plutarch was prompted to write a treatise, "On the Malice of Herodotus," wherein he renamed the "Father of History" the "Father of Lies." Plutarch, *Moralia*, Vol. 11 (Cambridge: Loeb Classical Library, Harvard University Press, 1965), 9. I view Herodotus' "lies" as myths —allegorical representations highlighting the essential variability of *nomoi*.

4. Herodotus, *The Histories* (Cambridge: Loeb Classical Library, Harvard University Press, 1981). All references to the *Histories* are from this edition, with occasional modifications in translation, and will be noted parenthetically by section number.

5. Seth Benardete, *Herodotean Inquiries* (The Hague: Martinus Nijhoff, 1969), 9.

6. Plato, *The Republic*, Allan Bloom, trans. (New York: Basic Books, 1968). All references to the *Republic* are from this edition and will be noted parenthetically by line number.

7. Cf. Benardete, *Inquiries*, 4. Professor Benardete once commented to me on the passage as follows: "What makes Herodotus look so Platonic is that in the context of this sentence he presents an astonishing thought: that no happiness exists if there is justice. In effect, Herodotus says: 'The reason why I am shifting from the issue of justice to this other issue [of happiness] is because political life, in its attempt to combine freedom and greatness, necessarily leads to injustice.'" According to Benardete, political happiness resides in the coincidence of freedom and greatness—an impossibility. I am in this regard, as in others, indebted to his Herodotean insights.

8. We recall that Plato's Thrasymachus is shamed for asserting that justice is the advantage of the stronger; he blushes. (350d)

9. Why does the queen wait all night to confront Gyges? The obvious implication is that the queen, having discovered Gyges, spends a night of pleasure with him. It is as if, under the cover of darkness when no one could see them, she is also removed from the laws of shame. But in the cold light of morning when all is made apparent, the queen becomes ashamed and offers her ultimatum in the name of justice.

10. We notice that Herodotus' Gyges combines the two definitions: he seeks his own advantage but then uses the law to preserve and protect the city. For Herodotus, bare injustice lays the foundation for justice.

11. Kirby Flower Smith provides an extensive note on the literary significance of magic rings throughout history. (Smith, "Tale of Gyges," 268-69.) In addition, Jeffrie Murphy provides valuable commentary on Plato's story, viewing it as a parable of moral humility. See Jeffrie Murphy and Jean Hampton, *Forgiveness and Mercy* (Cambridge: Cambridge University Press, 1988), 101-2.

12. The philosopher knows that if one were truly invisible, one would not wish to be king. Thus, the soul of Odysseus in the myth of Er chooses the private life. (620c)

13. Here, Plato's Socrates echoes and expands upon Herodotus' sentiment that human happiness is not to be found in any particular city, with its fleeting political greatness.

14. We are forced to question the veracity of Plato's Socrates, however, when we look to his comment in Book Four:

> I once heard something that I trust. Leontius, the son of Aglaion, was going up from the Piraeus under the outside of the North Wall when he noticed corpses lying by the public executioner. He desired to look, but at the same time he was disgusted and made himself turn away; and for a while he struggled and covered his face. But finally, overpowered by the desire, he opened his eyes wide, ran toward the corpses and said: "Look, you damned wretches, take your fill of the fair sight." (439e)

Is truth really the beautiful body of the queen or merely a naked corpse? What are we to make of men whose ascent to truth culminates in such a "fair sight"?

Chapter 3

Aristotle and the "City of Sows": Doing Justice to Plato

John T. Scott

An old story has it that when Plato gave the first reading of his *Republic* there was only one person left by the end: Aristotle. Whether the story is apocryphal or not, Aristotle's treatment of the "city in speech" of the *Republic* in Book 2 of his *Politics* makes it appear that Plato's best student nodded off for a while. The incompleteness of Aristotle's characterization of the "city in speech" of the *Republic* is as perplexing as the seemingly mundane character of his criticism is disappointing. Notably, Aristotle fails to discuss what Socrates identifies as the most novel feature of the city he is building with Glaucon and Adeimantus: the rule of the philosopher-kings. Aristotle instead focuses his critique on Socrates' proposals for the community of women and children and of property, making some rather obvious objections that hardly seem to plumb the depths of the dialogue he is treating.[1] What sort of justice has Aristotle done to his teacher?

Aristotle's chief criticism of the *Republic* concerns Socrates' presupposition that unity is the greatest good for the city, to which he objects that the city is not such a unity but is by its nature a kind of multitude. Aristotle appears to object to the extreme unity or "holism" of Socrates' city, and such is the standard reading of his critique of the *Republic*.[2] However, Aristotle's criticism goes further, and his neglect of the governing body of the Republic and his objection to Socrates' presupposition are related.

For Aristotle, because the city is a multitude composed of individuals and partnerships that differ in kind and that thereby generate competing claims to rule and to the justice of their rule, the debate over the regime the city should have is inherently contentious. In contrast, Socrates avoids the contention that lies at the heart of politics and ensures the unity of his city from the outset by adopting the principle of "one man, one art" in building the "cities in speech," beginning with the first city of the dialogue, the city Glaucon calls a "city of sows." The "city of sows" is paradigmatic for

Aristotle of the *Republic* as a whole. Several interpreters have noted the strange prominence of Aristotle's references to the "city of sows" in his discussions of the *Republic*.[3] However, they have not seen how those references lie at the heart of his criticism of Socrates' approach and serve him as a sort of antistrophe to the explication of his own political science. The significance of the "city of sows" for Aristotle is revealed when we consider that the "city of sows" is also paradigmatic for Socrates. Socrates calls the city denigrated by Glaucon as fit for pigs the "true" or "healthy" city because it is a harmonious unity in which each part naturally fulfills its natural role. Yet that is precisely Aristotle's objection: the city is not such a unity. The success of the principle of "one man, one art" eliminates the need for a ruling body in the "city of sows" and prevents injustice or justice in any meaningful sense from appearing. The continuing success of Socrates' principle would make a ruling body unnecessary in the later cities of the *Republic* by inoculating them against an outbreak of injustice—or of justice. Aristotle ignores the rule of the philosophers because it does not emerge naturally as an intrinsic and necessary part of the city.[4] For Aristotle, both Socrates' beginning principle and presupposed end reveal a misunderstanding of the nature of the political partnership that precludes him from giving an adequate account of the regime and, indeed, of justice.

Aristotle's analysis of regimes centers on competing claims concerning justice and specifically on the way in which the differentiated parts of the city generate competing claims to rule and condition the form of regime the city can have. Socrates' mistaken analysis serves Aristotle as an antistrophe for the explication of his own political science. Aside from the thematic analysis of the city of the *Republic* in Book 2 of the *Politics*, there are several discussions of and references to the "city of sows" that illuminate both Aristotle's critique of the *Republic* and his own political theory. I will begin with a discussion of Aristotle's critique of the *Republic* and then, after turning briefly to the *Republic* to defend Aristotle's reading of the dialogue, I will analyze Aristotle's discussion of regimes in the light of his references there to the *Republic*.

Aristotle's Critique of the *Republic*

Aristotle's thematic critique of the *Republic* is found in the beginning of Book 2 of his *Politics* within his discussion of "other regimes" held to be in fine condition—actual regimes and those spoken about by others (2.1. 1260b27-32).[5] The "city in speech" of the *Republic* is the first such regime discussed by Aristotle and the one he considers at the greatest length, as if it represented the most formidable alternative to his own politics. Aristotle does not at first glance appear to rise to the challenge, yet upon closer examination his critique of the *Republic* does reveal a searching examination of the nature of the political partnership and the organic place of the regime within it. "Regime" translates *politeia*, which has the narrow sense of the "governing body" (*politeuma*) of a city and the broader sense of the authoritative ordering or arrangement (*taxis*) of the city as a whole (see 3.6.1278b8-11). Given that Aristotle will not discuss the governing body or regime of the *Republic* (*Politeia*), it is odd that he says at the outset of Book 2 that he will discuss it among "other regimes" (*politeiai*). Aristotle's principal allusion to the philosopher-kings is dismissive. He claims that Socrates "has filled out the argument with extraneous (*exôthen*) discourses, particularly concerning the sort of education the guardians should have" (2.6.1264b39-41). But we will discover in examining Aristotle's critique of the *Republic* that he regards the regime or governing body of the "city in speech" to be "extraneous" to that city because its regime does not emerge as a necessary and organic part of the city due to Socrates' initial presupposition in building it.

Aristotle's discussion of the city of the *Republic* arises out of a schematic discussion of the city as a partnership (*koinônia*[6]): the citizens can be partners in nothing, some things, or everything. This analysis builds on the very beginning of the *Politics*, where Aristotle establishes that the city is a partnership, and the "most authoritative" partnership embracing all the other partnerships (1.1.1252a1-6). In Book 2 Aristotle begins to inquire: in what are the members of the city partners and to what extent?[7] Plainly, the citizens cannot be partners in nothing, for they are at least partners in a location (2.1. 1261b36-1262a1). If the citizens' sharing in nothing is an absurd extreme, the city of the *Republic* represents the opposite extreme of the citizens sharing in everything in common, including women, children, and property (2.1.1261 a4-9). Socrates would have his citizens hold everything in "common" (*koina*), making their "partnership" (*koinônia*) complete. Aristotle's critique of the *Republic* is an inquiry into what sort of partnership the city is or should be.[8]

Aristotle questions both Socrates' proposals and his presupposition regarding the end of the city that leads him to suggest them. His main criticism of Socrates' city concerns "the end which he asserts the city should have.... I mean, that it is best for the city to be as far as possible entirely one" (2.2. 1261a13-16; see Plato, *Republic* 5.422b-d). Aristotle devotes most of his discussion of the *Republic* to the practical difficulties of Socrates' proposals for eliminating the subpolitical partnership of the household through the community of women, children, and property in pursuit of the end of unity. Many of his criticisms are quite sensible, even obvious. For example, he remarks that the inhabitants of Socrates' city will suspect whose children are whose (2.3.1262a14-24) and he argues that people tend to care less for what is not exclusively their own because they do not have the requisite affection for it (2.3.1261b32-40, 2.4.1262b14-35, 2.5.1263a40-b5). He also claims that it is unclear whether Socrates extends his communistic institutions to the lowest class of the city, and objects that in any case the divide between the lowest class and the guardians and auxiliaries produces two cities in opposition to one another (2.5.1264a11-29).[9] Socrates' proposals either deny or overextend the natural self-love and affection which are the basis for the political community and which are instilled most importantly in the partnership of the household. As Aristotle says, "the source and springs of affection, political order, and justice are in the household" (*Eudemian Ethics* 7.1242a22-23). Even if Socrates' proposals were possible, they would undermine his presupposed goal of unity (1261a11-12).

Aristotle concentrates at such length on Socrates' proposals to eliminate the subpolitical partnerships based in the household because they reveal a conception of the political partnership that contradicts his own understanding. Aristotle teaches that the political partnership is made up of subordinate partnerships, including especially the household. "Every city is composed of households" (1.3.1253b1-3), Aristotle states in Book 1, thus dismissing Socrates' city.[10] The political partnership embraces the other partnerships and is the "most authoritative" (*kuriôtatê*) partnership because it aims at the "most authoritative good of all": "living well," or happiness (1.1.1252a1-6, 1.2. 1252b27-30; *Nicomachean Ethics* 1.2.1095a17-20). The natural end or completion of the human being is realizable only through the self-sufficiency possible in the political partnership. Aristotle therefore concludes that "man is by nature a political animal" and that the city is natural and is "prior by nature" to the individual (1.2.1252b27-1253a29). The authoritativeness of politics is architectonic in that politics aims at the greatest good of the political animal (*NE* 1.1.1094a1-1.2.1095b14). Architectonic arts or sciences direct the arts or sciences subordinated to them, they do not serve as the model for a sole form of rulership or rule over them as masters over slaves. The analogy holds in politics. The political partnership is authoritative over the subordinate partnerships and "embraces" them, but it is not the only form of rule. Aristotle argues this point at the beginning of the *Politics*, apparently arguing against Socrates in the *Statesman* (295c). Different partnerships have different proper forms of rule because they differ not in size but "in kind" (1.1.1252a7-16). Aristotle therefore turns to a discussion of the partnerships that come to make up the political partnership. The subpolitical partnerships of man/wife, parent/child, master/slave, household, and village vary in kind because they have differing immediate ends and because their parts or members are differentiated in kind. Rule over a female is—or should be—different from rule over a slave because females are not by nature slaves (1.2.1252b5-9). The city is a multiplicity composed of partnerships that vary in kind and is authoritative in that it most of all aims at the end ultimately aimed at by all the individuals and partnerships that make it up. When Aristotle criticizes Socrates for eliminating the subpolitical partnerships involving the household, he criticizes him for misunderstanding the nature of a city as a multitude and for conflating partnerships that differ in kind and in the forms of rule proper to them. In Aristotle's view, Socrates' proposal to eliminate the subpolitical partnership betrays a misunderstanding of the nature of the political partnership.[11]

Aristotle points to Socrates' misconception of the city in his main criticism concerning Socrates' aim in proposing to eliminate the subpolitical partnerships of the household. Socrates supposes that the city is or should be a unity. Aristotle counters this by claiming: "And yet it is evident that as it becomes increasingly one it will no longer be a city. For the city is in its nature a sort of multitude [*plêthos...ti*], and as it becomes more a unity it will be a household instead of a city, and a human being instead of a household; for we would surely say that the household is more of a unity than the city, and the individual more than the household" (2.2.1261a16-20). In character-izing Socrates' aim, Aristotle appears to refer to Socrates' remarks about how communism of women and children and property will bind the city together and make it "one," thus achieving the "greatest good" of the city (5.462a-b). Socrates describes such a city as being bound by "the community (*koinônia*) of pleasure and pain," making the city like a single human being since all its members feel pain and pleasure at the same time and toward the same things, all of them saying "my own" about the same things (5.462b-464b). Aristotle's criticism of Socrates' proposals to make the citizens say "my own" about the same things and his objection to Socrates' aim in doing so both involve a disagreement over what sort of "partnership" the city is.[12] Socrates somehow denies the nature of the city as "a sort of multitude." Aristotle explains what "sort of multitude" he considers the city to be when he remarks against Socrates: "Now the city is made up not only of a number of human beings, but also of human beings differing in kind (*ex eidei*): a city does not arise from persons who are similar" (2.2.1261a22-24). Aristotle's discussion in Book 1 of the *Politics* of the rise of the political partnership out of the subpolitical partnerships of the household is the basis of his criticism of Socrates here.

Aristotle imagines that Socrates does recognize that the city is made up of a number of persons but that he somehow does not realize that these persons differ "in kind." But surely Socrates realizes that the city is made up of human beings who differ "in kind." That different individuals are fitted by nature for different arts or different functions in the city is the very presupposition Socrates adopts in building the "city in speech."[13] Aristotle indicates how he means his criticism of Socrates' failure to understand the differentiated nature of the city when, after having said that a city does not arise from persons who are similar, he continues: "A city is different from an alliance" (1261a24-25). While artisans differ in their arts, they are not differentiated "in kind" in the way that Aristotle explains that the parts of the city differ in his discussion of the city and the subpolitical associations that make it up. Aristotle considers Socrates' city of artisans to be more like an alliance than a true city.

The inherent limitation of Socrates' presupposition in building his "city in speech" is indicated by Aristotle in an indirect fashion in his thematic criticism of the *Republic*. Socrates seeks to make his city a unity, but the unity he crafts cannot attain the sort of unity Aristotle considers a true city to be. "Those from whom a unity should arise differ in kind. It is thus reciprocal equality which preserves cities, as was said earlier in the [discourses on] ethics" (2.2. 1261a29-31). The *Nicomachean Ethics* contains the same remark (5.8.1132b 33-34). The discussion there concerns reciprocal exchange as a form of justice. A partnership for exchange, he explains, is formed by those who are unlike and in need of others. Exchanges in such a partnership are equalized by relative value. Aristotle's example should be familiar to Plato's readers: "There will be reciprocity, then, when the equalization of the exchange becomes such that a farmer is to a shoemaker as the product of the shoemaker is to that of the farmer" (5.8.1133a33-b1).[14] He also uses the example of an exchange between a carpenter and a shoemaker in this context. That Aristotle is alluding to the first city of the *Republic*, the city consisting initially of the farmer, house builder, weaver, and shoemaker, is made explicit in the parallel discussion in his *Magna Moralia* (1.33.1193b38-1194a25). However, while reciprocal exchange may "preserve" cities, it does not constitute them as cities, for it does not reach the question of what form of regime a city will have. These questions concern distributive justice, which Aristotle distinguishes from reciprocal exchange as a form of commutative justice. Distributive justice clearly raises political issues, especially regarding competing claims to rule, as is clear from both the *Politics* and *Ethics*. By remarking in his criticism of the *Republic* on reciprocal justice as it is found in the "city of sows," Aristotle suggests that, by modeling his city on the exchange of artisans,

Socrates will never raise the issues of distributive justice so central to politics.

The limitation of reciprocal exchange is suggested by Aristotle in the *Politics* when he explains his remark about reciprocal equality and, as in the *Ethics*, appears to allude to the "city of sows." Reciprocal equality preserves cities, he says, even among persons who are free and equal, "for all cannot rule at the same time, but each rules for a year or according to some other arrangement or period of time. In this way, then, it results that all rule, just as if shoemakers and carpenters were to exchange places rather than the same persons always being shoemakers and carpenters" (2.2.1261a29-37). Decisions about who should rule depend upon some decision about relevant equality or inequality among persons. Whether or not it is better for some always to rule because they are better, or for equals to rule by turns (2.2. 1261a37-b3) is a political decision about justice that transcends issues of reciprocal justice. Socrates' starting point of "one man, one art" in building his city precludes him from fully raising and confronting the difficult and related issues of distributive justice and the regime. For Aristotle, the "city of sows" is paradigmatic for the *Republic* as a whole.

The "City of Sows" in the *Republic*

In regarding the "city of sows" as paradigmatic, Aristotle follows Socrates' own lead. The first city of the *Republic* is a city of artisans who come together because of need. Glaucon objects to the city built by his brother, Adeimantus, and Socrates and says that they have been providing not for a human city, but a "city of sows." Socrates agrees to examine a "luxurious city" but says that he believes that the "true city" is the one he and Glaucon's brother had just described, a "healthy" city as opposed to the "feverish" one Glaucon wants to see (2.372d-e).[15] As the "true city" grows into the city of the armed camp with a specific warrior class and ultimately the "beautiful city" ruled over by the philosopher-kings, Socrates and his interlocutors try to prevent or purge the disease of injustice. The "city of sows" remains the paradigmatic city for the *Republic* as a whole, but there are numerous indications in the dialogue that Socrates (and thus Plato) sees some of the same limitations of his approach to building his cities as Aristotle does.

Socrates and his young interlocutors begin building a city in speech in order to see the origin and nature of justice. Glaucon and Adeimantus want to see whether the just life is worth living, what justice and injustice do to the souls of those who possess them. Socrates suggests that they look for justice in the larger entity of the city on the assumption that they will see "the likeness of the bigger in the *idea* of the littler" (2.369a).[16] The questionable assumption of the likeness of justice in the individual and in the city, or an even more questionable assumption of sameness (see 4.434d-435e), is based upon the essential likeness of the individual and the city.[17] The dubious parallel Socrates draws between the city and the individual makes sense of Aristotle's perhaps initially strange criticism that the unity Socrates seeks in the city makes it more like a household or even like an individual human being. Although the title of Plato's dialogue would appear to indicate that it is about the city or "public things" (a very literal translation of the title), the individual is in an important way the ultimate object of analysis and interest in the work. For example, the ultimate importance of the individual for the dialogue is indicated when Socrates concludes his discussion of the cycle of regimes in Books 8 and 9 by stating that the just man "looks fixedly at the regime within him" and that they have been laying up a pattern (*paradeigma*) for someone who "wants to see and found a city within himself" (9.591d-592b). Perhaps the most vivid conflation of the individual and the city in Socrates' presentation is his discussion of the "community" (*koinônia*) of pleasure and pain that he says would be created by his communistic proposals and would produce the "greatest good" of the city: unity. Unified in this fashion, the city would be like a single human being, or rather a single body.[18] This, of course, is the discussion upon which Aristotle concentrates his attention in his critique of the *Republic*. That Aristotle objects to Socrates' treating the city as an organic unity is fairly obvious, but less attention has been paid to the way Aristotle points out that Socrates stacks the deck from the very beginning of the building of the "cities in speech" by introducing the principle of "one man, one art," thereby ensuring that these cities will be the sort of unity to which Aristotle objects.

Socrates gets his companions to agree to watch a city come into being in speech. To begin their investigation, Socrates suggests an origin for the political partnership: "a city, as I believe, comes into being because each of us isn't self-sufficient but is in need of much" (2.369b). The most basic city, "the city of utmost necessity," would be made up of four or five artisans: a farmer, a house builder, a weaver, a shoemaker,and perhaps another artisan concerned with the needs of the body (2.369d). The city Adeimantus and Socrates found is based upon exchange: "It was for just this reason that we made a partnership (*koinônia*) and founded the city" (2.371b). They agree that since "each of us is naturally not quite like anyone else, but rather differs in his nature, different men are apt for the accomplishment of different jobs," they should adopt the principle of "one man, one art" (2.370a-b).

Socrates' adoption of the principle of "one man, one art" ensures that justice and injustice will fail to come to light in the "city of sows" and in the *Republic* as a whole. Having posited that their city of necessity will consist of four or five artisans, Socrates asks Adeimantus whether the artisans will put their products at the disposition of all in common or divide their time practicing different arts by themselves, "not taking the trouble to share in common, but minding his own business for himself." Adeimantus answers: "Perhaps, Socrates, the latter is easier than the former."[19] Socrates replies: "I myself also had the thought when you spoke that, in the first place, each of us is naturally not quite like anyone else, but rather differs in his nature; different men are apt for the accomplishment of different jobs. Isn't that your opinion?" Adeimantus agrees, and they adopt the principle of "one man, one art" (2.369e-370a). Close examination of this passage yields several surprises. Socrates gives Adeimantus the choice of each man doing his own art and sharing the products or each one "minding his own business." These divergent options actually converge when they adopt the principle of "one man, one art." "Minding one's own business" is how Socrates will later define justice, and by that he means each of the artisans in the city performing the art for which he (or she) was presumably intended by nature (see 4.433a-b).[20] There is no conflict between individual good and the good of the community in the "city of sows"; minding ones' own business coincides perfectly with sharing in common.[21] One could imagine justice—or rather injustice—arising in Socrates' city with an unfair exchange among its artisan residents, or what we might call with Aristotle a problem of justice as reciprocal exchange. Socrates eliminates any such conflict, as is seen in his answer to Adeimantus' suggestion that minding one's own business might be easier than sharing in common. Socrates responds that he had the same thought. We expect him to say that minding one's own business, which we initially understand as pursuing one's self-interest, is easier; however, what he does say is that each of us is suited by nature for a different art. Socrates gets Adeimantus to agree to this proposition, thereby avoiding the problem of the conflict between self-interest and common interest, and, thus, any serious consideration of justice. The success of the principle of "one man, one art" ensures that they will never see injustice or justice come into being in their city.

The success of the principle for apportioning arts is shown when Socrates and Adeimantus look for justice in the first city of the *Republic* and cannot find it. Supposing that their city has reached "completeness," Socrates asks Adeimantus where in the city justice and injustice would be. Adeimantus has difficulty answering. "'I can't think, Socrates,' he said, 'unless it's somewhere in some need these men have of one another'" (2.371e-372a).

Socrates does not agree or disagree, and the proposition is never examined. However, the principle of "one man, one art" has ensured that Adeimantus cannot find justice or injustice in the city built in accordance with it. The "need" we have of one another leads us to make exchanges, and justice would be found in the reciprocal equality or fairness of the exchanges, at least in the terms of Aristotle's discussion of justice. But this sort of justice is rather empty and hardly merits being called justice at all in any normal, "political" sense of the term. Apparently, Socrates' artisans in the "city of sows" know instinctively how many houses equal how many shoes (see *Magna Moralia* 1.33.1193b38-1194a25), just as they somehow know who is naturally suited for what art. They have no apparent interest in making an unfairly advantageous exchange nor in transgressing the limits of their arts.

Not only is there no justice or injustice in the "city of sows," but there is no governing body either. The two absences are related. There is no need for a governing body in the "city of sows" because of its very "health." If every artisan "minds his own business" and practices his art, then there is no need for politics in any ordinary understanding of the word. It is no wonder that its inhabitants sing of the gods (2.372b), for they are truly blessed.

Despite their lives of seeming blessedness, Glaucon objects that the inhabitants of the city his brother and Socrates have been building will "have their feast without relishes." The feast Socrates offers would suit a "city of sows" (2.372c-d). Glaucon seems to characterize the first city of the *Republic* this way because it is not a truly human city. The inhabitants of the "city of sows" are limited to the limited and satisfiable needs of the body (2.369d); they do not seem to experience any truly human desires. There is also irony in Glaucon's choice of name for the city. There are no pigs in the "city of sows." There is, it seems, no meat-eating in a city where they feast on onions, acorns, and other food fit for pigs. Glaucon demands "relish" (*opson*), that is, savory meats, to put on bread. Swineherds will be among the first artisans needed in the "luxurious city" Glaucon wants to see (compare 2.370d-e to 373c).[22] There are no swineherds in the "city of sows" in another sense as well, for its swinish inhabitants do not need governing. The "piggish" demand for the "relishes" would produce a feverish desire that must be reined in by rulers.

Socrates indulges Glaucon's desire to see "a luxurious city" come into being. "Perhaps that's not bad either," he says, appearing to recognize the insufficiency of the "city of sows": "For in considering such a city, too, we could probably see in what way justice and injustice naturally grow in cities." But will they? Despite its lack of both justice and injustice and any need for a ruling body, Socrates takes the "city of sows" for his model. "Now, the true city is in my opinion the one we just described—a healthy city, as it were" (2.372e). The city is "healthy" not only because of its physical moderation (2.372d), but more importantly because of the unity ensured by the strict observance of the principle of "one man, one art," which will later become the basis for their definition of moderation in the city and the individual (see 4.430d-432a, 442c-d). If Socrates can success-fully purge the luxurious city of its fever by adhering strictly to the rule of "one man, one art," then it too will display no justice or injustice and no need of a ruling body.

As Adeimantus' swinish city makes way for Glaucon's "luxurious" one, further artisans are needed. As the city grows and is gorged by the "bulky mass of things, which are not in cities because of necessity." Poets, beauticians, relish-makers, and cooks are added, and so are swineherds and doctors (2.373a-d). I noted above that swineherds suggest rulership; so do doctors, for there is a persistent analogy in the *Republic* and other Platonic dialogues between doctors who tend to the health of the body and rulers who tend to the health of the soul (see 3.405e ff.). But doctors are not needed where there is health, and so too rulers would not be required where there is no disease of the soul, or injustice in Socrates' sense.

Socrates does not add rulers at this stage, but since it oversteps "the boundary of the necessary," his new city will need warriors to seize a piece of their neighbors' land. At this point Socrates reiterates the principle upon which they are building their cities. They will not let shoemakers, house builders, or any of the other artisans practice the art of war, but only "the one for which his nature fitted him," and a new class of warrior-artisans, or "guardians," is needed (2.373d-374d). It is perhaps to this discussion that Aristotle refers in his allusion to the "city of sows" within his critique of the *Republic*. While discussing how "reciprocal equality" among individuals who differ in kind preserves cities, he considers whether a certain group should always rule or the citizens should take turns ruling. He suggests that where they are essentially equal in their nature it would be just for all to have a share in rule: by turns, "just as if shoemakers and carpenters were to exchange places rather than the same persons always being shoemakers and carpenters" (2.2. 1261a29-37). As noted above, such a decision raises questions of distributive justice and the regime, but no such questions arise here in Socrates' discussion. Although it will turn out later that a ruling class emerges out of the warrior "guardians" he adds to the city here, there is as yet no ruling body in their city. The question of justice has not yet arisen, nor has the question of the regime. These questions have not arisen for two reasons. First, the principle of "one man, one art" still reigns. Second, that principle reigns because it is ensured by the external power of the city's founders: Socrates and his young interlocutors. They are no longer "watching" a city come into being (2.369c) or "considering" it (2.372e), but they too have a "job" (*ergon*) in the city—or rather without it: "'Then it's our job, as it seems, to choose, if we're able, which are the natures, and what kind they are, fit for guarding the city'" (2.374e). The health of the city is guarded by its loquacious founders, who guard against the violation of the principle upon which it is founded and thus against the appearance of justice or injustice.

The second "city in speech" of the *Republic* finally gets a ruling body, but Socrates' rulers are not a necessary, organic part of the city; rather they are added to the city to ensure its health and its very possibility. They take over the role Socrates and his young friends have been exercising. They are therefore not a "regime" in Aristotle's sense: the authoritative arrangement that arises organically out of the partnerships that compose it and that gives form to the political partnership. Socrates separates the ruling class out of the class of warrior "guardians" he has been discussing, calling them "complete guardians" to distinguish them from their helpers, the "auxiliaries" (3.414b). They too are artisans fitted by nature for their art. Their art is that of "overseers" who care for the city and supervise an education designed to prevent the disease of injustice from arising (3.412a-c). A "throng of lies and deceptions" will be needed to bolster this education, notably the "noble lie," which gives cosmic support for the differentiation of functions in the city (3.414b-415d). By following the principle of "one man, one art" the city will, unlike other cities, "naturally grow to be one and not many" (4.423b-d). However, if the principle of "one man, one art" were successful, the city would remain "healthy" and there would be no need for a governing body. The rulers are again like doctors: only necessary where there is disease. Only the possible failure of Socrates' principle in building the city of the *Republic* leads him to introduce a governing body.

With their city supposedly complete Socrates and Adeimantus look for justice and injustice within it, but as in the "city of sows" they have difficulty locating it because the success of the principle of "one man, one art" prevents injustice and its opposite from arising. Proceeding on the highly dubious assumption that they can draw the four cardinal virtues out the city like balls out of a hat (427c-428a), Socrates bids Glaucon to get himself a lantern so that they can seek out justice. They first locate wisdom and courage in the two classes of the guardians and the artisans, then they find that moderation stretches throughout the whole city and is the unanimous opinion about who should rule (431d-432a). Moderation is therefore based upon the agreement upon the principle that everyone should practice only his own art or function in the city. If the city is moderate in this sense, it remains "healthy," and the pattern set by the "city of sows" has been followed. Having found the first three virtues, Glaucon has difficulty finding the object of their search: justice. "'Here! here!,'" Socrates shouts, explaining to Glaucon that justice has been "rolling around" at their feet "from the beginning." They find it in the principle upon which they founded the city, "that each one must practice one of the functions in the city, that one for which his nature made him naturally most fit." Justice, they conclude, is "minding one's own business" (4.432b-433a). Justice looks suspiciously like moderation, and indeed would not be necessary where moderation was practiced. The success of the principle of "one man, one art" has again precluded justice and injustice from appearing in their city.

In sum, Socrates' principle of "one man, one art" systematically avoids the issues of justice so central to Aristotle's consideration of politics in general and of regimes in particular. The regime of the *Republic* does not grow out of the differentiated parts that make up the city and that generate claims to rule and the justice of their rule, but in order to prevent these issues from arising. One might characterize the *Republic, the* dialogue on justice, as a grand attempt to avoid the issues of justice and of politics. In his own political science, Aristotle tries to avoid what he regards as Socrates' mistaken approach, the limitations of which are evident from a reading of Plato's *Republic* that sees in it more than a blueprint for a city.

Justice in Aristotle's Analysis of Regimes

Aristotle's analysis of regimes in Book 3 of the *Politics* emerges out of the problem of political justice and claims to rule that are seemingly absent in the *Republic*. His analysis might be characterized as dialectical: he addresses various views about justice and just claims to rule— even putting the opponents' disagreements into speeches. He then acts as a judge, adjudicating among competing claims by examining their strengths and weaknesses in the light of the proper end of the political partnership. Within his analysis of regimes, Aristotle refers to the "city of sows" in a way that illuminates why he believes that Socrates' treatment of the regime, and politics more generally, is deficient.

The debate over justice and the claim to rule is central from the outset of Aristotle's consideration of regimes in Book 3 of the *Politics*. He begins his consideration with a debate: "For one investigating the regime— what each sort is and what its quality— virtually [*schedon*] the first investigation concerns the city, to see what the city actually is [*ti pote estin*]. For as it is, there are disputes, some arguing that the city performed an action, others that it was not the city but the oligarchy or the tyrant" (3.1.1274b32-5). The debate over the identity of the city involves the question of the justice of the regime as the authoritative ordering of the political partnership. Those who do not believe that the regime is just reject it and claim that the actions of the regime are not to be taken for those of the city itself. This debate is particularly acute with revolutions (3.3.1276a6-16). Is the city the same city with a change in regime? Should the new regime be held accountable for the actions of the old one? Since the regime determines who is a citizen, the debate over the identity of the city is a debate over who are citizens, or more particularly, over "whether [they are so] justly or unjustly" (3.2.1275b34-7). Questions about the regime as the authoritative arrangement of the city necessarily raise the issue of justice, and that issue is inherently contentious in a partnership composed of parts that differ in kind. In Socrates' city there will be no debates over whether the city performed an action. Its unity is held to be its great strength against other cities, where there are such disputes (4.422e-423b). However, such a degree of unity is possible only if there is never any question as to who should rule; the success of the principle of "one man, one art" precludes any dispute about the city and its regime. Such disputes are the stuff of politics, however, and Aristotle begins his own consideration of the regime from a "political" viewpoint where the regime arises from the debate over justice.

In Book 1 of the *Politics*, Aristotle defined the city as the authoritative partnership composed of several subordinate partnerships, and at the beginning of Book 3 he says that for one investigating the regime "virtually" the first thing to investigate is the city, "what the city actually is." In referring back to his earlier discussion Aristotle suggests its limitation. We might say what was missing was politics. As Harry Jaffa remarks, "Aristotle's point of view in Book I is one of radical detachment from political life."[23] To learn that the city is composed of partnerships does not tell us what any particular city is. To learn that the city is the authoritative partnership does not tell us what any particular city is until we learn what its authoritative arrangement is, that is, until we learn what sort of regime it has. Aristotle's initial analysis of the city in abstraction from its regime suffers from the same limitation as Socrates' construction of the "city in speech" in the *Republic*.

The city is indeed a composite made up of parts, a partnership begun from our lack of self-sufficiency and our need for one another; however, the "material" of the city is, so to speak, inanimate without the "form" it is given by a regime. Aristotle therefore describes the parts of which the city is composed differently in his consideration of the regime from the description at the outset of the work. "We see that the entire activity of the political [ruler] and the legislator is concerned with the city, and the regime is some particular arrangement of those who inhabit the city. But since the city belongs among composite things . . . it is clear that the first thing that must be sought is the citizen; for the city is some particular multitude of citizens [*hê gar polis politôn ti plêthos estin*]" (3.1.1274b34-41; cf. 2.2.1261a18: *plêthos gar ti tên physin estin hê polis*). The "multitude of citizens" is not necessarily or even usually equivalent to the entire population of the city, but is restricted to "some particular multitude." A citizen is someone who shares in "decision and office," but who is a citizen varies from regime to regime. The citizen of a democracy will not necessarily be a citizen of an oligarchy (3.1.1275a2-33). The authoritative decision about who is a citizen defines the regime and above all makes a city what it "actually" is. Regimes differ "in kind" (3.1.1275a33-6), and so Aristotle concludes that a change in regime therefore produces an essentially different city for there is a change in form even if there is a continuity of inhabitants, or its "material." I will take up the relationship between the form and the material of the city in the next section. For now it enough to note that Aristotle concludes that "it is looking to the regime above all that the city must be said to be the same" or different (3.3.1276b1-15).

Aristotle's discussion of the types of regimes acknowledges the debate over claims to justice and the aim of the political partnership, and a reference to the "city of sows" within that discussion reveals once again that he believes that Socrates has misunderstood the nature of the city and its regime. As noted above, "regime" translates *politeia*, which has the narrow sense of the "governing body" (*politeuma*) of a city and the broader sense of the authoritative ordering or arrangement (*taxis*) of the city as a whole. Aristotle relates these two senses when he defines the "regime" as "an arrangement [*taxis*] of a city with respect to its offices, particularly the one that has authority over all [matters]. For what has authority in the city is everywhere the governing body [*politeuma*], and the governing body is the regime" (3.6. 1278b8-11). The governing body differs from city to city, and therefore there are several forms of regime. Those regimes that aim at the "common advantage" are "correct according to what is unqualifiedly just" while those that look to the advantage of the rulers are "errant" and "deviations from the correct regimes" (3.6.1279a16-20). Aristotle therefore divides regimes into "correct" and "deviant." Further, since the "authoritative element" must be "either one or a few or the many," he further divides regimes according to the number of their governing body, or citizenry more generally. This double division produces a schema of regimes: the "correct" regimes are kingship, aristocracy, and polity, and the "deviant" ones are tyranny, oligarchy, and democracy (3.7.1279a22-38). Aristotle's typology is rather schematic, abstract, even "Platonic" in its identification of ideal

types. We might characterize what is missing from this schematic presentation as the same thing as was missing from his discussion of the composition
of the city at the outset of his work: politics.

The various regimes are not ideal types, but arrangements of parts that
differ in kind and are ordered according to some view of justice and the aim
of the political partnership. Aristotle acknowledges the limitation of his
initial schematic presentation of the regimes when he states: "It is necessary
to speak at somewhat great length of what each of these regimes is. For
certain questions are involved, and it belongs to one philosophizing in
connection with each sort of inquiry and not merely looking toward action
not to overlook or omit anything, but to make clear the truth concerning each
thing" (3.8. 1279b11-15). An overly "philosophic" view of the regime will
not capture the effectual truth of the thing. The quantitative division of
regimes into one, few, or many fails to capture the animating principle of
oligarchies and democracies in particular. Oligarchy is the regime in which
those with property have authority and democracy is where the poor have
authority because of their numbers. Number is less important in defining
these regimes than material considerations.[24] "What makes democracy and
oligarchy differ is poverty and wealth; wherever some rule on account of
wealth, whether a minority or a majority, this is necessarily an oligarchy, and
wherever those who are poor, a democracy. But it turns out, as we said, that
the former are few and the latter many" (3.8.1279b39-1280a4). Aristotle will
discuss the relative proportion of rich to poor in different cities and the
bearing of that proportion on what form of regime suits that city in Book 4
of the *Politics*. At this point, he reveals how the form of regime is determined not only by the material of the city, but also by the competing
understandings of justice that emerge from those material conditions.

Aristotle discusses differing understandings about justice and claims to
rule in terms of the proper nature and aim of the political partnership and
rejects several sorts of partnerships that fall short of a true political
partnership in one way or another, including the "city of sows." He began his
consideration of the regime by noting that there are debates over the identity
of the city, its regime, and its citizens. Who are the citizens, or rather are
they so "justly or unjustly"? Having offered a schema of regimes and
suggested its defects, he returns to the central debate over the regime. "It is
necessary first to grasp what they speak of as the defining principles of
oligarchy and democracy and what justice is [from] both oligarchic and
democratic [points of view]." The oligarchs and democrats frame their
claims to rule in terms of justice. Their claims are not merely rhetorical, for
they speak to the aim of the political partnership, but they are partial claims.
"For all fasten on a certain sort of justice, but proceed only to a certain point,

and do not speak of the whole of justice in its authoritative sense." Aristotle phrases the democratic and oligarchic claims in the terms he uses in his ethical writings. "For example, justice is held to be equality, and it is, but for equals and not for all; and inequality is held to be just and is indeed, but for unequals and not for all; but they disregard this element of persons and judge badly" because of their partiality. "And so since justice is for certain persons, and is divided in the same manner with respect to objects and for persons ... they agree as to the equality of the object, but dispute about it for persons" (3.9.1280a7-19; see *Nicomachean Ethics* 5.6.1131a10-b9). The parties dispute about the relevant equalities and inequalities of persons that give them a just claim to rule. However, "both, by speaking to a point of a kind of justice, consider themselves to be speaking of justice simply.... But of the most authoritative [considerations] they say nothing" (3.9.1280a19-25). Both the democrats and the oligarchs fasten on a "certain sort of justice" in order to justify their view of the city as "some particular multitude of citizens," but their claims must be judged in light of the city as the "most authoritative" partnership aiming at the "most authoritative" good.

Aristotle elaborates in particular on the limitations of the oligarchic claim to rule. "For if it were for the sake of possessions that they participated and joined together, they would share in the city just to the extent that they shared in possessions, so that the argument of the oligarchs might be held a strong one." The oligarchs treat the city like a business partnership or a trade alliance. But Aristotle objects that the city exists "not only for the sake of living, but rather primarily for the sake of living well" (3.9.1280a24-32). Here he echoes his criticism in Book 1 of that errant household management—and, implicitly, political rule—which seeks to accumulate infinitely because it forgets the end of the partnership, and is therefore "serious about living, but not about living well" (1.9.1257b24-1258a2). Aristotle objects that the city is not an alliance, for whereas an alliance exists to prevent its members from suffering injustice from anyone or "for purposes of exchange and of use of one another," in a city the citizens not only have common offices but they "take thought that the others should be of a certain quality." By the "quality" of it members Aristotle means their "political virtue and vice" (3.9.1280a31-b6)—the regime-specific understanding of what makes a "good citizen" (see 3.4.1276b16-34). An alliance falls short of a true political partnership because it lacks a political "form": a regime and the shared view of justice it embodies. The oligarchic claim to rule betrays a similar lack. So does the "city of sows."

Aristotle alludes to the *Republic* within his discussion of the way in which an alliance falls short of a true political partnership. Every city must take care that its understanding of virtue and justice is shared by its citizens, for without such care "the partnership becomes an alliance which differs from others— from [alliances of] remote allies—only by location," and apparently from alliances of allies in close proximity not at all. "And law becomes a compact [*synthêkê*], as the sophist Lycophron says, a guarantor among one another of the just things, but not the sort of thing to make the citizens good and just" (3.9.1280b6-12). Aristotle could have said the same thing against Glaucon's suggestion (following the sophists) in the *Republic* that justice results as a compact against suffering injustice (2.358e-359b). Aristotle objects to the sufficiency of Glaucon's premise, an insufficiency to which Glaucon himself could be said to point in his criticism of the city his brother and Socrates construct. However, while like Glaucon's alliance against injustice the "city of sows" also lacks any concern for the justice of its members, it does so because there is no justice—or injustice—in the city. The inhabitants of the "city of sows" adhere naturally to the principle of "one man, one art," and their alliance need have no care for virtue. Having dismissed as insufficient an understanding of the political partnership reminiscent of Glaucon's initial suggestion about the origin of cities, Aristotle turns to Adeimantus' city. After a few remarks about the necessary but not sufficient characteristics of a city such as common location and intermarriage, Aristotle makes a reference to the "city of sows" when he discusses the possibility of an alliance among artisans who agree not to be unjust in their transactions: "for example, if one were a carpenter, one a farmer, one a shoemaker, one something else of this sort, and the multitude of them were ten thousand, yet they had nothing in common except things of this sort, exchange and alliance; not even in this way would there be a city" (3.9.1280b17-23). Compare the beginning of the "city of sows" in the *Republic*: "Won't one man be a farmer, another a house builder, and still another a weaver? Or shall we add to it a shoemaker or some other man who cares for what has to do with the body?" (2.369). Neither Glaucon's city originating in a compact against injustice nor the "city of sows" built by Socrates and Adeimantus aim in themselves at the proper end of the city and therefore reach the level of a political partnership.

Aristotle's reference to the "city of sows" within his discussion of partnerships that do not reach the level of the political partnership recalls his critique of the *Republic* in Book 2, and he continues his discussion with reference to that earlier critique. From his analysis of alliances he concludes that the city is not a partnership in location and for the sake of not commit-ting injustice and of transacting business. "These things must necessarily be present if there is to be a city; but not even when all of them are present is it yet a city, but [the city is] the partnership in living well both of households and families for the sake of a complete and self-sufficient life"

(3.9.1280b29-35). The city is made up of households and families, and Aristotle's critique of the *Republic* was largely concerned with Socrates' proposals to eliminate the subpolitical partnerships that aim at the self-sufficiency made possible in the political partnership. Households share in location and intermarriage creates connections among the households and "the pastimes of living together." Aristotle explains that "This sort of thing is the work of affection; for affection is the intentional choice of living together" (3.9.1280b35-9). In his critique of the *Republic* Aristotle remarked that Socrates' communistic proposals would produce a lack of genuine affection among its citizens and suggested that those proposals would be more useful for the lowest class of artisans—in order that they might be ruled more easily because of their lack of bonds (2.4.1262a40-b22). The affection generated by intentionally living together in households and families binds the city together in concord. "Living well, then, is the end of the city, and these things are for the sake of this end. A city is the partnership of families and villages in a complete and self-sufficient life. This, we assert, is living happily and finely" (3.9.1280b39-1281a2). And Aristotle criticized Socrates for claiming that his city would be "happy" even if its inhabitants were not (2.5.1264b15-23; see *Republic* 5.420b-421c). For Aristotle, the "city in speech" of the *Republic* is not a true city: it does not aim at the proper end of the political partnership and does not attain that end, or even the end of unity which Socrates presupposes for it.

The limitation of Socrates' city from Aristotle's point of view is related to its lack of a genuine regime. For Aristotle, the regime embodies a city's shared pursuit of justice as the whole of virtue and "living well" as the end of the political partnership. The end of the city transcends merely living together, Aristotle explains, alluding back to the very beginning of the *Politics*. The city is a partnership "for the sake of noble actions" (3.9.1281a2-4). What is considered "noble" will vary with the view of "political virtue and vice" held by the inhabitants of the city, and it is concern for the "quality" of the inhabitants in this regard that distinguishes a city from an alliance. The city is bound together by concord, a form of political affection or friendship based upon a shared view about the closely related matters of justice, virtue, and the end of that particular political partnership. The shared view that binds together the city is embodied in the regime and varies according to regime (see *Nicomachean Ethics* 8.9-11. 1158a30-1161b11). The "city of sows" lacks a regime and also lacks a shared view of justice, virtue, and the end of the partnership. It has no such needs if Socrates can preserve the "health" of the city based on the pattern of the "city of sows." Even if the "beautiful city" of the *Republic* possesses a governing body, a body conspicuously ignored by Aristotle, its regime is not an organic part of the city or representative of a shared understanding and affection. Aristotle states that "justice is a thing belonging to the city. For adjudication is an arrangement of the political partnership, and adjudication is judgment as to what is just" (1.2.1253a37-9). Justice does not belong to the "city of sows" or to the later cities of the *Republic*, and Socrates' city is not a city at all.

The Form and the Material of the City: Justice and the Regime

In his consideration of the regime in Book 3 of the *Politics*, Aristotle concludes that it is sharing in a regime that most makes a city what it is. The regime is the "form" of the city, and Aristotle considers the city to have changed when there is a change in "form" even where there is continuity in its "material": "it is looking to the regime above all that the city must be said to be the same" (3.3.1276a40-b15; see 7.8.1328a36-b23). Cities differ "in kind" or form (*eidei*) because their "constituent elements differ in kind" (3.1. 1275a33-6). This is the case whether one considers those constituent elements to be partnerships or citizens: partnerships differ in kind because the individuals who compose them do and citizens differ in kind because who is a citizen is determined by the regime, which itself differs in kind from other regimes. Dispute over what form the city should take is the stuff of politics and the centerpiece of Aristotle's analysis of regimes and claims to rule. But debate over just rule does not take place in the abstract, it arises from the fact that cities are made up of parts that differ in kind, as Aristotle says in opposition to Socrates. The dialogue about justice that constitutes politics is a dialogue with a concrete basis in the brute facts of the partnership in living and living well. Dialogue over justice in any particular political setting is conditioned by the materials out of which that city is composed, and the particular form that city can take depends a great deal on the materials out of which it is composed. "Form" (*eidos*) does not exist apart from material.[25] Within his discussion of the relationship of the parts of the city in Book 4 of the *Politics*, Aristotle again refers to the "city of sows." He suggests that Socrates fails to understand the relationship between the "form" and the "material" of the city in conditioning the theoretical and practical, political considerations about justice and the regime.

Aristotle's discussion of the way in which the parts out of which the city is made conditions the form it can take is found at the beginning of his analysis of the varieties of oligarchies and democracies and in preparation of his discussion of the possible mixture of those two regimes, the polity.

"Now the reason for there being a number of regimes," he states, "is that there are a number of parts in any city." He begins his analysis of the parts of the city here as in the *Politics* as a whole: with households. "For, in the first place, we see that all cities are composed of households, and next that of this multitude some are necessarily well off, others poor, and others middling, and that of the well off and the poor there is an armed and an unarmed element" (4.3. 1289b27-31).

The assertion that *all* cities are composed of households is an implicit criticism of Socrates' proposals in the *Republic*. Aristotle's assertion is not merely an empirical one, but carries with it the idea that households as the parts of which cities are composed necessarily generate claims to rule and therefore the regime. Poor and wealthy families provide the "material" for the democratic and oligarchic claims to rule. Similarly, certain families generate aristocratic claims to rule based on "good breeding" and on virtue (4.3. 1289b40-1290a5). These claims are very closely related to the oligarchic claim based on wealth, and generally family wealth, for being "well born" frequently means coming from a wealthy family and is also frequently taken to be a sign of virtue (see 3.12.1283a16-17; 3.13.1283a29-36; 4.8.1293b36-8; 5.8.1309a2-3). Aristocratic claims to rule— the best claim in Aristotle's eyes since it aims at the proper end of the political partnership (see 3.17. 1288a9-12, 32-41)— are therefore also generated to a large degree from the subpolitical partnership of the household. The same may be the case for kingship, which is very closely related to aristocracy in Aristotle's analysis, but given the similarity between Aristotelian kingship and Socrates' philosopher-kings I shall postpone discussing that form of regime and its emergence from the parts of the city.

Different claims to rule arise out of the different types of households that may be present in a city, and "of these parts all share in the regime in some cases, and in others more or fewer." The different arrangements of the parts of the city produce different types of regimes with different claims about justice and rule:

> It is evident, therefore, that there must necessarily be a number of regimes differing from one another in kind, since these parts differ from one another in kind. Now a regime is the arrangement of offices, and all distribute these either on the basis of the power of those sharing [in the regime] or on the basis of some equality common to them.... There are necessarily, therefore, as many regimes as there are arrangements based on the sort of preeminence and the differences of the parts (4.3.1290a5-13; see 7.8.1328a36-b23).

Aristotle objected to Socrates' presupposition that unity was the greatest good for a city that the city is in its nature a kind of multitude composed of parts that differ in kind, and now he shows how the existence of such parts generates claims to rule and regimes. By beginning with artisans and not households, Socrates could not generate a regime as an organic arrangement of the parts of the city.

Aristotle directly criticizes Socrates' failure to see that the form of the regime grows naturally out of the materials of the city and is conditioned by them, and once again the "city of sows" is paradigmatic for Aristotle of the *Republic* as a whole.[26] Aristotle the biologist compares the variety of regimes to a taxonomy of animals that orders them in accordance with the arrangement of their necessary parts, such as types of mouths, stomachs, sense organs, and so on. "[One may proceed] in the same manner in the case of the regimes spoken of. For cities are composed not of one but of many parts, as we have often said" (4.4.1290b21-40). Of course, one prominent place he has said this was in his criticism of Socrates' presupposition about unity being the greatest good for the city. Aristotle proceeds to construct a city. "Now one of these [parts] is the multitude that is concerned with sustenance, those called farmers. A second is what is called the vulgar element. This is the one that is concerned with the arts...." And so he continues, adding a marketing element, a laboring element, and then the warrior element (4.4.1290b40-1291a10). The impression that Aristotle is recreating the "city of sows" and then, with the addition of the warrior element, the next city of the *Republic*, the city of the armed camp, is confirmed when he turns to a direct criticism of the work. "Hence what is said in the *Republic*, though sophisticated, is not adequate. For Socrates asserts that a city is composed of the four most necessary persons, and he says that these are a weaver, a farmer, a shoemaker, and a builder," and then adds several other artisans. "All of these make up the complement of the first city, as if every city were constituted for the sake of the necessary things and not rather for the sake of what is noble, and as if it were equally in need of shoemakers and farmers" (4.4.1291a11-19). Further, Aristotle notes that Socrates' addition of the warriors comes only when the city encroaches on their neighbors (4.4.1291a19-22)— as if this were not a necessary part of the city, which is in fact the case in the *Republic* since Socrates adds the warrior-artisans only when the city becomes "feverish" (see *Republic* 2.373b-374b), implying that they would not be necessary if the city remained "healthy" and "true."

Most importantly, Aristotle objects to Socrates' failure to include a governing body as a necessary part of the city. "Moreover, even among four persons, or however many partners there are, there must necessarily be someone who assigns and judges what is just" (4.4.1291a22-4; see 7.8. 1328b6-14). But such a person was unnecessary in the "city of sows," and would be in the subsequent cities of the *Republic* if the principle of "one man, one art" succeeded. The "city of sows" was founded to care for the needs of the body (369d), which is one reason why Glaucon objects to it and so names it. Aristotle suggests that he shares Glaucon's objection and sees in Socrates' proposal a misunderstanding of human nature: "If, then, one were to regard soul as much more a part of an animal than body, things of this sort— the military element and the element sharing in [the virtue] of justice as it relates to adjudication, and in addition the deliberative element, which is the work of political understanding— must be regarded as more a part of cities than things relating to necessary needs" (4.4.1291a24-7). The "city in speech" of the *Republic* is like a body without a soul, and for Aristotle the "city of sows" is again paradigmatic for the *Republic* as a whole because he indicates that Socrates' starting point precludes him from giving an adequate treatment of both justice and the regime.

If the parts of the city differ "in kind," so too do the claims to rule that are generated out of those parts and the presence of competing but incommensurate claims to rule is precisely the problem of politics for Aristotle and the problem he believes Socrates avoids. Aristotle discusses the difficulty of incommensurate claims to rule just after his analysis in Book 3 of the democratic and oligarchic views of justice. "The political good is justice," he says, "and this is the common advantage" (3.12182b16-17). The political partnership (*koinônia*) must have something in "common" (*koinos*). However, the nature of the city as "a certain kind of multitude," as Aristotle describes it in opposition to Socrates, leads to debate over exactly what sort of arrangement, that is regime, is appropriate for the city. While the aristocratic claim would appear to be best since it most of all aims at the authoritative good aimed at by the political partnership (3.17.1288a9-12, 32-41), it is not the only claim. Furthermore it is perhaps not safe to make it the only claim, for reasons Aristotle suggests when he argues that Socrates' permanent ruling class effectively creates two cities instead of one (see 2.5.1264a24-6). While it is not reasonable for the citizens "to dispute over offices on the basis of every inequality," there are several reasonable claims. "It is reasonable, therefore, that the well born, the free, and the wealthy lay claim to honor," he concludes (3.12.1282b36-1283a22). However, these Aristotle reveals that these claims are ultimately incommensurate, and thus disputable. There is no way that these claims can be equalized through any sure proportion; their proportionate agreement is a political decision that is embodied in the form of the regime. Whereas Socrates avoided such debate by making his artisan-citizens engage in perfectly commensurate exchange, Aristotle sees the differentiated elements of the city as both the nature of the political partnership and the source of political dispute.

Aristotle addresses another potentially incommensurate claim to rule within his discussion of regimes that brings to mind the philosopher-kings of the *Republic*: absolute kingship based upon virtue and reveals his disagreement with Socrates. Aristotle considers several varieties of monarchy, including several existing forms, but the most important form of kingship from a theoretical perspective is absolute kingship based upon merit. "If there is one person so outstanding by his excess of virtue—or a number of persons, though not enough to provide a full complement for a city—that the virtue of all the others and their political capacity is not commensurable with their own . . . such persons can no longer be regarded as a part of the city." Such a ruler or rulers would appear to have an unassailably just claim to rule, as Aristotle says, and such a person would be like a god among human beings who was a law unto himself (3.13.1284a3-14; see 1.2.1253a3-5).[27]

Aristotle's seeming acquiescence to the justice of the claim by those of extreme merit might appear to move him closer to the Socratic understanding of just rule. However, upon closer examination his discussion rule reveals many of the same criticisms he has leveled at Socrates' approach in general. Aristotle states that such outstanding claimants cannot be regarded as part of the city even if they rule over it, and I have argued that he does not regard Socrates' philosopher-kings as an intrinsic part of his city. The philosopher-kings do not compose a genuine regime in Aristotle's sense, and neither does the rule of one or several persons with "excess of virtue." Such excess transgresses the boundary of politics, which includes human beings but not gods and beasts (1.2.1253a1-5). Aristotle indicates this transgression when he describes the rule of the absolute king over his subjects in terms of that of a master over a slave. Within his discussion of natural slavery, Aristotle emphasizes that mastery is not the same as political rule because mastery is properly rule over those who are slaves by nature and political rule is rule over those who are free and equal, or at least relatively so (1.7.1255b16-20). He describes rule over a slave as like rule of the soul over the body, so different are they in their natures (1.6.1255b9-15). The rule of the excessively virtuous king would be similar. And so too Socrates' philosopher-kings are likened to intellect ruling over the rest of the soul and body. But such rule is "excessive" by the normal standards of politics in Aristotle's analysis, and he even gives a somewhat sympathetic hearing to ostracism as a means for eliminating any "excessive" claims to rule, although he does conclude that the "natural" thing to do would be gladly to obey such a person (3.13.1284a18-b34; see 3.17. 1288a28-9). Yet, Aristotle still treats even the claim of kingship as a claim that emerges from the material of the city and whose rule is a "political" decision, in contrast to Socrates' philosopher-kings, who do not arise as an intrinsic part of the city and whose rule is not subject to considerations of justice or safety. Ultimately, however, Aristotle's treatment of absolute kingship might be characterized as Platonic in thrust. The claim of "excessive virtue" challenges the very limits of what one could reasonably consider "politics." After touching upon the depths the Platonic challenge, then, Aristotle returns to the field of politics and the case of persons who are similar and equal by nature (3.16.1287a12-14; 3.17.1287b39-1288a6). It is no accident that he terms "political rule" rule among relative equals with competing claims, for such equality is the normal parameters of politics and such claims are the stuff of politics.

Conclusion

Man is the political animal according to Aristotle because the completion of his nature and end is made possible by the political partnership (1.2. 1252b27-1253a3). Aristotle also points to speech as making man uniquely a political animal: for "speech serves to reveal the advantageous and the harmful, and hence also the just and the unjust. For it is peculiar to man compared to the other animals that he alone has a perception of good and bad and just and unjust and other things [of this sort]; and partnership in these things is what makes a household and a city" (1.2.1253a7-19). Partnership in a shared perception of justice and virtue constitutes the city *and* household, and the embodiment of that shared perception is the regime, the form of the city that animates and directs its parts. Socrates' beginning principle of "one man, one art" not only precludes his giving an adequate account of justice and the regime, but also fails to attend to the shared speech about justice that makes man a political animal.

"All the discourses of Socrates are extraordinary," Aristotle states: "they are sophisticated, original, and searching. But it is perhaps difficult to do everything finely" (2.6.1265a10-13). Such are in Aristotle's words "the discourses of Socrates"—not necessarily the works of Plato. Aristotle's attribution of the regime of the *Republic* to the Platonic Socrates, and not Plato, has been noted by numerous readers of the *Politics*, and his avoidance of Plato's name in his discussion of the *Laws* (2.6.1264b26-1266a30) suggest that Aristotle's target is the surface of his teacher's works.[28] His critique of the *Republic* may bring to the fore the lessons to be gleaned by a reader who takes the Platonic dialogue for more than a constitutional proposal. By himself appearing to take the *Republic* for such a work, Aristotle does not produce a mundane, misguided, or malicious critique. He produces a work intended to link theory and practice in a mutually beneficial dialogue. Plato's best student did not nod off, but meditated on how to do justice to his friend.[29]

Notes

1. For example, Susemihl comments on Aristotle's discussion of the *Republic* by saying: "its author had not the power, if indeed he ever had the will, to transfer himself to the innermost groove of Plato's thought" (*The Politics of Aristotle*, Books I-V [London, 1894], 32-33). Susemihl's judgment is cited by R. F. Stalley, who notes the incompleteness of Aristotle's treatment but (partially) defends Aristotle's treatment of Plato ("Aristotle's Criticism of Plato's *Republic*," in *A Companion to Aristotle's "Politics,"* David Keyt and Fred D. Miller, Jr., eds. [Cambridge: Blackwell, 1991], 182).

2. See Fred D. Miller, Jr., *Nature, Justice, and Rights in Aristotle's "Politics"* (Oxford: Oxford University Press, 1995), 205-10. Numerous interpreters have similarly objected to what they see as the holism or even totalitarianism of Plato's *Republic*, notably Karl R. Popper, *The Open Society and Its Enemies*, 4th ed. (Princeton: Princeton University Press, 1962); see Jacob Howland, *The Republic: The Odyssey of Philosophy* (New York: Twayne, 1993), 16-18. There is not much scholarly discussion devoted to Aristotle's critique of the *Republic* in particular, and "analyses of Aristotle's *Politics* largely ignore Book II, " as Arlene Saxonhouse notes ("Family, Polity, and Unity: Aristotle on Socrates' Community of Wives," *Polity* 15 [1982], 209, n. 15). Sustained treatments of Aristotle's discussion of the *Republic* include Martha Craven Nussbaum, "Shame, Separateness, and Political Unity: Aristotle's Criticism of Plato," in *Essays on Aristotle's Ethics*, Amelie O. Rorty, ed. (Berkeley: University of California Press, 1981); Darrell Dobbs, "Aristotle's Anticommunism," *Journal of Politics* 29 (1985), 29-46; Saxonhouse, "Family, Polity, and Unity," 202-19; Mary P. Nichols, *Socrates and the Political Community: An Ancient Debate* (Albany: State University of New York Press, 1987), Part III; R F. Stalley, "Aristotle's Criticism."

3. Saxonhouse remarks Aristotle's references to the "city of sows," but does not regard it as paradigmatic for Aristotle since she distinguishes it and the next city of the *Republic*, the city of the armed camp, from the city ruled by the philosophers, the "beautiful city" (*Fear of Diversity: The Birth of Political Science in Ancient Greek Thought* [Chicago: University of Chicago Press, 1992], 205, n. 19). Terence H. Irwin also devotes considerable attention to the first city of the *Republic* in a discussion of Aristotle's objections to Socrates' principle of economic specialization and his own defense of private property, but he also does not regard it as paradigmatic for Aristotle of the *Republic* as a whole ("Aristotle's Defense of Private Property," in *A Companion*, Keyt and Miller, 202-8).

4. See Leo Strauss, *The City and Man* (Chicago: University of Chicago Press, 1978), 122: "Since the rule of philosophers is not introduced as an ingredient of the just city but only as a means for its realization, Aristotle legitimately disregards this institution in his critical analysis of the *Republic*." In his "Aristotle's Anticommunism," Dobbs also defends Aristotle's neglect of the philosopher-kings but argues, against Strauss, that Socrates believes the philosopher-kings to be part of the intrinsic perfection of the regime and that Aristotle ignores the philosopher-kings because he believes that philosophers cannot arise in the city Socrates builds. Dobbs therefore sees a break between the "city of sows" and city of the armed camp on the one hand and the "beautiful city" ruled by philosophers on the other, and does not view the "city of sows" as paradigmatic for Aristotle of the "cities in speech" of the *Republic*.

5. All references are to Aristotle's *Politics* unless otherwise noted. I follow Carnes Lord's translation (Chicago: University of Chicago Press, 1984), altering it in places in accordance with W.D. Ross's edition: Aristotelis, *Politica* (Oxford: Oxford University Press, 1957). Citations to Aristotle are by book, chapter, and Bekker page and line numbers.

6. I translate *koinônia* as "partnership," following Lord, but its root sense of "sharing in common" should be kept in mind, and the term might also be translated as "community" or "association."

7. See Saxonhouse, *Fear of Diversity*, ch. 8.

8. See esp. Stalley, "Aristotle's Criticism."

9. Most scholars have been perplexed that Aristotle raises a question about the extension of communism to the lowest class, holding that it is obvious from the dialogue that it applies only to the two highest classes. For a defense of Aristotle's reading see Robert Mayhew, "Aristotle on the Extent of Communism in Plato's *Republic*," *Ancient Philosophy* 13 (1993), 313-21.

10. Saxonhouse, *Fear of Diversity*, 190 and n. 2.

11. Compare Susan Moller Okin, who argues that Aristotle's criticism of the communistic proposals of the *Republic* reveals the conservative or traditional bias of his "functionalist" view of the hierarchy of men over women (*Women in Western Political Thought* [Princeton: Princeton University Press, 1979], 84-86). Several writers offer a defense of Aristotle's view of diversity against such "functionalist" interpretations, e.g., Saxonhouse, *Fear of Diversity*, Part III; Judith A. Swanson, *The Public and the Private in Aristotle's Political Philosophy* (Ithaca: Cornell University Press, 1992).

12. See Stalley, "Aristotle's Criticism," 184-85.

13. As noted by Stalley, "Aristotle's Criticism," 189, and by Trevor J. Saunders in his commentary on the passage in his edition of Aristotle, *Politics* Books I and II (Oxford: Oxford University Press, 1995), 108-9.

14. Saxonhouse notes the allusion to the "city of sows" in this context, but does not pursue the analogy (*Fear of Diversity*, 205, n. 19).

15. Citations to Plato are by book and Stephanus number. I follow Allan Bloom's translation (*Republic*, 2nd ed. [New York: Basic Books, 1991]). Citations to the Greek text are to John Burnet's edition, *Platonis Opera*, vol. 4 (Oxford: Oxford University Press, 1902).

16. Bloom translates the Greek *idea* by the italicized "*idea*." The soundness of the analogy between justice in the soul and justice in the city presupposes the truth of the doctrine of the ideas presented later in the *Republic*.

17. See Strauss, *City and Man*, 91.

18. That even the individual human being is such a unity is questioned in the dialogue (see 10.612a). Relevant here would be the discussion in Plato's *Symposium* of the lack of wholeness due to the erotic nature of humans. As a number of Plato's interpreters have noted, the discussion in the *Republic* abstracts from *eros*.

19. In the second edition of his translation, Bloom corrects an error in the first edition, where "latter" and "former" were reversed.

20. Later in the *Republic*, justice as "minding one's own business" is described as pertaining not to "external business," but of minding one's business "with respect to what is within." Being just, then, binds together the parts and makes something "entirely one from many" (4.443c-d). Justice and even the regime continue to be understood in terms of the individual human being.

21. See Strauss, *City and Man*, 91, 94.

22. Strauss suggests that the "city of pigs" is so called because of its subhuman quality and notes the irony that there are no pigs in the city (*City and Man*, 94-95). The term Glaucon uses to characterize the city, *hys*, can be translated "pig," "swine," "boar," or "sow." I follow Bloom's translation of "city of sows" in part because of its euphony.

23. Harry V. Jaffa, "Aristotle," in *History of Political Philosophy*, 2nd ed., Leo Strauss and Joseph Cropsey, eds. (Chicago: University of Chicago Press, 1973), 94-95.

24. See Richard Mulgan, "Aristotle on Oligarchy and Democracy," in *A Companion*, Keyt and Miller, 316-17.

25. Aristotle criticizes the Socratic doctrine of the "forms" or "ideas" within his consideration of the regime when he alludes to Socrates' attempt, in Plato's *Meno*, to find a single form of virtue. Aristotle objects that the "city is made up of dissimilar persons" so that "the virtue of all the citizens is necessarily not single" (3.4.1277a4-11). For his criticism of the "idea of the good," see *Nicomachean Ethics* 1.4.1096a11-1097a14. For his general criticism of the doctrine of the ideas, see *Metaphysics* 1.6.987a30-988a18. The most extensive discussion of Aristotle's politics in terms of "form" and "material" that I have seen is Ronald Polansky, "Aristotle on Political Change," in *A Companion*, Keyt and Miller, esp. 326-32. See also Strauss, *City and Man*, 45-47.

26. See note 3, above. Nichols does not view the "city of sows" as paradigmatic for Aristotle of the *Republic* as a whole, but she discusses the passage at some length and stresses the complex makeup of the city and the relevance of that complexity for the choice of regime, in her *Citizens and Statesmen: A Study of Aristotle's "Politics"* (Savage, MD: Rowman and Littlefield, 1992), 91-92.

27. Aristotle will soon turn to a discussion of which is better, the rule of the best man or the rule of law (3.15-16.1286a8-1287b36), a discussion which leads to a broader consideration of the importance of the rule of law in any regime.

28. This is also suggested by Saxonhouse, "Family, Polity, and Unity," 205 and Swanson, *The Public and the Private in Aristotle's Political Philosophy*, 221. Following a more common course among scholars, Stalley notes that Aristotle consistently speaks of Socrates but argues that this does not necessarily suggest that he thereby means to distinguish Plato from Socrates. He does adduce a passage in which Aristotle attributes the communistic proposals of the *Republic* to Plato (2.12.1274b9-10) although he fails to note that the authenticity of that passage is highly contested ("Aristotle's Criticism," 183-84 and n. 5).

29. I would like to thank Judith Swanson and Aristide Tessitore for their comments and suggestions on an earlier version of this paper.

Chapter 4

The Divine Comedy of Homer: Defining Political Virtue through Comic Depictions of the Gods

Nick Janszen

The political lessons poetry offers are often overlooked because of preconceived notions about the value of poetry. Poetry is often considered to be of little value as a guide into the examination of fundamental political questions because at worst, it is understood to be simple fictional entertainment, and at best, it is assumed to be inferior to philosophical examination. Those who subscribe to the former evaluation will never appreciate the political truths to be gleaned from poetic genius, while those who subscribe to the latter evaluation will forever consider works of poetry as expressions of second class genius behind the systematic examinations of the fundamental questions of justice, morality, and the human condition found in works of pure philosophy.

I would suggest that at its best, poetry is potentially more powerful and more persuasive in its ability to define and promulgate justice than is philosophy because it more adequately expresses the tension between the rational and irrational parts of human nature. I would further suggest that the comic depictions of the gods in Homer's *Iliad* and *Odyssey* more completely and effectively teach the political virtues of justice than do philosophic examinations because Homer's comic depictions of the gods illustrate that justice consists of the strict adherence to rational principles, while simultaneously showing that due to man's passionate and irrational nature, it is impossible to prevent the commission of unjust acts. By illustrating in tales the fundamental tension between the rational and irrational parts of the soul, Homer ultimately teaches that the execution of justice requires the reconciliation of the irrational and rational parts of the soul, and not, as some would have it, the simple suppression of the irrational part of the soul. Furthermore, because poetry is capable of adequately expressing both the rational and irrational, it teaches the lesson that justice depends upon the reconciliation of these two parts of the soul much more effectively than philosophy can.

However, before exploring how Homer's works can exemplify political genius in poetry, it is necessary to examine briefly how the finest poetry can be understood to be superior to philosophy.

The Power of Poetry

In the *Poetics*, Aristotle defines poetry as a kind of imitation, and in his elaboration of the appropriate objects of imitation he describes the power of poetry. In book 2 he states,

> Since the objects of imitation are men in action, and these men must be either of a higher or lower type (for moral character mainly answers to these divisions, goodness and badness being the distinguishing marks of moral differences), it follows that we must represent men either as better than in real life, or as worse, or as they are.[1]

And in book 4, he adds, "Thus the reason that men enjoy seeing likeness is that in contemplating it they find themselves learning or inferring."[2] What Aristotle does not state, but clearly implies, is that the end of poetry is moral instruction. He does not question whether poetry should be used as moral instruction. He simply examines what kind of poetry is the most useful for moral instruction. Furthermore, because Aristotle constantly returns to Homer's epics as the models of great poetry, it is clear that he understands that the excellence of Homer's poetry is in part due to the moral instruction it contains.

In order to explain what he understands as excellent poetry, Aristotle subdivides poetry into tragedy, comedy, and epic. Of the three, Aristotle clearly prefers tragedy to epic and comedy because it more consistently conveys a single, morally unified imitation of noble actions while evoking the proper degree of pity and fear to foster a catharsis that encourages the audience to adopt a more noble standard of behavior. And while epic poetry runs a close second to tragedy because it has as its unified theme the imitation of the highest human good, Aristotle still finds it inferior to tragedy because it progresses episodically and includes some elements of comedy.[3] Least of the three is comedy. Yet, as Aristotle indicates, comedy has its ennobling elements, too. These ennobling elements are found in the higher of the two forms of comedy which Aristotle praises by expressing a preference for the ludicrous over lampooning. The ludicrous is preferable to lampooning because imitations of the ludicrous teach what kind of behavior is to be avoided by mocking the low in a general sense while lampooning fails to teach moral lessons because it simply ridicules particular individuals.[4] In short, Aristotle prefers tragedy because it creates a positive model of behavior for men to emulate while comedy only creates a negative model of behavior to be avoided.

What is most notable in Aristotle's subdivisions is not the categories of poetry that he defines, but his recognition of the philosophic power of poetry. Aristotle contends that poetry's utility lies in its ability to imitate what should be done as opposed to simply imitating what has been done. In his words: "it is evident . . . that it is not the function of the poet to relate what has happened, but what may happen . . . Poetry, therefore, is more philosophical and a higher thing than history: for poetry tends to express the universal, history the particular."[5] Clearly, Aristotle's praise of poetic genius is rooted in his recognition that poetry has the philosophic capacity to describe what man can become, as opposed to history, which is limited to describing what man has been.

From his subdivisions of poetic categories and his understanding of the power of poetry, it is easy to understand why Aristotle prefers tragedy. Tragedy is an imitation of the actions of noble men, and through exposure to it, men are encouraged to adopt the virtues and emulate the actions of these invented noble characters. Therefore, according to Aristotle, tragedy is the highest form of poetry because it is capable of encouraging men to become the best they can be by creating imitations of what they should be. But Aristotle overlooks something rather important. Even though he recognizes that the higher form of comedy, the imitation of the ludicrous, describes the universal, he fails to see the relationship between comedy and one of the highest human goods, justice. Aristotle fails to recognize that even those men who are raised in accordance with the strictest moral virtues will occasionally behave in an ignoble or ludicrous manner because they will, on occasion, allow their actions to be guided by the irrational part of their souls. Therefore, if a political community is to survive, it must not only encourage its citizens to adopt a noble standard for a moral guide, but it must also learn how to deal with those members who occasionally fall short of this ideal standard of behavior.

Comic descriptions of low behavior open up the possibility of teaching the citizens of a political community how to deal with injustice because comic depictions of the ludicrous not only reveal what behavior to avoid, but also teach how to resolve the conflicts caused by members of the community who fail to live up to the high standards of the community. Therefore, what Aristotle misses in his description of the power of poetry is that, in addition to being able to instruct citizens through descriptions of how men should behave in what constitutes noble behavior, poetry also has the ability to instruct citizens in the art of adjudication by providing examples of how the ignoble actions of individuals should be reconciled with the city's ideal standard of behavior. After all, if justice does not admit of the possibility of reconciling those who act unjustly with the city, the only course of action that remains for the administration of justice is to exile or execute the unjust. As a consequence of this line of reasoning, it should be clear that comic poetry is better suited to teaching justice than is tragic poetry because comic poetry reveals how the high and the low may be reconciled.

It is also in this capacity to illustrate how the high and the low might be reconciled that comic poetry proves to be superior to philosophy in the promotion of justice. Unlike philosophy, which advocates the moderation of those desires that lead to injustice by presenting rational arguments to the rational part of the soul, politically sound poetry seeks to moderate irrational behavior by speaking directly to the irrational part of the soul. Poetry does not have to simply announce that man should avoid irrationality after showing that irrational behavior is harmful and inconsistent with the human good; it can describe the consequences that befall those who succumb to irrational desires. Through the ludicrous actions and dialogue of its characters, comic poetry can reveal how men come to choose an unjust course of action even though they understand that their choice is immoral and harmful to themselves and their community. This is of primary importance because it reveals that the cause of injustice is rooted in the irrational part of human nature. And because the cause of injustice is incident to our human nature, to be just requires that we also recognize that injustice will always be with us.

Therefore, Aristotle was wrong to have faulted comedy for depicting "those who, in the piece, are the deadliest enemies...quit the stage as friends at the close."[6] Instead, Aristotle should have praised this element of comedy. For it is in the reconciliation of enemies that we find an ideal description of the execution of justice that is consistent with human nature and consequently attainable by the human political community. It is only through the execution of justice that the city can reconcile the tension between what it is and what it ought to be, and comic poetry illustrates how the low may be reconciled with the high.

Even though Aristotle repeatedly cites Homer as the foremost poet, he fails to recognize the utility of comedy in Homer's teachings on political virtue because he fails to recognize poetry's power to teach justice through comic resolutions and its depictions of the ludicrous. However, if we take a second look at those sections of Homer's poetry that Aristotle considers subordinate to tragedy, we will find that Homer's poems are not only useful in their ability to define and encourage the adoption of areté, but they also are useful in teaching how unjust actions can be justly adjudicated. In short, we will discover that Homer's comic depictions reveal his political genius because they display his understanding of the complex relationship among comedy, tragedy, and justice.

Homer's Political Genius

Stated simply, the execution of justice is the attempt to reconcile the individual who fails to live up to the public standard of virtue with the political community. Therefore, the execution of justice requires a sense of both tragedy and comedy. It requires a sense of tragedy because it is through tragedy that the community learns how human beings should behave. Adjudication also requires a sense of comedy because it is through comedy that we learn the reasons men fail to conform to the exacting standards of moral propriety. Therefore, in order to reconcile with the city one who would consciously violate the standards of the community, it is necessary to come to an understanding of how man's lower nature might be reconciled with his higher potential. It is this reconciliation of the comic and the tragic that Homer imitates when he presents the gods behaving in a ludicrous manner in both the *Iliad* and the *Odyssey*.

For the purpose of discussion in this essay I am going to limit my analysis to three characters and one event. The characters are Hephaestus, Ares and Aphrodite, and the event is Hephaestus' cuckolding as it is described by Demodokus in the *Odyssey*. This single episode concisely illustrates Homer's understanding of the relationship between comedy, tragedy, and justice.[7]

In lines 266 through 370 of book 8 of the *Odyssey*, Homer has Demodokus sing the song of Hephaestus' cuckolding by Aphrodite and Ares. The tale itself is short, but the explication is rich in its capacity to promulgate the principles of justice. In short, the story is this: Ares, the god of war, fouls the marriage bed of Aphrodite, the goddess of love, and her husband, Hephaestus, the god of artifice. Helios, the sun god who sees everything, reports the injustice to Hephaestus who lays a trap for the adulterous lovers. After setting a trap of golden threads that will bind the two lovers when they lie together, Hephaestus pretends to leave on a journey. As soon as he leaves, the two lovers attempt to take advantage of his absence and are quickly bound in Hephaestus' trap. Hephaestus returns and calls the gods to witness the injustice that has been done to him. He declares that he will not release the lovers from the bonds until he is reimbursed by Aphrodite's father, Zeus, for the gifts he gave her during courtship. When the gods who are gathered judge that Ares should pay the damages Hephaestus seeks, and the payment of damages by Ares is guaranteed by Poseidon, Hephaestus releases the lovers. The gods go their separate ways, and order is restored.

By itself, the story admits of all the elements of low comedy. It portrays sex, corruption, and a reversal of fortune. The plot progresses from a description of low desires and base actions. Yet, in the end, order is restored through the execution of justice. However, what is notable in this brief comic tale is more than the actions of the gods directly involved in this injustice, but the description of the other gods' reaction to this injustice. It is in examining the reactions of the various gods that we learn about Homer's complex understanding of justice.

The first point to note is that Ares and Aphrodite personify two of the passions that are often depicted as irrational and ignoble—erotic desire and the violence associated with war. The injustice they commit is a consequence of surrendering to the predominant passions that reside in their souls. And even though they are aware that their actions are unjust, they still succumb to their erotic desires. Their actions are consistent with the passions their characters personify because their adultery is best described as allowing the irrational part of their souls to guide their actions. Their behavior conforms to Aristotle's definition of the ludicrous which reads "Comedy is an imitation of characters of a lower type—not however in the full sense of the word bad, the ludicrous being merely a subdivision of the ugly. It consists in some defect or ugliness which is not painful or destructive."[8] The behavior of these two gods is ugly in the sense that it shows two gods refusing to moderate their desires even though they know that their desires run counter to the established standards of behavior. Furthermore, it becomes clear that the actions of these two gods conform to Aristotle's understanding that the imitation of the ludicrous should speak in general terms when we understand that this tale is not to be understood as an accurate depiction of what the gods are like. Instead, these gods should be understood as the personification of certain passions, and their actions should be understood as those which are likely to be taken by those who allow low passions to guide their actions.

The second point to note is that Hephaestus' actions conform to Aristotle's definition of tragedy, which is "an imitation of an action that is serious, complete and of a certain magnitude."[9] Clearly, the action of the story is complete in that it begins with Hephaestus learning of the adultery and ends with a just resolution of the conflict. The violation of the trust implicit in marriage qualifies as serious, just as the resolution of a violated marriage contract qualifies as a certain magnitude. But most importantly, the tale of Hephaestus' cuckolding conforms to the purpose of tragedy which Aristotle describes when he states that "a perfect tragedy should...imitate actions which excite pity and fear."[10] Aristotle explains what he means by saying that "pity is aroused by unmerited misfortune, fear by the misfortune of a man like ourselves."[11] Hephaestus' cuckolding is pitiful because he does nothing to warrant the injustice that is visited upon him, and Homer's audience can empathize with Hephaestus because, of all the gods, Hephaestus is the one who is most human. He was born imperfect, and in order to compensate for his limitations, he must rely on artifice. His cuckolding by a beautiful, erotically driven wife and her handsome, manly lover speaks to the fears of inadequacy that are incident to mortals who are aware of their own shortcomings.

Thus, by taking these first two points together, it becomes clear that this tale should not be understood to be a description of the gods as they are. Properly understood, this tale is a complex metaphor in which the cause of injustice is shown to be the natural desire to submit to the more irrational passions, and the ideal method of executing justice is shown to require the community's participation in meting out punishment to the guilty parties in order that they may be reconciled with both the injured party and community at large.

The third point to be taken from this story reveals Homer's political genius. Justice consists of reconciling the comic aspect of human nature with the tragic, and the process of reconciliation conveyed in this comic tale provides an ideal model for the adjudication of justice in a civilized community. Therefore, according to Homer's depiction of the gods, justice is a public, not a private, concern. The standard of justice depends upon a communally accepted standard of behavior, while the execution of justice requires the collection of evidence, the community's consideration of the evidence, a consideration of mitigating circumstances, and a judicious award of restitution by the community, payment of which is guaranteed by the community. It is of singular importance that the resolution of the conflict between the high and the low relies on restitution and not retribution because justice defined in this manner admits that there will be times when the members of the community will fail to live according to the high standard of the community. It is this oddly forgiving sense of justice that is necessary for civil society because only through the acceptance of certain shortcomings can individuals who fail to live up to the community's standards be reconciled with their community.

By taking each point separately, it should be easier to see how Homer conveys this teaching on justice through a comic portrayal of the gods. Having already noted that the commission of an unjust act in this tale is motivated by an overwhelming attachment to the low and that Hephaestus' righteous indignation conforms to the high standard of justice defined by tragedy, it is necessary to show how these polar opposites are reconciled through justice.

First, Homer shows through his tale that justice requires that the community share a common standard of accepted behavior. This is the crux upon which the execution of justice depends because without a commonly accepted standard of behavior, any behavior that runs counter to the majority's standard is not injustice, but individual expression. In addition, without a commonly accepted standard of behavior, there can be no punishment of an individual; there can only be the tyrannical imposition of majority will on the individual.[12] In the tale before us, the attempts of the two lovers to hide their affair reveal that they understand that adultery violates the accepted standard of behavior for members of the community. Furthermore, when Helios informs Hephaestus that he has been made a cuckold, and when Hephaestus calls the gods together to witness the injustice that Ares and his wife have inflicted on him, it becomes clear that the gods understand that the act of adultery is the community's concern. If justice were not a public concern, the violation of the marriage contract between Hephaestus and Aphrodite would simply be a private concern as would any attempts to resolve the conflict caused by the violation. Helios would have no reason to inform Hephaestus of the adultery, and Hephaestus would have no need to prove to the community that he had been wronged.

Second, Homer describes the elements necessary to the execution of justice. Most importantly, Homer teaches that equitable judgment requires the collection of evidence. After having Helios inform Hephaestus of the infidelity, he does not have Hephaestus confront either Ares or Aphrodite. Instead, he has Hephaestus set a trap. What is important to note, is that Hephaestus does not simply accept Helios' report as sufficient evidence of the adultery. Instead, he lays a trap to catch the lovers in the act. This shows Homer's audience that the collection of sure proof is essential to the execution of justice. Furthermore, it should be noted that the trap is not designed with retribution in mind because the trap does not harm the two gods. Instead the trap is designed to expose the two gods indulging their lower appetites. This teaches that justice does not take its bearing from retribution, but from a desire to uncover the truth.[13]

Homer also shows that the execution of justice is dependent upon community-defined sanctions. Through the discussion of the gods that takes place when they are called by Hephaestus to witness the injustice, Homer shows that adjudication is a public concern. By preventing Hephaestus from simply taking the execution of justice into his own hands, Homer shows that a noble character respects the community's standard of justice and when wronged will appeal to the community for restitution.

When the gods arrive at his home, Hephaestus pleads his case and presents his evidence. The basis of his argument is that he has been wronged by an intemperate wife, and the resolution that he demands is to have the gifts he employed to win Aphrodite restored to him by her father, Zeus. It is important to note that Hephaestus faults Aphrodite's intemperance and that the justice he demands is restitution, not retribution. Yet, by citing the cause of his wife's adultery, Hephaestus shows that he recognizes that succumbing to erotic desire is the cause of the injustice visited upon him, and by demanding restitution, Hephaestus shows that vengeance has no place in the execution of justice.

However, although Hephaestus appears to exemplify the appropriate actions of the just man, Homer reveals that Hephaestus' understanding of justice is imperfect by having the community modify the restitution to which Hephaestus is entitled when they award the damages he demands. Homer portrays the community awarding damages to Hephaestus by having them say, "No virtue in bad dealings. See, the slow one has overtaken the swift, as now slow Hephaestus has overtaken Ares, swiftest of all the gods on Olympus, by artifice, though he was lame, and Ares must pay the adulterer's damage."[14] And although the gods confirm Hephaestus' charge and award him damages, it should be noted that the party responsible for the payment of damages has been changed from Zeus to Ares. This reveals to Homer's audience that an important element of the execution of justice is appropriately assigning responsibility for restitution. It is the recognition of the importance of assigning blame that reveals the importance of shame in the execution of justice.

When Homer has Demodokus narrate, "among the blessed immortals uncontrollable laughter went up as they saw the handiwork of subtle Hephaestus,"[15] and "when they were set free of the fastening…[they] sprang up, and Ares took his way Thraceward, while she…went back to Paphos."[16] Homer shows the humiliation of the two gods that stems from the public exposure of their indiscretion. Therefore, Homer shows that in addition to the restitution demanded by Hephaestus, part of the punishment meted out to Ares and Aphrodite is the shame heaped upon them for yielding to their low desires.

In order to understand the role shame plays in the execution and promulgation of justice, it is necessary to consider briefly what shame is. Stated simply, shame is the public exposure of an individual's refusal to subordinate his lower desires to the higher, noble standards demanded by the community. Shame not only requires a commonly accepted standard of behavior, but in order for the threat of shame to serve as an effective incentive for citizens to restrain their irrational desires, it is necessary that anytime an individual fails to live up to those high standards, his actions should be publicly exposed. Clearly then, one reason that Homer presents for portraying justice as a public concern is that without the threat of public exposure, one of the primary incentives for restraining those natural desires that lead to injustice would be lost.

However, Homer does not simply moralize in the tragic sense and show that the behavior of Ares and Aphrodite is inexcusable. He shows that in order for justice to be served, it is necessary to take into account mitigating circumstances. He accomplishes this through the brief exchange that takes place between Apollo and Hermes. After having the gods declare that Hephaestus' demands are just and before the two adulterous gods are released from their bonds, Homer states:

> This was the way of the gods as they conversed with each other,
> but the lord Apollo, son of Zeus, said a word to Hermes:
> "Hermes, son of Zeus, guide and giver of good things, tell me,
> would you, caught tight in these strong fastenings, be willing
> to sleep in bed by the side of Aphrodite the golden?"
> Then in turn the courier Argeiphontes answered:
> "Lord who strike from afar, Apollo, I wish it could only be,
> and there could be thrice this number of endless fastenings,
> and all you gods could be looking on and all the goddesses,
> and still I would sleep by the side of Aphrodite the golden."
> He spoke, and there was laughter among the immortals ...[17]

Taken by itself, this exchange is quite funny; however, underlying the humor is a serious note. Both of these gods understand why Ares committed this indiscretion. Aphrodite's beauty is overwhelming. And even though Apollo and Hermes have concluded with the other gods that Ares was wrong to have slept with Aphrodite and that he must pay the adulterer's price, they empathize with Ares' decision to risk the shame and the penalties associated with acting on irrational erotic desires. Their recognition of the power of *eros* over the rational standards of justice shows that they are aware that as long as erotic desires exist, it is impossible to expect that the commission of unjust acts will be prevented.

This is the essential element of Homer's political teaching. He does not excuse injustice, but he describes its cause by displaying the power of the irrational part of the soul. It is the recognition of the power of the irrational part of the soul that allows us to understand why someone like ourselves might commit an injustice. And in this self-recognition, it is easy to see what depictions of the ludicrous share with perfect tragedy. Aristotle stated that tragedy is perfect when the members of the audience can empathize with the tragic hero because through their empathy, they can be brought to emulate the actions of noble characters. Likewise, good comedy is like good tragedy insofar that the mark of good comic poetry is that the audience can empathize with the comic characters. However, the purpose of comic poetry is not to encourage the audience to emulate the ludicrous behavior of its low characters. Comic poetry's purpose is to encourage its audience to recognize that they have the capacity in themselves to commit unjust actions. This recognition is essential if the community is to execute justice equitably because this empathy encourages men to recognize that the execution of justice is the act by which the community determines how the unjust individual can atone for his indiscretion and be reconciled with the community. This sense of justice is a far cry from the sense of justice encouraged by tragic poetry, in which those who fail to live up to the community's standard are simply condemned as being less than human. It is no less important to remember that the empathy fostered by ludicrous behavior does not excuse unjust behavior, but only gives us the capacity to comprehend the cause of unjust behavior. After all, even though Homer has Apollo and Hermes jokingly describe their envy of Ares' humiliation, Homer has both Hermes and Apollo condemn on rational grounds the violation of the marriage contract.

This brings us to the political lesson Homer would have us take from the comic depiction of Hephaestus' cuckolding. Not only do we learn from the example set by Ares and Aphrodite that we should not allow our erotic appetites to guide our actions if we are to live up to the ennobling standards that make living in a political community possible, but we learn that a just man will seek restitution instead of vengeance against those who have wronged him. A just man will choose the moderate form of executing justice because he understands that if a political community is to continue to live in accordance with the high standards it has set for itself, it is necessary that justice allow for the reconciliation of those who on occasion will allow their passions to rule their lives with those who wisely choose to be guided by reason.

Conclusion

Homer teaches through his comic depictions of the gods a more compre-hensive lesson about the execution of justice than either tragic poetry or philosophy is capable of teaching. He shows through his depictions of the ludicrous that injustice will never be eradicated because the cause of injustice is inherent in human desires. Yet, he does not simply excuse or accept unjust behavior as inevitable. Instead, he shows that the execution of justice should attempt to reconcile those who have committed injustices by publicly exposing their low behavior and setting the penalty through which they might atone for their injustices. Once they have atoned for their unjust acts, they are to be welcomed back into the community.

Tragic poetry cannot convey this complex political teaching because, by definition, tragic poetry seeks to ennoble the citizenry by providing them with examples worthy of emulation. By definition, tragic poetry cannot portray how the individual who fails to attain the high standards of the community might be reconciled with the community. Philosophic inquiry also falls short of being the best method of promoting justice because it is incapable of evoking the empathy necessary for the execution of justice in a manner that is consistent with civilized society among imperfect human beings. Comic poetry is better suited to promoting justice than either philosophy or tragedy because comic poetry is capable of evoking the necessary empathy for the unjust while portraying justice as a high but humanly attainable standard.

Notes

1. Aristotle, *The Poetics*, Francis Ferguson, trans. (New York: Hill and Wang, 1961), 2.1, 52.

2. Aristotle, *Poetics*, 4.5, 55.

3. Aristotle, *Poetics*, 12-16, 74-86.

4. Aristotle, *Poetics*, 9, 68-70.

5. Aristotle, *Poetics*, 9.1-4, 68.

6. Aristotle, *Poetics*, 13.8, 77.

7. A complete discussion of Homer's teaching on justice through the *Iliad* would require a much longer argument than is appropriate to this essay. Suffice it to say that the *Iliad* has two plots running through it—the tragic description of the rise and fall of Achilles' anger and the comic description of the restoration of order among the gods on Mt. Olympus. The second plot is often overlooked, which means that many overlook the political lessons found in the *Iliad*. The *Iliad* opens with the gods in conflict and concludes with the gods in harmony due to Zeus' manipulations. Through Zeus' machinations the gods are purged of their low and selfish attachments to particular mortals. By the end of the *Iliad*, instead of coming to blows over their petty alliances with mortals, the gods come together and cooperate for their common good. The transition from disorder to order on Mt. Olympus constitutes the just reconciliation of those gods who behave in a low and ludicrous manner with the noble standards of the divine community.

8. Aristotle, *Poetics*, 5.1, 59.

9. Aristotle, *Poetics*, 6.2, 61.

10. Aristotle, *Poetics*, 13.2, 75.

11. Aristotle, *Poetics*, 13.3, 76.

12. An important side note: As I have said before, poetry is potentially more effective than philosophy in promulgating justice. One reason for its effectiveness is that poetry is more accessible to the members of the community at large than philosophy is. If the entire

community accepts the same stories as the definitive moral tales, then it is certain that the entire community will share a consistent set of moral laws. For example, an entire community might be familiar with a common set of texts like the Bible, the Koran, or Homer's epics and, as a consequence, would be likely to share a common sense of justice based on what they had gleaned about justice through these texts.

13. In addition to showing that justice requires the collection of evidence, this example shows how artifice and cunning serve justice when properly applied. It is no accident that the simple stealth of Ares and Aphrodite is exposed by the more complex cunning of Hephaestus. And because it is the cunning of Hephaestus to which men might aspire, it is doubly important that an example be set for the proper use of such cunning.

14. Homer, *The Odyssey of Homer,* Richard Lattimore, trans. (New York: Harper and Row, 1967), 8.329-32.

15. Homer, *Odyssey*, 8.326-27.

16. Homer, *Odyssey*, 8.360-62.

17. Homer, *Odyssey*, 8.334-43.

Chapter 5

The Odyssey of Political Theory

Patrick J. Deneen

The Odyssey of the *Odyssey*

In common parlance, an "odyssey" means any prolonged journey replete with grave perils and inadvertent detours and delays, one implicitly comparable to the travails confronted by Odysseus in the first odyssey, the *Odyssey*, from which all odysseys take their name and their resonance. Yet, paradoxically, if Odysseus' journeys constitute the first odyssey, what can we make of his subsequent journeys and of the odyssey of the *Odyssey* itself—what shall we call these subsequent travels through vast space and time? From Odysseus' appearances in post-Homeric epic cycles to his frequent sightings in the plays and philosophy of democratic Athens; from his transformation into the stoic Ulysses of imperial Rome to his punishment in hell for *hubris* recorded by Dante; from his political portrayals by the bard of Stratford-on-Avon to Tennyson's scientific and colonial depiction, one realizes that Odysseus' odyssey merely began with the *Odyssey*'s conclusion.[1]

The history of Odysseus' many travails on the seas of literature outside the *Odyssey* is well remarked upon, even celebrated in recent incarnations such as James Joyce's *Ulysses*. If only in sheer volume of secondary literature alone, this modern retelling of the *Odyssey* in some senses rivals the original. Given such acute attentiveness to Odysseus' literary reappearances, the relative neglect of Odysseus' presence throughout the history of political thought is all the more remarkable. Perhaps while less pronounced—rarely, if ever, appearing as a lead character in political theory—Odysseus nevertheless even here continues his involuntary journey to strange and unforeseen places and into unexpected new roles and disguises. He appears in the myth of Er in Plato's *Republic*; as a model for Rousseau's *Emile*; and as a rapacious capitalist analogue in Horkheimer and Adorno's *The Dialectic of Enlightenment*, to mention but a few of the more obvious "political" portrayals. Given recognition of the *Odyssey* as a key source for earlier political philosophers, one can but wonder at contemporary dismissal of the epic.

Perhaps two causes can be proffered for political theory's relative neglect of the *Odyssey*. Where Homeric texts are considered, there is a longstanding assumption that the *Iliad* is the more political of the two epics.[2] This aspect, combined with the second cause, a contemporary preference for explicitly democratic politics, largely relegates Homeric thought to quaint, antiquarian, if dangerously authoritarian, status. As sensitive a critic as Alasdair MacIntyre makes precisely these assumptions in his treatment of the virtues of "heroic society" in *After Virtue*. Adopting the derisive stance toward antiquity of Enlightenment figures he otherwise chides, he divides human intellectual development into "childish" and "adult" stages. MacIntyre thereby dismisses what he characterizes as Homeric (specifically Iliadic) discourse by asking "the question as to whether the narrative forms of the heroic age are not mere *childlike* storytelling, so that moral discourse while it may use fables and parables as aids to the halting moral imagination ought in its serious *adult* moments to abandon the narrative mode for a more discursive style and genre."[3] Given the unfortunate language of developmental psychology here applied by MacIntyre, a largely *sympathetic* interpreter of ancient thought, to works of complexity and subtlety, it is hardly surprising that theorists antithetical to ancient thought are all the more likely to dismiss incipient political thought in Homer as either irrelevant or altogether nonexistent.

Yet closer examination of the *Odyssey* reveals a subtle if complex political theory, a conclusion shared by other sympathetic critics.[4] Odysseus' relationship to nature suggests that he approaches his world with an acutely political outlook, one which underpins his constancy in his attempt to return to family and community. His greatest trial comes not at the hands of a violent enemy, but from a kind goddess who offers him immortality. Resisting the temptation, unlike all other preceding mortals offered that forbidden existence, Odysseus unreservedly confirms his place with imperfect humanity. His *nostos* is finally achieved not by means of force—that *sine qua non* of nearly every other Homeric hero—but by that most political of means, persuasion. Nevertheless, he must remain a Homeric hero, for violence is also required in order to reinstitute justice amid the warlike conditions of Ithaca, where normally political solutions should suffice. Odysseus' flexibility—he is *Odysseus polytropos*, "Odysseus of many ways"—permits this most political of beings to act apolitically, but not antipolitically, as the situation demands. As such, he proves not to be an ideal ruler, but rather serves as a prototype for the founder of later political philosophy. If the *Odyssey* does not finally offer the portrait of an ideal king, it is perhaps because its final subtle lesson contains a "kernel of democracy," a subtle critique of the arbitrary power of the strong used against ordinary citizens, who eventually assert a form of rule.

The Nature of the *Odyssey*

The human position in the Homeric world is a precarious one. Everywhere and always the gods threaten oblivion: either on the sea, by land, on the battlefield, or in one's sleep, the gods function in a natural world that is more dangerous than nurturing. Yet, for all the arbitrary violence that nature visits on humanity, a surprisingly peaceful coexistence is nevertheless wrought by humankind with this seeming nemesis. As Vernant has written, *"de façon générale, l'homme n'a pas le sentiment de transformer la nature, mais plûtot de se conformer à elle."*[5]

Of all the heroes portrayed in both the epics, perhaps Odysseus' relationship to nature is the most ambiguous but hence the most revealing of the human condition, and of the place of politics in the human and natural spheres. The whole of the *Odyssey*—particularly inasmuch as the epic is suffused with chthonic locations, primal and powerful female goddesses, and a remarkable emphasis on the development of the human arts and sciences as a means of extracting sustenance from nature—marks a radical departure from the *mise-en-scène* of the *Iliad*. But of particular notoriety even in the *Odyssey* is an episode in Book 9, when, surveying an uninhabited island next to the island of the Cyclopes, Odysseus remarks in almost a personal aside on the island's inviting natural qualities, even its wealth:

> There is a wooded island that spreads, away from the harbor,
> neither close in to the land of the Cyclopes nor far out
> from it; forested; wild goats beyond number breed there,
> for there is no coming and going of humankind to disturb them,
> nor are they visited by hunters, who in the forest
> suffer hardships as they haunt the peaks of mountains,
> neither again is it held by herded flocks, nor farmers,
> but all its days, never plowed up and never planted,
> it goes without people and supports the bleating wild goats.
> For the Cyclopes have no ships with cheeks of vermillion,
> nor have they builders of ships among them, who could have made them
> strong-benched vessels, and these if made could have run them sailings
> to all the various cities of men, in the way that people
> cross the sea by means of ships and visit each other,
> and they could have made this island a strong settlement for them.
> For it is not a bad place at all, it could bear all crops
> in season, and there are meadowlands near the shores of the grey sea,
> well-watered and soft; and there could be grapes grown there endlessly,

and there is smooth land for plowing, men could reap a full harvest
always in season, since there is very rich subsoil. Also
there is an easy harbor, with no need for a hawser
nor anchor stones to be thrown ashore nor cables to make fast;
one could just run ashore and wait for the time when the sailors'
desire stirred them to go and the right winds were blowing (9.116-39).[6]

At first glance Odysseus appears here as transparently acquisitive, viewing each natural element of so-called "Goat Island" through the eyes of human development rather than with an appreciation of its simple natural state.[7] Yet, also present is a remarkably political aspect in his appraisal: what is most lacking is not economic development in itself, but those useful arts that undergird and afford the opportunity for political life. Other than the potential for food—and Odysseus is ever attentive to the needs of his stomach—the island's other obvious provision is that of "a strong settlement" comprised of laborers and artisans seeking together mutual protection and companionship. For, lacking the useful arts, in this instance shipbuilding, the Cyclopes cannot travel the "various cities of men, in the way that people / cross the sea by means of ships and visit each other." The course of normal, even natural, human relations drive people to visit each other, to speak and share knowledge, goods, and stories.

For Odysseus, the absence of people knowledgeable in the practice of such useful arts is indicative of a wider absence of *political* life, and as such he recognizes the deficiencies of the Cyclopes' social arrangements without having yet encountered them. Seeing the undeveloped state of this easily reached island, Odysseus rightly suspects that they might encounter on the populated island "a man who was endowed with great strength, /and wild, with no true knowledge of laws or any good customs" (9.214-15). His initial suspicion—one that might obviously have persuaded Odysseus from confronting Cyclops at all but for his combined selfishness for a guest-gift and for knowledge of what such creatures could be like (9.229)—is substantiated by his description to the Phaiakians of the Cyclopes' way of life:

. . . we sailed further
along, and reached the country of the lawless outrageous
Cyclopes who, putting all their trust in the immortal
gods, neither plow with their hands nor plant anything,
but all grows for them without seed planting, without cultivation.
These people have no institutions, no meetings for councils;
rather they make their habitations in caverns hollowed
among the peaks of high mountains, and each one is the law
for his own wives and children, and cares nothing about the others (9.105-15).

While the Cyclopes live in proximity to one another, they do not meet in order to deliberate, neither to settle conflict (which one imagines is settled through a test of strength) nor to satisfy what Aristotle described as the characteristics of "political animals," to see and to be seen, to speak and to listen, to rule and be ruled.[8] Odysseus' disdain for the Cyclopes is not, after a fleeting initial impression, provoked by a developer's greedy eye, but consists of Odysseus' understanding that humanity's ability to cultivate nature's bounty, to extend the flexible albeit naturally imposed boundaries over land and sea, is necessarily inseparable from the development of political life. Were food all that Odysseus desired, he might well have remained on Calypso's bountiful island, one that combines the plenty of Goat Island with the manicured splendors of the Phaiakian gardens.[9] Similarly, were the value of property his paramount interest, the unsettled island beside that of the Cyclopes clearly has more value *in potentia* than the already settled yet rocky Ithaca. But Odysseus craves more than merely material satiation—he longs for "sight of the very smoke uprising / from his country," or, short of return, "longs to die" (1.58-59). There is more in Odysseus' complex soul than the longing for material comfort: he too craves for his land, his people, his community, not merely the physical, even sexual satiation afforded by Penelope's superior, Calypso (5.215-24). So too is his outlook influenced by this overarching desire to return: his appraisal of Goat Island, far from being simply acquisitive, is fundamentally political.

Quite how political Odysseus' vision is becomes apparent when we compare his assessment of the Cyclopes to another similar political situation in the *Odyssey*. There is indeed another island described in the *Odyssey* that is remarkable for having "no meetings for councils" and where evidently "each one is the law for his own wives and children, and cares nothing about the others." This island, of course, is Ithaca itself, at least in the twenty years since Odysseus' departure before Athena prods Telemachus to call for a council meeting. As the aged Aigyptos reminds the assembled Ithacans, "Never has there been an assembly (*agora*) of us or any session / since great Odysseus went away in the hollow vessels" (2.26-27). Telemachus asks the gathering of citizens to assist him in curtailing the behavior of the ravenous suitors; until now, the affairs of the ruling family of Ithaca have been solely the concern of that family, even given the absence of their *basileus*, Odysseus. Indeed, Telemachus has matured under a type of political organization that fundamentally assumes all conflicts are private by nature and excuses his summoning the assembly as the indulgence of private concerns in a public setting: "nor have I some...public matter to set forth and argue, but my own need, the evil that has befallen my household (*oikos*)" (2.44-45). By calling the assembly through Athena's prompting, Telemachus

begins a process of education in which he will begin to see the entangle-
ments of public and private life, and to what extent a ruling family's
seemingly private concerns are never strictly without implications for the
polity at large. By extension, Odysseus vigorously pursued an explicitly
political role in Ithaca by regularly seeking out the counsel of Ithaca's
deliberative *agora*.

Knowing Nature: Gods, Beasts, and Political Animals

If Odysseus evinces something approaching disdain at the Cyclopes' lack
of political life—a disdain of a decidedly inhuman, even animal existence—further evidence suggests that such disdain derives from an
understanding that an unmediated relationship between humanity and nature
is largely impossible when one properly understands human limitations.
Borrowing from Aristotle's description of what constitutes a truly human
life, one can find in turn in the *Odyssey* the implicit acknowledgment that
"one who is incapable of participating or who is in need of nothing through
being self-sufficient (*autarkein*) is no part of a city, and so is either a beast
or a god."[10] *Autarkein*—literally meaning, and hence better translated as,
"self-rule"—is achieved through two possibilities that are not mutually
exclusive: one may be "incapable of participating" or one may be "in need
of nothing through being *autarkein*." How are we to understand Aristotle's
conditions of those not included in the partnership (*koinônia*) of the city?
Clearly, one must be human, or possessing of those qualities that entail full
humanity. Those that are literally "beasts or gods" are disqualified from the
possibility of political partnership through either their incapacity (clearly the
condition of the beasts) or their *autarkein* (clearly the condition of the gods).
Yet is there something in these two conditions that in fact draws these two
excluded categories into commonality?

In the *Odyssey* the gods and the beasts share one notable quality in
common: the innate ability to apprehend nature in an immediate and
unmediated fashion. Whereas humans constantly doubt the evidence of their
senses—and rightly so, given the propensity of gods to disguise themselves
as humans or beasts—the gods and the beasts of the *Odyssey* are never in
doubt of their senses, which afford them a direct conduit to a thing's
essence. Jenny Strauss Clay has shown the stark difference between human
and divine vision through an analysis of the word *eidenai*, which encom-
passes both the meaning "sight" and "knowledge" when referring to
immortal vision, and only "sight" when used to describe human vision: "the
gulf between divine and mortal *eidenai* reveals itself most clearly in men's

inability to see or recognize the gods. Hence men cannot have any sure knowledge of them."[11] Alternatively, the gods perceive one another at will regardless of disguise. Moreover, the gods possess a direct knowledge of nature's properties that is hidden to man except through divine assistance.

Acknowledgment of this divine knowledge of nature is indicated by a god's own admission of that knowledge and its revelation to an unapprehending human. The only use of the word *phusis*, or nature, in the entirety of the Homeric corpus occurs in the *Odyssey* when Hermes reveals to Odysseus the herb that will protect him from the transformative powers of Circe. Significantly, the godly knowledge of a natural property in this case will allow a human to remain unscathed by direct divine power—it is divine knowledge of nature, more than divine powers, that distinguishes the gods from men.

> So spoke Argeïphontes, and he gave me the medicine,
> which he picked out of the ground, and he explained the nature [*phusis*]
> of it to me. It was black at the root, but with a milky
> flower. The gods call it moly. It is hard for mortal
> men to dig up, but the gods have power to do all things (10.302-6).

Hermes explicitly contrasts the gods with mortal men by noting the difficulty that men have extracting the herb from the concealing earth. Yet, there is a certain commensurability between mortal and immortal physical ability, if the immortals nevertheless possess a distinct advantage in strength and skill.[12] What is implicitly *incommensurable* is the distinct immortal ability to see and know nature, which requires explanation to even the normally perceptive and resourceful Odysseus. Physically, human beings share many godlike attributes except the immortality of the gods; yet, in matters of apperception, mortal vision is enclosed in a fog that obscures true knowledge.[13]

As the immortal gods are capable of seeing and knowing the nature of divine and earthly things without mediation or effort, so are the beasts also endowed through their senses. In Book 17 of the *Odyssey*, Odysseus—disguised and unrecognizable to his closest friends, his enemies, even his family—is briefly glanced at by the hound Argos and is immediately recognized:

> There the dog Argos lay in dung, all covered with dog ticks.
> Now, as he perceived that Odysseus had come close to him,
> he wagged his tail, and laid both his ears back; only
> now no longer had the strength to move any closer
> to his master . . .
> But the doom of dark death now closed over the dog, Argos,
> when, after nineteen years had gone by, he had seen Odysseus. (17.300-4, 326-27)

Argos' sight ("he had seen," *idont'*, from *eidenai*) is remarkable: despite, on the one hand, his physical deterioration, emphasized by tick infestation atop a dung hill; and on the other hand, the passing of nineteen years without having seen his master, Argos is yet capable—without effort from his physically weakened body which cannot even lift itself—of easily recognizing Odysseus. Like the gods, the beasts possess senses that immediately comprehend a thing's nature, overcoming with ease those obstacles that would make even basic human comprehension impossible. Alternatively, mankind in the *Odyssey* is ever uncertain of a thing's nature: Noemon is confused whether it is a god or Mentor that has traveled with Telemachus on his sea journey (4.653-56), and likewise Odysseus himself expresses the difficulty of recognizing divine or mortal natures

> Antinoös, you did badly to hit the unhappy vagabond: a curse on you,
> if he turns out to be a god from heaven.
> For the gods do take on all sorts of transformations, appearing
> as strangers from elsewhere, and thus they range at large through the cities,
> watching to see which men keep laws and which are violent (17.483-87).

Odysseus here acknowledges the limits of human vision and suggests that justice must be pursued among human beings through laws, or human contrivances erected to assist mortals living amid uncertainty. The irony in Odysseus' statement is that at the moment he is disguised as a lowly beggar—not the god he warns Antinoös of, but decidedly not the form of human he appears either. Not only are mortals incapable of knowing the gods by sight—they cannot even trust their ability to recognize one another. This human uncertainty of their own senses drives them—unlike the gods or beasts—to embrace an admixture of nature and artifice, or politics, as the means to secure justice among each other.

Narration, Artifice, and Political Persuasion

Odysseus' vision, then, is a profoundly public, even political, outlook, not one solely directed toward self-maximization and individual achievement, but one seeking enrichment of his immediate friends and community through a mutual endeavor of compromise with human exigencies and natural limits. Even his one accomplishment of unsurpassed personal benefit is one that is inseparable from his political vision. This accomplishment—neither the outwitting of Cyclopes, nor the conquest of Circe; not the descent to Hades, nor even the almost single-handed defeat of 108 suitors—is to be found in the simple but astonishing narration of his own adventures to the Phaiakians.

It is this storytelling, both its content and its form, the words that disclose the man and the man telling the story, that move the Phaiakians to provide Odysseus with the two boons that Poseidon later bemoans:

> [The Phaiakians] carried him, asleep in the fast ship, over
> the sea, and set him down in Ithaca, and gave him numberless
> gifts, as bronze, and gold abundant, and woven clothing,
> more than Odysseus could ever have taken from Troy, even if
> he had come home ungrieved and with his fair share of plunder (13.134-39).

The Phaiakians have afforded him with more wealth than ten year's war could have procured, and a direct journey home that another ten year's effort could not accomplish. Twenty years of unsurpassed pain, sorrow, and failed effort do not equal in beneficence what one day's narration to the wealthy, powerful, and godlike Phaiakians can achieve.

His narration of his own story spanning Books 9-12 is both masterful and unprecedented—no other Homeric character tells more of his own story. Yet, for the significant departure Odysseus' own narration within the Homeric corpus represents—the poet in effect gives way to his character's version, one that may not necessarily be the same version the poet would have portrayed—endless perceptive critics have neglected to treat this narration as quite unique and meriting special, if suspicious, attention. For example, Richmond Lattimore—as intimate as any commentator with the Homeric texts, having translated both epics to English—summarizes that "in addition to the *authentic wanderings* of Odysseus recounted by the hero himself, there are five *false stories* told by the hero about himself" (emphasis mine).[14] Inasmuch as Odysseus has a penchant for lying and deceit on occasions when nothing is at stake—witness his cruel lies to Laertes after the suitors have been dispatched (24.303ff.)—the fact that Odysseus desires a great deal from the Phaiakians should give one pause before declaring his narration to be somehow inherently "authentic."[15] There are independent guideposts in the *Odyssey* indicating that certain events did indeed occur in addition to their presence in Odysseus' narrative. He did deceive Polyphemus and put out his eye, prompting the anger of Poseidon (1.68ff.); he did stay with Calypso for seven years and decline her offer of immortality (5.1ff., 136); his men did eat the kine of Helios and bring ruin upon themselves (1.8-9). These isolated moments are noted because outside of their definite occurrence according to an "objective" source in the *Odyssey* (meaning a god or the god-inspired poet), the specifics in Odysseus' narration might well be fabrication, and given his inclination toward deceit, almost certainly contain some embellishment, if not outright invention.

One story that should be approached with particular suspicion is the Cyclops episode, one whose peculiarities have long been noted by analysts, notably Denys Page in his classic examination *The Homeric Odyssey*. Page interprets the story of Polyphemus with careful attention to its folk tale elements, especially insofar as they differ from the many examples of this same basic folk tale of which 125 examples were collected in 1904 by Oskar Hackam. Page states that "there were various ways of telling that story [of the blinding of the evil shepherd], and our poet is not particularly careful to choose one way to the exclusion of all the others."[16] Specifically, he notes the changes made in the use of the weapon to put out Polyphemus' eye and the employment of lots to decide who will assist Odysseus in this matter.

Usually, as a means of effecting plot progression, the weapon used to put out the eye of the evil shepherd is the very roasting spit on which the shepherd's grisly dinner is cooked. Because Polyphemus does not cook his "dinner," but snatches up his prey and devours them raw, Odysseus must resort to using an olive club that lies unnoticed in the corner, thus ruining the logical economy of the original version (9.319-20). Even more strangely, while the folk tale also includes a scene in which the survivors use lots as in the *Odyssey*, it is consistently employed in the folk tale remnants to decide in what order the victims will be eaten, and not who will assist in the blinding of the shepherd. These two episodes are especially interesting because the skeleton of the normal plot progressions both exist in the *Odyssey*, but several changes are made, Page suggests, because the poet did not have full access or correct knowledge of the usual folk tale.

Yet, because Page does not note that the story is actually in Odysseus' words, not Homer's, he neglects a more interesting and even likely possibility: Odysseus purposefully makes up the changes. He has already demonstrated that in order to ingratiate himself to the Phaiakians, he will embellish freely, as he does in claiming that he, not Nausikaa, is responsible for his staying behind the procession in which she enters town (7.303-7; cf. 6.295ff.). In this episode we the audience know that in fact *Nausikaa* suggested that it would be more seemly for Odysseus to trail behind her party; might not such an effect be sought by Homer (using Odysseus' words) in the case of the Cyclops episode as well? Perhaps, given the commonness of the "evil shepherd" story as suggested by Page, Homer's audience was familiar with the story's normal elements, leaving the effect again of "putting one over" on the Phaiakians, but this time for a more personal reason—to protect his *own* reputation. Regarding the absence of a cooking scene, Page writes "we may conjecture that the cooking of the human victims, whether alive or dead, was rejected as being a deed of utmost barbarism, outside the law prescribed by tradition to the Odyssean story-teller. . . . [I]t is not surprising that some civilized communities have rejected it and substituted other weapons for the spit."[17] Here Page implicitly admits that in fact Homer may have known the full folk story of the blinded shepherd; and if it is possible that Homer would curtail his story for the sake of the "civilized" Greek audience, then it seems even more likely that such sensitive consideration would be extended by Odysseus to the cultivated Scherian audience, not forgetting that this is Odysseus' version of the events. The overall effect of the devious changes serves the emotionally fulfilling function of letting one's audience "in" (in this case *Homer's* audience) on a secret of which the other characters are unaware (*Odysseus'* immediate audience, the Scherians).

A revealing moment occurs in the midst of Odysseus' narration, one that interrupts the trance created by Odysseus' long trail of words precisely at the most daunting moment of the story, amid his description of his descent to Hades. Arete and Alkinoös break into the narrative, reminding us (Homer's audience) of the presence of, and the effect his narrative is having on, his fictive audience. Alkinoös publicly announces his intention to fulfill Odysseus' longings to return home along with a significant material reward to be raised from the property-holders of Scheria (11.348-53). Then, almost as an afterthought, much as a man being conned is given over to temporary doubts over the con man's character and must reassure himself that his suspicions are unfounded, Alkinoös says:

> Odysseus, as we look upon you, do not imagine
> that you are a deceitful or thievish man, the sort that the black earth
> breeds in great numbers, people who wander widely, making up
> lying stories, from which no one could learn anything. You have
> a grace upon your words, and there is sound sense within them,
> and expertly, as a singer would do, you have told the story
> of the dismal sorrows befallen yourself and all the Argives (11.363-69).

This moment, despite all its seriousness and high intentions, should cause us, as it likely caused its original audience, to break out in smiles and laughter: not only do we know that Odysseus is constantly making up "lying stories,"[18] but Odysseus has admitted as much to Alkinoös by describing both his tendency for theft (9.40ff.—the sack of the Kikonians) and his series of lies to Cyclops, in addition to the independent verification of his tendency toward deceit offered by Demodokus in his depiction of the Trojan Horse ploy (7.499ff.). To conclude, then, that Odysseus' narration of his own adventures constitutes his "authentic wanderings" is to admit to being as thoroughly duped as Alkinoös and the Phaiakians.[19]

Yet Alkinoös, upon closer examination, may additionally indicate that he knows or at least suspects Odysseus to be stretching his tale to fit the tastes of his audience, such that he qualifies his statement. It is not simply that Odysseus is exonerated of being a liar, but he is not "a deceitful or thievish man . . . from which no one could learn anything" (*eni de phrenes esthlai*— perhaps a generous translation of *phrenes* on Lattimore's part, but generally entailing the imparting of wisdom). In other words, Alkinoös does not dismiss the possibility that Odysseus is indeed a deceitful and thievish man, but one from whom in this case the audience has learned a great deal. There is here an implicit identification of Odysseus as a teacher, one not merely of deceit or theft—for what leader would reward such a teacher?—but rather one who deceives not merely for his own good, but for the good of the audience. Alkinoös goes on to compare Odysseus to a singer, to one who takes his inspiration from the immortal goddess herself, opening the pure and unmediated world of nature to the imperfect vision of humanity, distilled and refracted but still more essential than unaided senses can comprehend. Ironically, even paradoxically, Odysseus rivals Homer as the greatest epic poet of ancient Greece. Through language, even a form of persuasion, Odysseus achieves what force could not: *nostos* and untold wealth. More than the ploy of the Trojan Horse, Alkinoös' words indicate the transition of *bios* to *noos*, of force to mind, signaling the possibility for political philosophy rather than the arbitrary rule of the strong over the weak. Though not yet articulating the principle of just rule, of moderation, of limitation, Odysseus continuously *demonstrates* their possibility. That deception should go hand in hand with persuasion at its inception may indicate a more intimate link than coincidence.

Odysseus and Human Community: Choosing Death

Odysseus' alliance with poetry and the poet is appropriate, for through poetry Odysseus understands the true and only possibility for human immortality: not through nature, as is the case for the undying gods, but again through human artifice, now aided and ennobled by the goddess, through words and art. Like Tom Sawyer hearing his own eulogy, Odysseus is honored to hear his own future in the songs of Demodokus (8.72ff., 499ff.). His singular forbearance in sparing Phemios the bard indicates his esteem for poets (often taken to be a bit of Homeric propaganda). Phemios, in begging to be spared, perhaps unknowingly but rightly implores Odysseus in terms that appeal to Odysseus' sense of poetic destiny:

You will be sorry in time to come if you kill the singer
of songs. I sing to gods and to human people, and I am
taught by myself, but the god has inspired in me songways
of every kind. I am such a one as can sing before you
as to a god (22.345-49).

The link forged here between the gods and poetry is not infelicitous: for the Homeric society, poetry doubly partakes of the immortal world. The poet is both inspired by the Muse, figuratively becoming the outlet for the immortal perspective and, hence, capable of knowing that which humans are incapable of knowing. The difference between the narrative of Homer and that of Odysseus is striking in this regard; whereas Homer is ever confident of which god inspired a human to act in some fashion, Odysseus must admit to ignorance of where motivation originates.[20]

Odysseus is supremely conscious of the immortal yet wholly human possibilities of poetry because of his first-hand knowledge of the immortality he did not accept—life everlasting with Calypso. He is also remarkably the only mortal noted in the *Iliad* or the *Odyssey* who, when offered immortality, refuses that godlike state. Nevertheless, some critics have dismissed this singular instance. Alasdair MacIntyre, for example, argues that Odysseus' incredible refusal in fact represents a fundamental lack of choice, and hence does not merit admiration or wonder:

> The self of the heroic age lacks precisely that characteristic which . . . some modern moral philosophers take to be an essential characteristic of human self-hood: the capacity to detach oneself from any particular standpoint or point of view, to step backwards, as it were, and view and judge that standpoint or point of view from the outside. In heroic society there is no "outside" except that of a stranger. A man who tried to withdraw himself from his given position in heroic society would be engaged in the enterprise of trying to make himself disappear.[21]

MacIntyre is correct about the impossibility of achieving a standpoint of pure objectivity (both for ancients and moderns alike); yet, in considering Homer's heroes as incapable of *achieving* such removal from society at large, or objectivity, he similarly denies the *temptation* for objectivity, which nevertheless was no less powerful for the Homeric heroes than it continues to be for modern man. The desire to become a god (effectively or actually) is precisely that desire for unmediated objectivity or the direct and unmediated knowledge of nature.

Elsewhere Odysseus is explicitly offered such "detached" knowledge of the world, that clear unmediated vision only permitted to the gods. His hunger for this wisdom is manifest: he strains against the self-imposed and twice-fastened bonds that keep him from the Siren's offer:

Come this way, honored Odysseus, great glory of the Achaeans,
and stay your ship, so that you can listen here to our singing;
for no one else has ever sailed past this place in his black ship
until he has listened to the honey-sweet voice that issues
from our lips; then goes on well pleased knowing more than ever
he did; for we know everything that the Argives and Trojans
did and suffered in wide Troy through the gods' despite.
Over all the generous earth we know everything that happens (12.184-91).

Odysseus' *physical* temptation to fling himself off the ship to *know* the Siren's revelation reveals the power of this offer over Odysseus; the rotting corpses of other humans that lie about the water's edge further indicates this power over all humans (12.45-46). Even the very presence of those corpses is only known second-hand as related by Circe; Odysseus is too enchanted to notice, as one would have to be to ignore one's likely fate. Yet, having experienced the magnitude of this temptation for immortal vision, and having been told of its likely result, Odysseus is well-prepared for Calypso's offer; while still holding forth a temptation to the mortal who faces death, Odysseus' decision is an informed one.

The reality of the temptation that Calypso's offer entails should not be underestimated: at stake is Odysseus' eternal existence, either on the paradisiac island with the beautiful and unaging goddess Calypso, or among the immaterial shades in the cold necropolis, Hades. Within the epic itself we learn of Odysseus' existence on Calypso's island Ogygia at the outset of the epic (as related by Athena to Zeus, 1.48-59), and again return to his existence there after the *Telemachia* in Book 5. Yet, chronologically Odysseus' journey to Hades occurs *before* his exile on Ogygia, to be related later to the Phaiakians upon escaping Calypso in Book 11. Here again Denys Page's arguments become relevant, as he argues that the Hades episode is clearly interpolated given its ostensible dislocation from the rest of the work.[22] The episode is only dubiously connected to the epic by utilizing Circe in order to explain the purpose of the journey to the underworld. He must consult Teiresias, Circe informs him, who "will tell you the way (*hodon*) to go, the stages of your journey, / and tell you how to make your way home on the sea where the fish swarm" (10.539-40).

Page has asserted that two requirements must be fulfilled for Circe to make this demand of Odysseus: "first, that Circe is unable herself to supply this information, secondly, that Teiresias will in fact do what she says he will do."[23] It is in fact true that neither of these conditions is fulfilled to the letter: for while Teiresias does give Odysseus certain directions concerning the island of Thrinicia and advises him on the state of affairs in Ithaca, it is nevertheless clear that Circe also knows the steps of Odysseus' immediate path, and far more precisely than does Teiresias (12.37ff.). Nevertheless, Teiresias *does* afford Odysseus some information that Circe does not, and such that would not contradict the spirit of Circe's instructions. From Teiresias Odysseus learns the subsequent course of his life, including a prediction of his manner of death. While *hodon* does not yet clearly indicate the metaphorical sense of "way" or "path" that the word later accrues in Greek philosophy and Christian thought, such a possibility is not forestalled by its absence and is in fact suggested by the type of information that is provided by Teiresias. Thus, in a larger sense Teiresias does in fact explain to Odysseus his "way," not only in terms of his life-course, but also inasmuch as this knowledge has implications for his immediate journey home.

Teiresias' words are not fate: they are predictions based on what has preceded and knowledge of Odysseus' character but do not entail an external force that prevents all other possibilities. Thus Teiresias tells Odysseus that he has a "chance" of surviving to reach Ithaca, if "you can contain your own desire, and contain your companions" (11.103-4). Certain conditions must be met before certain outcomes can be achieved, but at all points Odysseus has a choice (within the parameters of *previous* choices, of course) *until* a decision is reached and the certain consequences are set in motion. Thus one suspects that if Odysseus had eaten of the cattle of Helios, he too would have died along with his men, just as he could have chosen to remain or die at any point on his journey, temptations often contemplated by Odysseus. It is this knowledge that Odysseus to some extent controls his own fate that indicates how Teiresias' advice will assist his journey home as much as Circe's subsequent advice helps him to get safely past some immediate dangers.

Odysseus' choice made with the knowledge of Teiresias' prediction of his eventual death is stressed indirectly at the outset of Book 5, where he for the final time refuses Calypso's offer of immortality. The first line of the book departs from Homer's usual description of Dawn's "rosy fingers" and instead reads: "Now Dawn rose from her bed, where she lay by haughty Tithonus..." (5.1). Homer calls attention to Eos' companion at this particular moment implicitly in order to contrast Tithonus with Odysseus, as both men are mortals with whom goddesses fall in love and offer immortality. Tithonus accepts, and Eos begs Zeus to grant him immortal life, to which Zeus assents—literally. Tithonus lives, but ages, decays, withers, eventually taking on the appearance of a grasshopper; he has been granted immortality without endless youth.[24] "Haughty" Tithonus accepts what is unacceptable for mortals to attain but which is nevertheless clearly tempting to normal mortal desires.[25]

Quite how tempting is subsequently revealed by Calypso in her complaints to Hermes who informs her of Zeus' decision to free Odysseus.

> You are hard-hearted, you gods, and jealous beyond all creatures
> beside, when you are resentful toward the goddesses for sleeping
> openly with such men as each has made her true husband.
> So when Dawn of the rosy fingers chose out Orion,
> all you gods who live at your ease were full of resentment,
> until chaste Artemis of the golden throne in Ortygia
> came with a visitation of painless arrows and killed him;
> and so it was when Demeter of the lovely hair, yielding
> to her desire, lay with Iasion and loved him
> in a thrice-turned field, it was not long before this was made known
> to Zeus, who struck him down with a cast of shining thunderbolt (5.118-28).

Along with Tithonus, other evidence is given of mankind's propensity to accept the favor of immortality when offered. Also indicated is the propensity of the gods to prevent such outcomes, either through subterfuge (in the case of Tithonus) or force (as with Orion and Iasion). Odysseus' decision not to accept Calypso's offer of immortality may be made as well with the knowledge of its likely consequences, as well as out of his desire to be reunited with Penelope and his community. The causes are fundamentally connected: both indicate an acknowledgment of the proper scope for human activity, not as ersatz gods, but as mortals whose very limitations sometimes cause them to crave more than their measure. Odysseus knows from Teiresias that he will die *if* he chooses to return home and reenter the flow of time. The choice is not foreordained, although Odysseus' eventual death is, if he decides to leave Calypso. His choice is made through his acceptance of his mortal position. Odysseus acknowledges as much as he begins his tale to the Phaiakians, thus framing his entire journey by his denial of Calypso's offer of immortality:

> But [she] did not at all persuade the *thymos* in my chest as
> nothing is more sweet in the end than country and parents
> ever, even when far away one lives in a fertile
> place, when it is an alien country, far from his parents (9.33-36).

The Homeric Gods, the Founder, and Justice

If Odysseus' *desire* to return to Ithaca reveals his embrace of the human condition of limitation and mortality, his *actual* return signals the possibility of the return of politics over violence in the Homeric world. The chain of violence does not cease on the shores of Troy, but continues unabated to the shores of Agamemnon's palace and to Ithaca. The *Odyssey* suggests the excessiveness of this chain of retribution; its inappropriateness finally in Ithaca—where political solutions should be the norm; and the mutual responsibility of the gods and men both in causing it, and finally in ending it.

In some senses, the continuation of violence has as its basis the very disagreement between the gods and men about the root causes of human action in general. Humans are ever accusing the gods, with good reason, of causing their strife and misery; even the argument at the basis of the *Iliad* is blamed on the gods by Agamemnon (XIX.134-39). Yet the gods too seek to avoid their participation in the perpetuation of violence. It is Zeus, in fact, who distances himself from the continuing chain of violence with some impatience at the outset of the *Odyssey*:

> "Oh for shame, how the mortals put the blame upon us
> gods, for they say evils come from us, but it is they, rather,
> who by their own recklessness win sorrow beyond what is given,
> as now lately, beyond what was given, Aigisthos married
> the wife of Atreus' son, and murdered him on his homecoming,
> though he knew it was sheer destruction, for we ourselves had told him,
> sending Hermes, the mighty watcher, Argeïphontes,
> not to kill the man, nor court his lady for marriage;
> for vengeance would come on him from Orestes, son of Atreides,
> whenever he came of age and longed for his own country.
> So Hermes told him, but for all his kind intention he could not
> persuade the mind of Aigisthos. And now he has paid for everything" (1.32-43).

Zeus' complaint against Aigisthos, one long celebrated and debated by critics, is rightly astonishing. While it reinforces the existence of humanity's capacity for choice over their individual fates, it seemingly denies the otherwise obvious presence of divine interference in the lives of men evident in both the epics. However, twice Zeus accuses humans of bringing misfortune upon themselves "beyond what is given" (1.34, 35); Zeus at least acknowledges a divine role in human affairs, just or unjust, that can be exacerbated by human choice. Such is in keeping with the general import of Teiresias' prediction: choice is limited by necessity, but within even this sometimes restricted parameter humans create their own fates. On the shield of Achilles, the gods are more in evidence in the city of war than the city of peace; the problem for the *Odyssey* is how to travel from one city to the other.

Despite the gods' constant *claim* to be attentive to justice among humans, and their occasional actions that would seem to effect a "rough justice,"[26] the gods are fundamentally inconstant in their enforcement of justice among humans. More baldly, the gods are arbitrary, and that arbitrariness *sometimes* deigns them to look kindly on humans, and sometimes not, but humanity finally has no way of apprehending from one moment to the next the inclination of the Olympians, just as they cannot apprehend the gods themselves.[27] Justice is then a human endeavor which the gods may alternatively help or hinder.

Yet notwithstanding such arbitrariness, the *Odyssey does* end in a just outcome (however rough), and the gods—specifically Athena, with the consent of Zeus—both open and end the poem in pursuit of that outcome. In between, we discover that it is Poseidon who has waged a petty and one-sided war against Odysseus for his eminently justifiable treatment of Polyphemus. Despite Polyphemus' savageness and *hubris* (9.275ff.)— including acts and words that would otherwise have called down the gods' wrath against ordinary humans—Poseidon is moved by his blood kinship with Polyphemus to punish the victim, Odysseus. If it is Athena's anger at Troy that initially endangers Odysseus' *nostos*, it is Poseidon's unconscionable vendetta that prolongs it for years.[28]

The cause of the gods' action finally to pursue justice is obscure. Only after Odysseus has languished on the island of Calypso for seven years does Athena finally broach the topic of Odysseus' homecoming to Zeus (1.45ff.). Ostensibly, her reason for waiting so long is her fear of Poseidon, who is now finally out of earshot among the Aithiopians (1.22-23); such forms the excuse she later gives to Odysseus for her long absence (13.341-43). Yet, Athena might have effected his return home long before Odysseus ever landed on the Cyclopes' island, or assisted in his escape there without resort to blinding. Rather, her absence *from the time Odysseus left Troy* is noted by Odysseus and serves to belie her excuse of Poseidon's anger as the single reason for her absence (3.316ff.).[29]

If Athena might have assisted Odysseus at any time before his encounter with Polyphemus—effectively forestalling the need to confront the suitors, who would not have gathered so quickly after the war's end—why then does she choose to act when she does, so long after Odysseus' embarkation and for no apparent reason? Nothing has changed in Ogygia—Odysseus still pines to return as he has since arriving there, and Calypso continues to hold him captive while offering him immortality. Homer does not explicitly tell us the cause of the strife but provides the clues needed to deduce the reason.

The answer lies in Athena's decision to go first to Ithaca, and not, as logic would demand, to free Odysseus. Her action does not necessarily indicate her concern for Odysseus, as many assume, but perhaps more for the breakdown of morality in Ithaca. The punishment of Odysseus for nine years, effected first by Athena and then unjustly prolonged by Poseidon, has

created an intolerable situation among the ordinary people of Ithaca. Even
the superficial veneer of decency that would normally attach itself to the
nobly born suitors has worn off: they not only gluttonously devour Odysseus' property, but threaten death to Odysseus, attempt to kill his son and
heir, and finally disregard pious warnings about their fate (1.160; 2.246-51;
4.668ff.; 20.364-83). Athena herself, on first arriving in Ithaca, is provoked
to ask Telemachus:

> Is it a festival or a wedding? Surely no communal dinner.
> How insolently they seem to swagger about in their feasting
> all through the house. A serious man who came in among them
> could well be scandalized, seeing much disgraceful behavior (1.226-29).

Her concern is admittedly for "a serious man's" perception of the suitors'
behavior, and the effect such unpunished disgraces would have on persons
of decency.

Appropriately, then, upon witnessing the rapid deterioration of morals on
Ithaca, Athena proceeds *not* to Ogygia to release Odysseus, but directly to
Ithaca, where she advises Telemachus to call the first *agora* in twenty years.
In the absence of a just leader, the gods must finally attempt to reinstitute
justice, not directly, but through the auspices of human institutions. As both
Zeus and Odysseus recognize, justice is finally a human affair. However, the
suitors' disregard of justice is by now so firmly established, and they are so
confident of acting without impunity, that the assembly is unsuccessful; it
merely hardens their determination to act lawlessly.[30]

The restoration of order requires not only *noos*—symbolized on Ithaca by
the aged Mentor—but also *biê*, both possessed in sufficient degree by
Odysseus. Telemachus the child notes that the citizens of the *polis* are
physically incapable of restoring order—"we ourselves are not the men to do
it; we must be / weaklings in such a case, not men well seasoned in battle"
(2.60-61)—and as such admits that persuasion, and hence politics, has
failed. If Odysseus throughout demonstrates a sympathy for political life, its
fellowship and the means of persuasion, it is ultimately his ability to act
apolitically and even amorally that will restore justice to Ithaca.

Such a conclusion gives pause: Odysseus has been portrayed throughout
as a man of moderation, engaged with political vision and his community,
and heedful of justice. Yet, he is also the consummate liar, a likely
desecrator of temples during the sack of Troy, a selfish commander who
exposes his men to unnecessary risk, a Homeric soldier capable of using
force. If the action of the *Odyssey* moves from lawlessness to justice—from
a violent world to one of moderation—the development of Odysseus'

character moves in the opposite direction, from moderation toward violence, from restraint toward anger. Odysseus by the end of the poem must become more *like* Achilles than his opposite; he must learn not to *control* his anger, a restraint he practices throughout the poem, but to *release* it.[31] As such, he must cease being "No-man," abandon *metis*, and become his own name, which has as its root the word "anger" or "pain."[32] Odysseus must found anew a political order, which calls forth a different skill than that with which he apparently ruled earlier through frequent assemblies.

It is Odysseus' ability ultimately to act amorally—exhibited in his most renowned qualities of endurance and trickery—that makes him the successful hero of the *Odyssey*, and of that world in which neither the gods nor man can be counted on to act justly.[33] If Odysseus' character is striking both for his sense of justice and moderation, and equally his ability to disencumber himself of these qualities, it is finally because Odysseus is more effective as a founder of a political community than as its long-term ruler. The Homeric hero—even Odysseus, who most expands the boundaries of the heroic code—is finally a dubious participant in political life because either violence or trickery is his *sine qua non* of activity, both of which can serve to found or destroy a community, but neither of which can serve as a long-term basis for its continuation. As Alkinoös does not fully trust Odysseus after his persuasive tale, so Odysseus indicates upon his return to Ithaca that he will not be a fully trustworthy and constant leader.[34]

Like Achilles' anger on the plain of Troy, so too when Odysseus' anger is finally released, it becomes difficult to control. The kinsmen of the suitors prepare to destroy Odysseus and his family, prolonging the long chain of retribution that dates back to before the war with Troy and continues unabated on the shores of the homecoming soldiers. Odysseus, too, prepares for civil war: the violence of destruction and restoration again become unidentifiable. Only by the gods' intervention can the chain be broken; having allowed it to proceed in the destruction of community after community, the general spread of *anomie* finally brings Zeus to stop it (24.482-86). Yet up to the very last line of the poem, Odysseus pursues retribution—when all the parties scatter at Athena's command to throw down arms, Odysseus leaps up to pursue them further (24.537-38). He must be stopped by the gods:

> But the son of Kronos then threw down a smoky thunderbolt
> which fell in front of the grey-eyed daughter of the great father:
> "Son of Laertes and seed of Zeus, resourceful Odysseus,
> hold hard, stay this quarrel in closing combat [*polemos*], for fear
> Zeus of the wide brows, son of Kronos, may be angry with you."
> So spoke Athena, and with happy heart (*thymos*) he obeyed her.

And pledges for the days to come, sworn by both sides,
were settled by Pallas Athena, daughter of Zeus of the aegis,
who had likened herself in appearance and voice to Mentor (24.529-48).

If Odysseus in these last lines "with happy heart" puts down his weapons, it is only after having disobeyed Athena once and receiving an explicit threat from Zeus. Odysseus is finally incapable of stopping the chain of violence himself; he is as much a link in a series as the rest of the heroes. He must be stopped by the gods and brought to the bargaining table—not only now to achieve homecoming, but to re-create a home. The institution of justice among humans, if created and maintained by humanity, is instigated perforce by the gods. Appropriately, following a demonstration of force, *biê*, politics is restored in the form of *metis*, in the person of Mentor.

These final lines of the *Odyssey* mark the end not only of homecoming, but of the entire circuit to Troy and back: it is the peace on Ithaca that ends the Trojan War. With that great invasion, political life had literally ceased, both for Troy itself, and at home as well. Its reinstatement must be effected by a founder of both Odysseus' profound sympathy for politics and his ability to act by the traditional amoral, apolitical heroic code when necessary. Justice is restored, prompted by the gods but organized and maintained through human, and thereby political, means. But if the gods aid in its creation, and Odysseus is its conduit, then as Teiresias predicts, and Dante later expanded, the founder may not long be able to remain in the community he founds, but may have to leave the community he creates to be maintained by the citizens of the *polis*.

The Kernel of Democracy

Even if we are persuaded that the gods are prompted finally to act on behalf of justice because the resulting *anomie* in Ithaca threatens mortal order, the question still remains as to *why* such *anomie* should trouble the immortal gods. Their physical existence is not threatened by Ithaca's unrest; indeed, the gods have hitherto delighted in both fomenting discord and joining mankind in its consequences. The gods' own social structure is notably marked by strife: while Zeus exercises final control over the panoply of the gods (primarily through the threat of physical violence, and not moral excellence—VIII.5-27; 209-11), he also avoids open conflict, and is even subject to deception by individual gods who by diverting his attention circumvent his preferences (XIV.243ff.).

As such, the most burlesque portrayal of the gods in the *Odyssey* is also arguably its most fitting, the song of Ares and Aphrodite's adultery (8.266-

367). By treating the subject of adultery, Demodokus' song touches on the source of the Trojan War, the tragedy of Agamemnon, and also alludes to the question of Penelope's fidelity that hangs over Odysseus' homecoming. Thus, a portrayal of the gods' own version of this breach of conduct is indicative of the difference between divine and mortal attitudes toward decency and justice.

Hephaestus, the god closest to mortal expression—being an artist and hence a mediator between nature and artifice—takes seriously his discovery of his wife's adulterous relationship with Ares, as might a human. He therefore devises a trap designed not only to catch the pair, but to humiliate them as well. The reaction of the other gods is illuminating: they admit sympathy not for Hephaestus' outrage, but for the adultery. Apollo asks Hermes, "would you, caught tight in these strong fastenings, be willing / to sleep in bed by the side of Aphrodite the golden?" to which Hermes replies:

"Lord who strike from afar, Apollo, I wish it could only
be, and there could be thrice this number of endless fastenings,
and all you gods could be looking on and all the goddesses,
and still I would sleep by the side of Aphrodite the golden" (8.339-42).

Unarguably a mirthful exchange, it serves in addition to reveal the gods' disregard for the forms of decency that must be followed by mankind to maintain order in a precarious world. The price of adultery for the Olympians is but momentary humiliation in their immortal lives—a harsh penalty by divine standards for whom honor (*timê*) is paramount—but a price the gods are willing to pay for playful iniquity. Alternatively, the price for humans who flout such civil standards is steep, often entailing blood-feud or war, estrangement, and death.[35]

The gods under normal circumstances are not prompted to act by norms of decency; thus, their personal stake in upholding an order of justice among mankind would appear tenuous. Yet Athena and (through her imploring) Zeus both act to restore order to Ithaca with unwonted intensity. *Why* they act finally is also suggested by the story of Ares and Aphrodite: recall that the adulterers flee from the scene in shame because their honor has been soiled. The gods are jealous of their honor; hence, human beings are continuously punished because they threaten the gods' honor. Thus, in view of Athena's sudden decision to restore justice in Ithaca, the equal possibility arises that the divine protection of honor may also prompt the gods occasionally to *uphold* human justice rather than perpetuate injustice.

This latter possibility is strongly suggested in Laertes' prayer upon hearing of the slaughter of the suitors and the return of his son. Through his words we witness the effect of unpunished injustice on common beliefs: "Father Zeus, there are gods indeed upon tall Olympos, / if truly the suitors have had to pay for their reckless violence (*hubris*)" (24.351-52). Laertes acknowledges the gods' existence because injustice has been punished; however, he also indicates by extension a prior and growing disbelief in the gods' existence arising from the unpunished *hubris* of the suitors. Such disbelief points to the cause of Athena's sudden action on behalf of justice: the indiscriminate rule of the strong over the weak has eroded any widespread belief in a just order. Jenny Strauss Clay, perceptive as ever in her assessment of hidden motivations in the *Odyssey*'s characters, also notes Laertes' implicit complaint:

> to extrapolate from what [Laertes] says, if the gods are never just, act only to protect their interests and according to whim, ultimately their very existence may be called into question. . . . Laertes' words suggest that men exert a kind of pressure on the gods to act justly, at least once in a while. Otherwise, there is a danger that no one will attend them.[36]

The gods' valuation of human honor places restrictions on how disregarding of justice they can finally be. Having observed, in Demodokus' song of Ares and Aphrodite, that the gods are only too willing to exist without governance of civic norms, we find it is the *human* demand for justice in their own lives that entices the gods to enforce these norms they themselves do not follow. The gods, without human worship, have no *raison d'être*; only their entanglement with humanity serves to ennoble their frivolous and fractious existence.

Noting this influence of human demands for justice on divine governance, Clay uncharacteristically does not pursue its implications. Yet, its resonance is unavoidable: the call for justice by ordinary people, prompting rulers to act not in their own interest, but on behalf of the common good, is a *democratic* response—rule with consideration of the *demos'* desires. The new foundation of Ithaca, initially demanded through the agora, finally agreed upon by warring parties, and both actions guided by the gods, is motivated and ultimately secured through the people's devices. Odysseus' "army" in the reestablishment of justice does not consist of Homeric warriors seeking to plunder a wealthy city; at his side stand a swineherd and a cowherd, both of whom have been praying continuously for a return of decency and justice. It is the prayers and the actions of these weakest characters that move the most powerful—the gods—to action.

The influence of the people's bestowal of honor as a control on the actions of the powerful is implicit even in the *Iliad*. There Sarpedon describes the obligation of honor that impels him to fight, even against his impulse to survive:

> "Glaukos, why is it that you and I are honored before others
> with pride of place, the choice meats and the filled wine cups
> in Lykia, and all men look on us as if we were immortals. . . . ?
> It is our duty in the forefront of the Lykians
> to take our stand, and bear our part of the blazing battle,
> so that a man of the close-armoured Lykians may say of us:
> 'Indeed, these are no ignoble men who are lords of Lykia,
> these kings of ours. . .,
> since they fight in the forefront of the Lykians.'
> Man, supposing you and I, escaping this battle,
> would be able to live on forever, ageless, immortal,
> so neither would I myself go on fighting in the foremost . . ." (XII.310-28).

The mechanism of honor—and goods—in exchange for battle is at base feudal. But remove the military imperative from the people's expectations—as finally the *Odyssey* does with the people's demands for peace—and a kernel of democratic rule is revealed. Sarpedon's partial vision also mistakes the role of the immortals in this mechanism: it is instead the very *fact* of their immortality that they are prompted to act on behalf of the people. Their endless existence is given content by humanity's attention; disregard their appeals for justice, and their immortality is rendered meaningless.

Of course, democracy proper is not to be found in the Homeric epics; indeed, defenders of Divine Right long used Odysseus' rebuke of Thersites as evidence against the wisdom of popular rule.[37] Nonetheless, the natural human—and, for Greece, divine—craving for honor would become a source in later political philosophy justifying at least an initial consideration of rule based on the common good. Unarticulated perhaps, hidden in the curious motions of gods and men, this early principle nevertheless functions in the pages of Homer. The audience of the *Odyssey* was not warriors and kings primarily, but common people whose continued struggle to survive natural, divine, and human cruelty demanded standards of civility, decency, and justice. Appropriately, the poet addresses only Eumaeus, the lowly but pious swineherd, directly as "you" (14.14, 55, 165, 360, etc.).[38] This simple audience's piety finally forces a response from the gods, and so marks the beginning of a longer odyssey—the education of both god and man in the ways of justice.

Notes

1. The best summary of Odysseus' many wanderings through the pages of literature remains W. B. Stanford, *The Ulysses Theme* (Oxford: Basil Blackwell, 1963).

2. As such, modern political theorists seem to follow the lead of the early ancients, who, according to James Redfield, "by 'poetry' . . . meant always, before anything else, the *Iliad*" (*Nature and Culture in the "Iliad": The Tragedy of Hector* [Chicago: University of Chicago Press, 1975]). Here I would disagree with Werner Jaeger's attempt to argue for the epics' equal significance for the ancients (*Paideia: The Ideals of Greek Culture*, Gilbert Highet, trans. [New York: Oxford University Press, 1945] I.43). Jaeger's own analysis, which examines the *Iliad* at twice the length as the *Odyssey*, seems to belie his own claim.

3. Alasdair MacIntyre, *After Virtue*, Second Edition (Notre Dame, Indiana: University of Notre Dame Press, 1984), 130. Compare MacIntyre's language to that of Marx in his description of ancient Greece:

> Why should not the historic childhood of humanity, its most beautiful unfolding, as a stage never to return, exercise an eternal claim? There are unruly children and precocious children. Many of the old peoples belong in this category. The Greeks were normal children. The charm of their art for us is not in contradiction to the undeveloped society in which it grew. (It) is its result, rather, and is inextricably bound up, rather with the fact that the unripe social conditions under which it arose, and could alone arise, can never return ("Introduction to the *Grundrisse*," in *The Marx-Engels Reader*, Robert C. Tucker, ed. and trans. [New York: Norton, 1978], 246).

4. See especially the essays by David Bolotin ("The Concerns of Odysseus: An Introduction to the *Odyssey*," *Interpretation* 17 [1989], 41-57), Mera J. Flaumenhaft ("The Undercover Hero: Odysseus from Light to Dark," *Interpretation* 10 [1982], 9-41), and Darrell Dobbs ("Reckless Rationalism and Heroic Reverence in Homer's *Odyssey*," *American Political Science Review* 81 [1987], 491-508).

5. Jean-Pierre Vernant, "Travail et nature dans la Grèce ancienne," *Journal de psychologie* 52 (1955): 18-38.

6. Throughout this essay I use the Lattimore translations of the *Iliad* and the *Odyssey*, which are almost uniformly true to the original Greek (Homer, *The Iliad*, Richmond Lattimore, trans. [Chicago: University of Chicago Press, 1951] and *The Odyssey*, Richmond Lattimore, trans. [New York: HarperCollins, 1965]). Occasionally, particularly regarding technical terms or words that will have later resonance in political theory, I have changed the translation and indicate the word in transliterated Greek following the English translation. Greek versions of selected passages are provided from the Loeb editions of the epics (*The Iliad*, A. T. Murray, trans. [Cambridge: Harvard University Press, 1924-25] and *The Odyssey*, A. T. Murray, trans. [Cambridge: Harvard University Press, 1919]).

Citations to the *Iliad* utilize a Roman numeral for the Book number and Arabic numerals for the line numbers (e.g., VI.11-12), whereas citations to the *Odyssey* will adopt Arabic numerals for both the book and the line numbers (e.g., 6.11-12).

7. Such is Horkheimer and Adorno's broader argument in *Dialectic of Enlightenment*, John Cummings, trans. (New York: Herder and Herder, 1972), 46-56.

8. *The Politics,* Carnes Lord, trans. (Chicago: University of Chicago Press, 1984), 1253d. Aristotle describes the social arrangements of the Cyclopes as a "village" (*komê*), a partnership (*koinônia*) that has not attained full self-rule and hence is not fully political (1252b22-27).

9. The lush description of Ogygia occurs at 5.63-74. The description of idyllic Scheria is found at 7.112-32. See Norman Austin on the significance of these voluptuous gardens regarding the ordering of the external world through artifice and nature (*Archery at the Dark of the Moon: Poetic Problems in Homer's Odyssey* [Berkeley: University of California Press, 1975], 149-58).

10. *Politics*, 1253a.

11. Jenny Strauss Clay, *The Wrath of Athena: Gods and Men in the "Odyssey"* (Princeton: Princeton University Press, 1983), 17-18.

12. Erland Ehnmark, *The Idea of God in Homer: Inaugural Dissertation* (Uppsala: Almquist & Boltrycken, 1935), 3ff. Similarly, Arthur W. H. Adkins writes: "in saying that the gods can do anything, the poet has no more in mind than 'if you think of anything which is very difficult for a man, a god can do it easily'" (*Merit and Responsibility: A Study in Greek Values* [Chicago: University of Chicago Press, 1960], 26, n. 4). The ability of humans to injure the gods in battle should indicate the physical similarity of gods and men (V.318ff., in which Diomedes injures Aphrodite, "a weakling goddess," and V.855ff., in which Diomedes, with the assistance of Athena, even injures Ares, himself hardly a "weakling" god).

13. See *Iliad* V.127-28: Human perception is constantly obscured by "mist before the eyes" which is only occasionally lifted by the gods.

14. Richmond Lattimore, "Introduction" in *The Odyssey*, Richmond Lattimore, trans. (New York: HarperCollins, 1991), 11.

15. Of the many critics who treat the episodes recounted by Odysseus, one of the few who have noted it with requisite suspicion is Stanford, *Ulysses Theme*, 64:

> In Books Nine to Twelve of the *Odyssey* Homer ostensibly delegates his task as storyteller to Odysseus. Now comes the problem: does Homer intend us to understand that Odysseus' narrative is factually as precise as it would have been were Homer himself narrating it, or does he intend us to take it as a Ulyssean (and sometimes even Autolycan) version of what "really" took place?

16. Denys Page, *The Homeric Odyssey* (Oxford: Clarendon Press, 1955), 3.

17. Page, *Homeric Odyssey*, 11.

18. Odysseus will subsequently demonstrate this renowned ability at some length during his secret return to Ithaka (13.256-286; 14.191-359; 17.419-444; 19.165-202; 24.302-308).

19. Here MacIntyre (*After Virtue*, 115) cites Fränkel approvingly: "Homeric . . . 'man and his actions become identical, and he makes himself completely and adequately comprehended in them; he has no hidden depths.... In [the epics] factual report of what men do and say, everything that men are, is expressed because they are no more than what they do and say and suffer'" (Hermann Fränkel, *Early Greek Poetry and Philosophy: A History of Greek Epic, Lyric, and Prose to the Middle of the Fifth Century*, Moses Hadas and James Willis, trans. [New York: Harcourt Brace Jovanovich, 1973], 79); see also Adkins, *Merit and Responsibility*, 48-49. Such an approach to the epics perhaps captures the qualities of the more conventional characters, although I suspect close examination of such characters would force MacIntyre to qualify his statement somewhat; but such an approach in the case of Odysseus is manifestly questionable. What Odysseus *says* is often quite the opposite of what he does, or even who he is. Such superficial readings of the epics have for too long been assumed to be the legitimate approach to the "transparent" intentions of Homer, aided of course by those who permit the dismissal of inconvenient passages which are therefore deemed to be interpolations.

20. Clay, *Wrath of Athena*, 10-53.

21. MacIntyre, *After Virtue*, 126.

22. Page, *Homeric Odyssey*, 21-51.

23. Page, *Homeric Odyssey*, 27.

24. This tale is told by the poet of the Homeric hymn, *Hymn to Aphrodite*.

25. MacIntyre (*After Virtue*, 126) is unwittingly correct to note that the attempt to achieve an existence of objectivity beyond one's own limitations would resemble for the Homeric hero "the enterprise of trying to make himself disappear," given Tithonus' shrunken demise. This suggestion is further reinforced by the meaning of Calypso's name, from the verb *kalupsein*, meaning "to cover" or "conceal." Such a fate is offered figuratively to Odysseus by "the Concealer," and concealment and disclosure is seen by some as the theme of the *Odyssey* (Agathe Thornton, *People and Themes in Homer's "Odyssey"* [London: Methuen & Co. Ltd., 1970]). For a subtle examination of *kalupsein*, Calypso, and Odysseus, see George E. Dimock, Jr., "The Name of Odysseus" in *Homer: A Collection of Critical Essays*, George Steiner and Robert Fagles, eds. (Englewood Cliffs: Prentice Hall, 1962).

26. Hugh Lloyd-Jones, *The Justice of Zeus*, 2nd ed. (Berkeley: University of California Press, 1983), 27.

27. H. D. F. Kitto, *Poesis: Structure and Thought* (Berkeley: University of California Press, 1966), 133-48; Clay, *Wrath of Athena*, 213-46.

28. B. Fenik, *Studies in the "Odyssey"* (Wiesbaden: Hermes Einzelschriften, 1974), 210.

29. Clay, *Wrath of Athena*, 186-212.

30. Kitto, *Poesis*, 138; Clay, *Wrath of Athena*, 233-34.

31. I am grateful to Professor David Davies for pointing out this contrast to me in conversation.

32. Dimock, "Name of Odysseus," 106-11.

33. Bolotin, "Concerns of Odysseus," 46.

34. Odysseus' gratuitous deception of his father, Laertes, is indicative of the difficulty he will have functioning in the peaceful community (24.244ff.). While he quickly breaks down over the sight of his father's agony, there was no cause in the first place to perpetrate the ruse—the suitors are dead, and he already knows from the soul of his dead mother that Laertes is loyal to his son's memory (11.187-96). His cunning is now merely cruelty without cause.

35. Austin, *Archery*, 161; Clay, *Wrath of Athena*, 139-40.

36. Clay, *Wrath of Athena*, 231-32.

37. Abraham B. Feldman ("Homer and Democracy," *The Classical Journal* 47 [1951-52]: 337-45), however, points out that Odysseus' words, "The rule of the many (*polykoiranouai*) is not a good thing. Let us have one governor (*koiranos*), one chief (*basileus*)" (*Iliad* II. 204-5), are to be understood in the context of battle: "[Odysseus] was trying to restore military concord among the Greeks in despair and tumult who were getting ready for flight from Troy. . . . [It is] a plea for obedience on the battlefield to a single commander, to save energy for victory (338).

Although Feldman's article is somewhat dated in its reliance on then-contemporary anthropological evidence, his general argument, particularly the extent to which decision-making in the epics is never simply tyrannical, but is rather consensual, remains pertinent.

38. Bolotin, "Concerns of Odysseus," 57; Clay, *Wrath of Athena*, 235-36.

PART TWO

Beginning from Law

Chapter 6

The Foundations and Defense of Law

Joshua Parens

Perhaps the most ready assumption of any reader of the *Laws*—if only because of its title—is that its primary purpose is to provide a philosophically criticized code of law.[1] Although the mere quantity of words is not a sufficient indicator of the leading subject of a great written work, it is worth noting that as E. B. England, the author of the most authoritative commentary on the Greek text of the *Laws* has observed, at least two-thirds of the *Laws* is taken up with "talk about the laws" as opposed to "actual legislation."[2] If jurisprudence is the art of "actual legislation," what is the bulk of the *Laws* concerned with when it is taken up with "talk about the laws"? First, I distinguish the jurisprudential art of inferring laws from the rhetorical art of defending the opinions and actions that law inculcates (the art of *kalâm*). I also distinguish the popular art of defending these fundamental opinions and actions, or roots, from the philosophic art of defending them. The latter art presupposes an inquiry into the purposes of the laws, i.e., political science; the former art does not. Thus, the "talk about the laws" that takes place in this Platonic dialogue proves to be twofold: First, it is an inquiry into the roots (political science); second, it is an art of defending them (*kalâm*).

Second, I clarify *why* the leading subject of the *Laws* is not jurisprudence but rather political science and *kalâm*. Jurisprudence presupposes that the lawgiver has already laid down the law. According to Alfarabi, Plato's objective is more profound than merely inferring laws on the basis of the preexisting purposes of the lawgiver. By inquiring into the purposes of law, political science enables human beings to revise the law and to defend it properly.

Third, I explain that the philosophic defense of the revised law or the philosophic art of *kalâm* takes the form of a *metaphysica specialis* or theology. This theology is frequently misconstrued as if it were intended to be a demonstrative *metaphysica specialis* rather than a rhetorical defense of law. Alfarabi shows in his *Book of Letters* that even the theology in bk. *Lambda* of Aristotle's *Metaphysics* (which is still viewed generally as his attempt to provide a demonstrative *metaphysica specialis*) is a piece of *kalâm.* Even the apparently apolitical *Metaphysics* cannot escape the political task of defending the law. Aristotle in bk. *Lambda*, like Plato in bk. 10 of the *Laws*, presents a theology in which the gods show little concern for human things. Indeed, the gods seem to have only one task: the guidance of perhaps the most regular feature of nature, the motion of the heavenly bodies. Although the political content of Aristotle's theology is nega-tive—astral gods are not concerned with the affairs of human beings—his theology is highly political. It promotes human self-reliance, especially in the realm of politics. Thus, the belief in astral gods promotes the formation of certain kind of souls. In sum, the purpose of this theology is essentially psychological or political.

Finally, I offer crucial textual evidence from the *Summary* that the intention of Plato's theology is essentially political rather than metaphysical.

Jurisprudence and *Kalâm*

In the *Enumeration of the Sciences*, Alfarabi defines the art of jurispru-dence (*fiqh*) as inferring decisions from the laws already laid down by the Lawgiver (*wâdi' al-sharî'ah*) as well as from his purpose in legislating. The Lawgiver's purpose is to inculcate belief in certain opinions and to command certain actions. Because religion and law are so inextricably bound up with one another in Islam, the opinions and actions that are inculcated and commanded are opinions "about God . . . and His attributes, about the world, and so forth, . . . actions by which God . . . is magnified, and . . . actions by means of which transactions are conducted in cities."[3] In the *Enumeration*, Alfarabi describes the political phenomena as he finds them in his commu-nity. The highest opinions—in this case the opinions about God—are the highest purpose of the Lawgiver. His highest purpose is not political. As has been suggested by others, this emphasis on the divine purpose is especially pronounced in the monotheistic religions. In such religions, the divine Law shapes political life for the sake of religion.[4]

After describing jurisprudence in the *Enumeration*, Alfarabi goes on to describe an art of "defending" (*nusrah*) these fundamental opinions and actions (or "roots") called *kalâm*. Of course, there are different ways of defending things. One may defend something with blind devotion and a willingness to use any weapons one might lay one's hands on. Or one might defend something only after having inquired into whether it is sound. The

Enumeration describes an art of *kalâm* of the former kind. The practitioners of *kalâm* (*mutakallimûn*) described therein willingly adopt arguments that "our intellects reject" and themselves eagerly deny "the testimony . . . of the objects of sense."[5] These *mutakallimûn* by denying the evidence of the senses and the intellect prove that they are not friends of the philosophic sciences. Consequently, Alfarabi describes the sciences he presents in the *Enumeration*, including *kalâm*, as the "generally known" (*mashhûrah*) sciences.[6] Although the art of *kalâm* described in the *Enumeration* is hostile to the philosophic sciences, is it not possible that there exists an art of *kalâm* that is not hostile to the evidence provided by the senses and intellect?

In the opening of the ninth discourse of his *Summary*, Alfarabi says that the earlier books of the *Laws* (bks. 1-8) presented a "discussion" (*kalâm*) of the roots of the laws. In other words, bks. 1-8 contain Plato's art of *kalâm*. Because Plato is a philosopher, his art of *kalâm*, unlike that described by Alfarabi in the *Enumeration*, does not contradict the guidance of the intellect or sensation.[7] Not only does Plato avoid using whatever weapon comes to hand, he also begins by inquiring into the soundness of the roots before he takes the field in their defense. The Platonic art may be called the philosophic, as opposed to the "generally known," art of *kalâm*.

Alfarabi's announcement that bks. 1-8 present Plato's art of *kalâm*, however, is somewhat disconcerting. The Athenian Stranger offers his leading theological arguments in bk. 10. Is not *kalâm* usually understood to be "theology"? There seems to be a ready solution to this whole problem. In the conclusion of the *Summary*, Alfarabi says himself that there were discourses or books of the *Laws* that he was not in a position to copy. The *Summary* breaks off its interpretation of the *Laws* early in bk. 9 (864c10). Alfarabi, it appears, was simply ignorant of bk. 10. He must go to great lengths, then, to describe Plato's art of *kalâm* in his summary of bks. 1-8. As Leo Strauss has shown in his "How Farabi Read Plato's *Laws*," however, Alfarabi is highly reticent about God or the gods in discourses 1-8. Above all, although the Athenian presents his brief version of the theological prelude to the laws as a whole in bk. 4, Alfarabi in contrast is nearly silent about God or the gods (in disc. 4). He describes the books he summarizes, bks. 1-8, as Plato's "discussion" (*kalâm*) of the roots of the laws. Why then is he not more taken up with "theology"? To understand this riddle of riddles in the *Summary*, recall that Alfarabi's foremost purpose is not to reproduce the content of the *Laws* but rather to describe what Plato "intended" (*qasada ilâ*) to explain. Although Plato presents certain fundamental theological opinions and actions (or roots) in bk. 10 as well as bk. 4, his intention in doing so is political. His account of the gods in bk. 10 should not be construed, as his scientific doctrine about gods or demonstrative *metaphysica specialis*.

In the popular religion described in the *Enumeration*, the fundamental opinions and actions are synonymous with the ultimate purpose of the Lawgiver. His highest purpose is to inculcate certain beliefs about God. In contrast in the philosophic religion described and defended in the *Laws*, the fundamental opinions and actions are not synonymous with the ultimate purpose of the philosophic legislator. The highest communal purpose of the philosophic legislator is instead the political well-being of the community. Alfarabi's object is to reveal the political purpose of Plato's *kalâm*. This inquiry into the political purpose of the law's roots is the element of the *Laws* that deserves to be called political science. The whole of the *Summary* deserves to be called political science.

Plato formulates a theology only in conjunction with an inquiry into the law's purpose. The popular *mutakallimûn* receive the religion they are given and defend it with unquestioning faith. In contrast, the philosophic *mutakallimûn* (like Plato) scrutinize their community's religious law with an eye to its political well-being. Because Plato's *kalâm* involves scrutiny or inquiry, the Athenian Stranger (the leader of the dialogue) describes bks. 1-8 as a process of "educating the citizens" (857e6). He contrasts this process of education with the juristic activity of inferring legislation. The inquirer into the purpose of the roots is compared to a doctor (who is a free man) treating free human beings. The latter engages the patient in a dialogue "using arguments that come close to philosophizing, grasping the disease from its source, and going back up to the whole nature of bodies" (857d2). As the doctor treats bodies, so does the legislator treat souls. Inquiring into the purposes of the roots is inquiring into the nature and the disease of the soul. This inquiry not only is a kind of prelude to the act of legislating, but it takes place within the preludes to the laws. Plato's free doctor was originally (in bk. 4) analogous to the prelude; the slave doctor was analogous to legislation proper. Thus, when in bk. 9 the Athenian describes his educational activity as a philosophic *mutakallim* on analogy to the activity of a free doctor, he is also alluding to the educational role of the prelude.

But in bk. 4 the prelude was said to be analogous to the free doctor not so much in his capacity as educator but as persuader. There the Athenian suggests that the prelude persuades where the law coerces. Alfarabi's interpretation of this passage in bk. 4 explains that preludes serve both an educational and a persuasive purpose. He describes a few kinds of preludes, only one of which is the Athenian's persuasive prelude. Alfarabi calls it the "imposed" (*taklîfiyyah*) prelude. Preludes of this kind "are like proclamations effected through discussion [*kalâm*] and clarifications by means of arguments [*mujâdalât*]" (disc. 4.16). The reader who attends to the bracketed Arabic terms will recognize this form of "discussion" as our art of *kalâm*. The other element the arguments, are specifically dialectical arguments (dialectic is called *jadal* in Arabic). The inquiry into the purpose of the laws takes on a dialectical form in the *Laws* and *Summary*. Alfarabi's dialectic, like Plato's, takes as the premises of its arguments commonly accepted opinions about divine law and its purposes. This dialectical inquiry into the purposes of divine law is political science. The intimacy of the relation between *kalâm* and political science is exemplified by the fact that "discussion" (*kalâm*) and "[dialectical] arguments" (*mujâdalât*) are merely two different aspects of the prelude to the law.

In the *Laws* even the inquiry into the purposes of the law (political science) is therefore not strictly rational or demonstrative; rather, it is dialectical. The purposes themselves are not strictly rational because the way of life advocated by the law is not strictly rational. Of course, if even the inquiry into the purposes is not strictly rational, we should hardly expect that the defense (*kalâm*) of this way of life would be strictly rational.[8] Although the purposes of the laws are essentially psychological rather than metaphysical, this does not make them rational. The closest the *Laws* comes to giving a rational description of a rational way of life is to point beyond the way of life advocated by the law to the philosophic way of life. (In contrast is the *Republic*, where the philosophic way of life is a prominent theme.)

In a discussion of *kalâm* that owes a great deal to Alfarabi's, Maimonides traces the historical origins of (generally known) *kalâm* in the Muslim community to the *kalâm* of the Christian community, especially in Greece and Syria where philosophic ideas had a wide currency. He suggests that *kalâm* arose in an effort to oppose philosophic opinions that "ruined the foundations (*qawâ-'id*) of their Law."[9]

In Alfarabi's community (as well as Maimonides'), popular *kalâm* views philosophy as an enemy of the law. This is inevitable in view of the subphilosophic character of law. This animosity, however, is especially marked in monotheistic communities in general. Indeed, it may account for the fact that these communities have an independent art of *kalâm*—in contrast for instance, to Plato's community. The animosity stems from each monotheistic community's claim to be the one true religion or divine law. This claim in turn stems from the belief that there is one and only one God rather than a loosely structured, often shifting pantheon of gods. The divine laws of the monotheistic communities lay claim to an incomparable degree of authority.[10] Any threat to the authority of such a law—and philosophy was perceived to be such a threat by the early Greek and Syrian Christians—was bound to evoke a greater response than it did in ancient Greece. Although a generally known *kalâm* did not have as distinct an existence in ancient

Greece as it did in Alfarabi's community, I intend to show that Plato's *Laws* contains his philosophic art of *kalâm*.[11]

Perhaps one may wonder why we (members of modern secular regimes) cannot merely dispense with *kalâm* so that we might pursue independently the dialectical inquiry into the purposes of the law's roots or political science. The reason is that this inquiry runs the risk of undermining the law's authority.[12] All written laws rest upon certain fundamental moral opinions, whether they are explicitly religious in character or not. Although Alfarabi defines *kalâm* as an art that defends a divine law or religion, one need not argue that the U.S. Constitution rests upon a tacit civil religion in order to show that as a regime ruled by written laws our regime requires something like Alfarabi's *kalâm*. In the *Enumeration* Alfarabi includes among the roots that *kalâm* must defend not only opinions about God and actions directed toward God but also "actions by means of which transactions (*mu'âmalât*) are conducted in the cities."[13] Even a regime, such as ours, that does not concern itself with its citizens' opinions and actions concerning God must provide a subphilosophic defense of its roots concerning human transactions. Written law as such requires a subphilosophic defense. Only if written law could become strictly rational could one make do without such a defense.

Why Are the Roots
the Theme of the *Laws* and the *Summary*?

Although legislation is the subject matter of the *Laws* as well as the *Summary*, both of these books focus on the highest aspect of legislation: namely, the defense of and the inquiry into the purposes of the roots.[14] As we saw above, this defense and inquiry are the activities of the philosophic *mutakallim*. Why, the reader may ask, is philosophic *kalâm*, rather than the act of legislation, the subject matter of the *Laws*? Every legislator should take up the subject matter of philosophic *kalâm* prior to legislating. To know what to legislate, the legislator must know what the purposes of legislation are. The act of legislation itself merely engages the limited kind of prudence that should be possessed by the jurisprudent.[15] Once the purposes of legislation have been determined, then one needs merely a certain amount of experience with human beings to know what laws should be laid down to achieve these ends.

Let us turn to the opening of the *Laws* to understand better why the subject matter of philosophic *kalâm* is the subject matter of the *Laws* and *Summary*. The Athenian Stranger asks his interlocutors (Kleinias and Megillus, a Cretan and Spartan, respectively) the following opening question: Who is the "cause" (*aitia*) of your laws, a god or some human being? As Alfarabi explains, this inquiry into the "cause" (*sabab*) is an inquiry into a specific kind of cause, namely, that of the "maker" (or agent, *fâ'il*). The interchange between the Athenian Stranger and Kleinias offers a heterogeneous answer: First Kleinias responds that it is most just to say that a god legislated the laws. Kleinias's answer seems to represent the most commonly accepted opinion among Cretans about the divine foundation of their laws. Thus, Plato begins (in a phenomenological manner) with commonly accepted opinion (rather than with metaphysical presuppositions). Second, the Athenian suggests that a hero, Minos, joined with Zeus in legislating for Crete. In contrast as if to denigrate the human role in legislation, the Athenian mentions only in passing Lycurgus's role in legislating the Spartan laws, so well known to the modern reader from Plutarch (632d4). The Athenian's mention of the semihuman hero, however, leaves us from the start with a heterogeneous and indecisive answer to the Athenian's own opening question.[16]

Why is it more just to say that the god, rather than some human being, legislated? The preliminary answer to this question is obvious. All people are more willing to obey a law that they believe is sanctioned, indeed legislated, by a god. The gods are more able to guarantee that the unjust—who, as anyone can see, frequently slip through the hands of the human authorities—will be punished. The gods should guarantee vengeance.

Leaving justice aside, who really legislates? This question also has an obvious preliminary answer for the modern reader. Let us restrain our desire for immediate answers, however. Although Plato and Alfarabi may have a similar answer to this question, the way in which they answer it is instructive. As I have said, Kleinias is led to answer in a heterogeneous manner the question of who is the cause of the laws. The very heterogeneity, and consequent insufficiency, of the answer leaves it as an unresolved matter. At first it might appear that this matter has been shunted into the background: The Athenian gains his companions' assent to undertake a discussion of the political regimes and laws. But as the dramatic setting—an ascent to the cave where Minos received from Zeus the laws of Crete—suggests, the questions of how, in what sense, and why human beings are said to receive their laws from gods will continue to be addressed, if only in the background, throughout the dialogue. It is for this reason that the *Laws* was described by Alfarabi's student Avicenna as the treatment of prophecy and the divine Law.[17]

Not long after the opening section on the "maker" of the laws, Alfarabi takes up the question anew in the form of an inquiry into the identity of the true legislator (disc. 1.14). In the passage Alfarabi summarizes (639a2 ff.), the Athenian attempts to draw analogies between the sober ruler's art of rule over the drinking party and the art of rule of a goatherd over a herd, a captain over a ship, and a general over an army. Alfarabi treats the sober art of rule over the drinking party as analogous to the legislator's art. Alfarabi piously asserts that the true legislator is distinguished from the false one by virtue of his having been created (*khalq*) and equipped for his purpose by God (*Allâh*). Alfarabi does not say that God reveals the law to the true legislator, but merely that the true legislator (the sober ruler) is endowed differently from the false legislator (drunk ruler) from birth, as the term *khalq* suggests.[18] Although the endowment of a human individual could be the result of a miraculous intervention by an omnipotent God, it could just as easily be the result of a God with knowledge of universals or nature or chance. Some human beings are capable of legislating "true laws" and some are not. This much is certain: Alfarabi does not say that God gives laws to legislators as a mysterious act of will. It remains unclear, however, who Alfarabi considers to be the maker of the laws.

At the opening of the *Laws* the Athenian appears to drop the question as to who makes the law. After having answered the question about the "maker" of the laws inconclusively (and after vaguely describing the subject matter of their future discussion), the Athenian turns from the question about the "cause" as "maker" or "agent" to the question about the "cause" as "purpose." Answering the latter question is an indirect way of answering the former. If a human being is capable of determining what the proper purpose of law is, then that person would not find it difficult to legislate—let alone to revise received legislation. In other words, if a human being is capable of determining what the cause of law is, in the sense of its purpose, then that human being should be capable of being the cause of law, in the sense of its agent. This inquiry into the purpose and, above all, into the agent of the law, which plays such a central role in medieval Muslim (as well as Jewish) political philosophy, is sometimes referred to as prophetology.[19] Once again, Avicenna's description of the *Laws* shows itself to be apt.

The Athenian does not begin the inquiry into the purpose of the laws by asking his interlocutors, "What is the proper purpose of law in general?" but rather by asking them, "What is the purpose of your laws—in particular, of your most distinctive laws concerning common meals, gymnastic, and the bearing of arms?" Yet citizens stand in such a relation to their laws that they, like Kleinias, transform a question about their own laws into a question about laws as such (625e7 ff.). For citizens are taught to cherish their own laws as the best. Why should one obey the laws of one's city if one believes that there are other laws that are better? In the following pages the Athenian shows Kleinias that either Kleinias does not understand the purpose of his own laws (630e-32d8) or his own laws do not have the proper purpose (634c-35b6). In either case, Kleinias is in need of an education as to what the proper purpose of law is. This education in the purpose, rather than in the art, of legislation is the primary subject matter of the *Laws* and the *Summary.* As I suggested earlier, the inquiry into the purposes of the laws is the part of political science that is indispensable to the philosophic *mutakallim.*

As we saw in section 1, the purpose of the philosophic law (including the laws proper and the preludes) is to cure the disease of the soul. Thus, proper legislation depends upon a proper understanding of the "whole nature of souls." The roots of the philosophic version of the divine law are specific opinions about God and the world, and so forth—namely, opinions that are compatible with the formation of certain kinds of souls. According to Thomas Pangle, "The science regarding soul is the same as the science regarding gods."[20] At least one possible meaning of this statement is that the kind of gods in which people believe determines to a great extent what kind of souls they will have. If people believe in an omnipotent God who is readily made jealous but who is merciful, they are likely to have humble souls. On the other hand, if they believe in a God who has a knowledge of universals and who suffers from no human passions, they are less likely to have humble souls. Of course, the humility or lack of humility of a city's population has a direct effect on its political life. Thus, the philosophic *mutakallim*'s concern with the soul translates into a concern with its gods. Once again, the difference between the way in which the philosophic *mutakallim* is concerned with the gods and the way in which the popular *mutakallim* is concerned with the gods is that the former focuses on that which promotes the right kind of souls and thus the political community's well-being, whereas the latter focuses on that which promotes the community's popularly accepted religious traditions.

What kinds of opinions about the gods, and thus about the human soul, are conducive to the political well-being of a community? This question will remain at the center of my inquiry throughout the rest of this study, especially in part 3. For the present let it suffice to say that a common but incorrect answer to this question is, that the community should depend upon the gods to give them victory in battle. Although such a vision of the gods might give rise to hopefulness among citizens about achieving victory in battle, it may fail to foster martial virtue by reducing human self-reliance. In general, one of the crucial ways, perhaps the crucial way, in which the philosophic *mutakallim* modifies the popularly accepted opinions about the gods is to reduce the amount of influence on political events popularly attributed to them. Certain philosophic *mutakallimun* have been so successful in reducing the political role of the gods that *kalâm* has come to be misconstrued as their demonstrative *metaphysica specialis.*

How Philosophic *Kalâm* Becomes Misconstrued as Metaphysical Doctrine

Aristotle is the leading example of a philosophic *mutakallim* who has been so successful in reducing the political role of the gods that his *kalâm* has come to be construed as his metaphysical doctrine. Indeed, the accepted modern interpretation of bk. *Lambda* of his *Metaphysics* is that it presents what he intends to be his demonstrative *metaphysica specialis.* In contrast Alfarabi explains in his *On the Purposes of Aristotle's Metaphysics* that bk. *Lambda* presents Aristotle's *kalâm.*[21] Alfarabi's own account of the intention of this *kalâm* is presented in the *Book of Letters*, his commentary on or interpretation of the *Metaphysics.* As Muhsin Mahdi has suggested, the second and middle section of the *Book of Letters* is a commentary on one brief but striking passage in *Metaphysics*, bk. *Lambda* (1074a38-bl4).[22] In this passage, Aristotle argues that in the most ancient religion among the Greeks there was a belief that the heavenly bodies are gods and that the natural whole is divine—a belief strikingly similar to the beliefs he defends in bk. *Lambda.* Modern human beings corrupted these purer beliefs by describing the gods as like human beings and animals to persuade the many "and as something useful for the laws and for matters of expediency." The usefulness and expediency for law of anthropomorphic gods is readily apparent: such gods give great immediacy to threats of punishment for disobedience to the city's laws.

Aristotle justifies his revised version of popular Greek religion by suggesting that his account of the astral gods is identical to the Greek religion that predated the anthropomorphic religion (*Metaphysics* 1074bl-14). In other words, he tries to persuade his reader that his account of the gods is more traditional than the tradition. He appeals to the prejudice in favor of tradition while revising the tradition. Alfarabi recapitulates this approach to *kalâm* in the *Book of Letters* in the following form: Philosophy precedes religion in time; philosophy is more traditional than the tradition.[23] Aristotle's claim that his theology is more traditional than the tradition has at least two politically salutary effects: he shields himself from persecution and, of greater interest at present, he revises the traditional understanding of the gods by substituting his more philosophic theology for the popular theology. He would be thoroughly irresponsible in making this substitution if the resulting theology could not at least accommodate a political teaching that would fill the political role traditionally played by the popular theology, namely, persuading the many "and as something useful for the laws and for matters of expediency." In other words, contrary to appearances, the *Metaphysics* must accommodate itself to politics even if it does not supply a political teaching. When one thinks of how that consummately political Socratic, Xenophon, portrays Socrates as arguing in favor of a teleological account of the whole (*Memorabilia* 4.3), one begins to wonder whether it is so implausible to suggest that even Aristotle's apparently apolitical teleological theology has a political purpose.

Alfarabi uses the myth[24] that philosophy precedes religion to defend philosophy in his community in the following manner: First if philosophy is older than religion, then it deserves the respect accorded the old. Second, religion not only emerges after philosophy but is an imitation of philosophy. And because often one religion follows another and the one that follows imitates its predecessor, the further a religion is from its origins in philosophy the more distant an imitation it becomes. Alternatively, sometimes a religion will emerge that is an imitation of a false philosophy. In either case, such an account of the emergence of religion makes it highly likely that one's present religion is only a distant imitation of the truth or of true philosophy. Consequently, one should not be surprised if adherents of one's religion attack contemporary adherents of philosophy because of the great divergence between philosophy and a distant imitation of philosophy.[25] One should assume that philosophers are unjustly accused when they are accused of heresy.

I am less interested here in the defense of philosophy that Alfarabi achieves with Aristotle's myth, however, than I am in how this argument is, as Aristotle says, "useful for the laws." By treating religion as an imitation of philosophy, Alfarabi makes it possible for religion to be made in the image of philosophy. "Metaphysics" is the means by which Alfarabi achieves this rationalization of religion. By replacing anthropomorphic gods with astral gods (or separate intellects or angels), Aristotle (and Alfarabi) considerably weaken the immediacy of punishment threatened by law. Indeed, Aristotle's political intention—although it is a negative political intention—is to transform the traditional gods, who like human beings have a personal stake in the affairs of human beings, into politically disinterested astral gods (very much like Plato's astral gods in bk. 10 of the *Laws*). On the other hand, by describing astral gods as the ruling part of a teleologically arranged whole, they offer some support to the law.

The Roots of the Laws Revisited

Book 10 contains Plato's *kalâm* in much the same way that Alfarabi says bk. *Lambda* of Aristotle's *Metaphysics*, contains Aristotle's *kalâm*. Alfarabi asserts, however, that Plato presents his "discussion" (*kalâm*) of the laws' roots in bks. 1-8 (disc. 9.1). To understand this apparent contradiction, we need only recall that although the roots and their purpose are both theological for the traditional *mutakallim*, the roots and their purpose are different for the philosophic *mutakallim*. For the latter, the roots are theological, but their purpose is political or psychological. Book. 10 does not contain the roots of Plato's law if one means by roots the ultimate purpose of law. Accordingly, Alfarabi says that what follows the opening of bk. 9—in other words, most of bk. 9 and bks. 10-12—"explains things that adorn and embellish the law and things that are consequences of the roots" (disc. 9.2). Insofar as the roots are the purposes of the laws, the laws are themselves the consequences of the roots. Most of bk. 9 and bks. 11 and 12 are taken up with legislation proper. Presumably, that which adorns and embellishes the law is what is left over once we take away most of bk. 9 and bks. 11 and 12, namely, bk. 10. Kleinias (a spirited soul) asserts that the theological prelude presented in bk. 10 is "just about [the] noblest and best prelude on behalf of all the laws" (887c). In spite of Kleinias's possible objections, however, the theological prelude to the law contained in bk. 10 is an adornment. (This is not to say, however, that adornments may not have substantial purposes. An account of the gods of the sort described in bk. 10 may be indispensable for the cultivation of the indignant or spirited kind of soul that will rule in the second-best city described in the *Laws* [see especially disc. 5.91].) By omitting a summary of bk. 10, Alfarabi merely omits the adornments. This is unproblematic because Alfarabi's *Summary* strives, above all, to reveal Plato's intention rather than to recapitulate his text. Plato's highest intention is to understand the psychological or political purpose of the best laws. In summarizing the first nine books of the *Laws*, Alfarabi reveals the psychological purpose (or roots) of the laws. The heart of the *Summary* is bk. 5, whose leading theme is how to honor the soul. Plato presents the purpose of bk. 10 in bk. 5.

In bks. 4 and 5, the Athenian presents his, as opposed to Kleinias's, version of the prelude to the law as a whole. This version of the prelude falls into two parts or preludes along the line separating bk. 4 from bk. 5: First in bk. 4 he presents a "prelude as regards the gods, those who come after the gods, and the living and dead ancestors" (724a). Second, in bk. 5 he presents a prelude as regards "how [human beings] should be serious and how they should relax as regards their own souls, their bodies, and their property" (724b). Alfarabi's interpretation of these two parts of the Athenian's prelude strips away the adornments of the law to reveal the purposes of the laws.

In his summary of the first part of the prelude, Alfarabi quickly undermines any inclination to view the account of the gods in this first part as belonging to the prelude to the law as a whole: He omits any mention of the striking opening of this part in which the Athenian announces that the god is the beginning, middle, and end of all things.[26] Alfarabi only notes that the gods are displeased with the arrogant human being (cf. disc. 4.9 with 716a4). Furthermore, he makes no mention, as Plato does, of people's need to sacrifice to, pray to, or serve the gods (cf. disc. 4.10 with 716c-18a). Their "support" is acquired, at least by the ruler, merely by his avoiding arrogance (which, as it so happens, is a way of serving other human beings rather than gods). The only things that Alfarabi suggests human beings need to care for are their own bodies, souls, and property; they should do so both for their own sake and for their family's sake (cf. 717c3). In other words, Alfarabi gives an account of the first part of the prelude (in bk. 4) that leaves it indistinguishable from the second part (in bk. 5). Finally, when Alfarabi turns to summarizing bk. 5, he does not mention the gods as those beings who must be honored before the human soul (disc. 5.1).[27] He merely notes that the human soul ranks third in divinity, and he chooses to add that the human soul is the noblest of things. What remains of the Athenian's prelude is an account of human being, and above all of the human soul. By reflection on this prelude one can begin to acquire the knowledge of the disease of the soul and the whole nature of the souls, i.e., of the true foundation of the revised divine law.

In modern political philosophy, Machiavelli initiated a concerted attack against religion. His loud declamations against Christianity led not to the revision of popular religion but to its near obliteration. If I am correct that politics can never be strictly rational, however, the ambition to obliterate religion was misplaced. Belief, which disappeared in one form, reappeared in another, in some ways less salutary, form.[28] At the same time, Machiavelli's loud declamations led eventually to an obliviousness of the need for philosophic *kalâm*. The ultimate result was not that *kalâm* was annihilated but that it became so intermingled with political science as to become indistinguishable from it—political science became ideology. Although positivism maintains an illusion of objectivity and neutrality, it has developed a decided preference for modern egalitarian political regimes. Such regimes are said to manifest the orderliness, symmetry, and equality characteristic of positivistic social science itself.

Under the illusion that modern Western culture is different in kind from all previous traditional cultures,[29] positivistic political science has become oblivious of the need for an art such as *kalâm.* In reaction, postmodernism would have us believe that political science is nothing other than *kalâm.* Thus, the postmodernists generally advocate the study of rhetoric rather than metaphysics and science. In contrast to both of these extreme positions, Alfarabi, through his interpretation of the *Laws,* describes both a dialectical inquiry into the purpose of law (political science)—which necessarily points beyond the rule of law to the rule of reason—and a rhetorical defense of law (*kalâm*). The rhetorical defense cannot be properly undertaken without a knowledge of the political science to which it is a supplement. On the other hand, political science is ill-equipped to make policy recommendations without a full recognition of the limitations political life places on rationality, limitations that circumscribe the subrational defense of law.

Notes

1. Cf. Ernest Barker, *Greek Political Theory,* 5th ed. (Strand: Methuen, 1960), 339. Despite his extraordinarily high estimation of the legislative sections of the *Laws,* Barker never really discusses the legislation.

2. Plato, *The Laws of Plato,* E. B. England, ed., 2 vols. (Manchester: Manchester University Press, 1921), 1:1.

3. Alfarabi, *Enumeration of the Sciences,* Muhsin Mahdi, trans., in *Medieval Political Philosophy,* Ralph Lerner and Muhsin Mahdi, eds. (Glencoe, Ill.: Free Press, 1963), 27 and *Ihsa'al-'ulum,* Osman Amine, ed., 2nd ed. (Cairo: Dar al-Fikr al-'Arabi, 1949), 107.

4. Leo Strauss, *What Is Political Philosophy?* (Glencoe, Ill.: Free Press, 1959), 164.

5. Alfarabi, *Enumeration,* in Lerner and Mahdi, 28-29 and in Amine (1949), 109-11.

6. Muhsin Mahdi, "Science, Philosophy, and Religion in *Alfarabi's Enumeration of the Sciences,*" in *The Cultural Context of Medieval Learning,* J. E. Murdoch and E. D. Sylla, eds., Boston Studies in the Philosophy of Science, no. 26 (Dordrecht, Holland: D. Reidel, 1975), 113, citing *Enumeration* in Amine (1949), 43 (lines 4-6).

This popular art of *kalâm* is usually referred to in English as "dialectical theology." The translation alludes to the dialectical style in which practitioners of *kalâm* present their theology. Although Alfarabi recognizes the need to present a theology in defense of the law, his *kalâm* shares little in common with traditional dialectical theology. Consequently, I have chosen not to use the English phrase to render *kalâm* in order to avoid misleading the reader into confusing the less popular art of *kalâm* developed by Alfarabi with the popular or traditional art of dialectical theology. For an extensive discussion of the popular art, see Richard M. Frank, "The Science of *Kalâm,*" *Arabic Sciences and Philosophy* 2 (1992): 7-37.

7. See Maimonides' assertion in *Guide of the Perplexed,* 1:71 (S. Munk, *Le Guide des Égarés,* 3 vols. [Paris: n.p., 1856-66], 98a) that the art of *kalâm* he offers to replace that of the popular art of *kalâm* will not contradict "the nature of existence [or contend] against sense-perception." (All page numbers referring to the Munk edition henceforth will be in brackets.)

8. See Strauss's assertion that the rhetoric used in the preludes in the *Laws* should not be confused with the truly philosophic rhetoric described in the *Phaedrus*. Leo Strauss, review of *Man in His Pride* by David Grene, in *What Is?* 301.

9. Maimonides, *Guide*, 1:71 [94b]. Also see Alfarabi, *Book of Letters*, in an unpublished translation by Muhsin Mahdi supplied by Mahdi in 1991, paras. 149-50, and in *Kitâb al-hurûf*, Muhsin Mahdi, ed. (Beirut: Dâr al-Machreq, 1969), paras. 154-55.

10. Maimonides, *Guide*, 1:31 [34b].

11. See Strauss, *What Is?* 139.

12. See Maimonides' statement above.

13. Alfarabi, *Enumeration*, in Lerner and Mahdi, 27 and in Amine (1949), 107.

14. This elevated understanding of *kalâm* as an aspect of the legislative art—indeed, the highest—should be distinguished from another presentation of what could be called a philosophic art of *kalâm* in Alfarabi's *Book of Letters*, para. 145, and 2:21 and 22 and in *Kitâb al-hurûf*, 152. In the *Book of Letters*, the philosophic art of *kalâm* is clearly subordinated to the philosophic legislative art. It appears to be limited in scope to the use of rhetoric. In contrast in the *Summary*, the philosophic *mutakallim* employs both rhetoric and dialectic. (He practices the latter, however, as a student of political science! The truly philosophic *mutakallim* needs to know the truth about what he is defending in order to defend it most effectively.)

Cf. the *Enumeration*, where *kalâm* also seems to be subordinated to political science. Note, however, that political science is purely analytic in the *Enumeration*: it analyzes political phenomena; it does not legislate. This reflects the fact that the *Enumeration* is descriptive of Alfarabi's own community, in which the law was not legislated by a political philosopher. (Perhaps philosophic *kalâm* shares a rank in the *Book of Letters*—a commentary on Aristotle's *Metaphysics*—similar to popular *kalâm* in the *Enumeration* because Aristotle presents an understanding of the arts and the sciences that is closer than Plato's to the everyday or popular understanding presented in the *Enumeration*.) For other accounts—such as the *Book of Letters*, where political science or political philosophy is not merely descriptive—see, for instance, *Attainment of Happiness*, in *Alfarabi's Philosophy of Plato and Aristotle*, Muhsin Mahdi, trans. (Ithaca: Cornell University Press, 1962), 46-47, paras. 57-58, where the (political) philosopher is identified with the (philosophic) legislator.

The only other discussion that comes close to the *Summary's* elevated understanding of *kalâm* is the discussion of the supreme virtuous ruler's art of dialectic—which is actually an art of rhetoric and dialectic—in the *Book of Religion* (in an unpublished translation by Charles Butterworth supplied by Mahdi in 1991), 7-8, para. 6 and in *Kitâb al-millah wa-nusûs ukhrâ*, Muhsin Mahdi, ed. (Beirut: Dar al-Machreq: 1968), 47-48.

15. Mahdi, "Science, Philosophy, and Religion," 140.

16. I have chosen not to mention Rhadamanthus here, though Kleinias mentions him in close connection with the Athenian's mention of Minos, because his role in legislating for Crete is vague, even according to Kleinias's own account. According to Pangle, Kleinias says that Rhadamanthus "regulated judicial affairs correctly," which may or may not mean that he participated in the act of legislation. Another possible reading of the Greek is that Rhadamanthus "distributed judicial penalties correctly" *(dianemein ta peri tas dikas orthôs)*, which makes it sound as if Rhadamanthus did not participate in legislating. For another Platonic reference to Rhadamanthus that supports this interpretation, see Plato, *Minos*, 318d-20d.

17. Avicenna, *On the Divisions of the Rational Sciences*, Muhsin Mahdi, trans., in Lerner and Mahdi, *Medieval*, 97.

18. Cf. Alfarabi, *Virtuous City*, in *Alfarabi on the Perfect State*, Richard Walzer, ed. and trans. (Oxford: Clarendon Press, 1985), 244-45, ch. 15, para. 10; and *Book of Religion*, 2, para. 1, and *Kitâb al-millah*, 44.

19. See, for instance, Strauss, *What Is?* 160.

20. Thomas Pangle, "The Political Psychology of Religion in Plato's *Laws*," *American Political Science Review* 70, no. 4 (1976): 1077.

Also see Strauss's suggestion that "the wisdom of the Platonic Socrates is ... [that] the true knowledge of the souls, and hence of the soul, is the core of the cosmology (of the knowledge of the things aloft)" in *Socrates and Aristophanes* (Chicago: University of Chicago Press, 1966), 314.

21. Alfarabi, *Maqâlah fî aghrâd mâ ba'da al-tabî'ah* [*On the Purposes of Aristotle's "Metaphysics"*], in *Tis' rasâ'il, risâlah* 2 (Hyderabad: n.p., 1926), 3. And see Mahdi, "Science, Philosophy, and Religion," 130.

Contrast this characterization of the subject matter of *Metaphysics, Lambda* as *kalâm* with Alfarabi's inclusion of the same subject matter within "metaphysics" (*mâ ba-'da al-tabî'ah*) in his account of the "generally known" sciences in the *Enumeration*, end of ch. 4, in *Ihsâ' al-'ûlûm*, Osman Amine, ed., 3d ed. (Cairo: Anglo-Egyptian Library, 1968), 120-23. It seems that this subject matter is "generally" mistaken for metaphysics. (The role played by *Metaphysics, Lambda* in Aristotle's arrangement of the sciences is already taken up by the popular art of *kalâm* in the *Enumeration.*)

22. See Alfarabi, *Kitâb al-hurûf*, editor's (English) preface, xi.

23. Alfarabi, *Book of Letters*, xi. Also see *Attainment* in Alfarabi, *Philosophy of Plato and Aristotle*, 44-46, para. 55.

24. Muhsin Mahdi, "Alfarabi on Philosophy and Religion," *Philosophical Forum* 4, no. 1 (1973): 1-25, esp. 12-15 and 19. The claim that philosophy precedes religion may in at least two senses be true and in one sense false (or mythical): Philosophy precedes religion insofar as demonstrative philosophy precedes philosophically revised religion, and false philosophies (which are not truly philosophy) precede popular religion. Philosophy actually follows religion insofar as demonstrative philosophy follows popular religion.

25. Alfarabi, *Book of Letters*, para. 149, 2:24 and in *Kitâb al-hurûf*, 153-54.

26. Strauss, *What Is?* 148.

27. Strauss, *What Is?* 148.

28. What may be less salutary about modern political beliefs is that they do not appear to be beliefs at all. Rousseau reminds us that, in spite of its negative character, tolerance is itself merely a belief.

29. See Ernest Gellner, *Reason and Culture* (Oxford: Basil Blackwell, 1992), 42.

Chapter 7

Hegel, the Author and Authority in Sophocles' *Antigone*

William E. Conklin

Introduction

In his study of Sophocles' *Antigone* in chapter 6 of the *Phenomenology of Spirit*,[1] Hegel concentrates upon the issue "what distinguishes human law from divine law?" In addressing this question, Hegel identifies four views of law. The first, the law of nature, ties individuals to institutions, not as a matter of morals or convention, but as a phenomenon arising from nature. Natural ties are fixed for eternity. Nature is believed, for example, to have set the feminine and masculine roles. Similarly, nature is considered to have tied the individual to the family. Hegel describes the family as "a *natural* Ethical community" of *immediate* determination (*P Sp* 450). The joining of the individual with the family is called a primitive *Sittlichkeit*. This ethical life is beautiful, coherent, and a unity of the one and the many.

Now, when Spirit passes from this natural unity to a consciousness of the individual in the actual world, philosophical or observing consciousness becomes concerned with the city culture (*P Sp* 441).[2] Spirit passes through a series of shapes which rend the former natural beautiful life asunder. In particular, natural harmony splits up into two further sets of laws: human law and divine law. Hegel suggests that the key to the split between human law and divine law lies in what consciousness understands as the natural difference between male and female. Nature assigns one gender to human law and another gender to divine law (*P Sp* 450). Male consciousness shifts from natural law to human law, whereas female consciousness moves from natural law to divine law.

Hegel makes this natural distinction within a wider thesis with which he introduces his discussion of ethical action in the *Phenomenology of Spirit* (464). To begin with, the Greek world is structured by a finite consciousness in contrast to a modern world of infinite spirit where a subject who is self-conscious structures an infinite process of recognition of contradictions between the subject and the object.[3] The finite spirit which works through both Creon and Antigone just cannot recognize them as contradictory. So, in paragraph 464, Hegel argues that individual and universal (state and family, nature and divinity, male and female) are opposites. Each proves to be "the non-reality, rather than the authentication, of itself and the other." In their opposition, they simply collapse into the absolute being-for-self of purely individual self-consciousness familiar to the modern world's *Recht*. *Recht* is Hegel's fourth view of law.

At the moment of consciousness when Sophocles' play, *Antigone*, is situated, neither human nor divine law recognizes the other as a superior authority.[4] Each knows that human laws involve divine laws, and vice versa. However, each takes itself to be the authoritative interpreter. For example, everyone knows that there is divine law.[5] Creon himself believes that divine law is in harmony with the city because the gods need the city as the locus of the divine laws and the city would dissolve if rebels were allowed to be buried. As Creon puts it when addressing the chorus for the first time, "[f]or I—be Zeus my witness, who sees all things always—would not be silent if I saw ruin, instead of safety, coming to the citizens" (192-93). However, Creon believes that he is the *authorized* interpreter of divine law because, being the head of the pyramid, he is closest to the intent of the author of the promulgated civil laws. According to Hegel, Creon and Antigone feel blindly and immediately obligated to his/her respective laws. Creon and Antigone fail to recognize that each is dependent upon the other for his/her very existence. As a consequence, the former beautiful harmony of natural ethical life collapses into strife. But when each consciousness, toward the end of the play, becomes conscious of its dependency upon the other, so too the reason for the existence of both human and divine law is undermined. An abstract universal world of legal status or *Recht* intervenes between the two, starting with Roman law as elaborated in the *Philosophy of Right*.

The important issue arising out of Hegel's background thesis, then, is why both Creon and Antigone consider their respective laws as authoritative to the exclusion of the other's view of authority? This issue does not suggest, by negative implication, that the critics of Hegel's difference thesis (namely, that the difference between human and divine laws lies in the natural difference of male and female) have been misdirected in their critique.[6] Nor do I wish to suggest that Hegel's own reading of *Antigone* is in error because, as Martin Donougho points out, one does not find a close reading of *Antigone* in any of Hegel's works. In this way, one cannot criticize Hegel for misreading the play.[7] Further, whether Hegel has misread the play is not important. By concentrating upon the issue of why both Creon and Antigone consider their laws as authoritative, I aim to complement the first aspect of

Hegel's general thesis: namely, that finite spirit which works through Creon and Antigone just cannot recognize itself as contradictory.[8]

Hegel supports his general thesis about human and divine laws by asking, in a sense, what makes human law *human* and what makes divine law *divine?* His answer, again, lies upon the acculturated gender difference of male and female. Instead of focusing upon the human and divine characteristics of law, I wish to ask what makes human law authoritative *as law* and what makes divine law authoritative *as law?* Taking my cue from Michel Foucault's "What Is an Author?"[9] I shall concentrate upon the relationship between the author and authority presupposed in the human laws. I shall argue that Antigone's divine law opposes Creon's human law in terms of its presupposed sense of authority. The tribe's members recognize divine laws as resting in an impersonal *Moira* or Fate, common to the Hellenes, as *experienced* through rituals and other personal experiences. The city-state's citizens recognize authoritativeness in terms of whether a law has its source in a juridical representer of an invisible author of the human laws. That invisible author dwells external to a hierarchical pyramid which vertically and horizontally links the author's representers together. The representers, of which the king is foremost, may interpret the human laws in an effort to reach closer to the intent of the invisible author. What becomes important, I shall show, is that philosophic consciousness observes how the characteristics of the two respective senses of authority clash.

The Immediacy of Written and Unwritten Laws

Philosophical consciousness observes a clash of legitimacy using a criterion of immediate acceptance by the ruled. Prior to *action*, a primitive *Sittlichkeit* permeates tribal society. The individual, as represented by Antigone, is unified in a beautiful harmony with the whole, as represented by Creon. Shared customary religious practices contribute to this primitive *Sittlichkeit*. The tribe or clan acts out the practices through rituals which rarely, if ever, need to be expressed, verbally or in writing. The individual immediately or intuitively knows the laws of action. This intuitive knowledge contrasts with a reflective *Sittlichkeit* of Plato's day where a citizen self-consciously exercises practical judgement or *phronesis* in arriving at action, much as Aristotle counsels in book 6 of the *Ethics*. Whether dwelling in a society bound by primitive *Sittlichkeit* or reflective *Sittlichkeit*, the individual is defined, not in terms of consciously posited rules as one observes in a Greek assembly, Roman or modern European law, but in terms of relationships, interactions, and expectations vis-à-vis the social group.

Hegel argues that these relationships support an identity of subject and object (*P Sp* 440, 441), individual and universal (*P Sp* 444). Through assimilation in a familial environment, individual conscience unites with community conscience. Loyalty to the social group makes physical force unnecessary. Such assimilation is exemplified when, faced with a sentence of banishment or death from the tribe's council of elders, an individual "voluntarily" leaves the community or eats the hemlock without ado.

Antigone's loyalty to the divine laws reflects this very sense of immediacy. She unhesitatingly abides by the divine laws, notwithstanding the risk that she will face death at the hands of Creon by doing so: "Die I must,—I knew well (how should I not?)—even without thy edicts," she admits to Creon (458-59). "So," she continues a moment later, "for me to meet this doom is trifling grief" (465). What she fears is not death but *the anguish* that would haunt her if she were to leave her brother's corpse to rot (458-70). In her words, "[n]ot through dread of any human pride would I answer to the gods for breaking *these*" (458).[10] To leave her brother's body unburied "would have grieved me" (468).

Creon experiences this same immediacy concerning the laws although, in his case, his immediacy lies with the city-state's posited or stipulated laws.[11] Creon sees himself as a representative of the city-state, the author of the human laws. He represents its laws. He is a representative because he has been duly appointed as king by the council of elders. The human laws, once formally promulgated in written form, exist "out there" beyond Creon, the representer of the laws. He *must* obey the laws just as all citizens *must* obey them. He possesses no choice in the matter. As a representative of the city-state, he identifies with the latter. It is not surprising that Creon would defend his action so vociferously in terms of the challenge that Antigone poses to everyone's immediate loyalty to the city-state. As Creon admonishes his son, Antigone had challenged that loyalty so necessary to the very existence of the city-state. Creon can say neither "yes" nor "no" to his law's commands any more than can Antigone to hers although this involuntary predicament exists for different reasons in respect to different laws. Creon and Antigone each live immediately under his/her laws. Neither recognizes the other's laws as playing a legitimate role in her/his own.

Again, Hegel explains the clash between Creon and Antigone in terms of the natural difference between the male's association with the city-state and the female's association with the family. The brother/son leaves the immediate, elemental, natural community of the extended family or tribe for the universal city. The mother, wife, and daughter remain at home in the family, whose members comprise the dead as well as the living. The woman of the family intuitively knows the divine laws. She is *not conscious* of them.

Rather, she has "the highest *intuitive* awareness of what is ethical" (*P Sp* 457).[12] The law of the family is an implicit, inner feeling which remains unexposed to the scrutiny of the daylight of consciousness, according to Hegel. Because human laws have evolved from the previous natural *Sittlichkeit* of the extended family or tribe, divine laws are prior in genesis. As such, divine laws belong to the world as a whole and not to any one city-state. Divine laws lie hidden in the background behind the city-state's human laws. Upon death, one is freed from the unrest of the accidents of one's sensuous or individual reality into "the calm of simple universality" (*P Sp* 451).

The fundamental issue, for Hegel, is his grounding of the distinction of human and divine law in nature. Male consciousness shifts from natural to human law, whereas the female consciousness rises from natural to divine law. As a result, the male separates himself from nature, and the woman remains embodied in nature. Furthermore, human law's genesis arises out of the natural world, just as life returns to the netherworld of divine spirit upon the death (a fact of nature) of an individual. Consciousness transforms nature in the real individual world in such a manner that each law complements and confirms the other (*P Sp* 462, 463). For Hegel, justice lies in an equilibrium between the two. When the divine spirit of a deceased body is not properly recognized by living family members, it wreaks vengeance upon the latter so as to restore the rightful place of the universals of the netherworld. The power of the netherworld is thereby integrated into the universal government of the nation. Peace (and justice) results.

Hegel is able to isolate the gender basis of human laws and divine laws because he focuses upon the question what makes human law *human* and what makes divine law *divine?* But my reading of *Antigone* suggests that the crucial issue for philosophic consciousness is the clash between the opposing senses of authority to which each of Creon and Antigone appeal, using Hegel's own criterion of immediacy for differentiation.

The Opposing Senses of Authority

Each of Creon and Antigone possesses an *internal* sense of obligation from *within* him/herself to obey his/her respective laws. Law is still *Gesetz* rather than *Recht*. The two sets of laws "command" each actor to proceed along irreconcilable lines. Neither actor conceives that the other's laws possess some legitimacy within his/her own. The question, then, is why does Creon consider human laws legitimate to the exclusion of the divine and why does Antigone consider her divine laws legitimate to the exclusion of the human?

Creon is a king of a city into which the pre-political Theban tribes have been organized. He has been duly chosen by the council of elders in contrast to kings who, in an earlier day, inherited their thrones. Against a social/religious practice wherebyafter a battle, the conqueror is obligated to allow the vanquished to bury the latter's corpses,[13] Creon posits an edict which proscribes anyone from burying the corpse of Polyneices, a rebel against Thebes. Creon unhesitatingly proclaims the edict. He pleads with the chorus that the act of rebellion is evil. The chorus defers to his authority to proclaim the edict. After all, Creon *represents* the city-state, and he acts out of duty in the interest of the city-state. The laws are presumed to be enacted by an invisible author who dwells beyond and above the city-state's pyramidal hierarchy.

I now wish to suggest that Creon presupposed a royalty model of authority.[14] This model claims that legal authority is drawn from a pyramidal hierarchy, with the king at the pinnacle of the pyramid. The pyramid represents the whole city. At each level of the pyramid, there rests a juridical official whose authority to act is drawn directly from the level of the pyramid immediately above. Each level sets down boundaries within which each official may legitimately act. The pyramid is formal in the stoic sense that procedural form, independent of the substance or significations of a law, posits which officials are qualified to act in the name of the whole. The laws speak for the whole, and the duty of an official is to administer the laws. But what is important in this view of authority is the assumption that an invisible author, who stands above and behind the pyramid, has imposed the laws on citizen and official alike.

Creon finds himself playing a *role*, as king, in such a pyramid. Although he is the head of the pyramid, he merely represents the expression (through the laws) of an invisible author. He has been duly chosen by the council of elders. Creon's authority is an *author*-ity. Once he has been duly appointed a representer of the laws' author, his policies and actions cannot be challenged as illegal because, whatever the content of the act, he acts as the laws' author *(author*-itatively). Interestingly, the sentry, Haemon, Teiresias and the chorus all initially recognize Creon as a duly appointed representer of the laws, although one is left to speculate whether the author is god, the city-state, or the city-state as god. Both Haemon and Teiresias begin their pleading with Creon with deference to him as king of Thebes. Immediately after Creon announces his edict to the community, the chorus replies, "Such is thy pleasure, Creon, son of Menoeceus, touching this city's foe, and its friend; and thou hast power, I ween, to take what order thou wilt, both for the dead, and for all of us who live (211-14)." When a citizen recognizes the king's edict as an appropriate expression of an official in the hierarchical pyramid, the citizen reaffirms the sovereign pyramidal order as a whole. It is with deference to the pyramidal order that Creon justifies and then enforces his edict that Polyneices' corpse be left unburied on the battlefield. And when Creon initially defends his view of authority to Haemon (636-79), the chorus again recognizes the representative character of Creon's edict: "[t]o us, unless our years have stolen our wit, thou seemest to say wisely what thou sayest" (680). At one point, the chorus even scolds Antigone for having challenged Creon's throne "where Justice sits on high" (853).

As Creon lectures to his son, Haemon, "if anyone transgresses, and does violence to the laws, or thinks to dictate to his rulers, such an one can win no praise from me. No, *whomsoever the city may appoint*, that man must be obeyed, in little things and great, in just things and unjust" (662-65).[15] So long as a representer acts within the boundaries of action allocated in the pyramidal structure, one cannot offend justice according to Creon (743-44). Nor may any other representer of the author legitimately prescribe to Creon how he should rule (734). Once his representative role has been delineated, Creon reasons, "do I offend, when I respect mine own prerogatives?" (743).

Accordingly, when a citizen such as Antigone attacks his edict, she does more than attack Creon as a duly appointed representer in the pyramid. She attacks the pyramidal structure of *author*-ity itself. As Creon puts it to her, "disobedience is the worst of evils. This it is that ruins cities; this makes homes desolate; by this, the ranks of allies are broken into headlong rout . . . . Therefore we must support the cause of order . . ." (674-79).

Creon is a *representer* of the author of the human laws, not the author itself. He represents the laws and their source at the top of the pyramidal structure in three contexts. First, as a duly appointed representer, Creon's actions legitimate the source of his own appointment: namely, the council of elders who themselves are representers of the ultimate author. Secondly, Creon insists upon recalling the council of elders in order to proclaim the edict before the council. He thereby recognizes the need to seek authority for the edict in a pyramidal and hierarchical system of representers. I have just noted how the chorus reciprocated by acknowledging Creon's *author*-ity to proclaim the edict. This second context renders Creon's edict an official act, rather than a personal, arbitrary, *ad hoc* utterance of someone who speaks from outside of the pyramid. Thirdly, Creon represents the human laws in that he must en-*force* them. He does not possess the *author*-ity to overrule a law—to say "no" to its enforcement. If he did, one could consider him as acting in the role of an absolute author. Creon possesses no choice but to *represent* the law's author by enforcing its will.

Each of the antagonists in *Antigone* recognizes the representative role of Creon within the pyramidal structure of the Theban state—each, that is, except Antigone herself.[16] This is so because Antigone shares a radically different conception of authority from Creon's and, given this different sense of authority, she refuses to recognize Creon as an authorized interpreter of the laws. From Creon's viewpoint, Antigone speaks *outside* of the authoritative discourse of the pyramidal structure. She is an *out*-law. She challenged the city's very pyramidal structure so essential to the enforcement of the invisible author's laws. Creon describes Antigone's disobedience of his edict as "the worst of evils" because "it ruins cities" (669-70); that is, "She transgressed the laws that had been set forth" (479). He asks incredulously, "[a]nd thou didst indeed dare to transgress that law?" As further evidence of Creon's identification with the human laws, Creon uses the words "edict" and "law" interchangeably. Moreover, whereas Antigone portrays justice as dwelling in the netherworld (451), Creon understands justice solely in terms of the *polis* (610, 743). In the latter reference, for example, he rhetorically asks whether he can possibly offend justice "when I respect mine own prerogative?" (743).

Antigone means authority in a radically different sense. She understands the legitimate source of authority in words which Aristotle later takes up as support for the unchangeable laws of nature as opposed to posited laws:[17]

> Yes, for it was not Zeus that had published me that edict; not such are the laws set among men by the Justice who dwells with the gods below; nor deemed I that thy decrees were of such force, that a mortal could override the unwritten and unfailing statutes of heaven (450-55).

For Antigone, Creon's proclamation just is not law. Rather, she calls it an "edict" (455). Laws are associated with the justice of the netherworld. As Hegel explains, the living members of a family owe a duty to the deceased because, by burying the corpse, death is no longer simply biological: death becomes a matter of heaven rather than of nature (*P Sp* 452). The burial raises the dead to the universality of spirit and thereby brings meaning to death. Any edict which violates this law of the netherworld is non-law. As Antigone rhetorically asks, "and by what laws I pass to the rock-closed prison of my strange tomb?" (849).

Antigone's radically different understanding of authority is exhibited in further passages in the play. Although she knows that she has transgressed Creon's edict (459-62), for example, she does not feel "grieved" for doing so (478). Indeed, it was not sufficient for her to sprinkle dust symbolically upon the corpse during darkness. She returns to the battlefield in open daylight in an even more open defiance of Creon's edict, fully knowing that she will likely be caught. Moreover, her sentence of death by starvation has not been made pursuant to a law; to be law, Justice of the netherworld must ordain a sentence. Instead, the sentence is the action of Creon, a mere mortal human who acts on his own outside of the authority of the heavens. As she indignantly states, "nor deemed I that thy decrees were of such force, that a *mortal* could override the unwritten and unfailing statutes of heaven" (452-53).[18] She believes that she is "a captive of *his* hands" (916), not those of the law.[19] Again, during her last speeches, she acknowledges that she had held the city's laws "in honour" because they had allowed a survivor to bury the corpses of the vanquished. But "*Creon* [not the law] deemed me guilty of error therein, and of outrage, a brother mine!" (910-17).[20]

The *Author*-ity of Creon

Antigone suggests that four factors support and, therefore, undermine Creon's claim to be a duly recognized representer of a super-author, the Theban state.

To begin with, some formal proceeding must *identify* an official as a legitimate representer of the author. The representer is sanctioned as a juridical representer by another representer higher in the pyramidal structure. So, for example, the council of elders has appointed Creon as king, both the council and the king representing the state/author at different levels of the pyramid. Creon initially recognizes this derivative authority when he summons the "council of elders" in order to announce the edict. As with the appointment of the king, so too the king's edicts must be publicly promulgated. This procedure provides *indicia*, for a citizen, that the edict has been enacted by a duly appointed representer at a certain place and at a particular time. If Creon had not publicly announced the edict before the chorus (which also represented the city-state) (193-215), a citizen would not be able to recognize the edict as *author*-itative. And if the edict had not been so recognized, then Creon's edict and subsequent sentence would have been outside of his *author*-ity. It is not a minor consequence that Creon's very first question of Antigone, upon the guard's complaint, is "[n]ow, tell me thou—not in many words, but briefly—knewest thou that an edict had forbidden this?" (446-47). Had Antigone responded in the negative, Creon would have restrained himself in his actions, one would presume. But Antigone responds in the affirmative: "I knew it: could I help it? It was public" (447). The public character of Creon's edict sets the stage for the citizenry in the chorus to assess the legality of Creon's action against Antigone.

Antigone offers a second condition for the *author*-itativeness of a human law: namely, a representer's utterance must receive public support. As Jebb points out, the Athenians of Sophocles' day would have considered that the city-state did not even exist if a ruler ignored the unanimous opinion of the community.[21] Without public support, a ruler rules as a *tyrannus* without constitutional authority. One can assess the extent to which Creon's conduct received public support in terms of the two stages of the legal proceeding which he conducted.

During the first stage of the proceedings, Creon investigates the alleged crime (by making inquiries of the guard, Antigone, and Ismene, for example) (236-330, 383-444), prosecutes the alleged crime (446-552) and judges against Antigone (575-80). During this first stage, the chorus fully supports Creon. It has been noted above that when Creon publicly declares his edict to the chorus, the chorus supports Creon with "[s]uch is thy pleasure, Creon, son of Menoeceus, touching this city's foe, and its friend; and thou hast power, I ween, to take what order thou wilt, both for the dead, and for all us who live" (211-14). Even when Creon explains his view of the divine laws (636-79), after his judgment against Antigone, the chorus fully supports Creon: "[t]o us, unless our years have stolen our wit, thou seemest to say wisely what thou sayest" (680). Haemon too defers to his father's wisdom (634-36, 682-85). When Creon cross-examined her, Antigone notes the support which Creon's edict received amongst the general public: "[b]ut royalty, blest in so much besides, hath the power to do and say what it will" (505). All Thebans, she admits, shared in this deference to Creon's power. Against a background of a stipulated law ("whereby I held thee first in honour" [915]) with respect to the corpse of the deceased, Antigone presumably acknowledges that Creon was the legitimate representer of the author of the human laws even as she readies herself for the final trip to the cavern.

This public support for King Creon begins to collapse, though, when Creon announces his sentence of death by starvation to Antigone. Haemon is the first to document the public unrest: "but I can hear these murmurs in the dark, these moanings of the city for this maiden"; "no woman," they say, "ever merited her doom less,—none ever was to die so shamefully for deeds so glorious as hers; ... deserves not she the reed of golden honour?" (692-97). Haemon describes this as "the darkling rumour that spreads in secret" (700). When Creon personalizes such a plea by claiming that Antigone is tainted with evil, Haemon again defers to the public's view: "[o]ur Theban folk, with one voice, denies it" (733). The dialogue—to the extent that it is a dialogue—deteriorates to the point where Haemon expresses a complete lack of confidence in his father: "[t]hat is no city, which belongs to one man"

(737); and then, again referring to Creon's unpopular stance, "[t]hou wouldst make a good monarch of a desert." (739)

Upon Haemon's exit, Creon revises the sentence from death by public stoning, as he had earlier pronounced, to starvation in a cave where nature, rather than the city, will take its course and thereby save the city from "public stain" (775-76). At this point, the chorus lends its full support to Antigone: "[b]ut now at this sight I also am carried beyond the bounds of loyalty, and can no more keep back the streaming tears, when I see Antigone thus passing to the bridal chamber where all are laid to rest" (801-4). The chorus proceeds to describe Antigone's integrity as "[g]lorious, therefore, and with praise" (817). She shares the doom "of the godlike" (837). The chorus ultimately urges Creon to "[g]o thou, and free the maiden from her rocky chamber, and make a tomb for the unburied dead" (1100). Even Teiresias, the loyal counselor of the state, cautions Creon that his acts "hath brought this sickness on our state" (1015). The gods have wreaked vengeance upon the citizenry as a whole: "the gods no more accept prayer and sacrifice at our hands, or the flame of meat-offering" (1021-22). Against all this evidence of public opposition, Creon maintains his position (1034-64), insulting Haemon and Teiresias in the process.

Antigone demonstrates a third condition for the author-itativeness of a human law. A representer of the author/state must act within preexisting, clearly demarcated boundaries. Out of concern that the sentry might have exceeded his own boundaries as a representer of the author/state, Creon accuses him of having taken a bribe. So too does he accuse the prophet, Teiresias. When Haemon, the chorus, and Teiresias question whether Creon has rightly acted in sentencing Antigone to death by starvation, they do so in terms of the preestablished boundaries of conduct for a representer of the author of the human laws, not necessarily the preestablished boundaries of *Moira*. They remind Creon again and again that he is not the only representer of the author of the human laws. Further, as a mortal, Creon can make whatever utterances he wishes. As a ruler, however, the boundaries of his *author*-ity to proclaim his edicts must be traced up to the representer on the next level of the pyramidal hierarchy, and from there to the next, and the next. Creon's sentence of death by starvation is ultimately a *personal* act, not the juridical act of a representer within the prior established boundaries of his *author*-ity for interpreting human laws. Haemon recognizes this important distinction when, upon urging his father to reconsider the sentence of death by stoning, he exclaims "[t]hat is no city, which belongs to one man" (737). Creon reacts in a manner which exposes that he has, indeed, exceeded the boundaries of his *author*-ity: "[i]s not the city held to be the ruler's?" (738). Haemon concludes that Creon has exceeded the boundaries of his *author*-ity, for Creon has left no room for any other representer, including the citizenry itself, in the state: "[t]hou wouldst make a good monarch of a desert" (739).

Ironically, Creon himself speaks as just another mortal with his own prejudices, feelings, insecurities and personal limitations—not as a duly *author*-ized representer of the author state. He turns to the chorus to call his son just a boy who is "the woman's champion" (740), a "woman's slave" (756). Haemon describes his father's judgments as "vain" and "unwise." With each challenge from Antigone, Haemon, the chorus, and Teiresias, Creon's initial, reasoned defense succumbs to a vindictive, emotional, polemical name-calling. What could be more out of character in a rational hierarchy than to have a juridical representer make vain, unwise, personalized, and prejudiced decisions? Even Teiresias confirms the personal character of Creon's sentence of starvation when, after unsuccessfully attempting to persuade Creon to withdraw his sentence, Teiresias remarks that Creon has openly forced violence against the gods (1072). By his own speech, Creon removes the royal cloak of his own being.

Creon's error, it seems, is to delude himself into believing that he is more than a representer of the author of the human laws; that he is the author itself. As an author, he could legitimately carry on a monologue. But as he was only one representer of several in the pyramidal hierarchy (the sentries being other representers, for example), each representer had to listen to the others.[22] Creon refuses to do so. He refuses to address the other representers—the sentries, Haemon, and Tireisius—in a dialogic and reasonable language shared among representers of the author of human laws. This would be required if he himself were only one of many officials in the hierarchical pyramid whose role it was to administer the author's laws. Haemon exasperatingly complains upon hearing his father call him a "woman's slave" who uses "wheedling speech," "[t]hou wouldst speak and then hear no reply?" (758). Creon is not the last representer to consider himself the author of the laws in Western culture. His own words remind one of Louis XIV: "*L'État, c'est moi.*" Creon erroneously believes that a monarchy with positive law has surpassed the authority of a clan hierarchy. Paradoxically, in her final appeal, Antigone addresses the chorus as the legitimate representer in the city's pyramid: "[s]ee me, *citizens of my fatherland*, setting forth on my last way, looking my last on the sunlight that is for me no more" (805).[23] From her point of view, the legitimate representer of civil society is the clan council which, in contrast to days past when the king did not have to listen to anyone, legitimates the king's very position in the hierarchy of *author*-ity. As the council's nominee, the king must start to listen.[24]

There remains one final characteristic of Creon's *author*-ity as a represen-ter of the author of human laws. A representer can carry on a dialogic relation with other representers, as Haemon complained that Creon had failed to do. But, vis-à-vis a citizen subject to the human laws, the re-presenter may speak in a monologic manner. As such, the citizen passively listens without an opportunity of reply.[25] There is a risk of a lack of consensus between ruler and addressee/citizen. In order for the addressee to understand the representer's utterance as representative of the author/state, it is not enough that the addressee be able to recognize the utterances as juridically promulgated from within the boundaries associated with its representer. Since the source of the human law is *external* to the ad-dressee/citizen, something more is needed than its formal promulgation, its source in an appropriate representer and its enactment by that representer within the legitimate boundaries of *author*-ity. That something is *force*.

Antigone, Ismene, the sentries, the chorus, and Haemon realize that Creon may supplement his edict with physical force, just as Plato advises in the *Statesman*,[26] Aristotle counsels at the end of the *Ethics*,[27] and Derrida argues with respect to *Recht*.[28] At the very start of the play, Antigone realizes that "who so disobeys in aught, his doom is death by stoning before all the folk" (35). Ismene urges her sister to remember, "first, that we were born women, as who should not strive with men; next, that we are ruled of the stronger, so that we must obey in these things, and in things yet sorer" (60-63). Ismene admits that she has neither the physical nor the psychic strength to defy the city (79).

Creon too is quick to remind all concerned that physical force conserves the *author*-ity behind the human laws. For example, he promises at an early stage that whoever proves his loyalty to the state, the king will honor in death and life (220-22). Creon threatens his sentries with death unless they uncover who began to bury Polyneices' corpse (305-10). The threat of force is implied in Creon's lecture to Haemon: the orders of an *author*-ized representer "*must* be obeyed, in little things and great, in just things and unjust" (665). Creon does not need to go on to describe what will happen if a citizen does disobey an order. Haemon responds to Creon by describing how the fear of physical force lies behind the citizenry's dread of Creon's utterances: "[f]or the dread of thy frown forbids the citizen to speak such words as would offend thine ear" (690-91). Creon, in turn, watches whatever they say or do. Indeed, throughout the play, the chorus does not question that a representer may exercise force in order to en-*force* his otherwise legitimate edicts. The chorus emphasizes just how difficult it is for a citizen to oppose the representer's authority to use force: "[r]everent action claims a certain praise for reverence; but an offence against power cannot be brooked by him who hath power in his keeping" (873-74). The eventual concern of the chorus is that Creon has exercised the wrong kind of force (death by starvation). As such, it believes that this, in turn, has taken Creon's action beyond the legitimate boundaries of his *author*-ity.

We are left, then, with the question of what Creon means when he exclaims that his "life is but as death" (1320). Creon is still Creon. He remains a mortal, just like other mortals. But he is no longer a juridical representer of an author in the pyramidal hierarchy. The formal trappings of *author*-ity have evaporated from him as evidenced in his loss of recognition in the eyes of the people as well as of other officials as a legitimate representer in the juridical hierarchy. A civil *Sittlichkeit* has collapsed. He is no longer *King* Creon in the sense of possessing the legitimacy which had earlier come with his crown as king. What is left is concrete particular as opposed to the universal form of juridical representer associated with the en(-forcement) of human laws. Creon's life is but as death because he had formerly identified his concrete particularity so deeply with his role as a juridical representer of the author/state that, once his role in the pyramidal hierarchy had been de-legitimized, spiritual death resulted. After all, he had been an official of Oedipus' court before his own,[29] although he had been king for only one and a half days. In playing a role as a representer in the pyramidal hierarchy, his being had been abstracted out of the immediacy of primitive *Sittlichkeit* to such an extent that he could not return to the former unity which he had shared in the natural community of the tribe/clan before the schism between the divine and human laws. He was reduced to particularity (less than citizenship). Put another way, the cloak of representer in the state's order had been withdrawn from him so as to leave him naked, reduced to particularity. But, because of his alienation from particularity as a representer in the hierarchy, Creon could no longer "find" himself as he had once been. Once the veneer of representer is removed, Creon dies spiritually.

The Authority of Antigone's Divine Laws

The problem is that Antigone's conception of authority simply does not recognize Creon's as having weight, as authority. The immediacy of her loyalty to the divine laws is so overbearing that she simply will not allow Creon to redefine her. She is, as the chorus put it, a "mistress of thine own fate" (819). She has pressed her own conception of authority to the point that "[t]hou hast rushed forward to the utmost verge of daring; and against that throne where Justice sits on high thou hast fallen, my daughter, with a grievous fall" (853-55). Antigone has withstood the terror which the human laws have imposed upon her. She has retained a "self willed temper" (874), even though it has brought her physical ruin. To the very end, her sole concern is "what law of heaven have I transgressed?" (920).

How does the authority of the laws of heaven differ from the authority of human laws? At first sight, the characteristics of the former seem similar to the latter. Both seem to have a pyramidal hierarchy with a mythical author external to the pyramid. For human laws, who is the author of the laws is unclear: it may be the city-state, a transcendental god, or the city-state as god. For divine laws, one might consider Zeus as the author. The pyramids possess vertical layers with each representer possessing discretion to rule within the posited boundaries of its *author*-ity. When Zeus and his *comitatus* conquer and expel Cronos from beyond the horizon, Zeus remains a permanent superlord.[30] He delegates *author*-ity to his brothers, Hades and Poseidon. Various children and followers are delegated still lesser fiefdoms. Apollo ventures off to conquer Delphi, Athena to conquer Poseidon and to gain Athens. Each god/goddess rules alone under his/her jurisdiction. The presumed super-author, Zeus, possesses particularly great power in ousting or assimilating all foreign gods. Zeus dispenses fate and upholds the spheres of activity of all his subservient gods/goddesses.[31] With Homer's influence, the Olympian gods become international rulers, not the gods of a particular tribe or locality. They rule by enforcing an overbearing set of universally shared divine laws.

It is at this point that the authority of the divine laws departs from Creon's conception of the authority of the human laws. For, whereas the representers in the pyramidal hierarchy of the human laws represent a personal author—however invisible—of the laws, Zeus is *not* the invisible author of the divine laws. Indeed, Jean-Pierre Vernant suggests that Zeus and the other gods are "powers," not "persons."[32] Rather, the Greek gods are subordinate to an *impersonal* force called *Moira* or destiny.[33] *Moira* is authorless. *Moira* dwells beyond the gods. *Moira* is a remote power that neither Zeus nor any other god has created. Nor may Zeus and the Greek gods withstand the hold of *Moira*. *Moira* destines the jurisdictional boundaries of each god. If a god exceeds its limits, *Nemesis* will wreak havoc upon the Hellenes. Cornford points out that the primary meaning of *Moira* in the *Iliad* is the allotment of jurisdiction to each god.[34] The word "destiny" is derived from this meaning of *Moira*. *Moira* (destiny), *Nemesis* (avenging anger), and *Dikê* (justice) are grounded in the allotted place of a god in the cosmic order.

The Greek people are bonded through *Moira* as manifested in their living experiences. *Moira* works through the citizen in a manner that offers a place for the citizen in the cosmic order and in tribal society. Its emotive force is felt as inevitable. Legal obligation (to the divine laws) is itself an aspect of this inevitability. As the one sentry admits to the other sentry before announcing to Creon the news of a violation of his edict, "for I come with a good grip on one hope,—that I can suffer nothing but what is my fate" (235). So too, Antigone continually speaks as if *Moira* leaves her no freedom of choice. She *must* follow the divine laws or *Nemesis* will wreak dread upon her. "My life," she resignedly encourages Ismene, "hath long been given to death, that so I might serve the dead" (560). And as Teiresias urges upon Creon, "[m]ark that now, once more, thou standest on fate's fine edge" (996). The chorus too acknowledges how *Moira* works through Antigone in that it suggests that Antigone did not even have personal responsibility for her actions. The chorus attributes the blameworthiness of her death sentence to her father's, Oedipus', crime of incest: "[t]hou hast rushed forward to the utmost verge of daring; and against that throne where Justice sits on high thou hast fallen, my daughter, with a grievous fall. But in this ordeal thou art paying, haply, for thy father's sin" (853-56). And a few minutes later, the chorus reminds the addressee that a Greek citizen simply cannot escape from the hold of *Moira*: "[b]ut dreadful is the mysterious power of fate; there is no deliverance from it by wealth or by war, by fenced city, or dark, sea-beaten ships" (952-55). Even Creon succumbs to the inevitable control of *Moira*. When the chorus urges him to free Antigone and to bury Polyneices, he finally agrees but with a resignation of the inevitable determination by *Moira*: "[a]h me, 'tis hard, but I resign my cherished resolve,—I obey. We must not wage a vain war with destiny" (1105). And, upon realizing that his own fate is death, he again defers to *Moira*: "[o]r, let it come, let it appear, that fairest of fates for me, that brings my last day—aye, best fate of all! Oh, let it come, that I may never look upon tomorrow's light!" (1328-29). And once more, "and yonder, again, a crushing fate hath leapt upon my head" (1346). The protagonist (Antigone) and the antagonist (Creon) recognize that the source of the authority of the divine laws is not an identifiable author as it was with the human laws. An *impersonal* power manifests itself in all godly and human experience.

Because the divine laws are authorless, it is impossible for a mortal being to identify the time and place when a particular law was enacted. Indeed, unlike the formal public procedure surrounding the promulgation of a human law, one cannot describe a divine law as having been promulgated. As Antigone emphasizes in her defence, "no one knows when they were first put forth" (457). And, as the chorus explains, "[t]hy power, O Zeus, . . . a ruler to whom time brings no old age, dwellest in the dazzling splendour of Olympus. And through the future, near and far, as through the past, shall this law hold good" (611-13). Indeed, the very conception of space and time

underlying divine laws contrasts with the quantitative and abstract conception of space/time presupposed in the promulgation of a human law, at least
since Galileo. The Frankforts explain that Greek tribal thought cannot
abstract a concept "space" from the very *experience* of space/time.[35]
Experience incorporates concrete orientations which refer to localities with
"an emotional colour." Space is not unambiguously fixed. And time does not
have a uniform duration of qualitatively indifferent moments. Each phase of
"time" is charged with a unique emotional value and significance. Thus, we
cannot even describe divine laws as having been "enacted" or "promulgated." As Antigone describes in her defense, "[f]or their life is not of to-day
or yesterday, but from all time, and no man knows when they were first put
forth" (455-57). A mortal simply cannot recognize divine laws in terms of
a quantitative and abstract space/time spectrum as we do today.

It is not surprising, then, that unlike human laws, divine laws are unwritten. For that matter, they may also be unspoken. For, they are without an
author who might represent them in a code or in an utterance. How, then, are
the divine laws discovered? They are "discovered" or, better, assimilated
through lived experiences, not least the experiences shared through
ceremony and ritual. In contrast to the Christian transcendental god and our
modern metaphysical truths, the Greek gods are not independent of the
social life of the Greeks.[36] The divine laws are transferred from one
generation to the next through actions of the body rather than through
conceptions of the mind. For example, after a battle, the survivors collect
and bury the dead without discussion. And the initiated young men (*Kouroi*)
become men through rites or sacred performances.[37] Indeed, the antagonists
in Sophocles' play do not talk about whether a divine law exists concerning
the burial of the dead. They do not debate, for example, whether it can be
discovered unwritten in some code or remembered through an utterance of
an elder wise man. Rather, the divine laws live through the presentative
experiences of tribal members. Basically, Creon demands that Antigone be
humiliated. It is *her* brother's body against which Creon's edict is directed.
Her loyalty to the divine laws possesses a personal character: the divine laws
address *her* experience just as she addresses the divine laws. Against this
experiential background with Creon's conduct, Antigone just intuitively
knows the divine laws without having to discover evidence of them in some
textual "authority," written or verbal, coded or customary.

Antigone's addressive experience with the divine laws contrasts with
Creon's interpretative act. Because Creon enunciates the signs of the human
laws, the other representers in the pyramidal hierarchy go to the *enunciator's*
interpretation of them. After all, Creon, who seems to be the external source
of the posited signifiers, is closest to what the enunciated signifiers *mean*. As

such, the meaning of an edict is believed to be represented by what Creon says. That is, the edict is presumed to have an exact or literal signified associated with Creon's signifiers. This very association of meaning with Creon as the legitimate representer of the author of the human laws may well lie behind Creon's uncompromising insistence that his edict *must* be obeyed.

But any claim to a denotative character for *meaning* is absent in the context of divine laws. For, first, as argued above, there is no identifiable author of the signs of divine laws. Rather, there is a multiplicity of interrelated roles and jurisdictions associated with *Moira*. Secondly, the meaning of the divine laws is presentative.[38] The addressive experiences of the listeners count in the meaning-forming process of the divine laws. Antigone's addressive experiences with the divine laws is not idiosyncratic to *Antigone*. Socrates explains the origins of the charges against him in the *Apology* in terms of his addressive experience with the divine sign generated from his friend, Chaerephon's, journey to the Delphi. And Oedipus' driven and very personal search for the meaning of Phoebus' words to Creon in *Oedipus the King* reflects Oedipus' addressive experience with the divine laws.[39] As a tribe brings meaning into a sign, the divine sign system becomes alive. Antigone insightfully remarks that the divine laws are in fact *alive*, "[f]or their life is not of to-day or yesterday, but from all time" (457). *Moira* is not imposed upon Oedipus, Socrates, or Antigone. *Moira* brings the unconscious to consciousness. The divine laws are alive because the divine laws are manifested through the living experiences of tribal members.

It seems reasonable to conclude that divine laws reflect a different discourse from that of human laws. The divine laws are unwritten. They are sometimes not even communicated through spoken word. Rather, the meaning of the divine laws is left to addressees of a particular tribe in a particular era to experience divine laws. The discourse of human laws, focusing as it does upon formally promulgated edicts of an invisible author's representers in a pyramidal hierarchy, contrasts with the unwritten discourse of the divine laws. In her loyalty to her brother and to the unwritten discourse of the divine laws, Antigone withstands all efforts by Creon to assimilate her into the discourse of the human laws. But in the process, Antigone ceases to be a corporeal reality.

Conclusion

An addressee of Sophocles' *Antigone*, then, is left with two radically different senses of authority. Both Creon and Antigone felt immediately bound to their respective laws. But neither Creon nor Antigone recognized the other's laws as authoritative. As such, each moment of consciousness was lacking in self-consciousness and, therefore, in infinite spirit. Hegel associated the distinction between human laws and divine laws in the respective social roles of male and female in civil society. I have argued that the distinction between the two sets of laws lies in the *cultural* difference between an *author*-ity of representers of an author of human laws and the authorless impersonal *Moira* of divine laws which is manifested through the addressive experiences of tribal members. This cultural difference represents a shift from a tribal discourse to the discourse of the city-state. The former concentrates upon the experiential meanings which a tribe brings into the signs "of a myth" as learned bodily through ritual and ceremony and through personal experiences. The discourse of a city-state seeks out legitimate conduct as posited within boundaries of different vertical stages in a pyramidal order. At each stage, there rests an identifiable representer of a super-author who is presupposed to exist external to the pyramid of juridical agents. If the conduct of a representer or other mortal lies within such boundaries, then such conduct is *author*-itative and, therefore, law in the sense of the authority of authored human laws. But if the conduct of a god or any mortal lies within the jurisdictional boundaries experienced as *Moira*, then it is authoritative in the sense of authority in divine laws. A mortal's action in the one sense directly contravenes the law in the other.

Another way of putting the distinction is to ask why Creon's interpretive acts, rather than Antigone's, should carry force. The answer, from the viewpoint of human laws, is that Creon is a representer whose own edicts are authoritative in three contexts: first, he is duly appointed as a representer of the author/state; second, his representativeness is legitimated by the public support which he achieves as reflected in the views of the chorus, his son's assessment of the views of the public, and the assessment of Teiresius; and third, he represents the laws in his en-*force*ment of them. In each context, one finds Creon in a hierarchical pyramid with a presumed author situated beyond the pinnacle. Four factors reinforce Creon's position. First, in order to be *author*-itative, his utterance must be formally and publicly promulgated. Secondly, in order for the *author*-ity to be efficacious, the public must do more than understand Creon's, the representer's, intent. The public must accept it as legitimate. I argued that the public accepted Creon's sentence of death by stoning as a legitimate sentence. However, the public's support deteriorated at the point when Creon changed the sentence to imprisonment in a cave with minimal food and water. Thirdly, as a representer, his conduct must lie within the preexisting boundaries of the sphere of action delegated to his representative position in the hierarchy. Finally, his ability to en-*force* his utterance ultimately ensures its *author*-itativeness. Creon's sentence of death by stoning and, then, death by starvation lacked the second, third and fourth conditions of *author*-ity for human laws. With a sentence without public support and in excess of preexisting boundaries of action and with a "head" representer unable to en-*force* his edict, Creon became a king in name only. Creon could no longer legitimately represent the super-author dwelling behind the pyramid. As a result, his immediacy with the human laws was shed. What remained was a naked particularity.

The sense of authority in the human laws fundamentally differs from that of the divine laws. Whereas physical force constitutes and conserves the human laws, the divine laws are enforced through guilt and dread. The chorus, Antigone, and, toward the end, even Creon acknowledge this dread. Further, whereas the pyramidal hierarchy of the human laws presupposes that an author enacts the laws, the divine laws possess no such au-thor—mythical or otherwise. Zeus himself is subject to *Moira*. *Moira* is a blind *impersonal* force beyond the control of gods or humans. Since there is no author of the divine laws, no god can act as a representer of a super-author. Nor can any ruler claim to possess denotative or exact meanings for the signs of the divine laws.

Most importantly, divine laws reflect a different discourse from that of human laws. The divine laws are unwritten. They are sometimes not even communicated through spoken word. Rather, they are transferred through ritual, though experienced as having a point. Creon effectively demanded that Antigone and her family be humiliated. It was *her* brother's body to which burial rites were not granted. Unlike the formally promulgated laws of the city-state, Antigone experiences the divine laws as possessing neither an identifiable beginning nor ending. Their legitimacy cannot be traced to an author external to human experience, as is the case with the human laws. Instead, it is left to addressees of a particular tribe in a particular era to interpret the divine laws through their living expereinces just as I, an addressee of *Antigone*, am left to interpret the legend of Antigone. The discourse of the human laws, focusing as it does upon formally promulgated edicts of representers in a pyramidal hierarchy, contrasts with the discourse of unwritten myths of the divine laws. In her loyalty to the discourse of the divine laws, Antigone withstands all effort by Creon to assimilate her into the discourse of the human laws.

Philosophical consciousness is left, then, with Hegel's thesis intact: namely, divine law and human law (universal and individual, divine and human) are opposites in which each proves to be the non-reality of itself and the other (*P Sp* 464). That is, neither authenticates the other. Rather than representing a clash of the natural difference between male and female, however, the contradiction rests in radically different conceptions of authority. Neither sense of authority recognizes the other as playing any part in its own meaning. Neither authenticates the other. Each proves to be a non-reality. Philosophical consciousness is left, then, with Creon who cannot be, Antigone who ceases to be, and the city-state whose mythic authorship is saved. Only God can save the King.[40]

Notes

1. References to Hegel are to the *Phenomenology of Spirit*, A. V. Miller, trans. (Oxford: Oxford University Press, 1977), cited hereafter by paragraph number as *P Sp*.

2. For the difference between philosophical consciousness and observed consciousness see generally Hans Georg Gadamer, "Hegel's Inverted World" in *Hegel's Dialectic: Five Hermeneutical Studies*, P. Christopher Smith, trans. (New Haven: Yale University Press, 1976), 36-37.

3. In the *Zusatz* to paragraph 433 of his *Philosophy of Mind* (William Wallace, trans. [Oxford: Oxford University Press, 1971], 174), Hegel remarks that the Greeks and Romans did not know that man as such, man as this universal "I," as rational self-conscious-ness, is entitled to freedom. On the contrary, with them man was held to be free only if he was born free. With them, therefore, freedom still had the character of a natural state. That is why slavery existed in their free states and bloody wars developed in which the slaves tried to free themselves, to obtain recognition of their eternal human rights.

4. References to Sophocles' *Antigone* are to the Richard C. Jebb translation (*Sophocles: The Plays and Fragments*, Part 3 [Amsterdam: Servio Publishers, 1962]).

I have also consulted the Elizabeth Wyckoff translation in *Sophocles I*, David Grene, trans. (Chicago: University of Chicago Press [Phoenix Books], 1984) and the Robert Fagles translation in Sophocles, *The Three Theban Plays* (Harmondsworth, Eng.: Penguin, 1982, 1984).

5. See, e.g., note 16 below.

6. This critique is set out in Luce Irigaray, *Speculum of the Other Woman* (Ithaca: Cornell University Press, 1985), 214-26 and Patricia Jagentowicz Mills, "Hegel's *Antigone*" in *The Owl of Minerva* 17 (1986), 131-52. For a criticism of the latter see Heidi M. Ravven, "Has Hegel Anything to Say to Feminists?" in *The Owl of Minerva* 19 (1988), 149-68. The most comprehensive study of the issue is Martin Donougho, "The Woman in White: On the Reception of Hegel's *Antigone*" in *The Owl of Minerva*, 21 (1989-90), 65-89.

My argument poses the following issue for the above: "Is the author at the apex of the hierarchic pyramid in Creon's sense of authority the very male whose monologic language of sameness Irigaray critiques?" More generally, "is the pyramidal structure of *author*-ity reflective of a male dominated culture and, if so, how?"

7. Donougho, "Woman in White," 65-89.

8. It may well be that although Hegel's general thesis is applicable to the Greek world to the extent that neither law recognizes the other as authoritative, his claim that they collapse into a unified being-for-self under Roman law is in error.

9. See especially his essay "What Is an Author?" in *The Foucault Reader*, Paul Robinson, ed., (New York: Pantheon, 1984); "Two Lectures" in Michel Foucault, *Power/Knowledge Selected Interviews and Other Writings, 1972-1977*, Colin Gordon, trans., (New York: Pantheon, 1980), 78-108.

10. Jebb's emphasis.

11. Ravven also describes how the relationships of Antigone to the family and of Creon to the city-state possess a "natural" character in this sense of immediacy. "Has Hegel Anything to Say?" 149-68, especially 154-55.

12. Emphasis Hegel's.

13. This is the opinion of Jebb in the "Introduction" to his translation, Part 3, xxii-xxiii.

14. Foucault makes a reference to this in "Two Lectures," 94-95, and again in "Governmentality" in *The Foucault Effect: Studies in Governmentality*, Graham Burchell, Colin Gordon and Peter Miller, eds. (Chicago: University of Chicago Press, 1991), 91-92.

15. Emphasis added.

16. This is not without ambiguity, however. At one point when all other arguments have failed to dissuade his father of the inappropriateness of his sentence, Haemon appeals to the supremacy of the divine laws (742-47). Similarly, although it scolds Antigone for having challenged Creon's throne "where Justice sits on high" (853), the chorus also acknowledged earlier that the divine laws are supreme: "[t]hy power, O Zeus, what trespass can limit?" (605). Moreover, toward the end of the play, the chorus suggests to Creon "how all too late thou seemest to see the right!" (1270) Wyckoff translates "the right" as "Justice."

17. In one of the three sets of passages where Aristotle is said to explicate a philosophy of natural law: *Rhetoric* I.13.1373b12-13 (*The Complete Works of Aristotle*, Jonathan Barnes, ed., 2 vols. [Princeton: Princeton University Press, 1984], II).

The other passages are in the *Nicomachean Ethics* V.7.1134b18-1135b and the *Politics* I.2.

18. Emphasis added.

19. Emphasis added.

20. Emphasis added.

21. Jebb, *Sophocles*, "Introduction," xxiv, n. 12.

22. In contrast to the city-state of Thebes, authority in clan thinking simply belonged to the father.

23. Emphasis added.

24. The theme of reasonableness is discussed by Martha Nussbaum in *The Fragility of Goodness: Luck and Ethics in Greek Tragedy and Philosophy* (Cambridge: Cambridge University Press), ch. 3.

25. The distinction between a monologic and dialogic language is drawn from Mikhail Bakhtin, "Speech Genres and Other Essays" in, Vern W. McGee, trans. (Austin: University of Texas Press, 1980); and *The Dialogic Imagination*, Michael Holquist, ed., Caryl Emerson and Michael Holquist, trans. (Austin: University of Texas Press, 1981).

26. *Statesman*, 293d-297e.

27. *Ethics*, 1179b5-19.

28. Derrida, "Force of Law: The 'Mystical Foundation of Authority'" in *Cardozo Law Review* 11 (1990): 919-1045.

29. Indeed, Oedipus had trusted him enough to have him go to the Delphic Oracle for the purpose of learning what could be done to eradicate the plague.

30. This is discussed in Gilbert Murray, *Five Stages of Greek Religion*, 3rd ed. (NewYork: Doubleday Anchor Books, 1951), 45-50.

31. This point is discussed by F. M. Cornford in *From Religion to Philosophy: A Study in the Origins of Western Speculation* (NewYork: Harper & Bros., 1957), 26.

32. Jean-Pierre Vernant, *Myth and Society in Ancient Greece*, Janet Lloyd, trans. (New Jersey: Humanities Press, 1974), 98.

33. Vernant, *Myth and Society*, 12. Also see the discussion in R. P. Winnington-Ingram, *Sophocles: An Interpretation* (Cambridge: Cambridge University Press, 1980), 150-55.

34. Vernant, *Myth and Society*, 16.

35. H. and H. A. Frankfort, "Myth and Reality" in H. and H. A. Frankfort, John A. Wilson, Thorkild Jacobsen, *Before Philosophy: The Intellectual Adventures of Ancient Man* (Harmondsworth, Eng.: Penguin, 1949), 29-36.

36. Vernant, *Myth and Society*, 100-1, 220-21. Also see generally, Johan Huizinga, *Homo Ludens: A Study of the Play-Element in Culture* (Boston: Beacon, 1950), ch. 4.

37. Murray, *Greek Religion*, 29.

38. Heidegger distinguishes between the presentative experiences associated with *Moira* and the representative character of meaning since Plato, which grasps being under a concept. See "Moira" in Martin Heidegger, *Early Greek Thinking: The Dawn of Western Philosophy*, David Farell Krell and Frank A. Capuzzi, trans. (Cambridge: Harper & Row, 1975, 1984) ch.3.

Gilbert Murray misses the presentative character of the meaning-forming process of tribal myths when he suggests that the gods "are *only concepts*, exceedingly confused cloudy and changing concepts, *in the minds* of thousands of divine worshippers and non-worshippers. They change every time they are thought of, as a word changes every time it is pronounced." *Greek Religion*, 29 (emphasis added). So, too, does Roland Barthès miss the *presentative* experience in tribal myths when he argues that myths are connotative or second-level stories of the tribe. Connotative meaning is re-presentative. It does not honor the emotive experience of the listener who brings meaning to bear in his/her living experiences. "Myth Today" in *Mythologies* (Paris: Edition du Seuil, 1957).

39. Oedipus had sent Creon to Delphi in order to inquire as to how to rid Thebes of the plague. Upon his return, Oedipus asks Creon to repeat precisely the words of the oracle. Creon replies, "Phoebus our lord bids us plainly to drive out a defiling thing, which (he saith) hath been harboured in this land, and not to harbour it, so that it cannot be healed" (95-99). Oedipus, who is but "a stranger to this report" (220), demands to know the name of the murderer, even though Phoebus had made no mention of a murder. His demand is softened with the assurance that any informant will be allowed to leave the land unhurt. A leader of the chorus offers some information to the effect that certain travellers were said to have killed Oedipus' father, Laius, only to have Oedipus reject it as mere rumor. Oedipus cross-examines Teiresias' "dreadful" interpretation of the moral of the story: "Now, Phoebus—if indeed thou knowest it not from the messengers—sent answer to our question that the only riddance from this pest which could come what if we should learn aright the slayers of Laius, and slay them, or send them into exile from our land" (305-10).

Oedipus still drives on to understand the meaning of the Delphic oracle. He searches out evidence from his wife/mother, Iocasta, as well as from the shepherd who, in Oedipus' infancy, had refused to enforce Iocasta's order to drown Oedipus. Iocasta begs Oedipus to stop his search for the meaning of the sign: "[f]or the gods' sake, if thou hast any care for thine own life, forbear this search! My anguish is enough" (1060-62). Oedipus' search for meaning—"my origins face-to-face"—leads him to recount a further story which he had received as a youth (780).

40. Following my original presentation of this essay to the Society for Greek Political Thought, a draft was presented to the Canadian Philosophical Association Annual Meeting, Charlottetown, PEI, June 4, 1992, and as the Northrop Frye Lecture, Victoria College, University of Toronto, May 31, 1994. I am grateful to Walter Skakoon and H. S. Harris, who read and commented on earlier drafts.

Chapter 8

Aristotle on How to Preserve a Regime: Maintaining Precedent, Privacy, and Peace through the Rule of Law

Judith A. Swanson

One of the fundamental questions Aristotle addresses during his inquiry into how to preserve regimes is whether law or men should rule. To appreciate his answer, which is effectively that both should rule, is to appreciate that he means, by the rule of law, constitutional law. Aristotle not only concludes that the primary function of constitutional law is preservative, but discovers that the sorts of laws and legal provisions necessary for a lasting regime are those that maintain precedent, privacy, and peace.

Preserving the Private

Although the fundamental conclusion of Aristotle's discussion of indispensable laws, that a city cannot last without securing order, may be obvious, what securing order requires is not always accepted or understood. Because not all human beings respond to argument, order requires cultivating habits in them that overcome or guide their passions (*NE* 1179b23-1180a5).[1] By embodying reason and either the promise of reward or the threat of punishment, laws have the power to cultivate habits, in effect judging for individuals. In contrast to Locke's view that laws should fence off a private sphere, they should, according to Aristotle, cultivate not only public but private habits that do not seemingly bear on a city (*NE* 1180a2-4). If the habits laws encourage are reasonable, then the thinking person will understand the rationale for them. For such a person, laws are not so much a substitution for his judgment as a great convenience or "salvation" in that they save him the trouble of always choosing conduct (*Pol* 1310a34-36). In any case, the aim of law should be to render everyone—the thoughtful and the thoughtless, the rulers and the ruled, the minority and the majority—supportive of the regime, for anyone might be the source of its destruction (*Pol* 1294b36-40, 1337a14-17).

Aristotle maintains nonetheless that laws should require individuals to exercise their own judgment over many matters of conduct, public and private. Indeed, the aim of the rule of law is not to command citizens to perform certain actions but to stipulate subscription to the qualitative conditions of the regime. Contrary to Hannah Arendt's and Richard Bodéüs's interpretations, legislators are not architects whose aim it is to control or preclude all significant political action but educators whose aim it is to encourage a way of life.[2] Laws cannot fabricate that way of life because they cannot make persons choose correctly. They can only try to make them understand the benefit or virtue of certain choices. As Aristotle says, human beings can only "become good *through* laws [*dia nomon*]" (*NE* 1180b25). Accordingly, he believes that the excellence of the citizens, not simply of the laws, determines the excellence of a regime (*Pol* 1332a33-35).

The Rule of Law versus the Rule of Men

If Aristotle deems certain sorts of law or legal provision necessary to the existence of any city, then it would seem that he would deem the rule of at least those laws superior to the rule of men. In fact, his debate over the question of whether laws or men should rule supports that conclusion (*Pol* 1286a7-24, 1287a16-b26). The debate is indeed of less interest for its unsurprising general conclusion—that both laws and men should rule—than for its finding about the nature of the laws that should rule.

The central points of the debate are as follows. The main advantage of rule by men is that men can deliberate over particular cases; its main disadvantage is that self-interest, prejudice, or ambition may influence deliberation. The main advantage of rule by law is that laws are impartial; its main disadvantage is that laws cannot judge individual cases. Aristotle raises a couple of red herrings to make very clear the actual advantage of each sort of rule, which in turn persuades us of his conclusion.[3] A political order needs both the discretionary ability of men and the impartiality of laws because the universal is not just in all cases and men are not always impartial. What is more, laws and men can rule cooperatively only if the men are more lawlike and the laws more like men: justice requires reasonable men and flexible laws (*Pol* 1282b1-6, 1287a25-27, b5-8, 25-26, 1292a32-34).

Of most interest is the conclusion that only a certain kind of law should be superior to the rule of men. Although laws that a regime cannot survive without should not be replaced by the rule of men, they should be sufficiently flexible so as to be tailored to the particular conditions of a regime, and written down.

As for the reasonable men that Aristotle thinks should rule along with law, it must suffice, in light of the focus of this article, to note that, in addition to being habituated by preservative or constitutional law, men can become reasonable by pursuing "leisure" or the liberal arts (*scholê*).[4]

The Rule of Law

To see that Aristotle means by 'the rule of law' the rule of preservative laws, one must begin with the law-versus-men debate in the *Politics* and then draw on the *Nicomachean Ethics, Metaphysics*, and *Rhetoric*. Aristotle introduces the question of whether law or men should rule with the paradox that passion or prejudice may permeate law; law may be oligarchic or democratic, for example (*Pol* 1281a34-38). In his continuing discussion, he completes the paradox. Law can permeate or influence men in two ways. A man may hold law or a general principle in his mind or may be habituated to the spirit of the laws of his regime (1286a16-17, 1287a25, b25-26). Since law may be impassioned, that habituation may not be wholly desirable. Law may, however, also be dispassionate (1286a17-19, 1287a28-30, 32, b4-5). With this claim, Aristotle clarifies the debate without eliminating the paradox. The rule of law is distinct from the rule of men insofar as it is good law. Aristotle does not need to make his definition of law explicit because both *nomos* and *dike*, like "law" and "justice," connote rightness.[5] Nonetheless, by the fourth century B.C. the primary sense of *nomos* was "written statute"; like "law" for us, *nomos* had a primarily positivist connotation.[6] Aristotle therefore treats the difference between law and justice,[7] and therewith that between good and bad law, in the *Nicomachean Ethics*.

Aristotle's discussion of natural and legal justice indicates how laws can be impartial even though they are necessarily made by men who are subject to desire or spiritedness (*Pol* 1286a19-20, 1287a31-32). Laws may derive from either the passions or the intellects of men. Insofar as they derive from intellect or knowledge, they derive from what is universal and unchanging (*NE* V.7, 1180a21-22, b20-22, 25-27, 1141a7-8, 21-25; *Met* 1074b26-28; *Pol* 1332a31-32).[8] Nothing guarantees that men will formulate laws objectively, but the activity of lawmaking conduces to their objective formulation because, first of all, it is a slow process, allowing time for reflection. Second, "love, hate, or personal interest" is less likely, and "the truth" is more likely, to influence their formulation because laws apply not to present particular cases but to a category of cases in the future (*Rh* I.1.7). Third and most important, legislators formulate laws from "laws resting on custom" or long-standing precedent. These serve as the political conduit of a kind of natural law (making universals accessible to the non-noetic).

The debate in Book III of the *Politics* over whether law or men should rule does not, then, weigh rule by any sort of positive law against rule by discretion; it weighs rule by a particular kind of positive law, law based on universal or natural law, against rule by discretion. Further evidence for this claim is as follows: Aristotle declares toward the end of the debate that "laws resting on customs are more authoritative, and deal with more authoritative matters, than laws resting on writings; so even if it is safer for a human being to rule than laws resting on writings, this is not the case for laws resting on custom" (1287b5-8). What are customs (*ta êthê*) according to Aristotle? In the *Rhetoric*, he observes that there are two sorts of laws, particular and general. In one place he states that, "by particular, [he means] the written law in accordance with which a city is administered; by general, the unwritten laws which appear to be universally recognized" (*Rh* I.10.3). Particular appear to correspond with written and general with unwritten laws, or more precisely with unwritten, universally recognized, laws—leaving open the possibility that there are unwritten, not universally recognized laws—though it is not clear whether Aristotle would call such laws particular or general. Later, he clarifies himself: "By particular laws I mean those established by each people in reference to themselves, which again are divided into written and unwritten; by general laws I mean those based upon nature" (*Rh* I.10.3). But if general laws are universally recognized unwritten laws, then they must form part of every particular community's unwritten laws. Unwritten laws include both universally recognized laws, laws based on nature, and the unwritten rules of a particular community.[9] Natural law and custom are somehow fused.

Testimony that natural law and custom intertwine is that a city cannot exist without attending to "the divine," a city's "first" as well as "fifth" need (*Pol* 1328b2-3, 11-12, 1322b31). Apparently, "the divine" has two meanings. A city cannot last unless it heeds the naturally divine precepts, which can be known through reason, and the conventionally divine precepts, which can be known through myths (*NE* 1178b21-23; *Met* 1074b1-14). A city should above all abide by the natural truths. The natural truths reveal paradoxically, however, that human beings need other truths, or piety. Thus, reason or natural law conveys the need for customs.

Although natural law teaches the *need* for customs, customs may or may not particularize natural truths. Customs may be practices people have simply opined to be good (e.g., men should carry weapons and purchase their wives) or they may be practices people have come to know to be good, expressing natural precepts (e.g., a society cannot exist without rulers and ruled). "Laws resting on customs are more authoritative . . . than those resting on writings" (or contemporary legislation) (*Pol* 1287b5-6) because they are more likely to express natural precepts. Natural precepts are precepts societies cannot last long without heeding; they have therefore already been discovered and become embodied in customs. Legislators should thus sort out the truly good customary laws from the others by examining "collections of laws and political systems," seeking out those laws that derive from custom or that appear to be ancient and, of those, the laws that are common to all political systems. Laws that are neither simply ancient nor simply widespread, but both ancient and widespread, have stood the test of time and circumstance (*NE* 1180b20-22, 1181b6-9; *Rh* I.4.13).

Such a search yields two results. Legislators discover all the laws or legal provisions that are necessary for a regime to exist; they find embodied in ancient, widespread laws what has already been discovered and rediscovered an infinite number of times (*Pol* 1329b25-34). In addition, they see the many ways these fundamental laws can be tailored and enacted to suit various circumstances. By familiarizing themselves with traditional constitutional laws then, legislators can find the measures that will keep their own regime in existence for the longest time possible (*Pol* 1288b28-30).

Aristotle therefore clearly opposes the belief, promoted by the creatively-dressed Hippodamus, that innovation is politically salutary (*Pol* 1267b22-1268a14). From the progressive's or rationalist's point of view, new ideas are essential to political progress, and old ideas impede it. To rely on tradition for answers to political problems constitutes a failure of imagination or of creative effort. In contrast, according to Aristotle, politics calls not for imagination but for prudence, the ability to detect what works. Indeed, a regime that arises "directly out of those that exist" (*Pol* 1289a1-4) is more likely than a new one to be just and to last.[10]

Aristotle's Argument against Changing *Patrioi Nomoi*

Aristotle gives several arguments against overriding traditional laws (*patrioi nomoi*)—laws resting on custom (*Pol* 1268b26-1269a27).[11] As usual, he presents his arguments dialectically, in this case presenting first and as persuasively as possible arguments in favor of changing long-standing laws.

The first argument is that, since arts and sciences such as medicine have benefited from moving away from traditional practices, so would politics (*Pol* 1268b34-38). As Jacques Brunschwig points out, Aristotle presents this argument in a "quasi-syllogistic way" (*p* and *q*, therefore *r*) rather than as a simple hypothetical implication (if *p* and *q*, then *r*). Thus, Aristotle's premises are accepted and his argument is contained in the form; hence he announces his conclusion as evident. Aristotle's second argument is that, "in general, all seek not the traditional [*to patrion*] but the good" (1269a3-4). Brunschwig notes that this statement underscores the opening proposition of the *Politics*—that the city aims at the supreme good. Aristotle's challenge is also forceful and would have shocked his contemporaries because the adjective "patrios" had a "strong laudatory connotation." Furthermore, Aristotle observes that, because it is impossible to codify everything with precision, "it is not best to leave written [laws] unchanged" (1269a8-9). Since Aristotle does not specify the extent of change written laws may require, we must assume, Brunschwig argues, that he would sanction any change—minor or profound—as long as it rendered the law more precise. From these arguments "it is evident," Aristotle says, "that some laws must be changed at some times" (1269a12-13).[12]

Aristotle then presents his arguments against changing laws. First, he says that laws should not be changed for the sake of effecting only small improvements because it would habituate people to the dissolution of laws (*Pol* 1269a 15-16). The order law achieves by remaining unchanged compensates for any small sacrifice of justice because order is a kind or a part of justice. Thus, he points out that "the argument from the example of the arts is false. Change in an art is not like change in law; for law has no strength with respect to obedience apart from habit, and this is not created except over a period of time. Hence the easy alteration of existing laws in favor of new and different ones weakens the power of law itself" (1269a19-24). Since the premise of the earlier syllogism is false, so is its conclusion. Perhaps not altogether by accident, Aristotle thus avoids risking shock to his contemporaries. He ends the section by raising and at once setting aside two questions: "If [laws] are indeed to be changeable, are all to be, and in every regime? And by anybody, or by whom?" (1269a24-26). That he does not answer these questions here or elsewhere seems to indicate, as Jacqueline de Romilly observes, that they are rhetorical.[13]

Brunschwig insists, however, that leaving the debate on this note gives a dogmatic interpretation to an aporetic text. For, with respect to even these last remarks, Aristotle is not as conservative as he could be. In saying that laws should remain unchanged if a change would effect only a small improvement, for example, he implies that laws should be changed if the change would effect an improvement that is other than small. Brunschwig also points out that, although Aristotle says in this passage that the only way laws can elicit obedience is through habit, he says in Book V that they may do so also through education. The implication is that, because people can understand reasons for laws, they can obey new laws immediately. Finally, countering de Romilly's claim that Aristotle ends the passage as if having reached a conclusion, Brunschwig infers that the rhetorical close signifies that no conclusion is reachable once and for all. The question of whether it is good to change laws must be addressed continually by legislators in every regime. The real question, then, is not whether laws should change, but where, when, and to what extent. For, Brunschwig argues, according to Aristotle there is no natural law; that is, "in refusing to take invariability as a criterion of naturalness . . . Aristotle does not let the distinction between nature and law become absorbed in the distinction between rest and movement."[14]

A few responses to Brunschwig are in order. Although in recommending that legislators forgo changing laws just to effect small improvements Aristotle may be implying that they should make changes if great improvements would result, he is not saying that the *changes* should be great. Changes should be made only if a cautious change can bring about a significant improvement (*Pol* 1269a13-14). Second, although Brunschwig is correct to note that laws may elicit obedience by way of education, he does not comment on his own (correct) observation that education through habituation is a necessary condition of living justly. People are not likely to be reasonable without habituation (*Pol* 1253a32-33). Even the best populace should be habituated (*Pol* 1334b8-10): "We need to have been brought up in noble habits if we are to be competent students of what is noble and just, and of political questions generally" (*NE* 1095b4-6). Since regimes should not discount the importance of habit, they should not discount the importance of leaving laws unchanged.

As to Brunschwig's claim that Aristotle does not put forth a doctrine of natural law, it is misleading to conclude that he therefore believes that all law is variable. Aristotle indeed teaches that justice resides in concrete decisions rather than in general rules. Yet, as Leo Strauss points out, "one can hardly deny that in all concrete decisions general principles are implied and presupposed."[15] Aristotle implies that universally valid principles exist when he states that "all is changeable; but still there is such a thing as what is natural and what is not" and observes that "nature" intimates what is "best" (*NE* 1134b29-30, 1135a5). This is not to deny that circumstances may justify suspending these principles but to underscore that political decisions should ensue only from an earnest attempt to uphold them—a difference between Aristotle's and Machiavelli's views. In short, the requirements of natural law do not vary, the requirements of justice do.

Aristotle suggests that earlier "discoveries . . . taught by need" (*Pol* 1329b 27-28) intimate the principles of natural right. It has been discovered that all political orders need the following: sustenance, arts, arms, funds, religion, and deliberation (*Pol* 1328b5-16, 1322b29-37). Our ancestors have also discovered that a political order may fulfill its own needs by establishing the several kinds of law, which will be discussed.

Soft Laws: Marital, Health, and Population Laws

Legislators should aim to bring about a healthy populace by in effect superintending the bodies of citizens (*Pol* 1334b25-26). This can be done by way of marital, health, and population laws.

Marital Laws

Marital laws should be conducive to the procreation of healthy offspring and to the health of the couple (*Pol* 1334b32-1335a35, b29-37). If men marry around the age of thirty-seven and women around the age of eighteen, then their bodies are in their primes, their sexual desires are mutual, and their reproductive years coincide.[16] Further, they and their children are more likely to be healthy, since very young mothers often have difficult births, resulting even in their deaths; young men impede their own growth by having intercourse; and very young or old parents tend to give birth to physically and mentally defective children.[17] Finally, parents should be sufficiently older than their offspring to benefit them and win their respect but young enough to benefit from their children's assistance in old age.

Laws should not, however, require men and women to marry at certain ages. In fact, couples should "study what is said by doctors and experts in natural [science] in relation to procreation" (*Pol* 1335a39-40); men and women themselves should make an informed judgment as to when to marry and have children. One might infer from Aristotle's discussion that laws should at most make it advantageous for couples to marry at certain ages. Such laws might include a dowry law or a law imposing a fine on all single males over fifty (a modern equivalent being a higher tax rate for single persons).

Marital laws should also encourage monogamy by discouraging adultery (*Pol* 1335b38-1336a2). Adulterers, men as well as women, should be punished if their actions interfere with the conceiving and raising of children. Apparently, punishment should be no more severe than revocation of political privileges, such as eligibility for public office; in any case, the stigmatization should be appropriate to the offense.

Legislators should only loosely legislate or legislate around marital relations, presumably because they are private. To make judgments in such matters for individuals would discourage them from their spousal and parental responsibilities and deprive them of opportunities to use their own judgment, such opportunities being necessary to the cultivation of judgment.

Health Laws

Laws should also encourage fitness through moderate exercise. Moderation is important not only presumably because over- and underexertion impair health but especially because the condition of the body affects one's character or soul and ability to pursue liberal activities (*Pol* 1334b25-28). If one is routinized by and sleepy from a schedule of rigorous exercise, like an athlete, then one cannot learn or enjoy liberal pastimes (*Pol* 1335b5-11, 1339a7-10). And if men train all the time, like the Spartans, they are apt to want to prevail over others, a desire that serves war but not the rest of life. Physical prowess and the courageous disposition it engenders are not ignoble, but their nobility derives from their capacity to serve and protect the higher moral and the intellectual virtues.[18] The end of war is peace, and the end of peace, leisure (*schole*), for which is needed moderation, justice, and the virtues of the mind. Men need moderation and justice especially during peacetime, for good fortune tends to make them arrogant (*Pol* 1333a30-b16, 29-31, 1334a11-b4). Contrary to Arendt's interpretation, Aristotle thus gives no indication that ordinary political life requires citizens to have "a fiercely agonal spirit," that "the virtue of courage is one of the most elemental political attitudes."[19] When legislating health and other laws, legislators should regard temperance as more of an aim than courage, not least because it is required to live privately as well as to live well in public.

Like marital laws, health laws should only encourage rather than mandate certain conduct. Fines should apparently be the severest penalty for noncompliance (equivalent policies exist today, such as higher insurance premiums for smokers). Moreover, positive as well as negative incentives should be used to encourage compliance. The receipt of a blessing, for example, might be made contingent on walking a mile to a temple. Furthermore, it may be appropriate for laws to encourage only select groups to exercise. Oligarchies might fine the wealthy but not the poor for not exercising, for example, since the poor get enough exercise by laboring (*Pol* 1297a32-34); or legislators might deem it appropriate to situate only the goddess of childbirth a mile from the city, thus encouraging only pregnant women to walk the distance every day (*Pol* 1335b 14-16).

Legislators should use such devices to bring about not only a healthy populace but the sort of political participation that secures polity or aristocracy (*Pol* 1297a38-b1).[20] An oligarchy should not penalize the free poor for not exercising and should encourage the rich to exercise, for example, in order to give the poor more time to serve on juries or attend political assemblies. Likewise, a democracy should distract the free poor from political participation through similar measures.

Population Laws

If marital and health laws succeed, the population increases. Aristotle therefore spends an entire chapter advising legislators to restrict the number of citizens (*Pol* VII.4). He agrees with the common view that a city must be great if it is to be happy, but believes that the greatness of a city, like that of any other animate or inanimate thing, lies not in its magnitude but in its capacity to perform its function. A huge ship is not great if it cannot sail. The function of any city is to achieve self-sufficiency and order. If it has too few members, it cannot achieve self-sufficiency; if it has too many, it cannot achieve order. Order requires that the rulers fulfill their function, which is to enforce the laws and to make just decisions, and that the ruled fulfill theirs, which is to obey the laws and to elect rulers on the basis of merit. Experience shows, Aristotle says, that overpopulated cities have difficulty securing obedience to the laws. But the point can also be established theoretically: law is a system of order, and orderliness, which is a part of beauty, presupposes limits.[21] Further, rulers cannot rule justly and citizens vote justly unless they are familiar with each other's characters, an unlikely state of affairs in a populous city. Aristotle also theoretically grounds the connection between ruling and population size: ruling and legislating are arts, and like other arts they require suitable materials. A carpenter cannot build a house with three planks, a painter cannot paint a portrait on the side of a barn. He has already made this point with respect to household management: "There is a limit with respect to what exists for the sake of the end" (*Pol* 1257b27-31). Finally, a moderate-sized population makes it easier to marshal and command forces for war; a city's preservation may depend directly on order.

Aristotle recommends two laws as means to limit population: one fixes the number of children allowed to each couple, and one prohibits the raising of deformed children (*Pol* 1335b19-26). If a couple conceives beyond the limit, then the embryo should be aborted (but before "perception and life arises"). If a deformed child is born, then it should be exposed. Aristotle realizes that not all parents would comply with such laws, but he does not say what the consequence for noncompliance should be.

One is thus reminded of his earlier recommendation that legislators leave the upholding of marital and health laws largely to the judgment, or one might say the conscience, of individuals. Good marital, health, and reproductive practices should be more a matter of custom or habit, not only because they are essential to the preservation of a city, but because their being matters for private judgment is essential to the city's goodness.

Laws to Prevent Domestic Conflict: Economic and Penal

In addition to a healthy populace, all cities need arms, both to keep domestic peace and ward off external aggression (*Pol* 1328b7-10). Aristotle indicates his belief that internal discord, in the form of either faction or crime, threatens the existence of a regime more than war does by his greater attention to the causes and prevention of the former. He may have been persuaded of the destructiveness of domestic conflict by Plato, whose Socrates observes that "the name faction is applied to the hatred of one's own, war to the hatred of the alien."[22] In any case, legislators should make sure to establish a police or guard as well as a military.

Causes and Signs of Faction and Crime

In order to institute other measures to preclude civic conflict, legislators need to recognize its signs, causes, and facilitating circumstances (*Pol* 1302a 18-22). The chief cause of conflict is the desire for money and recognition. Men fight with one another even to the point of demanding constitutional change in order to gain or avoid losing either (1302a31-34). Legislators should realize, at the same time, that most people probably do not seek both profit and honor, since most tend to prefer one thing above all else, believing that it will bring happiness (*NE* 1095a18-24). In fact, most people prefer money and what it can buy—namely, pleasure—to recognition and what it can bring—namely, power. Consequently, they would usually rather attend to their private business than hold public office (*Pol* 1308b34-37). Appreciating that people prefer to participate in public life to different extents, rather than assuming that everyone wants to, is important to preserving a regime. A practical arrangement would assign offices only to those desiring recognition or power, or, in other words, would accommodate a range of desires for privacy.

In regimes not so arranged, civic conflict is more likely to occur. The chief sign of such trouble, to which legislators should be alert, is the widespread perception of inequality—either when many perceive an inequality of condition, believing themselves to have less wealth or fewer prerogatives than those they consider their equals, or when they perceive an inequality among persons, believing themselves to have the same or less wealth or power than those they consider inferior. Such groups may complain to gain their perceived due, equality or superiority (*Pol* 1301b26-27, 1302a24-31). The desire for justice does not, however, necessarily coincide with self-interest; men may wrangle because they think *others* lack their due in wealth or prerogatives (1302a38-b2). Whether seeking justice for themselves or for others, they may be doing so unjustifiably, since their perceptions may be mistaken (1280a9-16, 1282b18-23, 1302a28-29, 40-b1). Most people are poor judges particularly of their own situations; they may not in fact merit what they desire. But they may be mistaken also about the situations of others, who may in fact merit the wealth and prerogatives they have. Aristotle thus implies that legislators should respond to the demands of citizens only if they coincide with those of justice, which is the common advantage (1282b16-18).

Legislators should also recognize situations and conduct that remind men of their relative material and political status and thereby give rise to disputes. Arrogance in rulers, for example, can make the ruled want to overthrow them; rulers who are overly fearful of the people, though, may unnecessarily suppress them and so incite faction. Then there is always the possibility, of which legislators should be aware, that a person or persons either inside or outside the government has potentially disruptive monarchical or dynastic aspirations (*Pol* 1302b2-5, V.3).[23]

The predominant philosophical point to emerge from these remarks is the distinction between the sense of justice and the feeling of envy. On this point, Aristotle and a contemporary liberal philosopher, John Rawls, agree: they both argue that, though "the appeal to justice is often a mask for envy," a genuine "sense of justice" is not, as Freud claims, "the outgrowth of envy and jealousy."[24] Envy cannot be the basis for, or accompany, the sense of justice, because, like some other feelings such as spite, it does not have a mean; some sentiments, not their excesses or deficiencies, are themselves base (*NE* 1107a 9-14). In contrast to Rawls, however, Aristotle does not think that politics should proceed from the assumption of universal rationality.[25] Although human beings can be educated to recognize that equality of distribution is not the same as justice, education will not eradicate envy and legislators should thus use other means to mitigate it.

The Middle Class

One measure Aristotle recommends to preclude conflict is increasing the middle class (*Pol* 1296a7-9). When the middle class predominates, people perceive existing inequalities to be less great (1295b29-33, 1308b30-31). The poor do not feel as poor because they see that the middle class also has less than the rich, and the rich are less fearful of the poor because they see that the middle class also has property interests. Moreover, those of middling means do not envy the rich because they are not in want and do not perceive themselves as greatly unequal to them. In short, the middle class is neither envied nor envious. According to both rich and poor, this makes those of middling means trustworthy, objective judges, and thus worthy of ruling (1297a5-6, *DA* 424a6). Rich and poor also welcome the rule of the middle class because their alternative, to join forces against it, is not in their interest; depending on which is in the minority, their collaboration would eventuate in the submission of one class to the other—the rich would enslave the poor or the poor would reduce the rich to their level by distributing their property (1296a1-3, b40-1297a5). Furthermore, there is no guarantee that this new aggregate could predominate over the middle class.

But how can a regime increase its middle class? We know that legislating property redistribution, as Phaleas recommends, is not a solution, because individual initiative and lack thereof would soon reestablish inequality. Aristotle proposes a few ways laws might help achieve parity of income (*Pol* 1309a14-25). Without redistributing the income of the wealthy, they might restrict family inheritances and allow only one inheritance per individual. In addition, a regime could allot the better-paid public offices to the poor. Such laws are desirable in that they do not alter the fundamental nature of the regime (1296b34-38). But it is doubtful that they alone can effect much of a redistribution. By raising this doubt, Aristotle calls to mind his recommendation that all regimes accommodate a market economy.[26] He helps confirm that he believes the market should effect redistribution when he includes "an abundance of money" on his list of things a city cannot exist without (1328b 10, 1322b32-33). The constitutional laws of a regime should provide for a market just as they should provide for a military or any other political necessity. Maintaining a market is a way of increasing the middle class without weakening the authority of the laws by continually changing them. Citizens are not likely to resist incremental redistribution which they largely control and which does not alter the fundamental nature or constitution of the regime.

Aristotle makes clear, then, that the aim of increasing the middle class is not homogeneity or even increased political participation but avoidance of civil disobedience and, thus, preservation of the regime. Increasing the middle class is a means, not an end; if measures taken to favor the middle class (such as inheritance and tax laws) create conflict, then they should not be maintained. The regime's stability is paramount, and the sign of stability is the prevailing support of the regime by its citizens (*Pol* 1309b14-18, 1294b36-40, 1296b14-16).

Criminal Punishment

Another way regimes should safeguard themselves against civil disobedience and other criminal activity is by instituting a penal system. Its presence should deter some of the criminally inclined and its punishments may discourage recidivism.

Aristotle does not seem to recommend severe punishments for crimes, mentioning in the *Politics* primarily fines, exile, and "dishonor" (probably, public stigmatization by revocation of political privileges) as penalties for breaking laws. He does discuss the matter of guarding prisoners but does not give examples of offenses warranting incarceration (perhaps, then, they are few) (*Pol* 1321b40-1322a29, b35). Nor does he mention capital punishment. He apparently thinks that physical punishment other than incarceration is appropriate only for the very young (1336b7-11). But other arguments compete against these. That the many are usually poor (1279b37-38) suggests that fines are a futile way to punish them. The suggestion that beating is appropriate for punishing only the very young occurs in the context of a discussion of the best regime, in which all older persons are virtuous. Aristotle describes "the many" in much the same way that Hobbes describes all human beings—as seekers of pleasure and avoiders of pain. By nature, fear of pain, not shame, motivates them to reasonable conduct. Indeed, in the *Nicomachean Ethics*, Aristotle says that the many yield not (at least initially) to argument but to force (*bia*) or the threat of force, compulsion (*anangke*) (1179b11, 28-29, 1180a4-5). He also claims that retributive justice entails returning "evil for evil" (1132b34-1133a1), except in the case where one party is an official (1132b28-30), and apparently endorses a proposal put forth by Plato that the pains (*tas lupas*) inflicted to punish a transgressor of the law should be those "that are most opposed to the pleasures he desires" (1180a12-14). Although this implies fines rather than incarceration or other physical punishment for tax evaders, embezzlers, and other "white-collar" criminals (and presumably an amount proportional to the amount stolen—that is, to the amount of pleasure sought), it implies equally that murder should beget execution, and in the way the murder was carried out,[27] and that the punishment for rape should be castration or some such debilitating measure (today, perhaps pharmaceutical). One is reminded of the injunction in *Exodus* 21:23-25. But Aristotle advances "an eye for an eye" not only on behalf of (divine) justice but with a view to deterrence (*Pol*

1332a11-14). He may not present the above extrapolations because they are unseemly.

In sum, Aristotle's recommendations for preempting domestic conflict—maintaining a police force, increasing the middle class, and instituting a penal system—are designed to maintain obedience to the laws and not otherwise to make better men. Nonetheless, civil obedience is a precondition of virtue, order, a precondition of justice.[28]

Laws Concerning War

A city needs not only to suppress internal conflict but to defend itself against attack from outside (*Pol* 1328b7-10, 1333b40-41). Given that the ability to ward off aggression is basic to the survival of anything, Aristotle's recommendation that a regime institute a standing militia is not surprising. This preservative precaution hardly needs to be pointed out to legislators. What legislators might be less certain about is whether offensive wars are necessary to the survival of a regime. This they must know in order to allocate adequate resources to the military and to have a sense of the extent to which they should prepare a regime for war.

On the one hand, Aristotle denounces the laws of Sparta and Crete for their pronounced concern with domination; they make war a way of life and victory the aim of the regimes. He also gives the impression of disapproving of the Scythians, the Persians, the Thracians, the Celts, and others for admiring and honoring the power to dominate. In the same tone, he reports laws and customs that reward men for killing enemies (*Pol* 1324b5-21). In addition, he points out that it is not lawful to conquer and rule neighboring regimes without regard to their wishes, for it disregards their free status, their ability to rule themselves. It is indeed noble to rule over free persons, but such rule cannot be achieved by sheer might. In sum, a regime preoccupied with war harms both itself and others (1324b22-34, 1333b26-36).

On the other hand, an offensive war is justified in two cases: when a free people is in need of outside leadership, and when a people has no potential to rule itself (*Pol* 1333b41-1334a2). Assuming the leadership of these peoples is justified because it benefits them. Although, in the first case, people's consent is not required to justify hegemony over them, the people might be grateful to outside leadership for ordering the regime; in effect, their consent may follow rather than precede the intervention. Moreover, if such people are free, such hegemony should be temporary, removed once their ability to rule themselves has been restored. In the second case, since the naturally slavish cannot reason on their own (1254b22-23, 1260a12), consent per se cannot be forthcoming. But natural slaves do not object to proper mastery: "he is a slave by nature who is capable of belonging to another" (1254b20-21).[29] The summary point, however ironic, is that aggression over neighboring peoples is justified only if accompanied, or at least followed, by prudence and moderation. If peoples who are not ruling themselves pose a threat to a neighboring regime, and the instability of a neighboring people is great or persistent, then intervention is not only noble but necessary. In any case, although a regime may or may not be justified in using force against such peoples for the sake of its own self-preservation, their unpredictability justifies a regime's being *prepared* for an offensive war. Aristotle does not, then, justify so much offensive war as military preparedness for offensive war, as a means to survival.

His teaching to legislators about war might be put as follows. Next to a virtuous populace, the noblest end a regime can achieve is peace. Peace is noble because it facilitates virtue, but it is also necessary for the preservation of a regime. To achieve peace, a regime must be prepared to wage both defensive and offensive wars. But the nature and extent of military preparedness must be compatible with peace and civilian, liberal pursuits. The nature and extent of any aggression must be such as to allow civilians to continue or at least to return to living in a liberal way. War must always serve peace, and peace, virtue (*Pol* 1325a5-7, 1333a30-b3, 14-16, 29-31, 38-1334a 10).[30]

Religious Laws

As noted earlier, religion is fifth and penultimate in Aristotle's list of things that must be present for a city to exist (*Pol* 1328b11-12). Religion should be part of a city, but should not be part of government (1299a17-19, 1322b18-19). Though Aristotle seems to be among the first political philosophers to advise the separation of church and state, he does not uphold a strict or modern version of that doctrine. His list of a city's indispensable items suggests that religion should be as separate from government as are the military and the economy; laws should establish nonpolitical offices to maintain it.[31] Priests, like generals and market managers, should be accessible and responsive to government but should function independently. Just as government should be able to command the military (to go to battle) and to impose higher sales taxes, so it should be able to instruct the religious establishment to induce people to pay revenues, to exercise, or perhaps to have more or fewer children (1330a8-9, 1335b14-16). Such inducements are necessary in ordinary cities because of the recalcitrance of most citizens to reason.[32] The presence of "the gods," or the promulgation of myths that explain their presence, can be as effective as the presence of a police force and a penal system in eliciting subscription to the laws.

But religion is superior to the threat of force (and perhaps therefore listed by Aristotle after arms, second only to political offices) in that it does not seek to suppress passions but to provide a means by which they can be expressed without endangering the regime. Religion can fuse *pathos* and *ethos* without (unlike rhetoric) the use of *logos;* it moves people to comply with the laws without requiring them to follow arguments.

Religion can render citizens not only obedient to the laws but respectful of authority in general and fearful of shame, attributes belonging to "free persons" (*Pol* 1331a40-b1). It therefore belongs even in the best regime. Since the proximity and counsel of priests tends to edify citizens, Aristotle recommends that most places for worship be conspicuous and near the citizens' recreational area (excepting those places required by religious law to be removed from the city) (1331a24-35). In general, at any rate, legislators should remember that laws should remind citizens of the gods.[33]

In either case, whether serving mere obedience or virtue, preservation or a higher justice, religion should serve the regime, not vice versa; for once religious aims displace political ones, privacy is endangered. Religion that does not recognize the sanctity of the human realm aspires to obliterate the distinction between public and private. Thus the fundamental laws of a regime should ensure that religion remains civil.[34]

Political Laws: Offices and Entitlement

The last, most important item on Aristotle's list of things a city cannot exist without, "the most necessary thing of all," is a public system of judgment or "offices" (*Pol* 1328b13-14, 1291a22-24, 34-36). The discussion suggests that they are the most important constitutional provision because they compensate for law's inadequacy to judge particulars; the rule of law is perfect or complete (only) in the sense that it provides for its own deficiency (1292a32-34).

Government needs many offices, but only two general sorts—deliberative and judicial. By judicial offices Aristotle means civil and criminal court posts, including juries. By deliberative offices he means the political offices. The deliberative element should have authority over foreign policy (matters of war and peace and alliances), over the laws, over (judicial) cases calling for severe punishment (the death penalty, exile, or confiscation), and over the appointment and auditing of officials (within government as well as appointments to military, religious, bureaucratic, and other such posts) (*Pol* 1298a3-6). Thus, the deliberative offices have legislative and higher judicial functions. What is more, not only "deliberation and judgment concerning certain matters" but "particularly command" characterize political offices (1299a25-28). Aristotle not only assigns an executive function to what he calls the deliberative element but seemingly paradoxically says that its main function is to execute.[35] This makes sense, however, given his teaching that regimes should arise out of those that exist. The fundamental laws of a regime are given to men (in *patrioi nomoi*) to be executed, but their perpetuation and preservative function depend on their being adjusted to circumstances and thus on human discretion. It seems then that nature sanctions the sovereignty of deliberation for the sake of itself—for the sake of perpetuating the actualization of natural law and perpetuating human nature. To perpetuate the actualization of its universals, it is not enough for nature to make them felt or to impose them on human beings; it must give the agents of their actualization some authority over them (*NE* 1134b18-1135a5). Ironically, then, the rule of *patrioi nomoi* is superior to the rule of men in that it accommodates and invites their rule as a means to perpetuate itself; the rule of men is not inimical to but in fact the catalyst of the rule of law. In sum, Aristotle wants to demonstrate that there cannot be purely executive, legislative, and judicial functions. Executors must judge, and legislators and judges must execute.[36]

The Preservative Tasks of Rulers

Aristotle's references to both "legislators" and "political rulers" (or "experts in politics") in his political works proposes a division of labor within the deliberative offices, evidently between those who have authority over the laws—the preservative laws—and those who rule otherwise. Like legislators, other rulers should seek to preserve the regime.[37] In chapter 8 of Book V of the *Politics*, Aristotle discusses the preservative tasks of rulers.

First of all, for a regime to exist, its inhabitants must perform specific actions necessary to the regime's functioning. The objective of political rule, which issues commands, is to ensure the performance of such substantive actions. But it can achieve this only if rulers and subjects recognize the authority of the laws by subscribing to them. In that the activity of ruling postulates association in terms of laws (*Pol* 1270b29-31), it must seek to preserve them. The commands of rulers should not transgress the laws even in a minor way, for minor transgressions eventually transform the regime (1289a19-20, 1307a40-b6, 30-34). Rulers are thus responsible for seeing that the activities law mandates as private remain private.

That ruling presupposes law indicates that the validity or authenticity of commands derives from law. An authentic command reflects the spirit of the laws; oligarchies issue oligarchic commands, democracies democratic ones, and so forth. Simply, an authoritative, or just, command respects or expresses law (*Pol* 1289a18-19).[38] As Aristotle explains, there are two sorts of good political order or, literally, good rule according to law (*eunomia*): when the laws of a regime are obeyed, and when they are both obeyed and the best (1294a4-6).

The next most important preservative task of rulers is to maintain good relations with one another and with the ruled. The first they may achieve by treating one another "in a democratic spirit of equality." As Aristotle says throughout his political works, democratic principles should obtain among the equally capable; the best place for democracy is *within* government or the governing class. Office holders might restrict their tenure, for example, to give their peers turn in office or a particular office. (This tenure should, however, be the longest possible to take advantage of experience; *Pol*

1261a38-39.) In aristocracies and oligarchies, such a rotational policy prevents the concentration of power in a particular family; in democracies, it prevents the rise of demagogues (1308a3-7, 10-24).

In Book IV of the *Politics*, Aristotle hints that the best way for rulers to maintain good relations with the ruled is to maintain their privacy. Political rule should direct all or a part of the citizenry only in certain matters, such as war or the supervision of children (1299a20-22). Book V, chapter 8 explains more ways rulers should keep the ruled content. They should appoint to political posts those among the ruled who demonstrate leadership ability or ambition, for example (1308a7-9). Such appointees as well as those already in government should, however, be advanced by degrees, not only to test their ability to uphold certain responsibilities but to prevent old boy networks, nepotism, and the like (1308b10-18). In addition, rulers may assign the least authoritative, nonpolitical offices to the ruled. The well-off in a democracy and the poor in an oligarchy could, for example, be assigned to religious, military, bureaucratic, judicial,[39] and penal posts (1322b31-36). These posts differ with respect to the amount of "experience and trust" they require. If distributing civil service appointments or pseudo-political power among the ruled satisfies their desires for recognition, then it is presumably another way—in addition to instituting a police, a penal system, and a free market economy—to safeguard a regime against civil disobedience. It should be noticed, however, that rulers, not laws, should distribute authority to the ruled (on an ad hoc basis); such distribution should not be a constitutional provision or, as we would say, a right. At any rate, rulers should not generally appease the ruled by granting them political power (1309a31-32, 1321a31-32), for it would not preserve the regime. Finally, rulers should also (indirectly) treat the ruled fairly by keeping their own salaries moderate (1308b31-33).

In the remainder of the chapter, Aristotle lists other general preservative measures. Rulers should keep alive or not try to dispel fears about the security of the regime that grip a populace, for such fears make the latter more protective of and willing to defend the regime. Rulers should intervene in disputes among the distinguished members of a regime, for these can escalate into faction.[40] Rulers should adjust property qualifications for office to take into account fluctuations in the value of currency.[41] And they should rely less on devices than on the laws to control who participates in the regime. This apparently miscellaneous list of tasks might be condensed into the general maxim that rulers should err on the side of caution, or always rule conservatively.

The Expert in Politics

Rulers can best achieve their conservative objectives if they employ a conservative mode of discourse. By employing this mode, which is rhetoric properly understood, they will persuade the ruled to obey their commands and policies. Since proper rhetoric combines *logos* with *ethos* and *pathos*, a rhetorician not only demonstrates his point logically but reveals his character and appeals to the characters and emotional state of his audience (*Rh* I.2.3). An effective appeal requires accepting uncritically, not examining in Socratic fashion, the common opinions of an audience or the public morality.[42] A ruler who refuses to accept this morality but proceeds to try to persuade is a mere sophist or dogmatist. One who insists on examining prevailing beliefs is not an expert in politics but a philosopher or skeptic.

Rhetoric, then, depends on the character of a populace, which in turn depends on the nature of the laws.[43] In contrast to the Sophists, Aristotle implies that law must regulate the arts because the reason inherent in law, unlike the reason inherent in the arts, is of the highest sort.[44] For the art of ruling to subordinate itself to the rule of law, it must—like the other arts—recognize its limits (*Pol* 1257b25-28). Experts in politics should not try to remake the world with causes or ideologies. Their virtue and justice relative to the regime and affection for it compel them to carry out the laws (1309a34-37, 1270b29-31), issuing commands only over particulars to achieve equity (*NE* 1137b27-32). In addition to love for the regime, love for their work—not an agonistic desire for power—motivates them (*Pol* 1309a35), though industry may look like the quest for power to others.[45]

Aristotle's conception of political rule thus contrasts with a prevalent unreflective liberal view, derived primarily from Hobbes and Locke, according to which "power is the capacity . . . to subordinate the wills of others to one's own will" and is a "cause of antagonism in society." On this view, "the more one man's desire for power is satisfied, the more will his fellows' wish for it remain frustrated."[46] Aristotle instead teaches that rulers can in fact satisfy the ruled by exercising their power prudently, can even make them glad to be ruled and to be able to attend to their own affairs (*Pol* 1321a31-39, 1297b6-8, 1308b34-37).

Monarchy versus Aristocracy

If, as Aristotle seems to imply, only the prudent should be entitled to hold political offices, then should not a human being whose prudence surpasses that of everyone else be entitled to hold all the offices—that is, to be king? Indeed, according to P. A. Vander Waerdt, Aristotle argues that if there exists a man so virtuous as to be able to govern alone, he should do so, for this would allow all citizens to devote themselves to the liberal arts.[47] It is indisputable that the rule of one supremely virtuous man appeals to Aristotle (*Pol* 1284b32-34) and likely that it appeals to him for the reason Vander Waerdt suggests, but Aristotle indicates several problems with such an arrangement, the main one being that, unlike a plurality of offices, a single office cannot be counted on to ensure the sovereignty of deliberation.

First, who should be king is not likely to be evident, for "it is not as easy to see the beauty of the soul as it is that of the body" (*Pol* 1254b39). Second, because of this difficulty, even good men may not agree on who is preeminent among them. Third, even if an outstanding man were detected and unanimously nominated to rule, he would be reluctant to claim the honor of ruling over all, preferring to give the honor to a friend (*NE* 1169a29-30). Although such a man would prefer to give up riches, honors, and offices to friends, he "would choose . . . to live nobly for a year, rather than for many years in a chancy way" (*NE* 1169a23-24); despite his preferences, he would rise to the occasion if called on. Short-term rule by an outstanding man is thus morally possible for him. Ordinary men might also agree more readily to be ruled by one man for just a year. On the other hand, rule of even the best man might get better—an argument for his continued rule (*Pol* 1261a38-39). The assumption of the existence of several exceptional men also undercuts the argument for monarchy, since it is not evident that we should assume the possibility of the existence of even one who is "like a god among human beings" (*Pol* 1284a11, b30-31). Even if we suppose with Vander Waerdt, as it seems we should, that Aristotle is recommending for king one whose virtue is heroic rather than philosophical,[48] such virtue seems to be unattainable by Aristotle's own account. Vander Waerdt says that, although "heroic virtue . . . transforms men into gods and places them beyond the sphere of human virtue and vice," such virtue is nonetheless humanly possible because it "is an excess of [human] virtue (*aretes huperbole*)."[49] But Aristotle indicates that this superhuman virtue must remain an aspiration, for every human soul necessarily has the passionate element (*Pol* 1286a18-20), which is able to pervert or twist even the best men (*aristous andras*) (1287a28-32); not even their passions always accord with virtue.

Aristotle therefore favors aristocracy over monarchy: "The judgment of a single person is necessarily corrupted when he is dominated by anger or some other passion of this sort, whereas it is hard for all to become angry and err at the same time" (*Pol* 1286a33-35). If, then, there are several persons who are "excellent in soul, just like the single person," they should rule, since they would be "more incorruptible" than the individual (1286b2-3, 1286a31-33); in other words, "if it is just for the excellent man to rule because he is better, two good persons are better than one" (1287b12-13).[50] Accordingly, Aristotle describes the regime in which virtue is honored above all as an aristocracy, not a monarchy (1273a41-b1, 1278a18-20), and states: "If, then, the rule of a number of persons who are all good men is to be regarded as aristocracy, and the rule of a single person as kingship, aristocracy would be more choiceworthy for cities than kingship . . . provided it is possible to find a number of persons who are similar" (1286b3-7).[51]

The Status of Democracy

Legislators cannot assume that several men equally preeminent in virtue exist in most regimes; it would be "a work of chance" if they existed in any regime (*Pol* 1332b16-23, 1331b21-22; *Rh* I.1.7). What qualification, then, should preservative laws establish for holding office? Only virtue legitimately entitles human beings to rule others, but a city needs wealth and manpower (1296b17-19); since virtue is scarce, regimes should allow also the wealthy and the people (those who are neither wealthy nor virtuous) to hold offices. It should be noticed, first, that this argument for allowing those who are less than virtuous authority does not appeal to justice or fairness (only persons who are similar deserve equal treatment; 1332b27). Second, Aristotle does not think that all those allowed authority should be allowed the same kind and amount of authority, as will be discussed. Third, he cautions us not to confuse a system that grants all free persons entitlement to participate in the regime with democracy. Democracy does not, in theory or in practice, allow all to rule.[52]

Aristotle arrives at the formal definition of democracy by reasoning (1) that democracy is the opposite of oligarchy, (2) that oligarchy is rule by the propertied, and therefore (3) that democracy is rule by those who lack a significant amount of property or are poor (*Pol* 1279b7-9, 17-19, 39-40). The poor tend to be the majority; the majority is—not by definition but by accident—poor (1280a3-4).[53] Thus even in actual democracies not everyone, but rather the majority, rules (1291b37-38, 1317b3-7). There is therefore confusion about what democracy is; it is rule by the poor, but since the poor are also many, it is thought to be rule by the many (*Pol* III.8). The many in particular reject the definition of democracy as rule by the poor, believing that number constitutes a just claim to rule. They maintain that whatever the majority resolves is just, since each of the citizens has a say. In their view, majority rule is a mark and defining principle of a free regime (1317b3-11, 1291b34-38).

In addition to empowering the poor majority, democracy in principle allows one to live as one wants. Like most human beings, democrats regard freedom as the greatest good. But they reason that, since not living as one wants is characteristic of a person who is enslaved, living as one wants is characteristic of a person who is free. Thus, they prize freedom of expression above all else—above wealth, family, or virtue. From their presuppositions that living freely is the greatest good and living as one wants is living freely, they claim the right to political freedom; that is, they claim that living freely requires freedom from any government interference and, failing that, the freedom to rule and be ruled in turn. They accept rotational rule because, in distributing authority to every citizen without regard to personal merit, it upholds the democratic notion of justice as equality (without regard to equality in what things) (*Pol* 1317a40-b4, 11-17; *NE* 1131a12-29).

Notable characteristics of democracy include "election to all offices from among all"; "having all offices chosen by lot, or those not requiring experience and skill"; "having offices not based on any property qualification, or based on the smallest possible"; "the same person not holding any office more than once, or doing so rarely"; "having all offices of short duration . . . where . . . possible"; and "having all or [persons selected] from all exercise judicial functions" over "the greatest and most authoritative matters" (*Pol* 1317b17-1318a3). Thus, many offices do not require any knowledge, experience, or wealth, and most offices, because of their short tenure, do not enable one to acquire any knowledge, experience, or wealth. In other words, in a democracy an ignorant, inexperienced, and poor majority rules.[54]

Yet this characterization does not take into account Aristotle's discussion of the merits of collective judgment, which points out that, although the individuals constituting most multitudes lack virtue, they may by acting in concert surpass in virtue and thus judgment individuals superior in virtue (*Pol* 1281a42-b5). This cannot, however, be said about all multitudes, since some are beastly (1281b15-20). That a multitude only *might* have good judgment means that it is not safe to have it fill the highest offices, for it might commit injustices or simply make mistakes (1281b26-28).

In sum, it becomes clear that Aristotle indicts democracy, and even more particularly the democratic character: "Low birth, poverty, and vulgarity" characterize the many (*Pol* 1317b40-41).[55] Lacking self-restraint and prudence and insisting that living by no standard is the best standard, they live deviantly. Democracy is thus itself, in a word, a deviation (1279b4-6).

Polity

The form of regime second best to aristocracy is polity, in which the minority—the wealthy and the virtuous—as well as the majority are entitled to hold office. Although the shortcomings of democracy suggest that the majority should not be given any authority, denying it to them would necessarily fill the city with enemies, risking rebellion (*Pol* 1281b28-30). Moreover, a multitude, regardless of its other positive or negative attributes, is a multitude of bodies, which a city needs for defense. Defense may not be forthcoming if the multitude is dissatisfied with the regime. If the multitude were shrewd, then it would stake its claim to rule not on majority opinion or freedom but on "military virtue" (1279b1-2).[56] But the many believe that the only way to serve themselves is to rule themselves, not to contribute to the needs of the regime.[57]

Although Aristotle's conclusion—that a regime, in order to survive, should allow money and free birth as well as virtue to entitle human beings to office—is a concession to the scarcity of virtue, a practical argument, he believes that a regime should seek justice or proportionate equality as much as possible within the limitations imposed by nature or chance. It may do so by making its deliberative offices open only to the virtuous or educated and the other, predominantly judicial, offices open to others.[58] Such a policy may contribute to the duration of the regime as well. But polity is a durable form of regime also because it can be tailored to the attributes of a particular populace: in some polities, more offices must be open to free birth than to wealth or virtue; in others, more to wealth than to virtue. Still, legislators should aim for a good mixture: "It should be possible for the same polity to be spoken of as either a democracy or an oligarchy"; but where possible a polity should "be spoken of most particularly as aristocracy" (*Pol* 1294b15-16, 1294a23-24).

Polity lies between democracy and aristocracy, then, in recognizing but differentiating all claims to office.[59] Democracy overlooks that a city cannot be self-sufficient without expertise (*Pol* 1277a5-11, 1273b5, 1261b14-15). How can individuals be "partners and helpers" to one another[60] if no one is very good at anything because all are at once free to live as they want but required to be available for political office? Falling short of self-sufficiency, not to say justice, democracy is not a durable sort of regime (1332b28-29, 1253a1, 1326a12-13). By contrast, polity is more viable (1294b34-40).

How can a regime distribute the most important offices to those worthy of them without instilling resentment and provoking unrest among those not worthy of them? Aristotle indicates that this task may be less difficult than it might seem. Contrary to Hobbes's later claim, not all people have an unceasing desire for power after power. In fact, "no one would ask for office unless he were honor-loving" (*Pol* 1271a15-16).[61] Desire for political recognition is not universal; some desire gain or pleasure instead or more. Legislators should not assume, then, that those not honored with office or an important office will be envious of or hostile toward those so honored.

Three sorts of people in particular prefer not to participate in political life. The poor would in fact rather work than either hold office or go to war.[62] They "are even glad if someone leaves them the leisure for their private affairs (*tois idiois*)" (*Pol* 1297b6-12, 1308b35-36, 1318b12-17). The well-off are not always inclined to public service; having to or preferring to manage their business affairs, they sometimes swear that serving would cost them financially or impose other burdens.[63] Since the interests of the wealthy should be spoken for, a regime should not allow them to decline office, even if they pay a fine for not serving (1297a19-20). But it can be inferred that, if a regime is more in need of their money than of their service (or the services of all of them), then it should make the wealthy's preference and ability to pay work to its advantage. Those who shun public service the most, even more than the rich and the poor, are the philosophical, those who find the greatest happiness in the activity of the intellect; for such activity thrives in solitude (*NE* 1177a 12-b2; *Pol* 1267a10-11).

Although these different sorts of people desire particular ends—subsistence, wealth, thought—they all desire the opportunity to pursue a good. Privacy is, strictly speaking, a means to fulfill their desires; but insofar as means are bound to their ends, these people desire privacy itself as much as their particular ends. Further, insofar as the pursuit of their ends requires some form of virtue—industry, prudence, or the highest human capacity—they all desire privacy as if it were a potential to be realized. The paradox that the human desire for privacy makes political life possible thus emerges.

If there are, and surely there are, some among the less virtuous who demand to participate in political decision making, then legislators might do the following: either allow some number from the multitude to be elected to the deliberative body, or allow the people to consider issues that have already been considered by the members of a preliminary council, a council of law guardians or some such office. "In this way the people will share in deliberating but will not be able to overturn anything connected to the regime" (*Pol* 1298b27-32).[64]

Although the limited participation of the less virtuous serves a regime, the nonparticipation of the philosophical is not desirable; legislators should not welcome philosophers' reluctance to perform public service and should contrive a way to make them serve. Since public service interferes with the activity of philosophy, legislators should figure out a way for them to serve indirectly, a way for a regime to benefit from the wisdom of philosophers without invading their privacy. Perhaps that way is to learn from ancient law or custom: if the presence, writings, and teachings of philosophers influence ways of life, then those ways of life as embodied in laws and customs may transmit the political teachings of philosophers. Philosophers perform their public service posthumously by leaving a legacy of political ideas. Thus, a regime may leave philosophers undisturbed while benefiting from philosophical wisdom. By leaving philosophers alone, then, a regime ensures its future or longevity.

Notes

1. I use the following abbreviations for Aristotle's texts: *NE* = *Nicomachean Ethics*, *Pol* = *Politics*, *Rh* = *The "Art" of Rhetoric*, *Met* = *Metaphysics*, *DA* = *De Anima*, *AC* = *Athenian Constitution*. Translations are my own in consultation with several other translations.

2. Hannah Arendt, *The Human Condition* (Chicago: University of Chicago Press, 1958), 194-98, 223-30; Richard Bodéüs, *Le philosophe et la cité: Recherches sur les rapports entre morale et politique dans la pensée d'Aristote* (Paris: Société d'Édition 1982), 85-86, 108-14, 125-29. Aristotle makes this point in the last chapter of Book II of the *Politics*, where he distinguishes between legislators who were "craftsmen of laws only," such as Draco, Pittacus, and Androdamas of Rhegium, and those brought about "a regime as well," such as

Lycurgus and Solon (1273b32-33). The difference between the two groups is not, as might be thought, that the first merely added laws to existing regimes whereas the second founded wholly new regimes; both groups evidently relied on existing provisions (1273b41-1274a1, b15-24). (This stands as evidence, of which more follows in this article, that Aristotle does not regard legislators, even such celebrated ones as Solon, as founders of new modes and orders as did Machiavelli.) The difference is rather that the laws of Draco, Pittacus, and Androdamas only prohibited bad actions rather than encouraged good conduct and government. Aristotle praises Solon's legislation, and although he is not uncritical of the Spartan way of life, his point is to contrast the two ways of legislating and to proclaim in favor of bringing about a way of life. In doing so he is criticizing, as he does elsewhere, the liberal view according to which a regime is reducible to a contract. Rule by *lex* or contemporary legislative acts that are merely legal in intention and scope can achieve only a rights-based alliance; by contrast, rule by *nomos* aspires to bring about a just and good way of life. See *The Politics of Aristotle*, Ernest Barker, trans. (Oxford: Clarendon, 1948), lxxi-lxxii.

3. First, he says in effect that, although one might think that an advantage of rule by men is their ability to address difficult matters of justice, if laws cannot address difficult matters, then neither can a human being (*Pol* 1287a23-25). This observation reminds us that men make laws, but the point is that we should not confuse the ability to judge particulars with the ability to judge difficult matters. When measured by the latter, men are no better than laws. Second, one might think that an advantage of law is that it can oversee many matters at once; but Aristotle suggests that several persons could do so (*Pol* 1287b8-9). The law-versus-men debate thus leads to a debate over whether the rule of one or of a plurality is more choiceworthy, a debate discussed later in this article. For now, it suffices to say that, on balance, Aristotle argues that the rule of some is safer than the rule of one. He thereby puts to rest the thought that law is advantageous because of the scope of matters it can address.

4. For a discussion of Aristotle's concept of leisure, see chapter six of my book, *The Public and the Private in Aristotle's Political Philosophy* (Ithaca: Cornell University Press, 1992).

5. *Politics*, Barker, lxxi.

6. See H. J. Wolff, "'Normenkontrolle' und Gesetzesbegriff in der attischen Demokratie," *Sitzungsberichte der Heidelberger Akademie der Wissenschaften, philosophisch-historische Klasse*, no. 2 (Heidelberg: Jahrgang, 1970), 68-76.

7. See also *Politics*, Barker, lxxi.

8. See also *Politics*, Barker, 366.

9. As Martin Ostwald observes, the meaning of *agraphoi nomoi* (unwritten laws) varies according to context in Aristotle's works, referring to both particular and general moral norms. In fact, Ostwald concludes from his study of the phrase in Greek literature that it has no one meaning, referring in various contexts to ordinances sanctioned by the gods or nature, eternal or local moral codes, social pressures, and ritual regulations ("Was There a Concept *agraphos nomos* in Classical Greece?" in *Exegesis and Argument: Studies in Greek Philosophy Presented to Gregory Vlastos*, E. N. Lee, A. P. D. Mourelatos, and R. M. Rorty, eds. [Assen: Van Gorcum, 1973], 101-3).

10. As Eric Voegelin explains, because lawmaking cannot alter given material conditions, the lawgiver's nomothetic art will be oriented toward perfect actualization but concretely he must be satisfied with the best he can do. . . . Politics as a nomothetic science, however, did not have the task of transforming the imperfect forms into the best form. On the contrary, any such attempt was rejected as it would only lead to disturbances and revolutions. The perverse forms were to be accepted as they

existed historically; and the lawgiver's art should only minimize their evils in order to preserve and stabilize them. . . . the nomothetic therapy seems to have no other purpose than to make the perverse form as durable as possible (*Order and History*, vol. 3, *Plato and Aristotle* [Baton Rouge: Louisiana State University Press, 1957], 324, 358-59).

Clarifying Aristotle's position, P. A. Vander Waerdt notes that legislators should be guided by a "double teleology"—preservation and the good life (see Vander Waerdt, "The Political Intention of Aristotle's Moral Philosophy," *Ancient Philosophy* 5, no. 1 [1985], 79, 87-88). Voegelin merely emphasizes that in practice preservation must be the foremost legislative aim or that "perfection must be understood in relation to the range of action of a lawgiver" (*Plato and Aristotle*, 323; see also Pierre Pellegrin, "La *Politique* d'Aristote: Unité et fractures éloge de la lecture sommaire," *Revue philosophique de la France et de l'étranger* 177, no. 2 [1987], 137-59).

11. Aristotle's arguments may be understood to be commentary on the revision of the Athenian laws, completed in 403/2 B.C., which involved a debate over resurrecting ancestral laws. The revision incorporated some *patrioi nomoi* but declared others invalid; see Douglas M. MacDowell, *The Law in Classical Athens* (London: Thames and Hudson, 1978), 47-48 and Martin Ostwald, *From Popular Sovereignty to the Sovereignty of Law: Law, Society, and Politics in Fifth-Century Athens* (Berkeley: University of California Press, 1986), 165-67, 370-72, 406-16, 514-15. The *patrioi nomoi* were various sorts of laws—religious, secular, written, and unwritten—but parties to the debate focused on the ancestral constitutions of Solon and Cleisthenes (see *AC* 29.3; Ostwald, "Was There *agraphos nomos*?" 90-91 and *From Popular Sovereignty*, 146, 163-68, 514; MacDowell, *Law in Classical Athens*, 192, 194).

There was disagreement as to whether those ancient lawgivers had populist intentions. The populists (*demotikoi*)—who prevailed, instituting the regime which was still in existence at the time of Aristotle's writing—appealed to the ancient constitutions to justify the continuation of popular sovereignty. Others, led by Theramenes, appealed to the ancient constitutions to remedy what they regarded as the populist extremism of the late fifth century. Still others, though desiring oligarchy and thus the demise of populism, blamed Solon for the extreme democracy. Aristotle explains in the *Politics* (II.12) that populists and oligarchs (apparently both those party to the debate and those among his contemporaries) misinterpret the ancestral constitutions. Addressing the populists, he explains that Solon did not promote populism. Popular suffrage, which should not be confused with allowing the people to hold office, existed before Solon's time; he only continued it. Furthermore, he extended only judicial power to the people; that is, he believed that the people ought to have only the power to elect eligible candidates to office and access to jury seats by way of voluntary lottery. As Aristotle says, paraphrasing Solon himself, Solon granted the people "only the necessary minimum of power." Aristotle goes on to explain that it was the successors of Solon, the demagogues Ephialtes and Pericles, who increased the power of the people by perverting the Solonian constitution—for example, by reducing the powers of the oligarchic Areopagus and paying the people for jury service, thus encouraging the poor to volunteer for it. By later approving of Solon's legislation and even ranking him among the best legislators (*Pol* 1281b21-1282a41, 1318b27-32, 1296a18-19), Aristotle confirms his own views and his allegiance. He, too, thinks that Athenian democracy is too populist, but he criticizes oligarchs for blaming Solon and for not appreciating that Solon's laws promote the leadership of notables. See *Politics*, Barker, 88 n. 1, 380-81; *The Politics of Aristotle*, W. L. Newman, ed. (New York: Arno Press, 1973), vol. 2, 372-74, notes on 1273b27, 35, 39; Ostwald, *From Popular Sovereignty*, 370-72, 469; *Aristotle: The Politics*, Carnes Lord, trans. (Chicago: University of Chicago Press, 1984), 253 n. 98.

The point of this digression is to show that Aristotle's arguments against changing *patrioi nomoi* are consistent with and supportive of his critique of democracy and his understanding of polity (discussed later in the article), and to show that, although those debating the revision of the laws may have appealed to *patrioi nomoi* not in order to find historical truth but to promote their own political programs (Ostwald, *From Popular Sovereignty*, 372), Aristotle believes that *patrioi nomoi* do contain such truth; their best or indispensable provisions should be preserved, as Cleitophon (who was a member of Theramenes' party) recommended (*AC* 29.3). Aristotle concludes that legislators should err on the side of caution, changing *patrioi nomoi* only incrementally if at all. Thus, it might be said that "Aristotle revives the old conception of *thesmos* [the older Greek word for law deriving from a verb meaning 'to establish permanently'] but rationalises it" (John B. Morrall, *Aristotle* [London: George Allen & Unwin, 1977], 81-82).

12. Jacques Brunschwig, "Du mouvement et de l'immobilité de la loi," *Revue internationale de philosophie* 34, no. 133-34 (1980), 512, 522, 523, 527, 540.

13. Jacqueline de Romilly, *La loi dans la pensée grecque: Des origines à Aristote* (Paris: Société d'Édition, 1971), 220-25.

14. Brunschwig, "Du mouvement et de l'immobilité," 520, 530-35, quotation from 540.

15. Leo Strauss, *Natural Right and History* (Chicago: University of Chicago Press, 1953), 159; see also 160-62.

16. Although eighteen may seem by late twentieth-century Western norms too young an age for a woman to marry, Aristotle is in fact arguing against early marriage for women. In Athens at his time it was customary for girls to marry around the age of fourteen, the age at which they became legally possessed of their property. He apparently prefers the Spartan custom, according to which women marry a few years later; see W. K. Lacey, *The Family in Classical Greece* (Ithaca: Cornell University Press, 1968), 162.

17. In the case of children of aged fathers, Aristotle may mean that they are not only physically weak but also subject to emotion (*Politics*, Newman, vol. 3, 476, note on 1335b29).

18. Plato's Athenian Stranger advises legislators to rank the virtues in the following order: the intellectual virtues, moderation, justice, and courage (the divine goods), and then health, beauty, strength, and wealth (the human goods) (Plato, *Laws*, 631c-d).

19. Arendt, *Human Condition*, 35, 41.

20. See also *Politics*, Lord, 258 n. 44.

21. On the connections among beauty, order, and limits, see also *Met* 1078a36 (and b1) and Plato, *Philebus*, 64e, as suggested in *Politics*, Newman, vol. 3, 344-45.

22. Plato, *Republic*, 470b.

23. See also *Politics*, Newman, vol. 4, 296, note on 1302a34.

24. John Rawls, *A Theory of Justice* (Cambridge: Belknap, 1971), 539, 540. Rawls summarizes Freud:

> As some members of the social group jealously strive to protect their advantages, the less favored are moved by envy to take them away. Eventually everyone recognizes that they cannot maintain their hostile attitudes toward one another without injury to themselves. Thus as a compromise they settle upon the demand of equal treatment. The sense of justice is a reaction-formation: what was originally jealousy and envy is transformed into a social feeling, the sense of justice that insists upon equality for all (539).

Rawls cites Freud's *Group Psychology and the Analysis of the Ego*, rev. ed., James Strachey, trans. (London: Hogarth, 1959), 51ff.

25. Rawls, *A Theory*, 530.

26. See Swanson, *The Public and the Private*, ch. 4.

27. The reasoning being that the cessation of the murderer's life by the same means inflicts the amount and kind of pain most opposed to the amount and kind of pleasure he apparently took in the act.

28. As J. L. Stocks observes about Books IV-VI of the *Politics*, "we are here almost, but never quite, surrendered to that 'cogent expediency' on which in Edmund Burke's view all just government depends." To the extent that Aristotle surrenders in these books to realism and empiricism, he argues, as Stocks also points out, on behalf "of the relativity of political truth, of the necessity of concessions to democracy, of political institutions as the expression of social and economic fact, the adoption of stability and contentment instead of virtue as the test of success" ("Σχολη," *Classical Quarterly* 30 [1936], 186-87).

29. See Swanson, *The Public and the Private*, Ch. 2.

30. Aristotle follows Plato in denying that war is the proper end and most serious business of the *polis*. See, for example, Plato, *Laws*, 631b and *Republic*, 521a, as recommended by Newman (*Politics*, vol. 3, 332, note on 1325a7; see also 443, note on 1333a35, and Friedrich Solmsen, "Leisure and Play in Aristotle's Ideal State," *Rheinisches Museum für Philologie* 107 [1964], 209).

31. This is not to say that those holding political office cannot be religious or make the appearance of their being so serve their political objectives. Aristotle indicates that appearing religious can be politically effective when he advises the tyrant: "he must always show himself to be seriously attentive to the things pertaining to the gods. For [men] are less afraid of being treated in some respect contrary to the law . . . if they consider the ruler a god-fearing sort who takes thought for the gods, and they are less ready to conspire against him thinking that he has even the gods as allies" (*Pol* 1314b38-1315a3).

32. See also Leo Strauss, *The City and Man* (Chicago: Rand McNally, 1964), 22.

33. Jean-Pierre Vernant explains that the emergence of the polis in ancient Greece brought about the publicization of religion. Religion was no longer secret wisdom known by priests of a *gene*, but a body of public truths promulgated by official city cults. Temples were open, public, and visibly situated; they and their sacred holdings were to be seen—to be a spectacle providing "a lesson on the gods"; see *The Origins of Greek Thought* (Ithaca: Cornell University Press, 1982), 54-55.

34. Aristotle's contemporaries also regarded civil authority as more authoritative than religious authority. Civil courts judged violations of religious law, and the religious authorities (for example, the *eumolpidai* or the *exegetai*) had no standing in court; the presiding magistrates and juries were secular; see MacDowell, *Law in Classical Athens*, 193; Michael Gagarin, *Early Greek Law* (Berkeley: University of California Press, 1986), 14, 70; Ostwald, "Was There *agraphos nomos*?" 90 and *From Popular Sovereignty*, 165-71.

35. See also *Politics*, Barker, 193 n. NN.

36. For related and similar points, see Harvey C. Mansfield, Jr., *Taming the Prince: The Ambivalence of Modern Executive Power* (New York: Free Press, 1989), 46-71; 53-65 is an in-depth analysis of deliberating and judging as presented in Book IV of Aristotle's *Politics*. For a longer version, see Mansfield's "The Absent Executive in Aristotle's *Politics*," in *Natural Right and Political Right*, T. B. Silver and P. W. Schramm, eds. (Durham: Carolina Academic Press, 1984), 169-96. Mansfield points out that the need for the sovereignty of deliberation is why the deliberative offices must be plural (*Taming the Prince*, 58, 71). Mansfield explains reason's sovereignty as follows:

> Deliberation in [Aristotle's] account, unlike modern scientific reason, does not make its way solely on the basis of its own premises to create its own sovereignty. For Aristotle, deliberation must deal with things beyond human power and somehow bring them within human power. While facing the difficult, perhaps indeterminate, question of what is beyond and within human power, Aristotle does

at least avoid the necessity embraced by the modern schema of claiming that we are sovereign even when we give no thought to the matter at hand (54).

37. Not even political activity is wholly divorced from necessity; political rule, like mastery, cannot then be the noblest of activities (*Pol* 1325a26-27).

38. See also *Politics*, Lord, 256 n. 3.

39. The Athenians selected juries by lot from a permanent group of six thousand volunteers; see M. I. Finley, *Democracy Ancient and Modern*, rev. ed. (New Brunswick, NJ: Rutgers University Press, 1985), 117.

40. For instances of such disputes and possible modes of intervention, see *Politics*, Newman, vol. 4, 388, note on 1308a31.

41. See *Politics*, Lord, 262 n. 75.

42. Larry Arnhart, *Aristotle on Political Reasoning: A Commentary on the "Rhetoric"* (DeKalb: Northern Illinois University Press, 1981), 38, 41, 153-54. Put technically, the rhetorician constructs a proof; however, although the body of this proof, the enthymeme, is like the logical syllogism employed in dialectic (*Rh* I.1.11), it incorporates *ethos* and *pathos* in order to create trust or belief (*pistis*) in the audience. The rational can embody the emotional without becoming irrational (21, 22, 34, 114-15). On Aristotle's claim that the rhetorician should employ *logos*, *pathos*, and *ethos* together, see also William M. A. Grimaldi, *Studies in the Philosophy of Aristotle's "Rhetoric"* (Weisbaden: Franz Steiner, 1972), especially 58; Mary P. Nichols, "Aristotle's Defense of Rhetoric," *Journal of Politics* 49, no. 3 (1987), 664-68.

43. Arnhart, *Political Reasoning*, 24, 75.

44. Strauss, *City and Man*, 23-24; Strauss cites *NE* 1094a27-b6, 1180a18-22; cf. 1134a34 with *Pol* 1287a28-30.

45. For a similar point, see Mansfield, *Taming the Prince*, 49.

46. Roberto Mangabeira Unger, *Knowledge and Politics* (New York: Free Press, 1984), 64-65.

47. P. A. Vander Waerdt, "Kingship and Philosophy in Aristotle's Best Regime," *Phronesis* 30, no. 3 (1985), 249-73.

48. Vander Waerdt, "Kingship and Philosophy," 266-68. Aristotle cannot mean to propose that the philosophically virtuous person rule, because philosophy and politics are two different ways of life (*Pol* 1324a25-32).

49. Vander Waerdt, "Kingship and Philosophy," 267.

50. Thus it is not the case that Aristotle thinks the outstanding man should rule "regardless of the natural character or excellence of his subjects" (Vander Waerdt, "Kingship and Philosophy," 249).

51. Vander Waerdt cites this passage in support of his claim that both kingship and aristocracy are acceptable to Aristotle, and that their "relative rank . . . accordingly depends upon which of them is better suited to promote the way of life of the best regime" ("Kingship and Philosophy," 255). It appears rather that their relative rank depends on whether one of them is unrealistic. For arguments that Aristotle does not intend his notion of supreme monarchy to be a practical proposal, see W. R. Newell, "Superlative Virtue: The Problem of Monarchy in Aristotle's *Politics*," *Western Political Quarterly* 40, no. 1 (1987), 159-78, especially 161, 170, 175 and Mansfield, *Taming the Prince*, 23-45, 62, 70.

52. See also Mansfield, *Taming the Prince*, 56.

53. See also Strauss, *City and Man*, 36.

54. Or, as Strauss reasons, "if democracy is rule of the poor, of those who lack leisure, it is the rule of the uneducated and therefore undesirable" (*City and Man*, 36).

55. This remark is bracketed by Alois Dreizehnter in *Aristoteles' Politik* (Munich: Wilhelm Fink Verlag, 1970) and others (see *Politics*, Newman, vol. 4, 503, note on 1317b38; *Politics*, Lord, 265, n. 8), indicating an interpolation.

56. Especially since military virtue involves more than brute strength; by Aristotle's account, it involves at least *thumos* and perhaps also *sophrosunê*. Vernant argues that these are opposite military virtues; the warrior of the Homeric epic needed *thumos*, the hoplite, *sophrosunê* (*Origins of Greek Thought*, 63).

57. In claiming to rule themselves regardless of benefit, they reveal their tyrannical stubbornness. To the extent that a regime permits such assertion of will or "freedom," it shares in tyranny (Mansfield, *Taming the Prince*, 48-49).

58. Thus, we see that Aristotle agrees with Solon (see note 11 above).

59. Insofar as modern democracy recognizes merit—for example, requires lawyers, judges, and other civil servants to pass exams, or requires officials to be elected rather than chosen by lot—it "would have to be described with a view to its intention from Aristotle's point of view as a mixture of democracy and aristocracy"—in other words, as polity (Strauss, *City and Man*, 35). Because Aristotle realizes that the intention of elections (or exams) may not be fulfilled, he would consider them only a theoretically aristocratic mechanism (see *Politics*, Newman, vol. 2, 374, note on 1273b39).

60. Plato, *Republic*, 369b-c.

61. Fortunately for regimes, there are people who both are virtuous and want to perform public service (*Pol* 1291a34-b2, 1324a29-32; *NE* 1177a30-31); "actions directed to honors and to what makes one well off are very noble in an unqualified sense. . . . they are providers and generators of good things" (*Pol* 1332a15-18). Aristotle is not disparaging "honor-loving" per se.

62. Assuming that, as was the case in Athens, the per diem compensation for public service is less than what could be gained or earned in a working day (*Pol* 1297b11-12, 1318b13-16). There would, however, be those among the poor who would prefer the compensation to work—the elderly, the very poor, and, one might add, the lazy (see Finley, *Democracy*, 118).

63. See *Politics*, Lord, 258, n. 45.

64. As Mansfield observes, "in advising that the power of rejecting be conceded to the demos, Aristotle recognizes the naysaying *thumos* of human beings; and also, without making a point of it, he admits the necessity of decrees despite the sovereignty of deliberation." In other words, Aristotle concedes the power of human nature and nature "to decree limits to human choice." Thus, choice "must rest content with having the first word" (*Taming the Prince*, 57-58).

Chapter 9

Aristotle and American Classical Republicanism

Fred D. Miller, Jr.

Aristotle of Stagira (384-322 B.C.) had a far-reaching influence, direct as well as indirect, on modern political theorizing. This extended to the founders of the American political system in the late 1700s. As Richard Gummere has remarked, "No eighteenth-century statesman could escape the fine Hellenic hand of Aristotle, the student of politics rather than the metaphysician who puzzled undergraduates in the early colleges. His *Politics* is as relevant today as it was when he defined and discussed over one hundred constitutions. His formula was not the first but it is the best and clearest."[1] This observation is confirmed by the fact that James Madison (1751-1836) placed Aristotle's *Politics* at the top of a list of books that he recommended for congressional use in 1783.[2]

Aristotle's *Politics* is to a large extent concerned with the best constitution; indeed, half of its eight books (Books II-III and VII-VIII) are devoted to the study of the ideal political system. However, Aristotle maintains that the science of politics should not only investigate the best regime, but also study which constitution is best adapted for which persons and, further, what constitution is best for a given city-state, taking into account the limitations of its population and its resources. Following his teacher Plato (ca. 427-347 B.C.), Aristotle refers to the constitution that is best under the circumstances but not ideal as the "second sailing" (*deuteros plous*), which is a nautical metaphor for breaking out the oars when there is no wind to fill the sails.[3] The Greek idea of the second-best constitution prompted Pierce Butler (1744-1822), a participant in the United States constitutional convention, to remark, "We must follow the example of Solon who gave the Athenians not the best Government he could devise; but the best they would receive." The sentiment was echoed in *The Federalist*.[4]

The direct influence of Aristotle was especially evident in the thought of John Adams (1735-1826), whose writings, including most notably *A*

Defence of the Constitutions of Government of the United States of America,[5] contain extensive discussions of ancient authors. For Adams maintained that the justification of the American Revolution rested on "the principles of Aristotle and Plato, of Livy and Cicero, and Sidney, Harrington, and Locke."[6] His study of the classics along with modern European theorists led Adams to embrace a theory of government now widely called "classical republicanism." Recent scholars have argued that the American Founders were well acquainted with classical sources and used them, not merely as embellishments,[7] but as a source of practical wisdom, so that they could avoid the political failures of the Greeks and Romans. Some have gone so far as to argue that classical republicanism was a more dominant influence than the ideas of John Locke (1632-1704) and other modern political theorists. However, the Founders were eclectic thinkers, who freely appropriated political insights from ancient and modern thinkers alike, combining a Lockean theory of natural rights with classical and modern constitutional principles.[8] This is the approach of John Adams, who defended the republican form of government against the more extreme democratic form, drawing on Aristotle's theory of the second-best constitution. Adams not only borrowed principles from Aristotle, but also, as we shall see, he read his *Politics* carefully and critically.

Adams' *Defence* champions three principles derived from Aristotle's second-best constitution. First, Adams endorses in principle Aristotle's doctrine of *the rule of law*: "a government where the *laws alone* should prevail, would be the kingdom of God" (*Politics* III.16.1287a28-29); and "[o]rder is law, and it is more proper that law should govern, than any one of the citizens: upon the same principle, if it is advantageous to place the supreme power in some particular persons, they should be appointed to be only guardians, and the servants of the laws" (1287a18-22).[9] This is part of Adams' refutation of the allegation of Turgot (1727-1781) that republican theorists conflated political liberty with the rule of law. Adams correctly remarks that Aristotle did not assert "that liberty consists in being subject to the laws only." The republican thesis is rather: "Although there may be unjust and unequal laws, obedience to which would be incompatible with liberty; yet no man will contend, that a nation can be free, that is not governed by fixed laws."[10] That is, the rule of law is a necessary condition for the constitution of liberty which the American Founders were seeking.

Second, Adams favors Aristotle's *middle constitution* and underlying theory of virtue in *Politics* IV.11.[11] Adams quotes in full Aristotle's argument that the constitution that vests political authority in the moderately wealthy middle class will exemplify virtue, justice, political friendship, and stability. However, Adams cites this passage as part of a refutation of

Aristotle's own argument in *Politics* VII.8-9 that producers and merchants should be excluded from the citizenry of the constitution on the alleged grounds that they are insufficiently virtuous. Adams' immediate reaction to the latter argument is ironic:

> We must pause here and admire! The foregoing are not only the grave sentiments of Portenari[12] and Aristotle, but it is the doctrine almost of the whole earth, and of all mankind: not only every despotism, empire, and monarchy, in Asia, Africa, and Europe, but every aristocratical republic, has adopted it in all its latitude. There are only two or three of the smallest cantons in Switzerland, besides England, who allow husbandmen, artificers, and merchants, to be citizens, or to have any voice or share in the government of the state, or in the choice or appointment of any who have. There is no doctrine, and no fact, which goes so far as this towards forfeiting to the human species the character of rational creatures. Is it not amazing, that nations should have thus tamely surrendered themselves, like so many flocks of sheep, into the hands of shepherds, whose great solicitude to devour the lambs, the wool, and the flesh, scarcely leave them time to provide water or pasture for the animals, or even shelter against the weather and the wolves!

Adams grants that in the context of ancient Greek and Roman politics it was impossible for the classes occupied with production and exchange to assemble in a body to act in concert. However, he adds,

> since the invention of representative assemblies, much of that objection is removed, though even that was no sufficient reason for excluding farmers, merchants, and artificers, from the rights of citizens. At present an husbandman, merchant, or artificer, provided he has any final property, by which he may be supposed to have a judgment and will of his own, instead of depending for his daily bread on some patron or master, is a sufficient judge of the qualifications of a person to represent him in the legislature.

Adams adds that a representative assembly, fairly constituted, will be able to control the rich and illustrious, and even the king where there is one. He cautions, however, against the rule of the mob, which he notes is detrimental to liberty and the rights of mankind: "all history and experience shows, that mobs are more easily excited by courtiers and princes, than by more virtuous men, and more honest friends of liberty."

Adams mentions another argument deriving from Aristotle: "that farmers, merchants, and mechanics, are too inattentive to public affairs, and too patient under oppression." Adams concedes that such persons, especially "the most sober, industrious, and peaceable of them," are the least disposed to involve themselves in political or military affairs.

> The only practicable method therefore of giving to farmers, etc. the equal right of citizens, and their proper weight and influence in society, is by elections, frequently

repeated, of an house of commons, an assembly which shall be an essential part of the sovereignty. The meanest understanding is equal to the duty of saying who is the man in his neighbourhood whom he most esteems, and loves best, for his knowledge, integrity, and benevolence.

This prompts Adams to challenge Aristotle's allegation of moral inferiority:

The understandings, however, of husbandmen, merchants, and mechanics, are not always the meanest: there arise, in the course of human life, many among them of the most splendid geniuses, the most active and benevolent dispositions, and most undaunted bravery. The moral equality that Nature has unalterably established among men give these an undoubted right to have every road opened to them for advancement in life and in power that is open to any others. These are the characters which will be discovered in popular elections, and brought forward upon the stage, where they may exert all their faculties, and enjoy all the honours, offices, and commands, both in peace and war, of which they are capable.

Adams implicitly endorses the classical meritocratic principle of natural justice that political offices should be assigned to persons naturally qualified to fill them. He further contends however, that meritorious individuals are found in all walks of life and that they will be selected as representatives by means of the electoral process.[13]

Adams declares that "the dogma of Aristotle, and the practice of the world, is the most unphilosophical, the most inhuman and cruel, that can be conceived." He concludes that "this doctrine of Aristotle is the more extraordinary, as it seems to be inconsistent with his great and common principles," which form the basis for Aristotle's own defense of the middle constitution in *Politics* IV.11. Adams proceeds to quote the entire chapter starting from 1295a36, with the identification of the happiest or virtuous life with the middle life, and the claim that this life is most fully exemplified by the middle class. Adams complains, "These are some of the wisest sentiments of Aristotle; but can you reconcile them with his other arbitrary doctrine, and tyrannical exclusion of husbandmen, merchants, and tradesmen, from the rank and rights of citizens? These, or at least those of them who have acquired property enough to be exempt from daily dependence on others, are the real middling people, and generally as honest and independent as any . . ."

Adams' charge that Aristotle is inconsistent, however, is based upon a mistaken interpretation: he erroneously supposes that Aristotle is discussing the same constitution in both *Politics* VII.8-9 and IV.11. In fact, however, Aristotle is discussing the so-called "constitution of our prayers" in VII.8-9 and the second-best constitution (the "best" under the circumstances) in IV.11. (The distinction between the two constitutions is at IV.11.1295a25-

31.) It is not inconsistent for him, therefore, to admit the middle class to the second-best constitution while excluding them from the "constitution of our prayers." Aristotle's reason would be that the citizens of the ideal regime are great-souled persons (VIII.3.1338b3) but the middle persons are not great-souled (*Nicomachean Ethics* IV.3.1124b18-23). For moderately wealthy persons would not enjoy the blessings of nature and fortune required for the citizens to lead completely virtuous lives in the ideal state.

Adams is on firmer ground when he criticizes Aristotle for excluding producers and merchants from the ranks of the truly virtuous. Indeed, Aristotle's argument for the psychological and moral inferiority of persons engaged in these professions depends more on prejudice than empirical evidence. Moreover, Aristotle supposes without convincing argument that his quite general analysis of moral virtue is exercised in only a single lifestyle, similar to that of the traditional Greek aristocrat.[14] Adams objects that moral virtue and prudence can also be found in the husbandmen, artificers, and merchants of eighteenth-century America. These groups are qualified to be citizens and to elect the best among their number to be their representatives.

The third Aristotelian feature present in Adams' classical republican theory is the *mixed constitution*.[15] Here Aristotle's influence is less direct, however, because the concept of a mixed constitution, which Aristotle himself adapted from Plato, underwent significant further development afterward. In Aristotle's constitutional theory, mixture occurs often on the micro-level: the lawgiver designs mixed modes of deliberation, office, and adjudication which incorporate democratic, oligarchic and aristocratic standards for assigning political rights to the citizenry. No group has unchecked authority over the rest. For example, in an oligarchy the right to participate in deliberation over political matters, such as whether to declare war or make a peace, to pass laws and decrees, and so forth, was confined to those who could meet stringent requirements, e.g., a property assessment. In a pure democracy all free citizens could participate in the assembly and they had jurisdiction over all public matters. However, in a mixed constitution mode the right to deliberate would be partitioned: for example, all the citizens might have the right to deliberate about certain matters (e.g., the selection of officials), but membership in other deliberative bodies might be restricted (e.g., on the basis of property assessment or election). Aristotle discusses similar mixed modes in connection with jury courts and magistracies, for example, by entitling all to hold some offices but restricting eligibility to other offices; and by filling some offices by lot, but requiring election for others.[16] The aim is to promote the political participation, in some form or other, of the entire citizenry: "So it is evident that if one wishes to mix justly, one ought to bring together features from each [viz., democracy and oligarchy], for example, paying some for attending, and fining others for not attending; for thus all persons would share in [governing], whereas in the other case the constitution comes to belong to only one group of them" (IV.13.1297a38-b1). There are also checks in the system that prevent one group from acquiring unlimited authority over the rest. For example, it is characteristic of a polity to assign to the popular assembly the authority to pass decrees, but also to confer on a small body (sometimes called the "law guardians") the power to veto them (IV.14.1298b38-1299a1). This prevents one office or body from gaining excessive power.

Furthermore, Aristotle (IV.9.1294b18-34) characterizes the Spartan constitution (in spite of other reservations) as a mixed constitution, in that it combines features of democracy (for example, in the equality of education, common meals, and apparel) with those of oligarchy (for example, use of election rather than the lot). In his extended discussion of the Spartan constitution (*Politics* II.9) he remarks that it combines features of kingship, aristocracy, and democracy:

> If the constitution is to be preserved, all parts of the *polis* must wish that it exist and endure in the same way. Therefore, the kings are in this condition because of the honor they possess, the noble and good men because of the Senate (*gerousia*), and the people because of the office of ephors; for the ephors are selected from among all [the citizens] . . . (1270b21-26)

Here Aristotle seems to follow Plato's *Laws* III.691d8-692b1, which mentions these three elements and also describes the Spartan constitution as mixed and therefore enduring. These accounts evidently influenced Polybius (ca. 200-118 B.C.), who regarded the Spartan constitution and the Roman republic as paradigmatic mixed constitutions.[17] The Polybian constitution contained elements of each of Aristotle's correct constitutions: kingship (embodied by the consuls), aristocracy (the senate), and polity (the popular assembly). The mixed constitution possessed a stability lacking in the simple forms, because the different parts of the constitution could prevent each other from excessive action, thus establishing a system of checks and balances among the parts. On this theory mixture occurs on the macro-level: the constitution as a whole is mixed because each of its major parts is of a different type. Polybius' theory appealed to many modern theorists, including Algernon Sidney (1623-1683), who defended the proposition that "there never was a good government in the world, that did not consist of the three simple species of monarchy, aristocracy, and democracy," and offered illustrations from the ancient Hebrew government and modern states, including England.[18] The theory of the mixed constitution was further modified by Montesquieu (1689-1755), who developed the distinction, already hinted at in Aristotle's *Politics* IV.14-16 among three parts of the constitution: the executive, legislative, and judicial. According to Montesquieu, in order to protect the liberty of the citizens, these branches should possess separate powers and there should be a system of legal checks and balances among them.[19]

Adams regards the ancient mixed constitution, as described by Polybius,[20] as superior to a pure democratic system:

> Polybius's opinion of different orders, checks, and balances, in a commonwealth, is very different from that of Mr. Turgot. The Roman constitution formed the noblest people, and the greatest power, that has ever existed. But if all the powers of the consuls, senate, and people, had been centered in a single assembly of the people, collectively or representatively, will any man pretend to believe that they would have been long free, or ever great?

Nonetheless, the Roman republican constitution was a failure:

> The distribution of power was however never accurately or judiciously made in that constitution: the executive was never sufficiently separated from the legislative, nor had these powers a control upon each other defined with sufficient accuracy: the executive had not power to interpose and decide between the people and the senate.[21]

The task of the lawgiver—which in Adams' view had never been successfully carried out but would be fulfilled in the American constitutional convention—was to produce a perfect mixture of aristocracy and democracy by defining the authority of each branch of government with sufficient clarity that each possessed separate powers which could not be usurped by the others.[22]

Although Adams was steeped more deeply in the classics than most of his contemporaries, his aristocratic antidemocratic sentiments were to some extent shared by others.[23] For example, James Madison in *The Federalist* expresses the concern that the popular assembly not be permitted to grow too large. "In all very numerous assemblies, of whatever characters composed, passion never fails to wrest the sceptre from reason. Had every Athenian citizen been a Socrates; every Athenian assembly would still have been a mob." He also argues for the necessity of a senate "as a defence to the people against their own temporary errors and delusions." Such an institution can check the excesses of the more popular assembly "until reason, justice, and truth, can regain their authority over the public mind." He adds an allusion to the extreme democracy of antiquity:

What bitter anguish would not the people of Athens have often escaped, if their government had contained so provident a safeguard against the tyranny of their own passions? Popular liberty might then have escaped the indelible reproach of decreeing to the same citizens, the hemlock on one day, and statues on the next.[24]

Madison correctly contends that there are precedents for representative government in the Greek democracies, since many officials were elected. But the proposed American constitution differs from the ancient democracies "in the total exclusion of the people in their collective capacity from any share in the [American Governments]."[25] In Madison's view, the American constitution offered a more moderate form of republican democracy.

The framers of the American government certainly did not theorize it in Aristotle's terms. They rejected Aristotle's doctrines of communitarianism, authoritarianism and elitism in favor of Lockean liberalism and egalitarianism.[26] However, although the leading philosophical influences on the American Founders were undoubtedly Locke and other modern European theorists, Aristotle and other ancient writers also made an important contribution.[27] The eclectic character of the American revolutionary theorists is illustrated by Thomas Jefferson (1743-1826) in his letter to Henry Lee (1756-1818) on the Declaration of Independence: "All its authority rests then on the harmonizing sentiments of the day, whether expressed in conversation, in letters, printed essays, or in the elementary books of public right, as Aristotle, Cicero, Locke, Sidney, &c."[28] The Founders accepted Aristotelian principles, although these were reinterpreted in modern terms. For example, Madison in *The Federalist* invokes the eudaimonistic principle that in politics "the public good, the real welfare of the great body of the people is the supreme object to be pursued," so that a system of government is justified only to the extent that it promotes "the public happiness."[29] He argues further that "the principles . . . of justice and the general good" must be promoted by means of the separation of powers, that is, "by so contriving the interior structure of the government as that its several constituent parts may, by their mutual relations, be the means of keeping each other in their proper places." Through the separation of powers and the far-flung federal structure, "the society itself will be broken into so many parts, interests and classes of citizens, that the rights of individuals, or of the minority, will be in little danger from interested combinations of the majority."[30] Madison is here clearly asserting that the separation of powers and the system of checks and balances will prevent one group of the population from exploiting another and violating its rights.[31] Madison's justification for the federal constitution is thus akin to Aristotle's justification of the second-best constitution.

It is clear, therefore, that the American Founders were influenced by Aristotle's *Politics*. The long-term effects on American politics are more difficult to assess. For soon after the ratification of the U.S. Constitution, the revolutionary consensus broke down, and two principal political movements began to diverge: the Federalists and the Republicans (later Democrats). John Adams, Alexander Hamilton (1757-1804), and other Federalist leaders were aligned more closely with the classical view that the constitution must be mixed in order to balance the opposed interests of the propertied and non-propertied classes. In this view political rights and offices should be apportioned on the basis of criteria reflecting class interests: for example, a property qualification or poll tax for the electorate for certain offices. This party also favored fiscal policies that seemed to favor the wealthier class: such as tariffs and a national bank. In opposition James Madison, Thomas Jefferson, and other spokesmen for the Republicans emphasized the aforementioned view that the tyranny of the majority might be avoided through a system of representative democracy. Madison recognized that the political process could be subverted by factional interests, but he thought that this could be prevented by the appropriate checks and balances. However, as argued above, this is but an application of the general theory of the mixed constitution to the peculiar American context. Also, later in life, Jefferson distanced himself from the Stagirite:

> The introduction of this new principle of representative democracy has rendered useless almost everything written before on the structure of government; and, in a great measure, relieves our regret, if the political writings of Aristotle, or of any other ancient, have been lost, or are unfaithfully rendered or explained to us.[32]

Jefferson was correct to emphasize representative government, but he overlooked the continuing role of Aristotelian principles that had been explicated and defended by John Adams: such as the rule of law and the mixed constitution. Although the United States took a more democratic turn in the nineteenth century than many of the Founders may have anticipated, it can be argued that constitutional principles adapted from classical theorists such as Aristotle served to moderate this development, so that the United States escaped the fate of the French republic.[33]

Notes

1. Richard M. Gummere, *The American Colonial Mind and the Classical Tradition* (Cambridge: Harvard University Press, 1963), 175. A popular translation of Aristotle's *Politics* was by William Ellis and originally published in 1776; see Meyer Reinhold, *The*

Classick Pages: Classical Reading of Eighteenth-Century Americans (University Park, Penn.: American Philological Association and Pennsylvania State University, 1975), 117-20.

2. James Madison, "Report of Books," in *The Papers of James Madison*, Robert A. Rutland, et. al., eds. (Chicago: University of Chicago Press, 1962-77), vol. 6, pp. 76-77 (cited by Carl J. Richard, *The Founders and the Classics: Greece, Rome, and the American Enlightenment* [Cambridge: Harvard University Press, 1994], 140).

3. I defend this interpretation of Aristotelean political science in *Nature, Justice, and Rights in Aristotle's "Politics"* (Oxford: Clarendon Press, 1995), esp. ch. 5-8.

4. For political uses of *deuteros plous*, see Aristotle, *Politics* III.13.1284b19, *Nicomachean Ethics* II.9.1109a34-35; Plato, *Statesman* 300c2; compare Plato, *Phaedo* 99c9-d1 and *Philebus* 19c2-3. Butler was alluding Plutarch's life of Solon XV.2; see Madison's *Notes of Debates in the Federal Convention of 1787* (New York: Norton, 1987), 73; compare Jacob E. Cooke, ed. *The Federalist* (Middletown, Conn.: Wesleyan University Press, 1961), no. 38 [James Madison], 241.

5. (London: C. Dilly, 1787), henceforth cited as *Defence*.

6. John Adams, "Letters of Novangulus (1775)," in *The Papers of John Adams*, Robert J. Taylor, ed. (Cambridge: Harvard University Press), vol. 2, 230.

7. In contrast, Bernard Bailyn, *The Ideological Origins of the American Revolution* (Cambridge: Belknap, 1967), 24, sees the frequent citations of ancient authors as mere "window dressing." Bailyn argues that the dominant influences on the American revolution and founding were John Locke and more immediately eighteenth century libertarian authors, such as John Trenchard and Thomas Gordon.

8. The rise of classical republicanism (or civic humanism), and more generally the influence of Aristotle and other ancient authors on English and American political theorizing in the seventeenth and eighteenth centuries, is documented in Zera S. Fink, *The Classical Republicans: An Essay in the Recovery of a Pattern of Thought in Seventeenth Century England* (Evanston: Northwestern University Press, 1975); Richard M. Gummere, *American Colonial Mind*; Caroline Robbins, *The Eighteenth-Century Commonwealthman: Studies in the Transmission, Development, and Circumstance of English Liberal Thought from the Restoration of Charles II until the War with the Thirteen Colonies* (Cambridge: Harvard University Press, 1959); and Gordon S. Wood, *The Creation of the American Republic, 1776-1787* (New York: Norton, 1972). Along related yet different lines, J. G. A. Pocock, *The Machiavellian Moment: Florentine Political Thought and the Atlantic Republican Tradition* (Princeton: Princeton University Press, 1975) traces the evolution of "civic humanism" through the Italian Renaissance. Pocock goes so far as to describe the American Revolution as "a flight from modernity," and as a revival of "the ancient ideal of *homo politicus* (the *zôon politikon* of Aristotle)." The classical-republican interpretation of the American Revolution is challenged by Thomas S. Pangle in *The Spirit of Modern Republicanism: The Moral Vision of the American Founders and the Philosophy of Locke* (Chicago: University of Chicago Press, 1988), esp. ch. 4; and by Michael P. Zuckert, *Natural Rights and the New Republicanism* (Princeton: Princeton University Press, 1994), esp. ch. 6.

However, the evidence that Locke's natural-rights theory was a more important philosophical influence than the classics is consistent with the thesis that the American founders and their English contemporaries were eclectic thinkers who readily combined Locke with Aristotle and other classical sources. See also Forrest McDonald, *Novus Ordo Seclorum: The Intellectual Origins of the Constitution* (Lawrence: University Press of Kansas, 1985), ch. 3. Finally, Paul A. Rahe, *Republics Ancient and Modern*, vol. 3 *Inventions of Prudence: Constituting the American Regime* (Chapel Hill: University of North Carolina Press, 1992, repr. 1994) provides a valuable discussion of these issues.

9. Adams (vol. I, 126) cites James Harrington, *The Commonwealth of Oceana*, "The Preliminaries, showing the Principles of Government": "Government *de jure*, or according to ancient prudence, is an art, whereby a civil society of men is instituted and preserved upon the foundation of *common interest*; or, to follow Aristotle and Livy, it is an empire of laws and not of men." Adams was also influenced on the rule of law by Algernon Sidney's *Discourses Concerning Government* II.10, 30. On the role of this doctrine in American jurisprudence see Edward S. Corwin, "The 'Higher Law' Background of American Constitutional Law," *Harvard Law Review* 42 (1928), 149-85; (1929), 365-409.

10. Adams, *Defence*, vol. I, 124-25.

11. Adams, *Defence*, vol. III, 162-74.

12. Adams' discussion of Aristotle is part of a discussion of *Della Felicità di Padova* by Angelo Portenari of Padua, who had made use of the *Politics*.

13. Adams evidently assumes a different conception of virtue than that described in Aristotle's *Nicomachean Ethics*. On the difference between the Founders' conception of virtue and the classical, see Thomas Pangle, "Civic Virtue: The Founders' Conception and the Classical Conception," in *Constitutionalism and Rights*, Gary Bryner and Noel Reynolds, eds. (Provo, Utah: Brigham Young University Press, 1986); and Richard Vetterli and Gary Bryner, *In Search of the Republic: Public Virtue and the Roots of American Government*, rev. ed. (Lanham: Rowman & Littlefield, 1996).

14. However, *Politics* I.7.1255b37 implies that Aristotle's citizen will also be a philosopher. Cf. VII.14.1333a23, 32.

15. Adams in "Novangulus" alludes to the mixed polity of "Aristotle, Livy and Harrington"; cited in Wood, *Creation of the American Republic*, 206.

16. For a detailed discussion of Aristotle's sophisticated analysis of the constitutional modes (most fully expounded in *Politics* IV.14-16), see Miller, *Nature, Justice, and Rights*, 116-83.

17. Polybius, *Histories*, VI.3-10. Polybius (ca. 118-100 B.C.) may have been directly influenced by later writers, who were transmitting the ideas of Plato and Aristotle. The most popular translation of Polybius was by James Hampton (first published in 1756-72): see Reinhold, *Classick Pages*, 122. On the transmission of the idea of the mixed constitution from Plato and Aristotle to John Adams see Richard, *Founders and the Classics*, 124-39.

18. Algernon Sidney, *Discourses Concerning Government*, II.16.

19. Montesquieu, *The Spirit of the Laws*, XI.6.

20. Adams, *Defence*, vol. I, 169, cites a passage from Polybius' Book V included in Edward Spelman's English translation of the *Roman Antiquities* of Dionysius of Halli-carnassus. Polybius' theory is also described in an excerpt from Portenari quoted by Adams (vol. I, 172), and it forms the basis for the arguments of Machiavelli and Algernon Sidney, both of whom Adams discusses at length. See also Bailyn, *Ideological Origins*, 70-72 on modern English sources.

21. Adams, *Defence*, vol. I, 175-76.

22. Garry Wills has argued that the classical ideal of mixed government was opposed to the Founders' principle of separation of powers because mixed government theory requires that "all the interests should 'have a say' on all the issues" in *Explaining America* (New York: Penguin, 1981), 100. Richard (*Founders and the Classics*, 133-34) argues convincingly that Wills' interpretation is thoroughly mistaken and that theorists like Adams viewed the separation of powers as a necessary condition for a mixed constitution.

23. The abhorrence of Athenian democracy was pervasive among the American founders. Jennifer Tolbert Roberts argues this view was based on a somewhat distorted understanding that tended to equate the classical Athenian democracy with ochlocracy or mob rule (*Athens*

on Trial: The Antidemocratic Tradition in Western Thought [Princeton: Princeton University Press, 1994], 179-93).

24. *The Federalist*, no. 55, 374. Thomas Jefferson also criticized Athenian direct democracy and advocated a mixed government, cf. Richard, *Founders and the Classics*, 131-32 and 229 for references.

25. *The Federalist*, no. 63, 425-28; cf. *Politics* IV.4.1292a10-37.

26. John Adams was derided by his contemporaries as overly sympathetic to a classical mixed constitution modeled after the British and hence as making concessions to traditional monarchy and aristocracy. See Wood, *Creation of the American Republic*, 567-87.

27. See Meyer Reinhold, "Survey of Scholarship on Classical Traditions in Early America," in *Classical Traditions in Early America*, John W. Eadie, ed. (Ann Arbor: Center for Coordination of Ancient and Modern Studies, University of Michigan, 1976).

28. Letter to Henry Lee (May 8, 1825) in Jefferson, *Writings* (New York: Library of America, 1984), 1501.

29. *The Federalist*, no. 45, 309. McDonald (*Novus Ordo Seclorum*, ix-x) also conjectures that Jefferson's non-Lockean reference in the Declaration of Independence to "the pursuit of happiness" as a fundamental right may have ultimately derived from Aristotle. Rahe (*Republics*, vol. 3, 58-72) discusses in detail the tacit reliance of the American Founders on Aristotle's political science. Rahe correctly notes that the Founders did not share Aristotle's view that the proper end of the state was to make the citizens virtuous in Aristotle's sense (73).

30. *The Federalist*, no. 51, 347-48, 351.

31. Richard (*Founders and the Classics*, 139-41) argues that Madison tried to incorporate the classical principles of mixed government into the American constitution.

32. Jefferson, letter to Isaac Tiffany (August 26, 1816) in *The Papers of Thomas Jefferson*, Julian P. Boyd, ed. (Princeton: Princeton University Press, 1816), vol. 15, 66; cited by Richard, *Founders and the Classics*, 155-58, to which this paragraph is very much indebted.

33. An earlier version of this paper was presented at a meeting of the Society for Greek Political Thought, North American Chapter, on September 1, 1995, in conjunction with a meeting of the American Political Science Association, where I received valuable criticisms, for which I am most grateful. I also wish to thank Michael P. Zuckert and Paul Bullen for their very helpful suggestions.

Chapter 10

The Rule of Law or *Pambasileia*: Competing Claims for Rule in Aristotle's *Politics*

Clifford A. Bates, Jr.

I have argued that there are two peaks in the argument of Book 3 of the *Politics*.[1] The first peak is the democratic regime, which is arrived at after a debate between oligarchy and democracy which occurs in *Politics* 3.9-13. The second peak is the universal kingship (*pambasileia*) which begins in *Politics* 3.15 and concludes at the end of Book 3. Pambasileia literally means kingship over everything,[2] and Mary Nichols suggests that "Aristotle apparently coins" this word. She says it is "a combination of the noun for 'kingship' with the adjective for 'all.'"[3] The discussion of the *pambasileia*, the second peak, consists of three *logoi*, or arguments, where opposing claims about political rule are addressed. In these arguments, we discover Aristotle's comprehensive teaching concerning political philosophy—that the rule of the many restrained by law is preferable to the rule of the one best man.[4]

In this article I wish to address the first of these three *logoi* in *Politics* 3.15-17[5] to show that in this debate not only do we find Aristotle's missing critique of Plato's teaching about the philosopher-king,[6] but also an argument for the superiority of the rule of law. It is said by commentators on this section of the *Politics* that the teaching about the *pambasileia* has similarities to the Socratic-Platonic teaching about the philosopher-king as presented in the *Republic*.[7] Yet it is reasonable to consider that, contrary to Plato's suggestion of the possibility of a philosophic politics, Aristotle ultimately rejects such a politics in favor of one that is more practical.

The importance of the *pambasileia* section of the *Politics* is that it brings to an end the examinations of the basic forms of regime discussed in the beginning of Book 3. The concern that arises from the general examination of regimes, or classical political science, is to judge the political nature of various regimes. In doing so, we may be given a better understanding of the character of those regimes and the authoritative element that rules within them. The introduction of the discussion of the *pambasileia* appears to follow a similar track, a general exploration of the character of a particular form of regime.

Concerning the *pambasileia* section of the *Politics*, Martha Nussbaum muses that this section is "notoriously hard to interpret in a way that renders [the argument] consistent with [Aristotle's] insistence on shared rule."[8] Nussbaum then argues, after noting the difficulty of interpreting this section, for an interpretation that would make this section consistent with her claim that Aristotle insists that rule must be shared. I read her point as an argument for the mixed regime, a combination of the rule of the few and the many. She is not discussing political rule generically speaking.

Nussbaum seems to take too seriously the claim that the "polity" or mixed regime is the desired regime in Book 3, and she is not alone in the belief that Aristotle presents the "polity" as his best regime, if not in theory then in practice. Nichols, in *Citizens and Statesmen*, also holds this position.[9] But there are two arguments counter to Nichols' and Nussbaum's.

The first is that the "polity," the so-called mixed regime, is not the regime presented as the best regime, either practically or theoretically, in Book 3. There are two regimes presented as possible contenders for the best regime in Book 3—democracy and the *pambasileia*. As I have argued, neither the best regime of *Politics* 7 nor the aristocracy in 3.7 are contenders for the best regime.

Second, the inconsistency suggested by Nussbaum is an important hermeneutic clue that Aristotle gives to help the reader uncover the argument he is trying to make. In this light, I interpret the dispute between the *pambasileia* and the argument for the mixed regime as an important textual clue for concluding that the interpretation that the mixed regime is the best regime is false.

An Inquiry into Kingship

In *Politics* 3.14 Aristotle suggests a transition to "investigate kingship" (3.14.1284b36) after a digression concerning what to do with a "person of excessive virtue" (3.14.1284a4). This digression centers on the issue of whether it is right to ostracize such a person. The solution is that, in "deviant regimes," to ostracize a person of "excessive excellence" (*arete*) is both "advantageous [for the rulers] and just" (3.14.1284b24); "yet it is also evident, perhaps, that it is not simply just [to do so]" (3.14.1284b24-25). In the case of the best regime, "there is considerable question as to what ought to be done" to such a person of "excessive excellence" if he exists (3.14.1284b 26-27). The digression ends with the suggestion that such a person, if he were to exist, should be obeyed by everyone gladly (3.14.1284b32-33). He notes that to obey him "seems the natural course" (3.14.1284b32), and that these persons of "excessive excellence" when obeyed "will be a sort of permanent king in their *polei*" (3.14.1284b34).

The transition into an examination of kingship comes after the digression concerning what to do with the person of "excessive excellence." "What must be investigated is whether it is advantageous for the city or the territory that is to be well administered to be under a kingship or not, or some other regime instead, or whether it is advantageous for some and not for others" (3.14.1284b37-39).[10] This general set of questions establishes the tone for the whole inquiry. Aristotle raises the question of kingship to ask if such rule is "advantageous"—that is, best—for cities. Yet what immediately follows this question does not address it but is simply an account of the various forms of kingship. The four types of kingship (*basileia*) that Aristotle presents are (1) permanent kingship (3.14.1285a2-15); (2) barbaric kingship (3.14.1285a16-28); (3) elected tyranny (3.14.1285a30-b3); and (4) heroic kingship (3.14.1285b3-19).[11]

The conclusion of the examination of the varieties of kingship, which occurs prior to the discussion of the *pambasileia*, ends with the relisting of four types of kingships: (1) heroic kingship (3.14.1285b20-24); (2) barbaric kingship (3.14.1285b24-25); (3) dictatorship or elective tyranny (3.14.1285 b25-26); and (4) the Spartan form, which, "to speak simply, is permanent generalship based on family" (3.14.1285b26-27). In the original ordering of the varieties of kingship, the position of both heroic kingship and the Spartan form were switched. Also, it should be noted that all the varieties of kingship so far mentioned are under the restraint of law.[12]

After listing the four varieties of kingship, a fifth form of kingship is mentioned in which "one person has authority over all matters, just as each nation and each city has authority over all in all common matters with an arrangement that treats political rule as though it were a form of household management (*oikonomike*)" (3.14.1286b29-32).[13] This form of kingship is similar in character to the head of a household, but involves rule over a city or a nation or several nations (3.14.1286b32-33).[14] It is also important that no mention of law is made in the passage that introduces this form of kingship.

In chapter 14, the *pambasileia* and the Spartan, or an elected, kingship are said to be the two fundamental kinds of kingship that must be investigated (3.14.1285b35). Thus, Aristotle reduces the original five forms of kingship to two. In doing so, he implies that any discussion concerning kingship need only examine these two. He says that although the other forms of kingship have more authority over matters than the Spartan form of kingship, they have much less authority than the *pambasileia*. Because of this, Aristotle collapses the other four forms of kingship under the category of kingship limited by law and then compares restrained kingship to the extreme form of kingship, unrestrained by law, which he calls *pambasileia*. Aristotle states the two questions he wishes to examine: whether it is advantageous for cities to have a permanent general and whether it is advantageous for one person to have authority over all matters. (3.1285b37-86a1).

The first question is dismissed without examination; to examine the first question, Aristotle says, would require a study of the laws rather than of the regime. Also, the "permanent general" can arise in all regimes and not just in the one form in question (3.14.1286a4).[15] Therefore, with the dismissal of the first question, the proposed examination of Spartan kingship is also dismissed without further discussion. The latter question and the *pambasileia* alone remain for examination. This occurs because Aristotle states that *pambasileia* is a form of regime, whereas the first type, the Spartan, is not. This division opens the discussion for the *pambasileia* as such, and leads to the possibility of the political artist, or the politically disciplined man, suggesting that this man ought not to be ruled by anything. His nature is such that he is best suited (because of his supremacy of foresight) to rule over all human beings.[16]

First *Logos* (1286a7-b40)

The Best Man *vs.* the Best Laws

At this point Aristotle opens up the first *logos* with the question, "is it more advantageous to be ruled by the best man or by the best laws?" (3.15.1286a8-9). This question begins a dialogue between a partisan of the laws and a partisan of the best man.[17]

The partisan for the best man puts forth the argument against the laws: "the laws only speak of the universal and do not command with a view to circumstance" (3.15.1286a10-11). The laws cannot be superior since they only speak generally. Also, to rule in accordance with the written laws, argues the partisan for the best man, is foolish because it would be like requiring a doctor to treat sick people by a written set of instructions ("as it is done in Egypt") without regard to the individual circumstances of the patient in question (3.15.1286a12-15).

Another problem is that the laws cannot simply address problems that arise out of the consequences of implementation. That is, the laws cannot give order to what comes from the laws (3.15.1286b10). These objections suggest that something other than the laws needs to guide what the laws themselves cannot directly control or provide.[18] Judith Swanson reads "law" here not to refer to that derived from custom and the political character of the regime, but from natural law.[19] Such a position seems a gross misrepresentation of the text.

In Swanson's correct reading of Book 3.15-17 of the *Politics*—the debate between the rule of law and the rule of the wise king—Aristotle sides politically with the rule of law over that of human will, regardless of how wise or noble that ruler can be. In this she is correct. But she goes on to argue that the law being advocated in this debate is natural law rather than everyday, conventional law, *nomos*.[20] Putting aside the problems with ascribing a natural law teaching instead of a natural right teaching to Aristotle's *Politics*, the text in question—*Politics* 3.15-17—uses law (*nomos*) in its conventional meaning, or customary law. Although conventional law may be in accord with natural law, or the principle of natural right, it is not natural law *per se*. If Aristotle were arguing for the rule of natural law in this text, he would not have allowed the rule of law argument to win, because the rule of law argument is in fact the continuation of the democratic argument earlier in Book 3. Instead, if he were supporting an argument for natural law/natural right, he would have let the argument for the absolute rule of the wise king defeat the rule of law argument. The absolute rule of the wise king would seem to be the perfect embodiment of the rule of natural law/natural right.

To restate the argument made against the laws by the partisan of the best man: first, the difficulty of the laws is that they speak generally and, second, because they speak generally, they do not attend to the particular circumstances. Hence, the partisan for the best man concludes that the "regime" of written laws cannot be best.

In response to the attack on the rule of law, the partisan for the laws declares that "what is unaccompanied by the passionate element generally is superior to that in which it is innate" (3.15.1286a16-18). He argues that passion is not present in law but is necessarily possessed by every human soul.

The partisan for the best man interrupts, stating that such indeed is the case but that this problem is addressed "by the fact that he [the best man] will deliberate in a finer fashion concerning particulars" (3.15.1286a20-21). Also, as "the ruler must necessarily be a legislator, the laws must exist but they must not be authoritative" (3.15.1286a22-23). The laws cannot be authoritative because circumstances change. Issues of justice tend to admit of degrees of variation in circumstances that affect the outcome of the judgment. Laws cannot be authoritative because they are dependent on the particular type of regime a *polis* happens to have. The laws of a democracy are fundamentally different from those of an oligarchy, an aristocracy, or a kingdom. The same is true for the offices. The regime itself is prior to both the laws and the offices, and is thus fundamentally more authoritative than either.

The partisan for the best man admits the need for the laws but claims that they ought to be subordinate to the best man because he is best able to deliberate about circumstances, whereas the laws cannot. The laws cannot change themselves. Because what is right and wrong is determined by the given circumstances, the possibility arises that the laws may be in contradiction to what is right. Once the laws deviate from what is right, they become unjust. Therefore, the possibility of the unjustness of the laws supports the claim for the rule of the best man.

The partisan of the laws then asks, "as regards the things that law is unable to judge either generally or well, should the one best person rule, or should all?" (3.15.1286a22-25). The partisan for the laws, noting that the laws can at times be unjust and may be unable to deal with specifics, changes the question. He asks who is a better judge, the best man or the many? (3.15.1286a25). In response to this question, we see that the partisan of the laws also reveals himself to be a partisan of the many.

The argument for the laws is in fact the justification for the rule of the many over the laws, regardless of the best man's character. The partisan of the laws notes that any single person taken separately, like most human beings, might (or even, will) be inferior to the best man (3.15.1286a27). But, he argues, "the city is made up of many persons, just as a feast to which many contribute is finer than a single and simple one, and on this account a crowd also judges many matters better than any single person" (3.15. 1286a26-31). Here the partisan of the laws argues that the numerical strength of the many makes up for the defects of single individuals, and together the many's collective strengths will exceed even the best man's. This is similar to the argument made at *Politics* 3.11.1282a13-19.

The partisan of the laws goes further by arguing that the many are less corruptible than the one best man (3.15.1286a32). This is so, he argues, because they are like "water" and, as such, are "more incorruptible than the few. . . . The judgments of a single person are necessarily corrupted when he is dominated by anger or some other passion of this sort, whereas it is hard for all to become angry and err at the same time" (3.15.1286a33-35).

The partisan of the laws seems to make a comparison between the laws and the many. They (both the laws and the many) are said to be less corruptible by the passions than is the one best man. This is the case for the many because, to restate, it is harder to corrupt them than it is to corrupt one man. The partisan of the laws does not say that it is impossible for the many to be corrupt or to become angry, but that it is harder to make them corrupt or angry.

Experience tells us, however, that a corrupt people can be far worse than any single tyrant. Publius, in the *Federalist Papers*, clearly indicates this, by his concern about majority tyranny. But the partisan of the laws does not exaggerate the many's incorruptibility, so he limits the many: they "must be free people acting in no way against the law, except in those cases where [the law] necessarily falls short" (3.15.1286a36-37). The multitude ought to consist of the free men who do nothing against the law unless the law does not or cannot deal with the issue at hand (3.15.1286b35). The partisan of the laws also argues that the many are better able to judge well than the one best man simply because their number lessens the possibility for error due to mere passions.

So the partisan of the laws limits the many's judgment in that they must be, first, free men; second, obedient to the law; and third, careful to change the law only when it falls short. These three limits, or criteria for limiting the judgment of the many, point to the power of the many; if these are not present, the laws will be ignored, and the many will rule according to their whims. Hence, the rule of the many is potentially worse than, or at least as bad as, the bad rule of one man. The tendency of this argument is to downgrade the superiority of the rule of law in favor of the rule of the best man.

The partisan of the best man argues that the limits placed on the many by the laws are easily evaded by them. The partisan of the laws then poses the question: "if there were a number who were both good men and good citizens," then "is the one ruler more incorruptible or rather the larger numbers who are all good?" (3.15.1286a38-39). The partisan of the best man answers that it is clearly not one, because the many good will have difficulty with factions, whereas the single good ruler will be without factions (3.15.1286b1-2).

The partisan of the laws at first seems to ignore the problem of faction raised by the rule of the many. He instead raises the question whether the good man or the good majority is less corruptible. If there can be a good multitude, argues the partisan of the laws, then to argue that the good one is better than the good many will create a situation in which the many will rise up in factions (3.15.1286b1). Aristotle here suggests that those who believe themselves to be good or as good as the good single ruler will view his absolute reign as a slight to their excellence. In this light, they will strive for equal status with him.[21] However this does not deal with the question of how to address problems that occur because of factions within the many. I contend that Aristotle deals with factions and their problem in his discussion of the so-called "mixed regime" in *Politics* 4.7-9 and 4.11-16. What is discussed there is not a particular form of regime but what elements constitute a regime and how they can be made harmonious.

Instead of addressing the problem of factions in order to show that the rule of the many good is superior to the rule of the single best ruler, Aristotle raises the question whether it is more likely that there could be one good man or a good multitude. To clarify, the question is which is more possible, aristocracy—which at this point in the text he calls the rule of a good multitude—or kingship. If there could be a majority of good men, it would be better to be ruled by them than by one single good man. However, the principle that it is better to be ruled by the good simply, regardless of number, than to be ruled by the many is maintained, in light of the previous argument for the many's excellences—their excellences in judging, providing for the city's needs, and so on. This puts an interesting twist to the debate. The partisan of the laws has gotten the partisan of the best man to accept the premise that the rule of the many good men is better than the rule of the one good man (3.15.1286b5).

This establishes the direction for the argument that the rule of the many is simply better than the rule of one man. Since aristocracy is more choiceworthy than kingship—"provided it is possible to find a number of persons who are similar" (3.15.1286b7-8)—then the groundwork is laid for the rule of the many being better than the rule of a single ruler. Given this line of reasoning, the partisan of the best man has accepted the premise that the rule of the many good is better than the one good, which can be used to support a fundamentally democratic premise, that the many are simply better than either the one or the few. Thus, the possibility of a good multitude provides the basis to rescue the rule of the many—i.e., democracy—from its status as a merely base regime.

At this point, to avoid the trap set by the partisan of the laws, the partisan of the best man argues that only if the majority is seriously good can it avoid the creation of factions (3.15.1286b1).[22] The underlying argument is that the one good man can be seriously good, whereas it seems improbable that there can be a seriously good multitude.[23] However, if such a seriously good majority could exist, it would be an aristocracy. Yet, what is aristocracy? Is it merely the rule of the good men, as suggested above, or is it the rule of the few, who rule for the sake of the common good as suggested by *Politics* 3.1279a35? Recall that Aristotle earlier in Book 3 seems to reject the usefulness of the twofold typology of regimes—composed of the quantitative (e.g., one, few or many) and qualitative (i.e., its justice, or its rule for the common good) claims—established in *Politics* 3.7. His rejection takes the form of his making the case that what defines oligarchy is not that its rulers are few but that they are rich, and that they claim their rule is just simply because only the wealthy should rule (3.8.1279b11-80a6). Aristotle argues that the rule of the many rich is as much an oligarchy as the rule of the few rich. Therefore, the quantitative claim of the regime is not a basis to understand what type of regime one is examining. Instead, the qualitative claim of a regime, its claim about the best way of life, is the distinctive criterion for examining the varieties of regimes (3.10.1281a13-39). Therefore, what defines aristocracy is its claim that it is the rule of the best men (*aristoi*). But this claim is too generic. Would not all regimes claim that their rule is the rule of the best men? In this light, aristocracy then becomes merely the name of whatever actual regime is best.

Earlier in *Politics* 3, the rule of the many was not justified as better than the best man in judging because they were the virtuous multitude. Rather, it was justified in spite of the fact they were far from virtuous. So if one accepts the earlier position as valid, then the standard needed to rescue democracy from becoming a base regime may not be the possibility of the good multitude but the collective judgment of the multitude that is not overly slavish. This consideration should underlie any acknowledgment of the unlikelihood of a virtuous multitude.

To return, the partisan of the best man argues that the many good have to be excellent in soul, just like the single good man. But if one good man is hard to find, then a good multitude would be even harder to find. Also some even suggest that not only is a good multitude difficult to find, it is most likely that one could not even exist. It is stated that if the condition set forth is true, although the aristocracy of many good rulers is more choiceworthy in cities than kingship, its creation is highly improbable.

The History of Regimes

In response to these arguments, the partisan of the laws presents the history of regimes (3.15.1286b5) as an explanation for the superiority of aristocracy over kingship. Or, more correctly, the partisan of the laws presents the history of regimes to show the natural tendency for the rule of the many to come gradually into being over time and thus to prevail against both the rule of one and the few. The history of regimes begs the questions: Who is to rule? Is it to be the one or the many? As shown by the history of regimes, which is, properly speaking, the political history of the Hellenes, history tends to point toward the rule of the many.

An outline of the history of regimes presented at *Politics* 3.15.1286b8-21 goes as follows:

(1) kingship,

(2) "many similar with respect to excellence" ruling together,
(3) oligarchy,
(4) tyranny,
(5) democracy.[24]

The regime after kingship lacks a specific title, about which Aristotle notes: "But when it happened that many arose who were similar with respect to excellence, they no longer tolerated [kingship] but sought something common and established a regime [*politeia*]" (3.15.1286b11-13). Lord, in his translation of the *Politics*, reads *politeia* in this sentence as a reference to so-called "polity," the mixed regime of Book IV. Nichols agrees with Lord's interpretation of the passage.[25] Both Nichols and Lord translate *politeia* in a way that supports their interpretation of the text, that "polity" is either the best practical regime or the best regime. Instead of an argument for "polity," it seems more textually sound to interpret Aristotle as giving an account of the arising of political rule. Kingly rule as discussed in the history of regimes is heroic kingship—not *pambasileia*—and emerges through kinship bonds. The emergence of political rule comes from the moving away from the rule of the father in the household, which is the model for kingship, to the rule of equals ruling in turn. The emergence of the regime comes from the creation of political rule out of kingship. Thus, what is described in the above passage is not the emergence of a specific regime type but the emergence of political rule. Yet, if one assumes that the rule of the few good (i.e., virtuous) men is aristocracy, then this regime resembles aristocracy.

Returning to the history of regimes, it is clear that each step away from kingship gives more power to the many. Because the political communities become progressively larger, a reading of the history of regimes suggests perhaps that it is no longer easy for any regime besides democracy to come into existence (3.15.1286b21). Thus, what the history of regimes actually represents is an account of the coming together of human beings. Or, stated differently, it represents the development of human civilization.

First, the history of regimes shows that the process engenders an equalization (a leveling out) of excellence. I read this as a leveling out of virtue—i.e., human excellences expressed by skill and performance understood as one's nature. This leveling out occurs because of technology. Technology's ascent is seen in the predominance of the artisan classes in the polis. Also, the greater availability of the arts and their leveling effect make it difficult to perceive the differences—hence, the excellences—among human beings. The more the arts predominate in the political community (which is to say the more technology), the less apparent the differences among human beings become. As the differences become less apparent, even more human beings begin to look fundamentally equal. Therefore, people living in technological civilizations will no longer abide inequality, since in a technological order there appears to be no obvious differences among human beings.

The arguments made here appear to agree with what David Hume argued in his *History of England*, summarized in the *Essays*, that political liberty and equality arise with the arts.[26] This would argue against Rousseau's claim, in his *First Discourse*, that with the development of the arts and sciences mankind not only loses its natural freedom but its equality. Hume and Aristotle argue that the contrary occurs. In fact, Hume says that "progress in the arts is rather favourable to liberty, and has a natural tendency to preserve if not produce a free government."[27] This point leads to the next consequence of the history of regimes.

Second, acquisition and the prominence of self-interest promote the creation of democracies. Civilization tends toward the development of democracies and nothing but democracies (3.15.1286b19-21). The evidence from the development of civilizations indicates that the majority will rule in their own interest. Therefore, the end product will be either democracies or tyrannies.

Here, Aristotle sounds very much like Alexis de Tocqueville in *Democracy in America*, in which he argues that in the future only democracies or despotisms will be created as political systems. With this insight, we might see that the current debate concerning how much democracy is choiceworthy and/or inevitable begins with Aristotle's discussion. Aristotle shows that, not only does democracy seem to be inevitable but it is also choiceworthy. It is choiceworthy in that it meets the natural needs of the majority of human beings.[28] Aristotle in this section of the *Politics* suggests all the aspects of democracy that we today see as desirable. Yet Aristotle also gives a warning in the history of regimes about what tends to happen in democracies—the rule of law tends to erode in them in favor of the arbitrariness of the many's will. This suggests that Aristotle argues that the key to preserving the best form of democracy is to reinforce the respect of the rule of law in the many. The many must be made to love the law more than the articulations of their own interests. To preserve the regime allows their rule and that provides for their essential needs—the liberty to live as free men and to live in relative peace without the fear of violent death. Aristotle seems to suggest the ironic position that, in order to preserve the many's ability to rule and thereby to serve their self-interest, they must resist allowing their pursuit of self-interest to undermine the rule of law, which provides the very regime that allows them to pursue their interest in the first place.

We are again drawn back to address the following question: can there be a good multitude? Only in the earliest regimes could one find a good majority. Why? The text is silent on this question. Now, Aristotle wonders whether a seriously good majority is possible. The difficulty is obtaining a multitude that is good. To obtain a good multitude depends upon the particular route of development that a civilization has taken. Developments of civilization that lead to equality tend also to lead to factional differences. This is caused by the release of self-interest, which tends to destroy the unity originally fostered by equality.

Does the development of civilization that provides for the possibility of human equality also necessarily lead to factionalization, struggle, and the dominance of self-interest? The answer seems to be, yes, it must. But this leads to an even more fundamental problem. Democracy is said to be, by this argument, the natural end of human equality. Yet it is also a bad regime. If this is true, equality must be "bad," or else the premise that democracy is bad must be false. I suggest the latter is the case. Aristotle is trying to suggest, in his use of this dialogue, a teaching that democracy is not as bad as was suggested by the original typology presented in *Politics* 3.7.

The King and the Kin

At *Politics* 3.15.1286b21, Aristotle raises a fundamental question about kingly rule: "Should the family reign?" Even if kingly rule were best for the *polis*, would this hold for the king's offspring? What would happen if his offspring were like the many—i.e., like everybody else, prone to a desire for profit and self-interest rather than the desire for the best and the good? Should he choose the good or his own? Clearly, the principle of kingship would require him to choose the good over his own. Such a choice, however, is hardly credible, since it would require his going the principles of love of one's own.

The love of one's own seems to be something which nature promotes in all animals, hence in all human beings. The question of what the *pambasileia* should do seems fundamental in deciding its choiceworthiness as a regime. Should he give rule to another who is virtuous, or should he choose his own, less virtuous offspring? This problem places the love of the good and the love of one's own, both instilled by nature, in direct opposition to one another. However, in a contest between the two, nature seems to favor the love of one's own as more authoritative than the former. The point Aristotle makes is that it is not easy to believe that one can choose against one's own for the sake of the good. Again, it is a hard thing to believe because nature instills in us the love of one's own, and a conflict between the two claims suggests that nature does not provide an answer to this problem.

The claim of the *pambasileia* is that he must be superior by nature. The first difficulty is that to be human requires the preference for one's own.[29] The *pambasileia* would be required to love the good more than his own.[30] Can the superior man be superior to nature? Can the superior man overcome the love of one's own? That is not easy to believe, Aristotle notes. Therefore, human beings, the many, will not allow a superior man to be so hardhearted as to disavow his son or to prevent him from getting his inheritance—the kingship. However, not believing that one could deny his own leads us to the conclusion that it is likely that the many will not stand a person who could be so hardhearted. We can conclude from this line of argument so far developed that the people will then force the *pambasileia* to give his own son the inheritance.

It is reasonable, therefore, to suggest that the many will demand that the *pambasileia* choose his own. The requirement to choose one's own over what is best, of the good, is done out of the necessity to respond to the many's demand. The requirement to choose one's own at all costs is done to appease the many's sentiment that one should not reject one's own. It is hard for the many to believe that the choice of one's own is irrational. Because nature inclines one toward the love of one's own in both animals and human beings, there must be some sort of intelligibility—hence rationality—to it. Or to what extent is nature guided by reason? The conflict between one's own and the good points to a possible problem with teaching the benevolence of nature. If there is no rationality behind choosing one's own, then in what sense is nature intelligible or benevolent?

The second difficulty is the problem of persuasion or the difficulty of having to use force (power). The *pambasileia*'s rule is supposed to be accepted merely by the evident superiority of his nature. His nature is so evidently superior that all recognize it as being such: this is his claim to rule.[31]

Therefore, if the king has to rely on force, it would suggest the inability of nature to reveal what is naturally superior. It would also suggest that nature does not provide for the best simply to rule. The politically effective man is said to be superior as such. This assumption about the superiority of the politically effective man is brought about by what people believe about their general comprehension of human nature. If they can see clearly what is implied by nature, then the superior should rule. If they cannot perceive what is implied by nature clearly (like the difference between the natural master and the natural slave), then such a political rule would be problematic.

The first *logos* concludes with these two difficulties that concern the perpetuation of the *pambasileia* as a regime. As Nichols says, even if the *pambasileia* is the best regime, its "succession is a difficult problem."[32] The problem that is manifested here is similar to the problem that arose concerning the natural slave. Nichols argues that, "as in the case of masters and slaves, we cannot count on nature to produce like from likes."[33] This problem makes a regime's perpetuation subject to chance, and this is a political defect in any regime. Secession and perpetuation are critical to judging which regime is better. Democracy, on the other hand, escapes this problem; in a democratic regime, the continual existence of the many ensures that regime's perpetuation. Also, as long as law is maintained and respected by the many, the rule of law will be preserved.

Questioning the political efficacy of the *pambasileia* leaves in doubt the natural superiority of the *pambasileia*. People are either fundamentally equal, or they believe that they are fundamentally equal because the differences are not readily evident. Although Aristotle does not present this teaching in his own name, the argument as developed so far is that if people are generally equal, then law should rule. The premise is that the rule of law is favored by nature because human beings are fundamentally alike. Also, the doubts concerning the clear and evident superiority of any one man will weaken the fundamental claim of the rule for the *pambasileia*.

The remaining *logoi* of *Politics* 3.16-17 continue the partisans' debate between law and universal kingship, addressing the character of universal kingship, the analogy of the arts, the nature of law, the possibility of friendship, the happiness of the universal king, the differing natures of multitudes, the special excellence of the *pambasileia*, and obedience to the universal king. The debate concludes in an apparent tie, an *aporia*, where both the rule of law and universal kingship seem to have equally good arguments defending each claim that it is the best form of rule. But upon further reflection, one comes to the awareness that the political problem with *pambasileia* points to the superiority of popular rule restrained by law. This superiority arises out of the practical problems of universal kingship, which undermine the superiority of *pambasileia*, and therefore indicate that popular rule, i.e., democracy, restrained by law is the best regime, both in theory and in practice.

Notes

1. Clifford A. Bates, Jr., "Popular Rule, Political Excellence, Wisdom, and the Rule of Law: Democracy as Aristotle's Best Regime in 'Politics,' 3" (Ph. D. dissertation, Northern Illinois University, 1993).

2. W. L. Newman, ed., *The Politics of Aristotle*, (New York: Arno Press, 1973 [Reprint of the original Clarendon Press edition, 1887-1902]), vol. 3, 279.

3. Mary P. Nichols, *Citizens and Statesmen* (Savage, Md.: Rowman & Littlefield, 1991), 74.

4. Contrast R. G. Mulgan, "A Note on Aristotle's Absolute Ruler," *Phronesis* 19, no. 1 (1994): 66-69.

5. One of the only articles that addresses this debate directly is Thomas Lindsay, "The 'God-Like Man' versus the 'Best Laws': Politics and Religion in Aristotle's *Politics*," *Review of Politics* 53, no. 3 (Summer 1991): 488-509. Lindsay's specific comments in reference to the debate in the *Politics* text are both insightful and helpful, but I find that he stretches his argument when he attempts to tie this debate with Aristotle's teaching about the divine in the *Metaphysics*.

6. Dobbs argues that Aristotle's silence about the Philosopher-King is an implicit rejection of that teaching. I reject Dobbs' interpretation because, although he does not address the philosopher king, Aristotle does address the issue of the king who is simply best. Dobbs' argument is incorrect in that he fails to see the clear similarities between Socrates' Philosopher-King and Aristotle's presentation of the *pambasileia*, yet I believe that he is correct that Aristotle does not think this form of rule is the best. Darrell Dobbs, "Aristotle's Anticommunism," *American Journal of Political Science* 29, no. 1 (1985): 29-46.

On the other hand, Lockyer suggests that, in this section of the *Politics*, Aristotle presents an implicit criticism of Plato's teaching about Philosopher-Kings. Andrew Lockyer, "Aristotle: The *Politics*," in *A Guide to the Political Classics*, Murry Forsyth and Maurice Keens-Soper, eds. (Oxford: Oxford University Press, 1988).

7. Newell notes, "some commentators regard this aspect of Book 3 as a rather puzzling relapse into Platonism, as if Aristotle had suddenly conceded the possibility of the Platonic philosopher-king" (W. R. Newell, "Superlative Virtue: The Problem of Monarchy in Aristotle's *Politics*," *Western Political Quarterly* 40 [1987]: 159-79). The commentators to whom Newell is referring are Trevor J. Saunders, *The Politics* (New York: Penguin, 1991) and Sir David Ross, *Aristotle*, (London: Methuen, 1960), 255.

8. Martha C. Nussbaum, "Shame, Separateness, and Political Unity: Aristotle's Criticism of Plato," in *Essays on Aristotle's "Ethics,"* Amelie Oksenberg Rorty, ed. (Berkeley: University of California Press, 1980), 421. Also, P. A. Vander Waerdt ("Kingship and Philosophy in Aristotle's Best Regime," *Phronesis* 30, no. 3 [1988], 249-53) claims that this passage is either ignored or made into a historical support for Macedonian rule.

9. Note that the description of "polity" as a mixed regime does not arise in Book 3. The view of "polity" as a mixed regime is developed in Book 4. I argue that the so-called discussion of the mixed regime in Book 4 is not about "polity" or even about a specific form of regime but a generic discussion about what elements compose a regime. Although I do not support Nichols' argument about polity, *Citizens and Statesmen* is extremely helpful in reading most sections of the *Politics*.

10. Some interpreters of the *pambasileia* section see it as Aristotle's discussion of the importance of the prerogative powers of the executive. They read the discussion about kingship as a prelude to the discussion concerning the executive (or the offices) in Book 4.14-16. See Harvey C. Mansfield, Jr., *Taming the Prince* (New York: The Free Press, 1989) and Richard H. Cox, "Executive and Prerogative: A Problem for Adherents of Constitutional Government," in *E Pluribus Unum*, vol. 2, *Constitutionalism in America*, Sarah B. Thurow, ed. (Lanham, Md.: University Press of America, 1988). This interpretation tends to ignore the setting of the discussion of absolute kingship, a discussion examining the validity of the claims to rule of various regimes.

11. Newman is perplexed about the discussion concerning kingship. He notes:

We might have expected that more would be said about Kingship than is said, and that Aristotle would follow up his study of it with a study of Aristocracy. The kinds of kingship have been clearly distinguished, and why should not those of aristocracy be similarly enumerated? This is not done; on the contrary, Aristotle passes on to inquire in C.18 which is the best of the normal constitutions, and he finds that the best is kingship or aristocracy, whence he infers that, as the citizen of the "best state" is a good man, the citizen of a kingship or aristocracy will be brought into being by the education which produces good men (Newman, *The Politics*, vol. 3, xxxiii).

Also see Nichols, *Citizens*, 74-75.

12. See *Politics*, 3.14.1285a4, 1285a18, 1285a32, and 1285b5-6.

13. Newman notes at 1285b29 that "Aristotle forgets that he has included under the Lacedaemonian type of Kingship not only the hereditary but also the elective kingship (1285a15: cp. also C.15.1396b39)" (*The Politics*, vol. 3, 277). Commenting on 3.14.1285b31, Newman also suggests that "In saying that the rule over a household is a kind of Kingship (see above on 1278b37), Aristotle is thinking of the relation of a father to his children, not that of the husband to his wife or of the master to his slaves" (*The Politics*, vol. 3, 278). Also this view of kingship collapses household management and political rule in a way similar to what Aristotle himself criticizes in *Politics* 1.1.

14. This implies that the *pambasileia* is beyond the *polis*, that he is not limited by the *polis*, but may also rule an *ethnos* (nation) or a collection of *ethnê* (cf. Newman, *The Politics*, vol. 1, 268).

Newman translates *ethnos* as "nation." A more literal translation would be "people." "Nation" should be understood in terms of a tribe, i.e., the Navaho nation, and not in terms of the nation-state, i.e., Germany, Japan, etc. "Nation," I argue, should be avoided because the required use is archaic and the current usage might lead to misunderstandings.

15. This is why there is no need in the first two books to discuss either the laws or the ruling offices. There is no need for the laws or offices if there is a virtuous ruler: he supersedes the laws and the offices. The laws are a limit on his wisdom. This distinction will be discussed later in this paper. Compare Leo Strauss, *The City and Man* (Chicago: University of Chicago Press, 1978).

Another reason there is no need before this to discuss either laws or the ruling offices is that both are creations of the regime. The centrality of the regime in Aristotle's political science delays the inquiry into either law or the offices because their character is a function of the character of the regime, and thus derivative of it. Aristotle argues that the character of both law and institutions is shaped by the regime, and not the other way around.

16. On this point, Martha Nussbaum notes, "Several passages in the *Politics* seem to indicate that Aristotle agrees with Plato about the desirability of subjecting all citizens to someone divinely good and wise, disagreeing only about the possibility of setting up a polity [regime] that could deliberately cultivate such men as rulers" ("Shame," 421). Nussbaum misses the depth of Aristotle's argument here. It is true that on the surface of Aristotle's *pambasileia* argument, he is in agreement with Plato, but that is on the surface only because beneath the surface there are, I argue, many disagreements with Plato.

17. We should read the next three chapters of the *Politics* as a dialogue, not as part of a systematic treatise. Thus, we are able to go beyond what is obscured by the surface of the text in order to reveal what is underneath. By doing this, we are able to see the importance of this chapter of the *Politics*.

18. See Richard Bodéüs, *The Political Dimensions of Aristotle's Ethics* (Albany: State University of New York Press, 1993), 54-57, Eugene F. Miller, "Prudence and the Rule of Law," *American Journal of Jurisprudence* 24 (1979): 181-206, and Bernard Yack, *The Problems of a Political Animal* (Berkeley: University of California Press, 1993), 175-208.

19. Judith A. Swanson, *The Public and the Private in Aristotle's Political Philosophy* (Ithaca: Cornell University Press, 1992), 98-101. See also Chapter 8 above, especially pp. 155-59.

20. Swanson, *Public and Private*, 98-106.

21. See, *Politics*, 3.15.1286b11-13.

22. I argue that Aristotle sets aside the question of how to resolve the problem of factions until Book 4.

23. Earlier in Book 3 Aristotle discusses the problem with the possibility of the many having and exercising virtue. He notes, "It is possible for one or a few to be outstanding in virtue, but where more are concerned it is difficult for them to be proficient with a view to virtue as a whole, but (some level of proficiency is possible) particularly regarding military virtue, as this arises in a multitude" (*Politics*, 3.7.1279a39-b2).

24. Assuming the unnamed regime is aristocracy, the account presented is similar to the degeneration of regimes presented in Plato's *Republic* 8, except that timocracy is missing and tyranny and democracy are reversed in their order.

25. See Nichols, *Citizens*, 80.

26. David Hume, *Essays: Moral, Political, and Literary*, Eugene Miller, ed. (Indianapolis: Liberty Classics, 1985), 277-78.

27. Hume, *Essays*, 277.

28. Although discussing the teaching about democracy presented in *Politics* 6, Thomas Lindsay does make the interesting suggestion that "Aristotle perhaps anticipated a democracy somewhat resembling the modern liberal version *in practice*." He also suggests that "we modern democrats should give Aristotle" what was refused him by Hobbes, that Aristotle "anticipated, in key respects, the foundation from which Hobbes would launch liberalism" (Lindsay, "Liberty, Equality, Power: Aristotle's Critique of the Democratic 'Presupposition,'" *American Journal of Political Science* 36, no. 3 [August 1992]: 758, 760).

29. Nichols also sees this as a problem for the preservation of the *pambasileia* as a regime (*Citizens*, 78).

30. This is reminiscent of Aristotle's criticism in Book 2 of the *Politics* concerning the communism of wives and children in Plato's *Republic*.

31. At *Politics* 3.15.1287a1; Newman suggests that this line suggests that "Aristotle is thinking of a King like the King of the Persians (Hdt. 3.31), *allon mentoi axeurakenai nomon, to basileuonti perseon exeinai polieein to anboulatai*" (Newman, *The Politics*, vol. 3, 290).

32. Nichols, *Citizens*, 77.

33. Nichols, *Citizens*, 77-78.

Chapter 11

Aristotle's Legislative Science

Tim Collins

One of my favorite passages in Aristotle's *Rhetoric*, from Book II, chapter 12, describes the "youthful type of character" as "[looking] at the good side rather than the bad, not having witnessed many instances of wickedness. ...They have exalted notions, because they have not yet been humbled by life or learnt its necessary limitations. . . . All their mistakes are in the direction of doing things excessively. . . .They love too much and hate too much and the same with everything else."[1] Experience was a fundamental requirement for Aristotle's lectures on ethics and politics because a young person who lacked practical experience of life would not understand the content and point of the lectures, nor, because of their unsettled characters, would they derive the practical benefit of the lectures, whose entire point was "not knowledge, but action." (*EN* 1095a2-6) Even so, the typical student of the Lyceum, though beyond the *ephebe* stage and newly bearded, would still just be beginning to embark on a political career.[2] What kind of science of legislation is appropriate for these aspiring young statesmen?

I want to suggest that Aristotle's legislative science takes this audience into account, that the lectures on politics are intended to occur as they do for pedagogical effect, and that the structure of the discussion is meant to provide a conservative account of how regimes might, provisionally, develop into aristocracies. I say "provisionally" because I worry that my position will be taken to argue that "Aristotle was really Pol Pot." Aristotle was not an innovator or experimenter when it came to legislation. But he did believe in reform, and he did have a feel for the texture of psychological and institutional development over time. He viewed the legislator as a kind of physician, though with important disanalogies as well, and organized the *Politics* as an instructive course for young practitioners in both the bedside manner and prescriptions of lawmaking.[3] This paper will begin by describing the "bedside manner" of the legislator before turning to its primary emphasis, the prescriptive aspect of the legislative science.

The Frame of Mind of the Legislator:
Conservative Reform

In Book I of the *Nicomachean Ethics*, Aristotle announces that the task of political science and its practitioners is to make men good. (*EN* 1099b20-32) In Book VI, he reinforces this claim by attributing to political science and prudence the same state of mind, while distinguishing between their respective objects, the *polis* and the individual. He goes on to distinguish two aspects of prudence concerning the *polis*: "one, which is controlling and directive, is *legislative science*; the other, which deals with particular circumstances, bears the name that properly belongs to both, viz. political science."(1141b22ff., emphasis added) What does "controlling and directive" mean, and how does this branch, *nomothetikê*, differ from political science generally?

Book X provides us with some clues as well as a segue to the *Politics* when it makes the acquisition of the legislative science essential to producing a good disposition in others.(*EN* 1180b23ff.) There he criticizes the sophists for professing to teach political science without practicing it, and politicians for failing to pass their supposed knowledge down to their sons. But how much and what kind of practical experience was necessary to effectively study the science of lawmaking?[4] If I am right about the age of Aristotle's students, practical requirements of *political* experience, alone, would disqualify the overwhelming majority of the Lyceum from studying the *Politics*. What, then, is the purpose of the *Politics*? Aside from his criticisms of rival authorities claiming to teach politics, Aristotle is actually interested in the correct judgment that allows the expert to sift through collections of laws and "understand by what means and methods perfection is achieved, and which elements can be harmoniously combined."(*EN* 1181a26-28) This kind of judgment usually requires years of practical experience, but Aristotle wants to suggest that those who are willing to sift through collections of laws, even if they do not have "formed habits of mind," might improve their understanding.(*EN* 1181b9-12) In attempting to form these legislative habits, Aristotle is taking up the project begun in Plato's *Statesman* of teaching the subordinate arts of statesmanship—in this case the arts of legislation and education.[5]

The specific reference in Book X to the science of lawmaking as analogous to medical practice suggests parallels in the habits of mind required by practitioners of each art and the ways in which these habits may be inculcated. In neither case can one become qualified by reading handbooks on the subject.(*EN* 1181a32-b4) For this reason, the *Politics* should not be seen as a handbook, but rather as series of lectures which, though open to revision from students, seeks to exemplify the manner one finds in good doctors and lawgivers.[6] This is especially true of Book II of the *Politics*, which attempts "not only [to] describe statesmanship but also to practice it. . . ."[7]

The practice of statesmanship shares many of the attributes of the medical art. Martha Nussbaum suggests that, in addition to aiming at some kind of action, *value-relativity* and *responsiveness to the particular case* are characteristics, shared with medical science, that distinguish the practical sciences from mathematics or astronomy.[8] By *value-relativity* she does not mean a simple record of traditional or conventional social beliefs, but rather an approach that takes common beliefs seriously by subjecting them to the scrutiny of a normative idea like "health."[9] Similarly, the priority of particular cases, at least temporally in the dialectical sorting of Aristotle's method, reflects an appreciation for the *differences* of existing persons, beliefs, and practices.[10] This liberal (and medical) posture toward difference emerges in Aristotle's criticisms of Plato in Book II of the *Politics*, initiating a study of the legislator's disposition. In contrast to the Socratic principle that "it is best for the whole state to be as unified as possible," Aristotle argues that this craving for unity would actually destroy the regime. (*Politics* 1261a16ff.)[11] Difference within a *polis* is what allows for specialization and self-sufficiency. Thus a *polis* is by definition made up "of different *kinds* of men, for similars do not constitute a [*polis*]."(*Politics* 1261a24, 33-35, b13-15)[12] Nevertheless, differences must be woven into some sort of unity through education if it is to be a regime and not a mere alliance.(1263b37-38) Such a political education *through* differences places the burden of proof on the innovator out of respect for the human need for habits and stability; but, at the same time, it recognizes the need for development.[13]

The willingness to countenance differences requires a patience that innovators, with their penchant for simplistic quick-fixes and eagerness to see dramatic change, have failed to acquire. Aristotle believes their defect stems from the fact that they had "never taken any part at all in public affairs." (1273b29) Since the young legislator suffers this same defect, the critical study of their mistakes provides an opportunity for him to learn from them, and for Aristotle to inculcate the proper disposition toward reform. Aristotle argues that Phaleas begins *nearer* to existing constitutions than Plato, in that he primarily emphasizes economic redistribution through practices that are already in some sense familiar, like marriage portions.(1266a40-b4) And yet, as with Plato, Phaleas fails to appreciate the complexity of both human nature and the political system, ignoring how desires are connected to practices, such as birthrates and national defense. What is interesting about his analysis is that he does not dismiss the need to reform disparities of wealth, but recognizes, by sifting through previous accounts of economic reform, that economic redistribution has a persistent influence on political communities.(1266b15) Persistent questions, like established practices, deserve notice and counsel moderate solutions. But questioning, itself, stands in need of moderation, and Aristotle takes the case of Hippodamus as an opportunity to emphasize the importance of habit for the rule of law.(1267b23ff)

Hippodamus proposed legislation that would encourage innovation by giving public honors for inventions and allowing juries to qualify their verdicts to fit particular cases.[14] Aristotle feared that the constant interrogation and qualification of the laws would breed a habit of disobedience and an atmosphere of uncertainty, rather than the habitual respect for laws necessary for political stability. This concern, when taken with the earlier studies of Plato and Phaleas, issues into the central dilemma facing the lawgiver and Aristotle's response to it provides the essential example of the legislator's frame of mind, or manner.

> It has been doubted whether it is or is not expedient to make any changes in the laws of a country, even if another law be better. . . . [T]here is a difference of opinion, and it may sometimes seem desirable to make changes. Such changes in the other arts and sciences have certainly been beneficial; medicine, for example, and gymnastics, and every other art and craft have departed from traditional usage. And, if politics be an art, change must be necessary in this as in any other art. . . . [M]en in general desire the good, and not merely what their fathers had . . . Even when laws have been written down, they ought not always remain unaltered. . . . Hence we infer that sometimes and in certain cases laws should be changed; but when we look at the matter from another point of view, great caution would seem to be required. For the habit of lightly changing the laws is an evil, and, when the advantage is small, some errors both of lawgivers and rulers had better be left; the citizen will not gain so much by making the change as he will lose by the habit of disobedience. The analogy of the arts is false; a change in a law is a very different thing from a change in an art. For the law has no power to command obedience except that of habit, which can only be given by time, so that a readiness to change from old to new laws enfeebles the power of law. (1268b26-69b25)

Three things stand out in this passage: first, Aristotle's method of sifting through conventional opinions, giving them their due; second, the analogy and disanalogy with medical science; and third, the moderate position on reform Aristotle eventually reaches. Aristotle begins with "it has been doubted . . ." and proceeds to present contrary views of the desirability of change. The analogy with medicine allows him to infer that laws sometimes require reform, but also to distinguish the unique reliance of laws on habit. Failing to give any clear resolution to this deliberation, Aristotle places the reader in a moderate position toward reform. The student will see the political system as a kind of organism whose parts are connected (resembling a physician's perspective), requiring a certain level of stability and habitual continuity, and thus see the task of legislation as an art of piecemeal reform with existing practices.

When Aristotle turns to existing regimes in chapter 9 of Book II, he presents two points that in legislating for a regime have to be considered: "first, whether any particular law is good or bad, when compared with the perfect state; secondly, whether it is or is not consistent with the idea and character which the lawgiver has set before his citizens."(1269a30-35) Why wait until *after* the study of private legislators to suggest these guides? Why not state them as objectives up front as Rousseau would do in his *Emile*?[15] We noted previously that Aristotle saw the shift from Plato to Phaleas and Hippodamus as a movement *nearer* to existing regimes. Following this progression, the student comes to see the political system conservatively and thus when presented with the points would see them in their practical, as well as logical, order. In the practical context in which the student has been immersed, the question of consistency with the existing regime takes priority over the absolute goodness of a law. This practical priority shapes the student's frame of mind subtly, through the largely negative examples of private legislators's programs, so that when existing regimes of some merit are introduced, the tension between the two aspects of legislation can be fully experienced—as it would by men of practical experience.

The Spartan, Cretan, and Carthaginian constitutions are "justly celebrated" in Aristotle's view as good examples. (1273b25-26) Their goodness stems from the fact that all *mix* competing forces within the regime by giving groups (the poor, the rich, and the virtuous) a share in ruling, and thus a stake in stability.[16] Here is one significance of the legislator's two points of ref-erence—through proper mixing one can achieve stability (1270b21-24)—and in fact, we learn from Aristotle's criticisms of the Carthaginian constitution that the legislator has a *responsibility* to provide against disturbances by mixing, even if, like Carthage, all the groups are satisfied with their roles by a strong economy.(1273b20-22) Good legislation, not luck, should maintain stability. But this brings up the legislator's second point of reference—are the laws that will provide stability also "good" with reference to the best state?[17] To begin with, the stability that arises from "consent" of the major groups within the *polis* "is no proof of the goodness of the institution." (1272a40-b2) Instead, it is the stability of a regime whose forces are blended with reference to the potentialities of its constituent parts (not its wealth or isolation) that is the goal. That Aristotle is looking at the *potentials* of the parts also appears in his description of institutions in terms of their "*deviations* from the perfect state."(1273a2ff.) Sparta, for instance, values goods over virtue, and its constitution regards martial excellence but not the virtues of peace.(1271b1ff.) Similarly, Carthage is held defective because it chose its magistrates with an eye to both wealth and merit. (1273bff.) But surely, at least in the latter instance, the constitution would be more stable if the possibility of bribery were removed by a wealth requirement. Why, then, does Aristotle consider these regimes "defective" (suggesting reform) rather than differently oriented?

I think Aristotle views stability as a necessary, but not sufficient, end of politics which nevertheless is temporally prior in the growth of the *polis* toward what may be described as its "health," but what we commonly refer to as *excellence*. For this reason, stability will be the critical standard with regard to some institutions, while others will be referred to the best regime.[18] How is the legislator to know when to organize with reference to stability and integration or when to look to the best regime as a guide? If the conservative teaching of Book II has succeeded in situating the legislator within existing practices, so that the limitations of time and habituation are felt appropriately, he will be able to distinguish the necessities of stability from the potential for excellence. There is no principle to guide this decision, only a kind of "timing" which comes from the legislator's habits of mind, his conservative disposition toward reform. Before turning to how this timing plays out in Aristotle's "empirical" books, I want to briefly recap the main points in the legislator's frame of mind:

1. The legislator's activity aims at *practical action.* (Medical Analogy)

2. The legislator's method *begins with common beliefs* and gives *priority to particular cases* by respecting the differences of existing persons, beliefs and practices. (Medical Analogy)

3. Respect for differences requires the legislator to work with *existing practices* as his means of reform. (Criticism of Plato)

4. The legislator's frame of reference resembles that of the physician in that individual practices should be studied in relation to other practices that make up the *political system.* (Criticism of Phaleas)

5. The legislator's art differs from the physician's in its unique reliance on *habit.* Stability occurs over time and through habituation, so that, in order to maintain a general sense of predictability, any reforms will be *piecemeal*—leaving the system largely intact. (Criticism of Hippodamus)

6. The two points of reference for the legislator are stability and excellence. The legislator's conservative posture toward reform ensures that *standards of excellence will not precede the requirements of integration and stability* in the project of mixing contending forces. (Criticisms of Spartan, Cretan, and Carthaginian constitutions)

The Legislative Science:
Political Education and Prescription

Book III of the *Politics* is often said to contain the core of Aristotle's political science.[19] In it, he defines citizenship, classifies regimes in terms of correct and deviating regimes, evaluates different claims to rule, discusses the rule of law, and analyzes the identity of regimes in terms of change and continuity. This analytic task of setting out definitions for the parts of regimes and the references at the end of the book to the best regime have led some scholars to associate Book III with the account of the best regime in Books VII and VIII, suggesting that the "empirical" books in between disrupt the original study and belong to a later, less "idealistic" period in Aristotle's life.[20] Even for those who view the text as an integrated whole, the chapter is seen to center around the classification of regimes and especially a central question of political science: who rules? From the standpoint of the legislative science, however, Book II provides the formative influence and ensures that the legislator will glean a different message than the social scientist.[21]

The difference between the legislator's account of the remaining books and the political scientist's derives from the lawgiver's commitment to action. There is no esoteric teaching here, only the significances that attach to different aspects of the study as the result of one's frame of mind. Take, for instance, the question of citizenship. Aristotle's first definition, "one who shares in administration and holds office," satisfies the requirements of political science in that it is theoretically consistent with the understanding of political rule from Book I, as a kind of government where citizens "rule and are ruled in turn."(1252a15-16, 1275a22) But this definition could hardly be applied to an existing regime as the working guide to whom the legislator must include in his reforms. Such a principle would radically break the continuity with traditional criteria for membership. Consequently, Aristotle suggests a second, "practical" definition: one whose parents were citizens.(1275b22-23) Here is a practice in keeping with the "possibilities and dangers of local conditions."

The lawgiver's commitment to action carries with it a pedagogical consideration as well. In fact, it is this pedagogical concern that shifts the emphasis from the social scientist's question of who rules to the educator's interest in, first, of what the continuity of the state consists, and second, what kinds of education are appropriate.(1276b11, 1277a15ff.) That the two are related, as Aristotle suggests, will become clearer as we progress through books IV-VI, but for now we will follow his treatment. Aristotle is succinct about the first question,"the sameness of the [regime] consists chiefly in the sameness of the constitution, and it may be called or not called by the same name, whether the inhabitants are the same or entirely different."(1276b10-13) Like the tragic chorus, which may have the same actors as the comedy, the purpose gives the regime its identity.(1276b1ff.) Consider what this means in terms of the statesman's perspective. If the requirements of stability or virtue prompt the legislator to rearrange, significantly, the ruling offices, he in effect changes the *character* of the regime. In addition, since Aristotle defines "aristocracy" broadly—"it is so called, either because the rulers are the best men, or because they have at heart the best interests of the [regime] and of the citizens"(1279a35-38)—it includes those who might not be fully developed but have the right interests. Taken together, these moves transform the question of identity, the static classification of regimes correlated with the best examples of legal structures, into a study of the political education of regimes, of how they change and develop. The legislator's role in this education gives rise to a second question.

Aristotle argues that the citizen's excellence is always relative to the regime in which he lives, but that the excellence of the good man is perfect excellence and thus is always the same. (1276b30-35) This leaves the legislator with the pedagogical equivalent of the legislative dilemma between stability and excellence we saw earlier. Mary Nichols characterizes this discussion as "a rebuke to the one who claims absolute rule for himself." The reasons for this rebuke are worth quoting at length:

> [Aristotle] defines human goodness so that he excludes those who act as if they are self-sufficient, unable to be ruled along with others, as if they have no need of moderation or justice. We have also seen that he defines the citizen so that it includes the many. . . . His goals follow from his view that the city aims at both living and living well. . . . Aristotle is not, however merely incorporating the many into the city because of the lower end of the city and the outstanding individual because of its higher end. Rather, his political science brings the many into touch with the good life, which is possible for them as well as for the virtuous individual, just as it brings the latter into touch with the necessities that apply to him as well as others. . . . Human beings are commensurable; justice and friendship can therefore exist among citizens (*EN*, 1161a 32-34).[22]

Human beings are commensurable, but Nichols seems to have in mind, here, the kind of educative interaction that occurs in the master-slave relationship, where slaves are prepared for equality and freedom, implicitly replacing their differences with friendship.[23] And yet, though the political relationship brings common citizens *into touch* with statesmen, it is not clear whether they are being prepared for full participation or if their education amounts to a recognition of a kind of symbiotic relationship with each other, a welding together in a multifunctional (or dual) state through their common interest in its stability. From the standpoint of Aristotle's legislative science the question, "How are they to be transformed?" is intimately connected with the question "How *far* do they admit of transformation?" Both are included in Aristotle's express purpose for Books IV through VI: "we must proceed to speak of the perfect state, and describe how it comes into being and is established." (1288b3-5)

Books IV through VI, the so-called "empirical" books, show by their inclusiveness that the development of the best regime is not unilinear, but also that it need not rely on fortuitous circumstances. As Nichols writes, "in Books IV, V, VI, [Aristotle] teaches statesmen to transform their regimes in the direction of polities based on political rule."[24] I think Aristotle goes even further to attempt to develop both mixed regimes and eventually aristocracies, through polity, out of the common forms of democracy and oligarchy. This is possible because he thinks that through institutional reform and education the statesman can build a best regime on artful choice rather than luck, one of the marks of good legislation as we saw with Carthage. But this "prescriptive" aspect should not be separated from the conservative account Aristotle has provided thus far, and that is why he returns to the medical metaphor as he begins Book IV.[25]

To be specific, Aristotle illustrates his legislative project with the art of gymnastics. At first it appears that Aristotle discards the medical analogy, but when we look at what the new metaphor offers, we find that it includes not only what the medical analogy offered but also the major disanalogy with medicine—namely, the reliance upon habit.[26]

> For example, the art of gymnastics considers not only the suitableness of different modes of training to different bodies, but what sort is the best (for the best suits that which is by nature best and best furnished with the means of life), and also what common form of training is adapted to the great majority of men. And if a man does not desire the best habit of body, or the greatest skill in gymnastics, which might be attained by him, still the trainer or the teacher of gymnastics should be able to impart any lower degree of either. The same principle equally holds in medicine ... (1288b13-20)

The incorporation of the focus on habits is reinforced by the additional task of improving those who refuse their potential. There are no drugs or force in this medical art; rather, the physician-teacher relies on *persuasion*. "Any change of government which has to be introduced should be one which men, starting from their existing constitutions, will be both willing and able to adopt, since there is quite as much trouble in the reformation of an old constitution as in the establishment of a new one, just as to unlearn is as hard as to learn."(1289a 1-5) How is the project of teaching the citizens of democracies and oligarchies to want reforms, while removing the old lessons of deviant regimes, carried out?

We spoke earlier of a dilemma that was a pedagogical equivalent of the tension between needs of existing regimes and the standard of excellence. We can restate that dilemma now in terms of the explicit tasks Aristotle sets out at the beginning of Book IV. The statesman is told to consider both the best regime and that which is relative to circumstances. But how is the legislator to decide when to reform and when to preserve the current system? Aristotle does not address this difficulty directly, but rather points to a third task: to consider how any regime can be *preserved*.(1288b30ff.)[27] This prompts R. G. Mulgan to argue that there is a "problem in relation to [Aristotle's] stated intention of preserving all types of constitution."[28] The problem consists in the fact that the advice Aristotle gives, relative to democracies and oligarchies, requires that they moderate their regimes in ways that amount to *changing* the very character of the regime. This accentuates the legislator's dilemma between the claims of stability (or preservation of particular regimes) and the reform called for by the best regime.

I think there is a consistency to Aristotle's outline of the tasks of political science and that he answers the educational and constitutional dilemmas through the task of preserving regimes. From Book I we know that "what each thing is when fully developed we call its nature." (1252b32) Now, if the change in regimes conserves the highest development of the former regime, it could reasonably be said to have preserved the "nature" of the former regime in the transition.[29] This is exactly what happens in the most moderate forms of democracy and oligarchy as they blend into polity (1293b33ff.), and it explains why Aristotle thought that his counsel of moderation "preserved" deviant regimes. But if Aristotle counsels regime changes for the sake of preservation in the case of deviant regimes, why is preservative reform not applicable to all regimes short of the best regime?

Mary Nichols argues that in the course of "describing the middle class regime that is best for most, Aristotle speaks as if it were simply best."(98) Her chapter entitled "Turning Regimes into Polities" makes the case that "political rule . . . is the best way of life . . .," and since this life is manifested most fully in a polity—polity, and not aristocracy, is the best regime.[30] If it is the case that aristocracies are to be moderated so that they develop the virtues of a polity—deliberation, rule and being ruled—then all the regimes admit to reform; and, in addition, the statesman will be required to continually maintain the balance within polities and educate those being ruled for eventual participation. There is good evidence for this account in Aristotle's description in Book V of a mixed regime containing democratic and aristocratic elements. (1309a1ff.) Because this regime attaches no pay to office, the poor will continue to work, become rich, and thus become able to hold office. Here Aristotle does appear to "look forward to [the poor's] more responsible political participation," suggesting a primacy for an extension of the political life over that of exploitation, even for the sake of excellence.[31] Because Aristotle (a) blurs the boundaries between democracies, oligarchies, polities, and aristocracies; (b) considers both intra- and interregime reform as healthy or stabilizing; (c) thinks that the political life is the best life; and (d) sees the political life as distinctive of polity, which we know from the fourth task of political science to be the regime that is most appropriate for all cities, it appears that the majority of states can "in some way, attain the ideal."[32]

I agree with Nichols on (a), (b), and (d), but it is not clear that for Aristotle the political life is the best, nor that polity is the best regime. Nichols argues that the defects of aristocracy "are corrected . . . by moving toward more mixed forms of aristocracies, even toward polity, which more clearly gives the multitude a place in the regime and the ambitious the prerogative of statesmanship."[33] But to argue that one must extend participation for the sake of stability and political virtues does not preclude the possibility that that move is for the sake of future excellence. In other words, a movement toward the political life does not mean that that life is to be preferred to the life of contemplation and culture, but rather that it is a *necessary stage* in the development that cannot be short-circuited. Sparta, for instance, could moderate itself by giving the wealthy a larger place in the regime, becoming more of a polity, but this is the opposite of what Aristotle suggests, "[Spartans] err in supposing that [goods] are to be preferred to the excellence which gains them."(1271b10-12) Also the council of elders, as the institution of the wealthy, is criticized for allowing the wealthy to "canvass" for the office instead of appointing the worthiest, "whether he chooses or not." (1271a10-12) If polity is to be preferred to aristocracy, why are there no reforms for prerogatives in Book II?

An aristocracy that does not have a sufficiently stable base, for instance the one described in Book V as a democracy and aristocracy, like the Carthaginian constitution of Book II leaves too much to chance.[34] The temporal priority of stability in the legislator's criteria calls for a firmer foundation. The people of such a regime do not have the middle class habits of moderation and deliberation that make for stable politics (hence they might have great laws, but no one would obey them [1294a2-4]); consequently, when from their labor they begin to develop some wealth, and thus leisure for participation, the regime will have to be reformed to include those elements, but in a way that moves the regime toward polity. Polities are the schools of regimes, and it is over time that democracies and oligarchies develop the habits to become stable material for aristocracies. But polities already in existence and mixed regimes, "so-called aristocracies" in Book IV, ch. 7, usually fulfill the priority of stability and are subject, more rigorously, to the second criterion—excellence, or the best regime, aristocracy. The traditional notion of aristocracy, as rule of the best regardless of the ruled, is discarded in favor of a notion of aristocracy that arises out of polity.

All regimes can become polities, and polities are not all that different from aristocracies (1294a28-29). But if Aristotle saw these linkages and prescribed reform, why all the particular descriptions, the digressions, and the piecemeal disclosure of his program? In short, why not just line up the regimes on a continuum and state his goals up front? I think the structure of the *Politics* makes a substantive point about Aristotle's political science. Watching the text unfold is neither systematic nor linear, and while this is in part due to their being based on lectures, the disjointed progression parallels the lesson within the text closely.[35] Legislation for regimes is not zero-based constitutional construction, but is rather akin to prescribing an exercise program or teaching children—if one cannot countenance imperfection he is ill-suited to the task. Countenancing imperfection does not mean maintaining it, but rather understanding the forces at work in making it that way and the possibilities for change. I take this to be the meaning of the following passage in Book I: "In this subject as in others the best method of investigation is to study things in the process of development from the beginning."[36]

Conclusion

Aristotle's legislative science taught ambitious young men the contingency and complexity of legislation while tracing the growth of human societies to their natural end—aristocracy. By studying the particularities of existing regimes, showing their weaknesses and places of overlap, he taught these statesmen a kind of regard for existing systems of beliefs and laws, uncovering their principles of growth. To sum these principles up at the beginning would have been to treat his students as tablets, rather than as characters to be developed. The legislative science differs from political science in taking this developmental focus, inculcating a conservative disposition, and emphasizing the legislator's criteria for lawmaking— namely, stability and excellence. Like a physician, the legislator must take his bearings from the existing system, and even further, from how far that system will admit of persuasion. But this does not mean that he must reproduce it. "Two principles have to be kept in view, what is possible, and what is becoming: at these every man ought to aim. But even these are relative to age. . . .Thus it is clear that education should be based upon three principles, the mean, the possible, the becoming, these three" (1342b17-end).

Notes

1. Aristotle, *The Rhetoric and Poetics of Aristotle*, Rhys Roberts, trans. (New York: McGraw-Hill, 1984), 1389a-b.

2. Martha Nussbaum, *The Therapy of Desire* (Princeton: Princeton University Press, 1994), 55. For an opposing view on the age of Aristotle's audience, emphasizing their maturity and prepossession of practical knowledge, see Eric Voegelin, "Plato and Aristotle," *Order and History* vol. 3 (Baton Rouge: Louisiana State University Press, 1957), 300-1. See also Stephen Salkever's discussion of the intended audience for *politike* (social science), which includes "not only future lawgivers and political people,. . .[but] anyone concerned with making others better," in *Finding the Mean* (Princeton: Princeton University Press, 1989), 101.

Quotations from the *Nicomachean Ethics* (*EN*) are from J. A. K. Thomson, trans. (New York: Penguin, 1988).

3. On the medical analogies see Werner Jaeger, "Aristotle's Use of Medicine as Model of Method in His Ethics," *Journal of Hellenic Studies* 77 (1957): 54-61; G.E.R. Lloyd, "The Role of Medical and Biological Analogies in Aristotle's Ethics," *Phronesis* 13 (1968): 68-83; Salkever, *Finding*, 92-104; and Nussbaum, *Therapy*, chs. 2 and 3.

4. Aristotle himself had some second-hand knowledge of courts and statesmen but did not receive any real first hand tutelage until age thirty-seven, when he met the statesman Hermias in Assos. Werner Jaeger, *Aristotle: Fundamentals of the History of His Development* (Oxford: Clarendon Press, 1934), 113-15.

5. Plato, *Statesman*, 304a, 308d. The other subordinate arts are oratory, generalship, and the administration of justice. Aristotle drops the study of generalship in the *Politics*, and treats the others in the *Rhetoric* and *Ethics* respectively. In Book X of the *Ethics* he refers the educator to the science of legislation.

6. Nussbaum describes the practical contribution of ethical lectures to "someone who already has a thorough moral education, a relatively disciplined plan of life, and some experience of decision-making, . . ." as "individual clarification of ends and communal agreement concerning ends" (*Therapy*, 60). For a different view that advances the "clarification of ends" view without the constraints of communal agreement, see Salkever: "*politike*, theorizing about the human things, is perhaps best understood as an aspect of practical wisdom, as an inclination toward the universal that can clarify deliberation about our particular lives both by enriching our political vocabulary and by suggesting possible alternatives to political life as such" (*Finding*, 101) There may be some difference between ethical and political lectures in terms of the symmetry between teacher and student. While Aristotle's students probably have significant experience of ethical life by the time they come to his lectures, it seems unlikely that they would have much to "clarify" politically. The beliefs of the community provide limits to what can be taught, but nevertheless, there are lessons being taught in the *Politics*. For an interpretation closer to my own rhetorical perspective see Mary Nichols, *Citizens and Statesmen* (Savage, Md.: Rowman and Littlefield, 1992), 7.

7. Nichols, *Citizens*, 7. I would add to Nichols' account a pedagogical emphasis in Book II that is concerned with inculcating in statesmen the proper frame of mind in addition to the rhetorical concern for community stability and the linkage of disparate groups.

8. Nussbaum, *Therapy*, 61-68.

9. Nussbaum, *Therapy*, ch. 1, sec. 3 (on ordinary belief), 26; see esp. the example on 28.

10. Nussbaum, *Therapy*, 65. Aristotle writes that the doctor's primary responsibility is to "the health of this person: for he treats them one by one" (*EN* 1097a12-13).

11. Aristotle, *The Politics*, Benjamin Jowett, trans., Jonathan Barnes, ed. (New York: Cambridge University Press), 1988.

12. The distinction between *kinds* of people in a city lies behind the "aristocrat-democrat" interpretive controversy examined by Nichols in *Citizens* (1-12), and also at the heart of the more subtle disagreements between Salkever and Nussbaum on communal consensus (see n. 6 above). Salkever's notion of "the multifunctionality of political order," however, captures the texture of Aristotle's political framework in terms of tensions between the requirements of stability and those of virtue (*Finding*, 87-88).

13. Even Plato was criticized for complacency when he settled for a polity as his second-best regime (1265b33). Barnes translates *polis* as "state" (the literal meaning is "city"), and despite Stephen Everson's arguments for that translation, I prefer "regime" because it captures the compact sense of a way of life in addition to governmental offices. (xv)

14. Aristotle makes a point of describing Hippodamus as "a strange man, whose fondness for distinction led him into a general eccentricity of life, which made some think him affected . . ." (1267b22). This caricature resonates with the fascination for innovation and particularity that Hippodamus's proposals suggest. Aristotle also notes that he was the first person "not a statesman who made inquiries about the best form of government" (1267b30).

15. Jean-Jacques Rousseau, *Emile*, Allan Bloom, trans. (New York: Basic Books, 1979), 34-35.

16. Sparta is the first case analyzed, and it receives scrutiny for what Nichols calls its "sub-political" practices as well as its mixture of shares in governing—specifically, its treatment of slaves, women, and economic distribution (*Citizens*, ch. 2). These topics are omitted from the treatments of the Cretan and Carthaginian constitutions.

17. See the helpful discussion of this dilemma in a different context: Salkever, *Finding*, 85ff. Salkever writes:

If the sole business of politics were education in virtue, there would be no *aporia* con-cerning who should rule; only those who are most virtuous themselves and most capa-ble of recognizing and encouraging excellence in others would have a reasonable claim to citizenship. But since the *polis* must provide stability as well . . .[all free persons have a reasonable claim to citizenship]. . . .A determination will thus have to be made in each case concerning how far to modify the claims of excellence in view of the subordinate, though indispensable, requirements of stability and integration (86-87).

18. This duality of standards lies behind Salkever's notion of the "multifunctionality of political order" (*Finding*, 83-87) and Nichols' attempt to find "A Place for Beast and God" (*Citizens*, ch .2).

19. Nichols, *Citizens*, 53.

20. This is Jaeger's classic thesis in his *Aristotle.*

21. The distinction between the legislator's and the social scientist's view of the text parallels a similar distinction in Salkever between the *phronimos*, the wise citizen who has a "solid grasp of the possibilities and dangers of local conditions," and the social scientist, who studies human nature and the human good or goods (87).

22. Nichols, *Citizens*, 61.

23. Nichols, *Citizens*, 23, 82-83.

24. Nichols, *Citizens*, 85. This is not to deny that the empirical books contain a rich topography of the political landscape and that Aristotle is engaging in the classification and analysis of regime structures as well. The legislative science is a *part of* a larger political science which has theoretical clarification and understanding as its end.

25. Nor should the goal of building a best regime suggest a kind of utopian permanence. Aristotle always emphasizes the contingency that forms the backdrop of any human endeavor. See Martha Nussbaum, *The Fragility of Goodness: Luck and Ethics in Greek Tragedy and Philosophy* (New York: Cambridge University Press, 1986), Part 3.

26. See page 218 above.

27. There is a fourth task—to consider the regime applicable in all circumstances.

28. R. G. Mulgan, *Aristotle's Political Theory* (Oxford: Oxford University Press, 1977), 134.

29. This explains the educational, as well as the constitutional, question. "Now, to have been educated in the spirit of the constitution is not to perform actions in which oligarchs and democrats delight, but those by which an oligarchy or a democracy is made possible" (1310a20-23). Compare 1320a1-3, "[The legislator] must not think the truly democratic or oligarchic measure to be that which will give the greatest amount of democracy or oligarchy, but that which will make them last longest."

30. Nichols, *Citizens*, 203. Nichols writes, "In general, Aristotle's treatment of polity and aristocracy makes sense if his purpose were to favor an aristocracy that approaches polity over an aristocracy as traditionally conceived" (206, n. 32).

31. Nichols, *Citizens,* 118. This resonates with our earlier discussion of Carthage (p 221 above). Similarly, when he says "The legislator should *always* include the middle class in his government" (1297a35).

32. Nichols, *Citizens*, 206, n. 27.

33. Nichols, *Citizens*, 102.

34. 1309a1. Like the Cretan constitution it relies on an absence of pay for office (1272a 40ff.)

35. In fact, the lecture background would accentuate the pedagogical aspect of the books by spacing them out.

36. Aristotle, *Politics*, H. Rackham, trans. (Cambridge: Harvard University Press, 1932), 1252a28-30.

Chapter 12

Lawmakers and Ordinary People in Aristotle*

Paul Bullen

Aristotle says that while it is democratic for all matters to be deliberated upon by all citizens and oligarchic for all matters to be deliberated upon by only some, it is republican or aristocratic (i.e., correct) for some matters to be deliberated upon by some citizens and other matters to be deliberated upon by all.[1] Among the matters about which there must be deliberation, Aristotle lists laws and electing and auditing officials.[2] In this essay I extrapolate from things Aristotle says to the conclusion that he wants laws to be deliberated about by "some" and legislative officials to be deliberated about (i.e., elected and audited) by "all," at least in his second-best ideal.

Aristotle indicates that ekklesiasts (members of the popular assembly) and legislators are not the same people when he says that "the decision of the legislator is prospective and universal rather than partial, while the ekklesiast and the dikast [lay judge in popular courts] decide about what is immediately present and definite" (*Rhet* I.1.1354b5-8). He reinforces this position and gives a reason with his statement that "it is most proper for correctly established laws themselves to determine everything to the extent possible and for as little as possible to rest with the ones deciding (*hoi krinontes*) because, for one thing, it is easier to find one or a few who are prudent and capable at legislating or judging than it is to find many" (*Rhet* I.1.1354a31-b1). If "the ones deciding" include ekklesiasts (a position I defend in the appendix), this passage tells us that Aristotle expects the assembly to be filled with average people.

Most people, by definition, are average; it is, however, an empirical claim that average people (*hoi tychontes*) "are not given to deep thought, but are empty and vacant of all thoughts and, once stimulated, carried away by impulse."[3] Even if Aristotle produced models in which all citizens are good men, this is not an assumption of his realistic thinking. "While it is possible for one or a few to be outstanding in virtue, where more are concerned it is difficult for them to be proficient with a view to virtue as a whole" (III.7.1279a39-b1). "Good birth and virtue exist in few persons . . . . Nowhere are there more than a hundred well-born or good persons" (V.1.1301b40-1302a2). "It is not possible for a *polis* to be made up entirely of good persons (*spoudaioi*)."[4] Because average people are not "virtuous," Aristotle wants their power limited. At least one way he wants it limited is by laws which guide the exercise of their tasks as officials. He wants laws to do this in part because he expects lawmakers to be more prudent than average people.[5] We, in turn, can expect that Aristotle would not want the popular assembly to make the laws. This conclusion is possible even if we do not take "the ones deciding" to include ekklesiasts—as long as we make the safe assumption that, like the popular courts, the assembly includes a preponderance of average people. And Aristotle concludes his most populist chapter (III.11), in which he defends the idea of allowing average people some role in government, by saying that it is "especially evident that correctly established laws should be authoritative and that the official, whether one person or more, should be authoritative only concerning those things about which the laws are completely unable to speak precisely (on account of the difficulty of making clear, universal declarations about everything)."[6] The timing of this comment suggests to me that he is reassuring his audience that the power of average people will be restricted. Even if average people participate in governance, they are really subordinate to the good men who made the laws.

That the law should be the product of especially prudent people follows from the view that law is or ought to be "reason proceeding from a sort of prudence and intellect (*logos ôn apo tinos phronêseôs kai nou*)" (*NE* X.9. 1180a21-22) or, as Aristotle puts it in the *Protrepticus*, "a sort of prudence and reason proceeding from prudence (*phronêsis tis kai logos apo phronê-seôs estin*)."[7] Law plays a crucial role in Aristotle's social theory. Its primary function is not to control vice (i.e., to "rule"), but to make virtue[8]; and "it is not the average person (*ho tychôn*)" who can make laws capable of having this effect, "but if anyone can it is the one who knows (*ho eidôs*)," that is to say, the one who possesses legislative science and experience.[9] If those who deliberate about the laws should be citizens of above average prudence, and if the assembly is to be open to all citizens, a small council of "law guardians" would be a better place to make laws than an assembly.[10]

Nicomachean Ethics VI.8 compares the relationship between those who make laws (*nomoi*) and those who make decrees (*psêphismata*) to that between master-craftsmen and handicraftsmen (*cheirotechnai*) (*NE* VI.8. 1141b29), and the relationship between legislative science and practical political science to that between a master craft (*architektonikê*) and a subordinate craft (1141b25). This suggests that those who make laws and those who make decrees are different people, and that the latter should be subordinate to the former. Legislative science is concerned with universals (laws), while practical political science is concerned with particulars (decrees) (*NE* VI.7-8.1141b21-28). Although laws rule "universally," ekklesiasts must decide in particulars (*Pol* IV.4.1292a33-4, *NE* VI.8.1141b 25-28, *Rhet* I.1.1354b7-8).

How should people fit to be legislators be determined? Though laws are a deliberative matter, Aristotle would call the members of small councils of deliberators officials. He speaks, for example, of circumstances under which it might be advantageous to "allow all to advise, but have the officials deliberate."[11] The possible criteria for choosing officials from "some special persons" are property, family, virtue, or "some other such thing" (IV.15. 1300a16-17). Of these, Aristotle would prefer (relevant) virtue: prudence, justice, ability, political virtue, political capacity—or generally speaking, "merit."[12] As we saw, electing and auditing officials is also on the list of matters for deliberation.[13] While lawmaking is best handled by "some" (i.e., some kind of small council of wealthy or talented citizens; IV.14.1298a 40-b5, 15.1301a13-15), electing and auditing legislative officials is best handled by all (i.e., a popular assembly).

In III.11 Aristotle says that having "the multitude of citizens . . . [namely,] whoever is not wealthy and has no claim at all deriving from virtue . . . participate in the highest offices is not safe; for through unjust character they would necessarily act unjustly, and through lack of prudence they would necessarily make mistakes" (III.11.1281b23-28). Yet he says that denying all participation to the *dêmos* is risky. To exclude them completely is likely to make the *polis* "filled with enemies" (III.11.1281b30). "What is left, then, is for them to participate in deliberation (*bouleuesthai*) and decision (*krinein*)" (III.11.1281b31). The wording is similar to the definition of a citizen as one who has the right to participate in deliberative (*bouleuetikê*) or decisional (*kritikê*) office.[14] In III.11, as an example of deliberation and decision, Aristotle immediately mentions, in connection with Solon "and certain other legislators," electing and auditing officials (1281b31-38). In II.12 he had already approvingly said that "Solon seems . . . to have granted only the most necessary power to the *dêmos*, that of electing to office and auditing; for if the *dêmos* does not even have authority over this they would be enslaved and an enemy" (II.12.1274a15-18). If laws should be in the hands of "some," the electing and the auditing of officials should be in the hands of "all."[15]

Aristotle describes the best form of democracy, the one closest to a republic, as based on farmers. He particularly likes them because they are too busy to assemble frequently. Whatever interest they may have in "honor" rather than profit is satisfied if they are allowed to elect and to audit officials (VI.4.1318b6-22). "It is both advantageous to and customary for" such a democracy "to have all elect to offices and audit and judge (*dikazein*), but for persons elected on the basis of assessments to hold offices (and the greater offices from the greater assessments), or else to elect none on the basis of assessments, but rather those capable" of bearing the burdens associated with holding office, viz., the wealthy (1318b27-32; see II.11. 1273a24ff., IV.4.1291a36ff., V.8.1309a6ff.; *Rhet ad Alex* 2.1424a 12-20, 38.1446b21-23).

In addition to the stability that controlled popular participation brings,[16] electing officials is a task potentially suited to an assembly because under the right conditions people who are not themselves prudent can discern prudence in others. Aristotle approves of Hesiod's division of people into three kinds: "He who understands everything himself is best of all; he is worthy who also listens to one who has spoken well; but he who neither understands it himself, nor takes to heart what he hears is a useless man."[17] Aristotle shares a belief in this capacity of average people with Plato, who wrote that

> the many are not as deficient in their judgment about who among the rest are wicked or good as they are in the possession of virtue themselves; for there is a certain divine shrewdness even in bad persons (*kakoi*), such that very many even of those who are very bad can distinguish well . . . better humans from worse. (*Laws* 950b-c)

So, even if it is the *dêmos* that is doing it, voting can be an aristocratic method of selection.[18]

Still, certain conditions must obtain. Most important, participation must be collective. Solon and the other legislators, after all, "do not allow [average persons] to hold office alone" (III.11.1281b34). It is only when each average person has only marginal influence that average persons as a group can make good decisions.[19] Also, the *polis* should not surpass a certain size because "to distribute offices according to merit, each citizen must know what sorts of people the other citizens are; but where it turns out that they do not know this, then what pertains to offices . . . must go badly" (VII.4.1326b14-18).

Aristotle suggests the need for keeping one's eyes on the specific institutional arrangement of election when he says that traditional democracies can turn into extreme ones because of the wrong way of letting the *dêmos* elect officials: "Where offices are (1) elected to [as opposed to being assigned by lot] (2) by the *dêmos* (3) without assessments, those seeking office establish the *dêmos* as having authority over the laws in order to make themselves popular. This can be obviated or minimized by having election take place by tribe (*phylê*)" (V.5.1305a29-34). Aristotle is less prone to make specific policy recommendations, but Plato suggests a number of ways this electing could be done. Here is one, for choosing *euthynoi*:

> Each year . . . the entire *polis* should assemble . . . to present to God three men from among them. Each is to propose a man of not less than fifty years of age whom he considers to be the best in every way. . . . They pick out the half of the nominees who receive the most votes. . . . They are to judge among the rest by voting again, until three are left. In the first year they are to elect twelve such auditors (*euthynoi*), until each has attained the age of seventy-five, and afterwards three are to be added each year (*Laws* 945e-46c; see also one of the methods for electing law guardians at 753b-d).

I do not want to assert that Aristotle would endorse this or that particular arrangement, as much as indicate his desire to adjust the mechanisms to achieve the right results.[20]

Even with these precautions, Aristotle expresses doubt that collective prudence "can exist in the case of *every dêmos* and *every* multitude," although "nothing prevents what was said from being true of a *certain kind of multitude*" (III.11.1281b15-21), one that is "not overly slavish" (1282a 15-16). One wants him who "can listen to one who has spoken well" to vote, not him "who neither understands it himself, nor takes to heart what he hears." Aristotle recommends, then, excluding from citizenship artisans and laborers and possibly merchants and farmers (I.13.1260a36-b2, III.5.1277b 33-1278a26, VII.9.1328b33-1329a7, 1329a19-39), not to mention women, natural slaves, *perioikoi* (subordinate peoples, who are not slaves), and non-Greeks in general.

In his best *polis*, the multitude of citizens consists of men who have served as hoplites (heavy infantrymen) in their youth and are now supported by land farmed by slaves or *perioikoi* (II.9.1269a34-35, VII.9.1329a2-26, 10.1330a23-33). Under these conditions there need be no legal limit on which citizens can be nominated for legislative office, and the assembly should have the power to veto legislation (cf. IV.14.1298b32-1299a1). However, in the more likely situation that some unideal people are citizens, there should be an assessment required for higher office: "All the offices established by Solon were to be chosen from among the notables (*gnôrimoi*) and well-off persons (*euporoi*)"—from the first three classes (*pentakosiomedimnoi*, *hippeis*, and *zeugitai*); the fourth class, the laborers (*thêtes*), "had no part in any office" (II.12.1274a18-21), although they were allowed in the assembly and in the popular courts.

The multitude can also act as a check on those in higher office. Generalizing from the benefits of end-of-term audits (*euthynai*) in farmer democracies,

Aristotle says that

> to be left hanging (*epanakremasthai*), to be unable to do whatever comes to mind, has its advantages. The right (*exousia*) to do anything one wishes leaves [the political community] defenseless against what is base in each human. So [with checks] there necessarily results that most desirable of conditions in a constitution: good people (*epieikeis*) rule without falling into error, while the multitude (*plêthos*) is not deprived. (VI.4.1318b38-1319a4)

Even good people need limits to keep them from falling into the error of exploiting the multitude.[21]

This two-way policy of excellent men making laws which control ordinary men and ordinary men electing and putting a check on the excellent could perhaps be called "aristocracy with the approval of the multitude."[22] It is supported by Aristotle's recommendation that oligarchies convince members of the *dêmos* to participate in the deliberations of the assembly, while also limiting the power of that assembly by establishing a separate body of preliminary councilors or law guardians, "for in this way the *dêmos* will participate in deliberation but will not be able to undo anything to do with the constitution" (IV.14.1298b30). The assembly would only vote on decrees prepared by the preliminary council, or possibly even do no more than give advice (1298b26-1299a1). In republics the opposite happens with decrees (the few have veto power only). I would contend that with respect to laws it would be the assembly that has only veto power.

Aristotle says that to be a citizen is to be entitled to participate in an office that deliberates or makes decisions concerning the affairs of the *polis*. However, this definition may mislead since the *extent* of participation in deliberation and decision-making is not stated. What issues is one necessarily entitled to deliberate about? How much influence is one necessarily entitled to have in their resolution? The answer to both questions seems to be "not much." The content of citizenship is not quantified because the definition does not say who ought to be awarded citizenship in the first place. The appropriate extent of citizen power will depend on who is allowed to be a citizen. The baser the *dêmos,* the narrower and weaker Aristotle would want its influence to be. Perhaps the right account is that one can be a citizen in different degrees. One has the quality of being a citizen to the extent of one's right to participate in office. As a practical matter, the minimum standard of citizenship is the right to vote in an assembly which elects and audits at least some of the *polis*'s officials. Aristotle wants some average people to be citizens—but attenuated ones—so they will do no harm and do some good. Collectively they can make good decisions about some things, and they can act as a check on the political power of others. Although it is a task for the popular assembly to elect those officials, including the ones who make the laws, and hold them to account, under no realistic circumstance does a minimum definition of a citizen include the right to participate in the drafting of laws.

APPENDIX

That *Rhetoric* I.1.1354a31-1355a3 Applies to Ekklesiasts as well as to Dikasts

In the first chapter of the *Rhetoric*, Aristotle gives three reasons why lawmakers should minimize the discretion of *kritai* (decision-makers or judges) by being as precise and as comprehensive as possible in the laws they make (*Rhet* I.1.1354a31-b16). It is usually assumed that the *kritai* are dikasts. I want to argue that Aristotle is consistently referring to ekklesiasts as well. One reason readers may not see this possibility is that in the discussion leading up to the three reasons Aristotle is in fact talking about issues related to judicial rhetoric in particular. Another reason is that throughout the presentation of the three reasons he uses the words *kritês*, *krinein*, and *krisis*, which can be, and usually are, translated as "judge," "judging," and "judgment," respectively. This encourages the impression that the topic is still exclusively judicial.

Yet these words can have a broader application. (To avoid confusion, I will translate *kritês* as "decision-maker," *krinein* as "deciding," and *krisis* as "decision.") When distinguishing the three types of oratory, Aristotle says that those who listen to ceremonial speeches are *thêatai* (spectators), while both dikasts and ekklesiasts, who listen to judicial and deliberative speeches respectively, are *kritai*.[23] Officials are said to engage in deliberation, decision (*krinai*), and command (*Pol* V.15.1299a 25-28). The deliberative element of the constitution is said to make *kriseis* in five areas (*Pol* IV.14.1298a8; see also VII.8.1328b14-15). It is only when Aristotle uses *dikastês*, *dikazein*, and *dikê* that we can be fairly sure than he means judge, judging, and judgment (or trial) in the specifically judicial sense. Having made a case that these words *can* have a broader use, let me show why I think they actually do in *Rhetoric* I.1.

The *Rhetoric* opens with a discussion of the nature of rhetoric and the tendency of previous manual writers to emphasize secondary, nonrational matters (*Rhet* I.1.1354a11-18). This, we are told, is because in many courts irrelevant talk is allowed (1354a18-26) and previous writers have focused on judicial rhetoric at the expense of the more noble political kind (1354b22-

1355a3). Aristotle recommends that such speech be made illegal, as it had been for the Council of the Areopagos. If it were, litigants would have

> nothing to do outside showing that something is or is not the case or did or did not happen. Concerning [an act's] importance or triviality, justice or injustice, insofar as the legislator has not already determined this, the dikast should [come to] know this on his own, and not learn it from the litigants. (*Rhet* I.1.1354a26-31)

The only issue that should be of concern to the litigants is that of fact, mainly past fact.

Not only should procedural law leave litigants with little to do, but substantive law should do the same for dikasts. Anticipated where Aristotle said "insofar as the legislator has not already determined" (1354a29-30), Aristotle makes this latter point clear in the next sentence, saying that "it is most proper for correctly established laws themselves to determine everything to the extent possible and for as little as possible to rest with the ones deciding (*hoi krinontes*)" (*Rhet* I.1.1354a31-33; see Plato, *Laws* 876). It is the "ones deciding" and cognate words in the next sentence that I take to include ekklesiasts as well as dikasts. Although Aristotle brings up the importance of detailed laws from a consideration of the problems of popular law courts (and not of assemblies or of magistracies), he expands his subject matter to include the effect of laws on ekklesiasts. Although this is not made explicit until the third of the three points, it is hinted at in the second. The first, however, gives no clue of the broader application.

The first argument is that "it is easier to find one or a few who are prudent and capable at legislating or judging (*dikazein*) than it is to find many" (1354a33-b1). Here, Aristotle really does only mention the functions of adjudicating (*dikazein*) and legislating, which would legitimately encourage the belief that his concern is only with dikasts. There is no reason for the first-time reader to think that he is considering political deliberation too. It is what he says later that indicates that the subject has already broadened and that even this statement should or could be taken to include ekklesiasts.

Aristotle's second point is that "legislation comes from having thought over much time, while decisions (*kriseis*) are made offhand; so it is difficult for the ones deciding (*hoi krinontes*) to render well what is just and what is advantageous" (*Rhet* I.1.1354b4). The juxtaposition of "what is just" (*to dikaion*) and "what is advantageous" (*to sympheron*) suggests that both judicial and deliberative circumstances are being talked about since Aristotle says that advantage is the end in deliberative rhetoric, aimed at ekklesiasts, while justice is the end in judicial rhetoric, aimed at dikasts (*Rhet* I.3.1358b 20-29; see also b30-37; I.10.1368b3ff.).

In the third reason Aristotle is explicit. He says that the foremost reason that it is most proper for correctly established laws themselves to determine everything to the extent possible, and for as little as possible to rest with decision-makers, is that

> the legislator's decision (*krisis*) is prospective and universal rather than partial, while the ekklesiast and the dikast *decide* what is immediately present and definite. For them friendship, animosity, and private advantage are often entangled [with decision-making], with the result that they are unable to see the truth adequately: personal pleasure or pain clouds their *decision-making* (*Rhet* I.1.1354b4-11, emphasis added).

Aristotle here mentions an ekklesiast explicitly for the first time in *Rhetoric* I.1, and speaks of him as a *kritês*, making *kriseis*. Not only does he speak of the ekklesiasts deciding, but he even speaks of the legislators doing so.

In the next passage Aristotle adds to the earlier list of past and present fact ("that something is or is not the case or did or did not happen" [1354a28]), future fact:

> As we say, then, the decision-maker (*kritês*) ought to be made authoritative over the fewest [or: least important, *elachista*] other things possible: whether something did or did not happen [dikast] or *will or will not happen* [ekklesiast] or is or is not the case—these it is necessary to leave resting with the decision-makers (*kritai*). For the legislator is unable to foresee them. (*Rhet* I.1.1354b11-16, emphasis added)

As mentioned, future fact is a concern of deliberative rhetoric aimed at the ekklesiast: "An ekklesiast makes decisions about what will happen" (*Rhet* I.3.1358b4; see also 1358b3-4, 20-24), while a dikast makes decisions about past fact. Since Aristotle draws the same basic conclusion here, after having introduced ekklesiasts, as he did before his three reasons ("It is most proper for correctly established laws themselves to determine everything to the extent possible and for as little as possible to be left with the ones deciding" [1354a 31-33]), I think we can read back into the earlier statements an applicability to deliberative rhetoric and ekklesiasts.

A bit later in the same chapter Aristotle uses *kritai* to mean only ekklesiasts when he says that in the assembly "the decision-makers (*kritai*) themselves adequately guard against" being misled by irrelevant emotional appeals (*Rhet* I.1.1354b31-1355a3). In conclusion, then, the arguments presented in *Rhetoric* I.1 concerning the need for exact laws to minimize the discretion of decision-makers apply to ekklesiasts as well as dikasts. An important part of the rule of law for Aristotle is its rule over the assembled *dêmos*.[24]

Notes

* I would like to thank Russell Hardin, Richard Kraut, Bernard Manin, and Fred Miller, Jr. for their comments. This paper is dedicated to the late Arthur W. H. Adkins.

1. *Pol* IV.14.1298a9-11, 34-35, b5-8. References are to the *Politics* and, unless otherwise indicated, to works by Aristotle, using the following abbreviations: *NE* = *Nicomachean Ethics*, *Rhet* = *Rhetoric*, *Rhet ad Alex* = *Rhetoric to Alexander*, *Ath Pol* = *Athenian Constitution*. In this chapter "prudence" represents *phronêsis* (often represented by "practical wisdom"). At IV.14.1298a7-9, Aristotle says that the responsibility for making decisions (*kriseis*) about these subjects must be distributed such that either (a) all citizens are entitled to decide about all of them, or (b) only some citizens decide all of them, or (c) some citizens decide some of them while all citizens decide the others. Option (b) is subdivided into either (i) one group of "some" deciding all matters, or (ii) one group of "some" deciding some matters, with one or more other groups of "some" deciding the rest of the matters, and no matters being decided by all citizens. Aristotle indicates (IV.14.1298b5-13) a preference for at least some of the decision-making being carried out by the citizenry as a whole. Thus, he prefers option (c) to a variant option (ii) of (b) in which all citizens participate in decision-making but with no one area in which they all share.

2. According to IV.14.1298a3-7, "the deliberative element (*to bouleuomenon*) has authority concerning war and peace, alliances and their dissolution, laws (*nomoi*), [cases involving] death, exile, or confiscation, and the election and the auditing of officials." According to *Rhetoric* I.4.1359b19-24 "the important subjects on which people deliberate (*bouleuontai*) and on which deliberative orators (*hoi symbouleuontes*) give advice are basically (*schedon*) five in number: finances, war and peace, protection of the countryside (*chôra*), imports and exports, and legislation (*nomothesia*)." The main difference between the two lists is that the *Rhetoric* includes economic matters and does not mention capital cases or electing and auditing officials. According to the pseudo-Aristotelian *Rhetoric to Alexander*, "the subjects of public speeches are seven in number; for our deliberations and speeches addressed to the council or to the *dêmos* necessarily deal with either sacred rites or laws or the constitution (*politikês kataskeuês*) or alliances and agreements with other *poleis* or war or peace or finance" (2.1423a21-26).

3. *On Divination in Sleep* 2.464a21-24. On *ho tychôn*, see *Ath Pol* 27.4-5, *Pol* II.8. 1269a6, II.9.1270b29, II.10.1272a30, II.11.1272b36, V.8.1308a33, 1309a9; Xenophon, *Memorabilia* III.9.10. Based on the Greek word for chance or fate *(tychê)*, *ho tychôn* could be translated "any chance person," "first comer," "man on the Clapham Omnibus," "ordinary person," "person off the street," etc.

4. III.4.1276b37-38. This statement is part of a conditional sentence, but I take it to express Aristotle's belief.

5. Concerning Spartan ephors, Aristotle says that "although they are just average people (*tychontes*) they have authority in the most important decisions. Hence it would be better if they did not decide (*krinein*) according to their own opinion but according to what is written, that is to say, according to the laws" (II.9.1270b28-31). See also II.10.1272a37-39, b5-7.

6. III.11.1282b1-6. The laws rule ekklesiasts by making them liable to prosecution, should they propose decrees that could be construed as in conflict with the laws; see Demosthenes XXIII (*Against Aristocrates*) 87, 218 on Athenian constitutional law: "No decree of the council or of the *dêmos* shall have more authority than a law." See also, Demosthenes XXIV (*Against Timocrates*) 30 and Andocides I (*On the Mysteries*) 87 [11-12]. Cf. VII.2.1324b5-6.

7. Iamblichus, *Protrepticus* 6 (37.22-41.5) in Aristotle, *Fragmenta Selecta*, ed. W. D. Ross (Oxford: Clarendon, 1955), 33. English translations can be found at Anton-Hermann Chroust, *Aristotle: Protrepticus* (Notre Dame, Ind.: University of Notre Dame Press, 1964), 15, 64-65; and at *The Complete Works of Aristotle: The Revised Oxford Translation*, ed. Jonathan Barnes (Princeton: Princeton University Press, 1984), 2408. Aristotle makes similar comments in other places, though not in his own voice.

8. *Pol* III.9.1280b8-12; *NE* II.1.1103a17ff., b4, 3.1104b13-16, III.5.1113b23-1114a3, V.1. 1129b19-25, 2.1130b22-24, X.9.1179a33-1181b2.

9. *NE* X.9.1180b23ff. Aristotle contrasts *ho tychôn* with *ho politikos anêr* at V.8.1308a 33-34.

10. Aristotle generalizes that among boards of deliberative officials, the council (*boulê*) is democratic, the preliminary council (*proboulê*) is oligarchic, and law guardians (*nomophylakes*) are aristocratic (IV.14.1298b26-1299a1, 1299b30-1300a4; VI.8.1323a6-9). This, of course, depends on what one means by "council" etc. On the Council of the Areopagus as a guardian of the laws, see *Ath Pol* 3.6, 4.4, 8.4; Isocrates, VII (*Areopagiticus*) 37-42; Aeschylus, *Eumenides* 680-710. See also Xenophon, *Oeconomicus* VI.14-19; Plato, *Laws* 752d-755e, 762d-e, 766b, 767e, 770a-c, 772a-c, 775b, 779c-d, 828b, 835a-b, 840e, 847c-d, 855c-d, 871c, 957c-b, 961a-b; Cicero, *de Legibus* III.20.46-47. "It would be equally correct if we substituted for the Greek words 'Rule of the Many,' 'Rule of the Few' the expressions 'Rule by the Assembly,' 'Rule by the Council'" (J. W. Headlam, *Election by Lot*, 92, as cited in Leonard Whibley, *Greek Oligarchies: Their Character and Organization* [Chicago: Ares, 1975 (1896)], 157, n. 1).

11. IV.14.1298b33-34. In Aristotle's way of speaking it is quite possible to have deliberative *officials* (see III.1.1275a26-33, IV.14.1298a8-9, 22-23, 26-27, 30-31, b6-7, 27-30, 32-34, 35-1299a1, 1300b4-5, 15.1299a25-28, b30ff., VI.2 *passim*, VI.8.1322b12-17, 36-37, 39, 1323a6-9; Plato, *Laws* 767a-b), even though he appears to make the deliberative and official functions of the constitution mutually exclusive: "there are three parts in all constitutions . . . [namely,] the part that deliberates about common matters, the part concerned with offices, . . . and third, the adjudicative part" (IV.14.1297b37-1298a3).

12. On political virtue, which includes prudence, as a basis for office, see III.1.1301 a38-b1, 9.1281a4-8, 12.1283a21 (I take political and not military virtue to be intended here; cf. V.11.1314b22), III.13.1284a3-11, III.17.1288a9, V.1.1301a38-b1, VII.3.1325b10.

13. On electing and auditing officials, see II.12.1271a16-18, III.11.1281b33, 1282a26-27, IV.14.1298a6-7, VI.1.1317a5, 8, VI.3.1318a10, VI.4.1318b21-1319a4.

14. III.1.1275b17-19, 5.1277b37-38. According to the corrected definition, which appears at the end of III.1 (1275b13-19), these offices can be either "definite" (for a limited time) or "indefinite" (like regular ekklesiasts or dikasts). Apostle and Gerson are not only unliteral but interpretively incorrect in their translation of III.1.1275b17-20: "A citizen of a state is said to be a man who has the right to participate in legislative or judicial office of that state" (*Aristotle's Politics*, trans. Hippocrates G. Apostle and Lloyd P. Gerson [Grinnell, Iowa: Peripatetic Press, 1986], 73-74). "Judicial" as a translation of *kritikê* is perhaps understandable, but there is no justification for translating *bouleuetikê* as "legislative."

15. Aristotle mentions electing and auditing officials again at III.11.1281b33, 1282a1, 13-14, 26. Cf. VI.1.1317a8 vs. IV.14.1298a1. See also VI.4.1318b21-30.

16. While Crete's ten cosmoi and Sparta's five ephors both unfortunately "consist of average people (*tychontes*)" (II.10.1272a30), the Cretan constitution does not engender the solidarity that the Spartan does, because cosmoi are not elected from all the people, but only from certain families and the elders are elected from the cosmoi (II.10.1272a31-34). In Sparta "the people keep quiet because they share in the greatest office" by being eligible for

election to the ephorate (II.9.1270b18-19). "The [Spartan] *dêmos* shares in the greatest office and hence wishes the constitution to continue" (II.10.1272a31-33).

17. *NE* I.4.1095b10-13. Are average people like the quasi-rational part of the soul which, while not possessing reason itself, is able to obey reason (and hence deserves to be ruled politically, not despotically)? Although Aristotle makes a similar characterization of slaves, it seems to be in some way his view of ordinary free men. See I.5.1254b4-6, III.4.1277a 15-17, 1278b28-29, VII.14.1333a16-18; *NE* I.7.1098a4-5, I.13.1102b28-33; cf. *Pol* I.13. 1260b5-7.

18. On election as aristocratic, see II.12.1273b40-41, IV.9.1294b7-13, IV.14.1298a 26-28, and IV.15.1300b4-5 (and *passim* IV.15). Lot, by contrast, is democratic (VI.2.1317b 17-38, *Rhet* I.8.1365b31-32). See also *Rhet ad Alex* 2.1424a12-20. Taking his cue from Aristotle (and Guicciardini, Harrington, Montesquieu, and Rousseau), Bernard Manin provides his own reasons why the method of voting has aristocratic effects (*Principles of Representative Government* [Cambridge: Cambridge University Press, 1997]).

19. III.11.1281a39-1288a39. This bears comparison with the "jury theorem" of the Marquis de Condorcet (1743-94). "On matters of truth versus falsity, such as in a trial to determine whether someone is guilty of a particular crime, the average person has a view some fraction guilty and the remaining fraction innocent. Condorcet's *jury theorem* says that, if each person is more likely to be right than wrong, a larger jury is more likely to be right than wrong, a larger jury is more likely to yield the truth than is a smaller jury. Having only a judge yields the worst error rate. With a very large jury the odds of error are vanishing small" (Russell Hardin, *One for All: The Logic of Group Conflict* [Princeton: Princeton University Press, 1995], 206-7). Aristotle does say that "humans have a natural disposition for the true and to a large extent hit on the truth" (*Rhet* I.1.1355a15-17).

20. See a criticism of a particular sort of two-stage selection process (electing from those already elected) at II.6.1266a26-27. Aristotle says that the five Spartan ephors "should be elected from all, to be sure, but not in the way it is done now, which is utterly childish" (II.9.1270b26-28). Cf. II.10.1272a32-35 (Cretan cosmoi elected only from certain families).

21. Concerning the Spartan elders (*gerousia*), Aristotle says that "it is better that they not go unaudited, as they do now" (II.9.1271a5-6). And of the Cretan elders he says that "it is not safe that they should go unaudited" (II.10.1272a37).

22. Plato, *Menexenus*, 238d; see also Isocrates, VII (*Areopagiticus*) 26-27.

23. *Rhet* I.3.1358b4-6, 20-24; see *Pol* III.15.1286a21-28, VII.8.1328b13-15; cf. VII.8. 1328b22-23 (it seems that *anankaiôn* should be *dikaiôn* at VII.9.1329a4).

24. Martin Ostwald, *From Popular Sovereignty to the Sovereignty of Law: Law, Society, and Politics in Fifth-Century Athens* (Berkeley and Los Angeles: University of California, 1986), makes the following observation: "A new social and political order was created that retained the characteristic institutions of the Athenian democracy while subordinating the principle of popular sovereignty to the principle of the sovereignty of law" (497). He also states

> [I]t is no exaggeration to say that the reconciliation agreement [between the oligarchs at Athens and the democrats at Piraeus in 403 BC, after the overthrow of the Thirty and before the restoration of democracy], including the amnesty, represents a triumph of *nomos* not only over arbitrary government but even over the kind of popular sovereignty that found its extreme expression in the clamor of the masses at the Arginusae "trial" that "it would be a terrible thing not to let the *dêmos* do whatever it pleases" (509-10).

Further on, Ostwald concludes

> The written law . . . was now officially accepted as having precedence over

anything decreed by Council and Assembly to meet a particular situation, and any such decree was declared null and void unless it conformed to the code of written laws. There is evidence that this distinction was observed for most of the fourth century, except for the critical period between 340 and 338 B.C." (523-24).

Chapter 13

The Death Penalty in Plato's *Laws*

Brian Calvert

In 1981, Mary Margaret MacKenzie published her book *Plato on Punishment*. This was followed, two years later, by R. F. Stalley's *An Introduction to Plato's "Laws,"* which contains two chapters on Plato's theory of punishment. More recently, in 1991, Trevor Saunders brought out *Plato's Penal Code*, and this book has subsequently been commented on and criticized by Stalley.[1] While all of these authors make mention of Plato's use of the death penalty, they tend to refer to it incidentally, and there is no extended discussion devoted to the justifications offered by Plato for the execution of criminals. Nor is it the case, so far as I am aware, that any other study has concentrated solely on this particular issue. This is a gap which I shall attempt to fill, and in so doing my purpose will be twofold. I shall give an exposition of Plato's position, together with his reasons for holding it, which I shall try to make as clear and consistent as possible. At the same time my interest in Plato is not simply that of the intellectual archaeologist; I also want to explore how much of his position remains of interest and value for modern debates on the topic. This will mean that his account will be evaluated, in part, in terms of the theories of retributivism and utilitarianism, though I do not believe that the use of these theories will involve any undue distortion of his position. It will also mean that sometimes I shall take matters beyond what we actually find in the text to suggest where his account may be fruitfully linked in with ideas from contemporary thought. While some of these musings will certainly be speculative, I trust that they will not be pointlessly speculative and will be at least plausible extrapolations from what we actually do find in his writings.

Though a number of the dialogues makes some reference to capital punishment, by far the fullest account occurs in the *Laws*, and I shall confine my treatment to this work. After a brief review of the capital offenses described in the *Laws*, I shall turn to the justifications given for the imposition of the death penalty. Plato's defense contains a number of different features, some of which continue to be found in contemporary debates. Other points of contemporary interest are not discussed directly; yet at least in the case of some, he comes intriguingly close to dealing with them and certainly prepares much of the important groundwork. Not only this—there is an even more intriguing possible outcome. Despite the fact that Plato advocates the use of the death penalty for a wide variety of offenses, if we probe more deeply into the justifications given for the imposition of the penalty, we uncover some quite unexpected implications which may indicate that on his own terms Plato ought to be far more worried than he realizes about the extent to which he is willing to endorse the use of execution.

Capital Offenses—A Review

In this section I shall give a brief review of the main kinds of offenses that Plato claims should receive the death penalty. It would be helpful, though Plato doesn't adopt this procedure himself, to divide his capital offenses into two main categories, offenses against the state or community and offenses against individuals.

The first category can once again be divided into two parts. First, there are religious crimes, such as the robbing of temples (854c), unreformed atheism (909a), and practicing private religion (910d). Plato appears to regard these crimes as a subclass of offenses against the state because religion is viewed as an essential part of the very structure of his society, and any undermining of religion is to be thought of as an attempt to subvert the community. For this reason, he refers to temple robbery as one of a number of "impious deeds that bring about the ruin of the state" (854c).[2] There are also many other capital crimes against the state which we can designate as political. Among these are sedition (856), treason (856-57), private peace- or war-making (955b-c), and taking bribes while acting as a public servant (955c-d). Death is also the penalty for attempts to undermine legal procedures, such as obstructing the decision of a court (958c), sophistic perversion of justice (938c), and repeated perjury (937b-c).

As for capital crimes against individuals, Plato introduces a complex array. He follows current Athenian practice by distinguishing between intentional and nonintentional homicide, and makes deliberate murder of a citizen his prime capital offense (871a). He also follows current Athenian practice in ways which might strike the modern reader as bizarre or absurd. For instance, if someone is killed by an animal or an inanimate object, a trial is to take place, and if the animal should be found guilty it is to be executed

(873e). D. M. MacDowell,[3] however, cautions us not to be too hasty in dismissing such practices as ridiculous. Instead he thinks we should look on them in the same way we regard a modern coroner's court, where the aim is to determine the cause of death and to take whatever steps are possible to prevent the same thing from happening again. Another apparently curious example occurs at 869 where Plato says that if a person kills a parent in a fit of anger nothing less than death should be the penalty—in fact the killer deserves to die many times. However if the parent survives long enough to pardon the killer before he or she dies, the offense is to count as involuntary homicide, and a lesser penalty is to apply. Once again it seems here that Plato simply follows current Athenian practice. MacDowell[4] tells us that Demosthenes refers to this rule, though MacDowell adds that no instance has been recorded of such forgiveness actually being given. Though such a rule may well seem strange to Western minds, Roger Hood points out that a very similar rule is still maintained in Islamic law.

> Death is the punishment for premeditated murder if the victim's family seek retaliation (*Kisas*), but they may also pardon the murderer or accept "blood money"—compen-sation or forfeited rights of inheritance. The Koran appeals for such forgiveness, promising absolution of sins for those who extend a pardon.[5]

Other capital offenses against the person depend on the status of the victim and the assailant. If a person wounds a parent, brother, or sister with the intent to kill, death is to be the penalty (877b-c). However, if a citizen wounds another citizen not so related but again with the intent to kill, a less severe sentence applies. Considerations of social status are also apparent on a number of occasions when Plato is more severe on slaves than upon free citizens.

No mention is made of the method of execution to be employed. Nonetheless, Plato doesn't appear to be at all squeamish about recommending quite savage brutality in certain cases. For instance, if a slave deliberately kills a free citizen, he is to be scourged with as many lashes as the prosecutor instructs. Then Plato adds, "If the homicide survives the scourging, he is to be executed" (872b-c).

As the preceding brief review has made clear, Plato makes plentiful use of the death penalty. But on what grounds is such a procedure endorsed? To begin our answer to this question, we shall refer to three sections from the text.

(1) After describing the penalties appropriate for temple robbery by non-citizens (unlike citizens, non-citizens are not executed for such a crime), Plato then continues: "Perhaps paying this penalty will teach him restraint and make him a better man: after all, no penalty imposed by law has an evil

purpose, but generally achieves one of two effects: it makes the person who pays the penalty either more virtuous or less wicked" (854d). This passage illustrates an important element in Plato's theory, in that punishment is designed to benefit offenders by curing them of the injustice which infects their souls, and this view about the purpose of punishment is to be found in a number of the dialogues. MacKenzie refers to it as "humanitarian," a term used to emphasize that the theory is teleological. However, unlike utilitarian theories which stress that the aim of punishment is to benefit the community, the humanitarian theory is directed toward the well-being of the individual offender.

(2) The same theme is to be found in a longer passage a few pages later:

> when anyone commits an act of injustice, serious or trivial, the law will combine instruction and constraint, so that in the future either the criminal will never again dare to commit such a crime voluntarily, or he will do it a very great deal less often; and in addition he will pay compensation for the damage he has done. This is something we can achieve only by laws of the highest quality. We may take action, or simply talk to the criminal; we may grant him pleasures or make him suffer; we may honour him, we may disgrace him; we can fine him, or give him gifts. We may use absolutely any means to make him hate injustice and embrace true justice—or at any rate not hate it. But suppose the lawgiver finds a man who's beyond cure—what legal penalty will he provide for this case? He will recognise that the best thing for all such people is to cease to live—best even for themselves. By passing on they will help others, too: first, they will constitute a warning against injustice, and secondly they will leave the state free of scoundrels. That is why the lawgiver should prescribe the death penalty in such cases, by way of punishment for their crimes—but in no other case whatsoever.(862d-863a)

One initial observation can be made concerning the manner, in this latter passage, in which Plato refers to the purging of injustice from the soul of the offender. Sometimes his words suggest that the purpose is to effect a genuine reform in the offender, when he talks of making the criminal "hate injustice and embrace true justice." At other times he appears to be less ambitious; when he says that "the criminal will never again dare to commit such a crime . . . or do it less often . . ." he seems to think that, at least with some people, the most one can hope for is a change in behavior. This appears to reflect distinctions in the earlier passage: when he talks of making the offender "more virtuous," he is aiming at bringing about a change of character; when he refers to making the offender "less wicked," it seems that deterring the offender from acting in like manner in the future is what he intends.

The second passage also introduces some other considerations. Compensation or restitution is to be made to the victim for any damage, but such restitution is not to be thought of as a punishment. People who are to be absolved of any criminal responsibility because of insanity, for example, must still make good any damage caused by their actions (864e). In addition, as a device to promote greater social harmony, restitution is also designed to try to make criminal and victim "friends instead of enemies" (862c).

More central to our purpose, however, is Plato's contention that not all offenders will be amenable to treatment. Some will prove to be incurable, and the best thing for people in such a situation is that they die. Not only will their execution be for their own benefit, but in these circumstances and only in these circumstances, the death penalty will serve two additional purposes, namely deterring others from acting likewise, and protecting society by the elimination of such evil persons and the assurance that they never repeat their deeds.

(3) The final passage occurs at 933e-34c. Once more, we are told that restitution is to be made, proportional to the damage inflicted, and the offender must also pay a penalty "to encourage him to reform" (934a). This penalty, Plato adds, "is to be inflicted not because of the crime (what's done can't be undone) but for the sake of the future: we hope that the offender himself and those that observe his punishment will either be brought to loathe injustice unreservedly or at any rate recover appreciably from this disastrous disease" (934a-b). In addition to what we have seen before, this passage makes one further point. Any justification for the infliction of punishment depends on what effects it brings about in the future. By implication, retribution is rejected on the grounds that "what's done can't be undone." On the other hand, Plato also insists that damage can be compensated for—and, in this sense, what is done can be undone or made up for, an indication that we should make a clear distinction between restitution and retribution.

Humanitarian Execution

Let us now examine each of these facets in more detail, beginning with the claim that the purpose of punishment is to benefit the offender. In general terms this kind of theory has attracted a great deal of attention, and I do not wish to add anything to that debate.[6] Rather, what I want to do is to concentrate on what would appear to be a surprising or even paradoxical claim on Plato's part, namely that *execution* actually benefits the criminal. Normally, those who advocate the value of reform or rehabilitation regard the death penalty as completely incompatible with this aim. If we put a criminal to death, we could be accused of abandoning all hope that the criminal could ever be reformed or rehabilitated.[7]

Plato, however, does have a response to this accusation, one which depends upon the drawing of an analogy between injustice and mental illness. The unjust person suffers from a kind of sickness and is in need of a cure. Whenever it is possible to cure the offender, the purpose of punishment is to bring about that cure. But if a cure should prove to be impossible, it is better for the sufferer not to continue living because life is no longer worthwhile. Here then lies the crucial distinction: the curables are to live because punishment can be of some good to them, whereas the incurables are beyond all possibility of beneficial treatment in this life. They are like patients suffering from a terminal illness, and it is better for their sake that they die to win relief from their suffering.

In some cases, Plato tells us, people in such a predicament ought to take their own lives. He asks us to consider the situation of those who are tortured by an impulse to steal from temples. Such unfortunates are told to make every effort and use every device possible to free themselves from that impulse. Then he adds, "If by doing this you find that your disease (*nosêma*) abates somewhat, well and good; if not, then you should look upon death as the preferable alternative and rid yourself of life" (854c).

There is certainly something remarkable about this passage because Plato grants individuals a considerable degree of autonomy, which is unusual. While they are encouraged to seek aid from the moral leaders of the community, they are credited with sufficient knowledge to realize when they are beyond hope, and they are given the power to act upon their own diagnoses of their condition. It is not made entirely clear whether such drastic action is to be taken before or after the crime in question has been committed, but what does seem evident is that Plato regards it as falling under the rubric of justifiable suicide (873c-d). Such people would have their hands "forced by the pressure of some excruciating and unavoidable misfortune" or would have fallen "into some irremediable disgrace." What also seems to be the case is that this kind of self-imposed capital punishment is going to be a relatively rare occurrence. As far as we can tell, more common will be the situation in which the judges, after careful deliberation, decide that an offender is incurable and that, for his own sake, death is the most appropriate penalty (855c-56a).

An obvious question concerns the distinction between the curable and the incurable. We might expect Plato to institute some detailed procedure to determine the moral character of each individual offender. But what in fact happens is that Plato seems content to take the occurrence of certain kinds of actions, certain sorts of behavior, as sufficient to provide infallible indications of the state of mind of the individual. But even here there does not seem to be any consistent method. For instance, in the case of temple robbery, if citizens commit such an offense just once, they are to be executed as beyond all hope of a cure because their education and upbringing have failed to instil in them an abhorrence against committing such a deed, whereas non-citizens, who have not enjoyed the benefits of such an education, are to receive lesser sentences—they are not beyond hope. Here one offense is assumed to be a sufficiently reliable sign of an incurably evil character. In another case, a single repetition of the offense is the criterion; an atheist with a basically just character is to be sent to a reformatory for a period of no less than five years to mend his ways. If, on release, he is discovered to persist in his atheism, he is to be put to death (908e-9a). In yet another case, someone who is convicted of perjury three times is to be executed for the fourth offense (937c). Finally, in a passage cited earlier (862d-63a) no specific number is mentioned before the judgment about incurability is made. What we are told is that *all* offenders, including those who have committed serious or "great" (*mega*) crimes, are to be regarded as curable and treated accordingly—at least to begin with. It is hard to reconcile this position with the position that a single offense or a single repetition of an offense is to receive the death penalty. Given all this, we may surely feel sceptical about Plato's apparent confidence in thinking that he possesses a method to make reliable distinctions between the curable and the incurable. How can he be so sure in his judgment that certain individuals are totally beyond redemption?

At the same time, we should bear in mind that there are modern parallels to Plato's provisions. In the state of Texas, when juries are to decide whether to impose the death penalty, one of the considerations they must bear in mind is "whether there is a probability that the defendant would commit criminal acts of violence that would constitute a continuing threat to society."[8] Not surprisingly, there has been a lot of criticism directed at this provision, especially concerning the reliability of psychiatric judgments which are supposed to predict the future dangerous actions of offenders. It is not that I seek to minimize Plato's difficulties by citing this modern example; rather I want to indicate that some contemporary jurisdictions have bequeathed themselves the very same problem.

Nonetheless, if a Texas jury approves a death sentence in the belief that the criminal is probably incapable of rehabilitation, it is not likely (and certainly not required) that the jury thinks that the justification for the execution is that it will be of benefit to the criminal first and foremost. But for Plato, as we have seen, a justifiable execution must fulfill the function of benefitting the criminal by relieving him of an incurable psychological burden, and this makes it both tempting and natural to view his use of the death penalty as a kind of state sanctioned euthanasia. Let us pursue this line of thought.

Typically, we find three features that characterize situations where it has been contended that euthanasia is justifiable:

(a) the person involved is suffering from an incurable illness which has reduced the quality of life to an intolerable level of misery;

(b) death provides the only viable way of securing relief from the suffering;

(c) the sufferer wishes to die;

A brief comment on these features: often a distinction is drawn between active and passive euthanasia, but in the present context only the active form is relevant. If the third feature is added to the first two, we have what is usually described as voluntary euthanasia. This type is distinguished from involuntary euthanasia when it is impossible to determine the wishes of the sufferer, generally because the sufferer is either very young or is in a comatose state. An additional category which is also sometimes mentioned but seldom if ever defended is that of nonvoluntary euthanasia. In this case, the person involved has no desire to die and makes his wishes known, but death is imposed contrary to his wishes.

Let us now apply this to what we have found in the Platonic scheme.

(1) The first type of execution which was described earlier as a sort of state-sanctioned suicide bears the closest similarity to voluntary euthanasia, possessing all three features noted above.

(2) The second and most typical case is where execution is imposed and carried out by the state. As we have seen, according to Plato this kind of case will possess the first two euthanasia-making features, but will be unlike voluntary euthanasia in that the state rather than the individual takes the initiative in the decision. However, if we suppose that at least sometimes the criminal comes to concur with the verdict because she agrees with the judgment that her unjust and miserable life is not worth continuing, the case now resembles more closely the situation of voluntary euthanasia, and in practice becomes much like the first case.

(3) Let us now imagine a third possible case. The state sentences a criminal to death in the belief that the criminal is incurably unjust, but this time the criminal does not acquiesce in the decision because she doesn't regard herself as incurable and has no desire to die. Here the state insists that the first two features apply, but the criminal denies it. When the state carries out an execution in these circumstances because the judges maintain their belief that it is for the criminal's own good, this is a situation which is akin to non-voluntary euthanasia.

It is of some interest to note that Plato does not discuss a scenario where this kind of conflict might occur, even though the circumstances that give rise to such a conflict certainly exist in his scheme of things. For instance, the basically just but unreformed atheist might well insist that his soul is not plagued by incurable wickedness, and it is hard to believe that Plato did not even contemplate such a situation. What he does seem to assume, however, is that the judges will be better qualified to know if someone is beyond all hope of reform or rehabilitation than that person himself. Yet if this is his assumption, it surely should have bothered him more than it does. As we have already seen, Plato is perfectly prepared to grant the authority to an individual to take his own life, if that individual believes himself to be incurable. As we have also seen, this means that he credits that individual with sufficient knowledge to decide whether he is beyond hope, as well as the autonomy to act on his decision. But now all such considerations are set aside. This might be understandable if we were able to believe that Plato has given his judges the means to know best what is most conducive to an individual's own well-being. As we saw earlier, the criteria Plato offers for distinguishing the curable from the incurable are far from satisfactory, and don't justify our putting any great trust in the superior competence of the judges.

Even without these problems, this third category of humanitarian execution would probably seem far too paternalistic to win much sympathy from contemporary thinkers. The analogy with nonvoluntary euthanasia makes it too reminiscent of some of the more barbarous Nazi programs. By contrast, the first two kinds can pose some challenges for contemporary abolitionists; if a plausible case can be made to justify instances of voluntary active euthanasia which possess the features (a) through (c) noted above, one can at least raise the question whether the same considerations might not also make voluntary execution plausible. A number of years ago, Sidney Hook and Jacques Barzun did raise the question in a purely theoretical way, and favored the idea that a criminal sentenced to life imprisonment ought to be permitted to choose the death penalty instead. In his reply Hugo Bedau who, not surprisingly, was far from sympathetic to these suggestions, noted that this sort of proposal always tends to occur when mercy killing is advocated as a social policy.[9]

A full discussion of this topic is impossible here. All I want to suggest at this point is that parts of Plato's argument for humanitarian execution are not quite so bizarre and paradoxical as they at first appeared, and that they can serve to stimulate us to address an issue that continues to have some importance in the whole debate about capital punishment. At the same time, of course, it should be admitted that those who favor voluntary euthanasia and, perhaps, voluntary execution put a high value on individual freedom of choice, and this modern liberal doctrine is not at all characteristic of Plato.

Digression on the Insanity Defense

There is an interesting and important passage at 864d-e which deserves more attention than it has generally attracted. Plato interrupts his catalogue of capital crimes and punishments to make clear that certain classes of people should not be held responsible for their actions. "A man who commits one of these crimes might be suffering from insanity (*maneis*), or be as good as insane because of disease (*nosos*), or the effects of advanced senility, or because he is still in the years of childhood." In such cases if clear evidence is shown to the court that a person fell into one of these categories when the criminal act was performed, that person is not to be held liable for her action or suffer any punishment. Restitution must still be made, and in the case of homicide a period of exile is imposed for purposes of ritual purification, but these are not the same as punishments.

To consider this in more detail: there are really two distinguishable categories, firstly those who are insane, and secondly those who, for the purposes of the law, are not really different from the insane, and who, while grouped together, are quite diverse—namely the very young, the senile, and those who are afflicted by an unnamed disease.

To begin, let us briefly consider this second category. While no exact time for the age of majority is mentioned, here Plato is setting down a provision that minors are not to be held responsible for their actions, and so are not to be executed. Presumably the reason is that they lack the necessary knowledge that what they have done is unlawful or they lack the necessary self-control to refrain from committing what would otherwise be capital crimes. But because of their young age they are capable of being reformed or rehabilitated. While the senile may be excused for some of the same reasons, there would appear to be one obvious difference—it is more doubtful that the senile could be persuaded to change their ways.

Now let us turn to insanity. Apart from a few rare and relatively trivial cases, Greek law did not recognise insanity as a defense. K. J. Dover tells us that Greek attitudes concerning insanity are complex, but that the Greeks tended not to distinguish the mad from the bad (one reason for this being the belief that someone who is mad may be answering to a god for an undetected misdeed).[10] However Plato clearly regards insanity as a condition that should absolve a person from responsibility in the most serious situations—and for this he is congratulated by Richard Sorabji for making an advance that Sorabji calls exceptional for his time.[11] Sorabji also points out that in this respect he is much more advanced than Aristotle, and that he is really the first to formulate what has subsequently become known as the insanity defense. Unfortunately, because this passage is so brief, it is impossible to tell what Plato regards as the disabling factors in insanity—ignorance, blameless lack of control, or perhaps both. This makes it difficult to effect any useful comparisons with later attempts to formulate a satisfactory legal criterion of insanity. One can only speculate. Still, it does seem to mark an advance, and, moreover, it gives us a better impression of the operations of the judges. They are now to assess the circumstances concerning insanity in each particular case in order to determine whether a particular individual should be excused, rather than suppose that because a person performs an action of a certain kind, the person must be insane.

Despite this (and herein lies the reason for placing this digression in the place it is), the important advance made by Plato raises another serious problem. It is very difficult to see how on Plato's own terms these people are to be distinguished from the morally incurable—especially since Plato typically thinks of injustice in terms of a medical analogy. The word for disease (*nosos*) which has been used here to describe an excusing condition is virtually the same word as the term which was used at 854c to designate an incurable moral ailment (*nosêma*) which is not an excusing condition.

One difference seems to be that people who are now morally incurable once had it in their power not to be incurable; that is, at one time they still had the capacity to change their character. Certainly within the text there is plenty of evidence to support this idea. There are many passages (some of which were cited earlier) that insist that the purpose of punishment is to reform the offender as well as to serve as a warning to others. Clearly there is a presumption of the possibility of change. Perhaps Plato, like Aristotle, thought that after a certain stage a personality becomes fixed, and that when this stage has been reached, there is no longer any possibility of reform or character change and the person concerned should be regarded as incurable. Unlike the person who is insane and never had the power to bring about change of character state, the morally incurable did at one time possess such power.[12]

However this is to locate the explanation of one's character exclusively on the side of nurture, education, and upbringing, and to suggest that the generation of injustice depends solely upon such causes. But Plato also seems to hold that some people are born with characters like "hard shells" and are so intractable by nature (*phusei*) that they are incapable of being softened by the influence of the laws (853d). Now if Plato believes that at least some people could be partly (or even totally) morally incurable because of something like a natural defect over which they have no control, the previous means of distinguishing the morally incurable from the insane is no longer available.

Another point: the incurably unjust are miserable, and since life is a terrible torture for them, death is preferable. If the life of the insane is also miserable (do they not suffer from an incurable malady?), why should Plato not recommend that for their own good their lives should be terminated? So while in one sense Sorabji is quite right to commend Plato for introducing a version of the insanity defense, the problem is that it becomes a source of confusion because no clear difference is apparent between the morally incurable and the insane.

Deterrence

So far deterrence has only been mentioned in connection with capital offenses, where Plato claims that it serves as an important side benefit of executions. As a justification for the imposition of the death penalty, deterrence continues to loom large. However, in modern times a pressing question has been whether the death penalty is a more effective deterrent than other forms of punishment, such as imprisonment. Now while Plato has nothing to say himself directly about this more modern question, I believe it would be of some value to follow up how close his treatment in fact comes to addressing the issue. As I hope to show, he does come tantalizingly close.

First, no reader of the *Laws* can have the least doubt that Plato employs imprisonment as the penalty for a wide range of offenses. The length of the terms varies according to the seriousness of the offense, and he also seems to envisage different kinds of penal institutions (cf. 909-10, 855). As we should expect, the primary purpose of imprisonment is to benefit the offender. For instance, the 'reformatory' at 909a is intended to cure the basically decent atheist of his erroneous beliefs. At the same time, we should not suppose that reform is the only purpose: prisons also perform the function of deterrence. It must be conceded that Plato doesn't explicitly give prisons this purpose, but it is surely a legitimate inference from what he does say.

At the beginning of Book IX, by way of a general preamble to his penology, Plato tells us that since there will inevitably be people who will break the law, the list of penalties is designed as a threat to deter potential wrongdoers from crime (853b-c). Since imprisonment is one of the penalties, it follows that imprisonment is designed to act as a deterrent. Later, at 855b, if someone is unable to pay a fine, the punishment is to be "a prolonged period of imprisonment which should be open to public view." The public character of the penalty, we may surely suppose, is intended to stress its purpose as a deterrent.

However this is only to begin an answer to the more modern question. Even if it is granted that imprisonment has deterrent value, does Plato really make the least move in the direction of asking whether imprisonment is of comparable deterrent strength to the death penalty? A passage that shows the most promise of casting some light on this issue is to be found at 907e-9d, where Plato stipulates the penalty for the worst kind of atheist. Such a person, he tells us, deserves to die many times for his crimes, but death is not in fact the penalty prescribed. Instead this kind of cunning and dangerous atheist is to be sentenced to solitary confinement for life in a special prison in a remote region of the country (909b-c). The justification for imposing this penalty is not specified, but we can make some progress to determining the justification intended by noting what Plato excludes from consideration.

Plato plainly regards this kind of offender as one of the very worst, and we might expect him to be described as someone whose incurable wickedness was manifestly obvious, in which case we should expect Plato to proceed as he so often does in these situations, and to stipulate that for the offender's own good death is to be the prescribed penalty. However, in this particular instance, the absence of the death penalty indicates that the penalty actually laid down is not motivated by humanitarian criteria. Consequently we can be reasonably sure that, whatever the justification turns out to be, we can exclude considerations that are designated to benefit the offender. (On the other hand, the basically decent but unreformed atheist—certainly a far less serious offender in Plato's eyes—is to be executed. Presumably humanitarian concerns play their usual role in this case, and the sentence is intended in part to be for the offender's own good.)

It should also be noted that Plato's language in this passage contains some elements of retributivism. The heinous and abominable crimes committed by the worst kind of atheist are worthy of (*axia*) and deserve more than one or even two deaths, and the prison to which they are consigned takes its name from the word for retribution (*timôria*).

But despite the presence of these elements, there are reasons for thinking that in this case deterrence has come to occupy the primary position. Since Plato clearly views the atheism in question with utter abhorrence, he is especially anxious to take every step to prevent its occurrence. To do this, it is necessary for him to muster the most terrifying threats possible, and the grim form of imprisonment he describes is intended to fulfill this purpose. Why exclude death? It may be that his humanitarianism supplies the answer. In his eyes execution usually provides some compensatory benefit to the criminal by putting him out of his misery. So in order to maximize the threat against this worst of crimes, Plato may be seeking to exclude any penalty that contains any conceivable element of benefit to the offender. The kind of civil death involved in solitary confinement and the absence of any relief from the life of misery caused by extreme wickedness—such a state may well strike Plato as worse than death. In other words, it certainly appears that Plato may regard this form of imprisonment as providing a more potent deterrent threat than death.[13]

Now this is to take matters further than Plato himself takes them. Of course, he does not say that imprisonment is to be the penalty in this case because he thinks that it has a comparable or even more powerful deterrent effect than the death penalty. However, though the matter is not addressed explicitly, all the materials necessary for addressing it are implicitly there, and there seems no reason in principle why Plato should not have discussed the more modern question. Moreover if the issue can be raised in connection with one capital crime, there is no reason, from the point of view of deterrence alone, why it should not be raised for other capital crimes.

There is a related question. Plato doesn't simply justify execution for humanitarian reasons or because of its value as a deterrent. It also rids us of incurably vicious offenders (863a) and so protects society by ensuring that such offenders do not repeat their crimes. Similarly nowadays the death penalty is sometimes defended on the grounds that it affords the best form of protection for society. Then the question is raised—can imprisonment provide sufficiently acceptable levels of protection so that this concern can be adequately met? Once again, Plato does not address the issue directly; however given the descriptions in 909, he seems to envisage institutions where security would be extremely tight, and he does not appear to contemplate the possibility of any escape from them.

Why does Plato not press matters further than he does? Some might seek to explain this by taking the position that at this time incarceration as a penalty was uncommon or even unknown, and for this reason questions about its effectiveness as a deterrent would not arise. Stalley[14] tells us that it wasn't generally employed, except for people awaiting trial or sentence. Sorabji[15] agrees, and describes Plato's use of imprisonment as an original invention, primarily designed for moral re-education. However the authorities are by no means agreed on this, and Harrison[16] and MacDowell[17] adopt a different position. They insist that while it may have been used less commonly then than in modern times, it certainly did exist as a perfectly viable penalty. Both cite *Apology* 37b-c as one item of evidence, where Socrates considers, only to reject, imprisonment as an alternative penalty to execution. For our purposes, however, it is not essential to adopt any particular stance in this dispute.

(1) If imprisonment was a well-established practice, which Plato takes over (and perhaps extends), we might still wish that with respect to

deterrence or protection he had raised the modern question of whether it is as effective as the death penalty.

(2) But if Plato really is an innovator, the same question arises. If he is recommending the use of imprisonment as a punishment, could he not have explored its potential more thoroughly, and asked whether it might have served some of the functions of execution equally well?

Retribution

In a passage which was cited earlier in full (862d-63a), Plato says that if anyone commits an offense *great or small* (*mega ê smikron*), every effort is to be made to encourage the offender to mend his ways. Later he adds that if we find someone who resists all treatment, he is to be condemned as incurable and sentenced to death. If we conjoin these two parts of the passage, the consequence seems outrageously severe, in that the repetition of small offenses is made sufficient reason for execution. Is a person who persists in breaking the law forbidding the planting of trees too close to a neighbor's property, or who repeatedly fails to restrain his cattle from straying (843d-e), to be liable to the death penalty? Is the unrepentant bachelor (774a-d) who refuses to obey the marriage laws to be executed for his incurable stubbornness? What surely strikes us as wrong here is that such penalties seem so patently unfair (or even absurd) because they look to be out of all proportion to the offense. It is this feature of proportionality, where the severity of the punishment fits the seriousness of the crime, which has been traditionally supplied by retribution. If Plato's theory is completely nonretributive in nature (as would seem to be the case here), this seems to be the cause of considerable difficulties.

A common complaint about utilitarian or humanitarian theory is that there is no inherent requirement for the penalty to be proportioned to the crime. If there is a fit, it will be incidental—that is, when the fit just happens to fulfill utilitarian or humanitarian purposes. There are no essential limits imposed by such theories: as Plato puts it, "we may use absolutely *any* means to make him hate injustice and embrace true justice" (862d). Given this latitude, it becomes permissible for the legislator to introduce the most severe penalty for relatively trivial offenses.

This passage from the *Laws* with its indirect rejection of retribution is not isolated. MacKenzie[18] argues at length that while retributive themes occur quite frequently in his eschatology, in his "philosophical" writing Plato repudiates retribution, not indirectly but quite explicitly. A section from the "great speech" in the *Protagoras* is often quoted: ". . . he who desires to inflict rational punishment does not punish for the sake of a past wrong which cannot be undone; he has regard to the future and is desirous that the man who is punished, and he who sees him punished, may be deterred from doing wrong again" (324b, trans. Ostwald). Similarly in the *Laws* (933d-34a) there is a reiteration of the position that "what's done can't be undone," where Plato denies that any act of injustice once committed can be "uncommitted," as it were.

Yet despite the official repudiation we do find elements of retributivism in the *Laws*, nor are these confined simply to the eschatological passages, as MacKenzie would contend.[19] On a number of occasions there is a specification that the penalty match the deed. One good example of this occurs during part of the treatment of homicide. Plato believes that premeditated murder is worse than a killing that happens on the spur of the moment during a fit of anger, and that the penalties imposed should reflect this difference. In his own words, "something which resembles a greater evil should attract a greater punishment, whereas a lesser penalty should be visited on that which resembles a lesser evil" (867b-c).[20] Another instructive passage is to be found at 876e, where Plato tells us that examples of penalties to be imposed have been laid down for judges to imitate "to stop them exceeding the due limits of justice" (*tou mêpote bainein exô tês dikês*). If judges were to operate simply using utilitarian or humanitarian requirements, there would be nothing to prevent their going to all kinds of excess in order to promote those ends. But here Plato plainly sees that what justice (i.e., retributive justice) demands may not be consistent with utilitarian or humanitarian considerations. Hence it is necessary to lay down some fixed penalties which are to serve as upper limits in order to prevent the imposition of penalties that could be out of all proportion to the nature of the offenses.

So despite the official rejection of retribution, there is also clear evidence that elements of some important features of retributive theory do find their way into Plato's thinking. It is perhaps a pity that the importance of the retributive contribution wasn't recognized more explicitly as a check. If it had been, then the excesses of the passage with which this section began would surely have been avoided.

A few final words on some difficulties in Plato's treatment of retribution. We've already indicated that there is evidence in the *Laws* that Plato wishes to preserve the retributive feature of proportionality. However, he runs into some problems because he cannot always make his mind up whether the penalty should be proportional to the actual as opposed to intended outcome of criminal activity. Consider, for instance, a section beginning at 876e where he tries to assess what ought to be the appropriate penalty for cases where one person wounds another. A particularly vexing situation is that of a citizen who deliberately attempts to kill another citizen, but who only succeeds in wounding him. What should the punishment be? He begins by saying that such an attack should be treated in exactly the same manner as a premeditated murder—and here the *intended* outcome is what counts. But then he immediately checks himself, and says we should respect his luck and his "guardian angel" (*daimôn*) which intervened to save him from complete disaster. In the end a lesser penalty is prescribed than that for premeditated murder, and so the *actual* outcome is made the determining factor. If we find Plato less than satisfactory on this matter, we have the same problem today. In some jurisdictions, death is the penalty for premeditated murder, but attempted murder receives a lesser penalty. We may well wonder whether luck or even plain incompetence on the part of the criminal should play the part it does.

Conclusion

On the final page of his book, Saunders makes some significantly revealing remarks. He describes himself as having made an attempt to do his "best for Plato" by providing us with a consistent account of his penology and penal code. But he goes on to add

> Consistency, however, does not protect from criticism. The major drawback of any penology such as Plato's is that to permit "any" method of punishment which will prevent the criminal from offending again is an unconscionable infringement of his status as a responsible person . . . Such an extreme reformative position has to be tempered by some notion of desert, which permits suffering to be imposed only in some reasonable relationship to the gravity of the offense.[21]

Saunders goes on to conclude that even if Plato's theory strictly excludes any such features, because his language and concepts sound much like those of conventional retributivism, it is more than likely that at least in the early stages the operations of the Magnesian state will be conducted in ways which moderate the extreme forward-looking provisions, by taking due account of desert and proportionality. But, one might respond to Saunders, the paradoxical outcome would appear to be that as the Magnesian officials become more attuned to Platonic philosophy, the moderating elements will gradually disappear, so making the new state less immune from criticism.

As we saw earlier, however, such desperate maneuvering can be avoided if we abandon the position that Plato's theory is to be interpreted so as to exclude retributive features, though it certainly would have been preferable if Plato had given them a more explicit recognition. Such recognition would have meant that his account could have been saved from one obvious source of censure, namely the use of execution as a penalty for repeated trivial offenses. The principle of proportionality would ensure that execution would be restricted to only very grave crimes. In itself such a modification would require a very minor change and would continue to keep retributive considerations in a supplementary position in his whole theory.

The potential for strikingly significant change occurs when we assess his position on deterrence and the protection of society. As we have seen, in the case of what Plato regards as one extremely serious crime, he seems to think that a specially severe form of incarceration will prove a more effective deterrent than execution. If this is true in the case of one serious crime, there appears to be no reason why the same deterrent purposes could not be achieved for all serious crimes by the use of imprisonment. Doubtless, this is a surprising development, but not apparently excluded by the logic of the position he has adopted.

Yet, paradoxically perhaps, the feature which would appear to exert the greatest influence upon Plato to retain the death penalty is his humanitarianism. Assuming that he can overcome the various difficulties involved in giving a satisfactory definition of the incurables, as long as he believes that those who are irremediably unjust are better off dead because of their misery, it is difficult to see that he would change his mind on this. Of course, there does remain something strange about his contention that the unjust are better off dead. If he had retained one position suggested by Socrates at the end of the *Apology* that death is an annihilation of consciousness, it might be easier to believe such a state to be preferable to a life of psychological torture. But much of his eschatology emphasizes that the agonies of the unjust continue after death. It may be true that according to the doctrine of the *Gorgias* the unjust who are dead are slightly better off than those who are alive because in the afterlife they can no longer cause misery but only suffer it. However in the *Laws* (870e), as we saw, the story is that certain malefactors are fated to suffer the very same wrongs they inflicted, and so, albeit unwillingly, they play a part in causing an endless process of wrongdoing.

From the perspective of a modern reader, this aspect of Plato's theory will probably seem the least plausible. With the possible exception of cases where a criminal requests execution, a possibility referred to earlier, it is difficult to see how the infliction of the death penalty could be claimed to benefit the criminal, and while such a claim is undeniably prominent in Plato's account, it is unlikely to win much sympathy.

However, if the other elements in his theory are to be viewed as I have suggested, the results have the potential to be most intriguing. While superficially Plato endorses a high rate of execution, due recognition of the check imposed by retributivism would lead to more severe restrictions in its use. Then again, if he had only explored more thoroughly the alternative function that imprisonment could perform in terms of its being an equally or more effective source of deterrence and protection for society—which he does in one case—he might well have come to some startlingly different conclusions. It would be too much of an exaggeration to suggest that Plato would ever have been an abolitionist, but parts of his theory push him further in that direction than he seems to have realized.

Notes

1. R. F. Stalley, "Plato and the Theory of Punishment," *Polis* 10 (1992): 113-28 and R. F. Stalley, "Punishment in Plato's *Laws*," *History of Political Thought* 15 (1995): 469-87.

2. Here and elsewhere I use the translation of the *Laws* by T. J. Saunders (Harmondsworth, Eng.: Penguin Books, 1970).

3. D. M. MacDowell, *Athenian Homicide Law* (Manchester, Eng.: Manchester University Press, 1966), 85-89.

4. MacDowell, *Homicide Law*, 8.

5. Roger Hood, *The Death Penalty* (Oxford: Clarendon Press, 1989), 18.

6. For a good review of the issues involved, see Stalley, "Punishment in *Laws*," 470-75.

7. This particular issue has certainly perplexed the commentators; Saunders (*Laws*, 181-83) wrestles with it, but is reduced to offering a number of tentative suggestions about how execution might be said to benefit the offender, and Stalley speculates that it might prevent offenders "from sinking even lower into viciousness and helps them to avoid the penalties which await the wicked after death" ("Punishment in *Laws*," 469). While there is certainly something to be said for Stalley's suggestion, it does not cover the case of those offenders mentioned at 870e who are condemned by their very act to be engaged in an endless cycle of offenses.

8. Hood, *Death Penalty*, 94.

9. *The Death Penalty in America* (2nd. ed.), Hugo Bedau, ed. (New York: Doubleday, 1967), 146-65, 214-31.

10. K. J. Dover, *Greek Popular Morality in the Time of Plato and Aristotle* (Oxford: Clarendon Press, 1974), 126-29.

11. Richard Sorabji, *Necessity, Cause and Blame* (Ithaca: Cornell University Press, 1980), 266.

12. Further complications are introduced in some of the eschatological passages. For instance, at 870e Plato tells the tale that in their next life on earth murderers are preordained to suffer the same treatment they inflicted on their victims: hence, some people are fated in advance to commit incurably wicked deeds—and the cycle continues.

13. On this point, Plato's position can be compared with that taken by J. S. Mill. One of Mill's arguments in favor of retaining capital punishment was that any comparable alternative, such as hard labor for life, would be more cruel than death and it would be kinder to execute. While Plato agrees that some forms of imprisonment are worse than death, for him this is a reason not to execute society's worst offenders. Also worth noting is a difference between Plato and modern abolitionists who contend that the death penalty has no uniquely effective deterrent or protective value. These abolitionists believe that death is indeed a more severe penalty than imprisonment. They also maintain that if two penalties that differ in their severity are equally effective in accomplishing certain purposes, there is no justification for preferring the more severe. One should only use as much force as the circumstances require.

If this interpretation is correct, it may help answer a problem mentioned by Saunders, when he says that "it is difficult to see what other reason Plato can have for letting the more harmful offenders go on living, when he has explicitly said that they 'deserve' to die many deaths" (*Laws*, 159).

14. R. F. Stalley, *An Introduction to Plato's "Laws"* (Oxford: Blackwell, 1983), 138.

15. Sorabji, *Necessity*, 295.

16. A. R. W. Harrison, *The Laws of Athens* (Oxford: Clarendon, 1971), 177.

17. D. M. MacDowell, *The Law in Classical Athens* (London: Thames and Hudson, 1978), 256-57.

18. Mary Margaret MacKenzie, *Plato on Punishment* (Berkeley: University of California Press, 1981), chs. 11, 13.

19. One basic feature of retributive theory is correctly pointed out by Saunders, namely that punishment must be for an offense. "It should be noted that nowhere in the *Laws* is one punished simply for *being* unjust: one has to commit an offense first" (*Laws*, 191, n. 183).

20. Given his commitment to seeing Plato's theory as a genuine medical penology, Saunders attempts to interpret this and similar passages which refer to proportionality solely in terms of psychic injustice, though he has to concede that "Plato is capable of talking occasionally in terms of penalties that 'are worthy of' or 'fit' the crime, without reference to mental states so as to appear to be operating on some retributive theory of punishment" (*Laws*, 194). Similarly, in his comments on the punishment meted out to a person guilty of involuntary homicide, where in the very nature of the case there is no injustice in the soul of the perpetrator of the deed, Saunders is compelled to engage in some fancy footwork to persuade us that what Plato describes as punishment shouldn't really be construed as punishment (*Laws*, 223-24).

21. Saunders, *Laws*, 356.

Index

Adams, John, 183-91
adultery, 73-79, 103-4, 160
Aphrodite, 73-74, 76-79, 89n12, 104-5
Arendt, Hannah, 154, 160-61
aristocracy, 55, 61, 63, 161, 170-72, 175-76, 185, 187-89, 190n26, 197n1, 202-4, 213, 215n12, 220, 222-24, 229, 230n10, 232, 234
Aristotle, *Eudemian Ethics*, 44; *Nicomachean Ethics*, 44, 46, 47, 50, 57, 59, 60n25, 131, 136n17, 141, 153-56, 159, 162, 163, 165, 169, 171, 172-73, 175, 183, 186, 187, 213, 214, 215n10, 220, 230-31, 232n17; *Rhetoric*, 136n17, 155, 156, 170-71, 213, 229, 231, 235-37
assembly, popular, 188, 189, 229-31, 234-35
Athenian Stranger, 115-16, 118-20, 124-25, 160n18
Athens, 157n11, 159n16, 175n62, 189-90, 230n6, 237n24, 244-45, 256
authority: of law, 9, 117-18, 130-49, 164, 169-71, 199-200, 230; political, 55-56, 168-70, 173-74, 184, 187-89, 197-98, 229n2, 230n5, 231-32, 237

Bodéüs, Richard, 154, 199n18

city in speech, 36, 41-43, 47-54, 59, 63
common good, 5, 11, 14, 18-19, 73n7, 105, 106
constitution, 153, 197n11, 215, 217-23, 231n11, 232n16, 234, 235; American, 118, 183, 190-91; best, *see* regime, best; mixed, 187-90
convention (or custom), 28-32, 35, 37-38, 129, 156-59, 162, 176, 198-99
Crete, 118-19, 166, 217-18, 223n34, 232n16, 233n20, 234n21

deliberation, 88, 154, 169, 171, 175-76, 187, 199-200, 214n6, 223, 229-31, 234-37, 248
democracy, 17-18, 56-57, 61, 84-85, 103-6, 157n11, 161,169-70, 173-75, 187-91, 196, 199-200, 203-6, 208, 221-23, 231-33, 237n24

election, 174, 187-88, 229-30, 232-33
equality, 8, 17, 46-47, 50, 57, 61, 65, 125, 163-64, 169, 174-75, 186, 188, 205, 206, 220

faction, 162-64, 170, 191, 201-2, 206
Federalist Papers, The, 183, 189-90, 201
Foucault, Michel, 131, 134n14

Glaucon, 3-5, 8, 11-13, 16, 18, 20, 21n37, 27-28, 32-38, 41-42, 47-48, 50-53, 58, 63

happiness, 3-4, 6, 18, 19, 21-23, 29, 37, 44, 162-63, 175, 190
Hobbes, Thomas, 165, 171, 205n28
Hippodamus, 157, 216-18
Homer, *Iliad*, 69, 73n7, 89n13, 95, 99, 103, 105-6, 143

Jefferson, Thomas, 190-91
judiciary: office or function, 119n1,
    168-70, 174, 175, 235-37; power,
    157n11, 189

kingship, 21-22, 55, 61, 64-65, 134,
    140, 171-72, 185, 188, 190n26,
    195-200, 202-4, 206-8
Koran, 76n12, 245

law: divine, 114, 117-18, 120-21, 125,
    129-31, 133, 144-48; human, 130-
    33, 135-36, 138-48; natural, 129,
    136, 155-56, 158-59, 168, 199; rule
    of, 64n27, 126, 153-59, 168-69,
    171, 184, 191, 195, 198-203, 205,
    208, 216, 237; traditional (*patrioi
    nomoi*), 157-59, 168-69; unwritten,
    156, 157n11; written, 118, 156,
    237n24
lawmaking (or legislation), 113, 116,
    118-21, 124, 154n2, 155-59, 216-
    17, 221, 224, 229-31, 233-35, 236-
    37
legislative science, 213-25, 230-31
legislator, 116-20, 154-69, 173, 175-
    76, 199, 213-20, 222-24, 229, 231,
    236-37, 257
Locke, John, 171, 184, 190

Machiavelli, Niccolò, 125, 154n2,
    189n20
Madison, James, 183, 189-91
Mansfield, Harvey, 27n1, 169n36,
    171n45, 172n51, 174n57, 176n64,
    197n10
medicine, politics as, 51-52, 116, 157,
    198, 213n3, 214-16, 218, 221, 253,
    258n20
middle class, 164-66, 184, 186-87,
    222-23
Miller, Fred D., Jr., 41nn1-3, 56n24,
    60n25
monarchy. *See* kingship
Montesquieu, 189, 232n18
myth, 22, 32, 38, 123, 143-45

Nichols, Mary, 7n12, 21n35, 27n1,
    41n2, 62n26, 195-97, 204, 207-8,
    215nn7, 12, 217n16, 218n18,

219n19, 220-23
nomos, 28, 37-38, 154-57, 168n34,
    199, 237n24
Nussbaum, Martha, 41n2, 140n24, 196,
    198n16, 213nn2, 3, 215, 221n25

Odysseus, 36n12, 83-103, 106
oligarchy, 55-57, 60-61, 63, 157n11,
    161, 169-70, 173,187-88, 195, 202-
    3, 221-24, 229, 230n10, 234,
    237n24
Ostwald, Martin, 156n9, 157n11,
    168n34, 237n24

Pangle, Thomas, 119n16, 121, 184n8,
    186n13
participation, political, 161, 163-64,
    170, 173-77, 182, 187, 213-26, 219-
    20, 222-24, 229n1, 230-35
partnership, political, 42-46, 48-49, 52-
    61, 63, 65, 71-80, 84, 87n8, 88, 90,
    94-98, 102, 116-17, 121, 123, 132,
    134, 138, 142
philosopher, 3, 8-23, 32, 34, 36-38, 41-
    43, 115, 118, 171, 172n48, 175-76,
    187n14, 195, 259
philosopher-king, 3, 8-23, 36, 42, 43,
    47, 64-65, 195
poetry, 69-72, 76n12, 79-80, 94-95
Plato, *Apology*, 146, 256, 260; *Gor-
    gias*, 260; *Laws*, 65, 113-26,
    160n18, 167n30, 188, 230n10,
    231n11,232, 243-61, *Republic*, 3-
    23, 27-28, 32-38, 41-54, 57-66,
    83, 117, 162, 167n30, 195, 204n24,
    207n30; *Statesman*, 44, 141, 214,
    221, 222
polity, 43, 55, 60-61, 157n11, 161,
    174-75, 184-86, 187-88, 196,
    215n13, 221-224. *See also* regime,
    mixed
Polybius, 188-89
privacy, 7, 12, 17-19, 35, 36n12, 87-
    88, 153-54, 160-63, 168-70, 175-76
property, 7, 18, 41-43, 45, 56, 87, 93,
    125, 164, 170, 173-74, 185-87, 191,
    231
prudence (or practical wisdom), 28,
    118, 131, 157, 167, 171, 174, 176,
    184, 187, 214, 215n6, 229-33, 236

About the Contributors

Clifford A. Bates, Jr., earned his Ph.D. from Northern Illinois University in political philosophy and has been a visiting scholar at Brown University.

Paul Bullen received his Ph.D. in political science from the University of Chicago, where he is now doing post-doctoral work. He has taught constitutional law, comparative legal systems, and legal theory at Roosevelt University, and leads an Internet discussion list on Aristotle's *Politics*.

Brian Calvert is an associate professor of philosophy at the University of Guelph, Ontario, Canada, and the author of a number of articles in Greek philosophy, the philosophy of religion, and social philosophy.

Tim Collins recently defended his dissertation at the University of Virginia and teaches government and history at Campbell University in North Carolina.

William E. Conklin is Professor of Law at the University of Windsor in Ontario, Canada.

Patrick J. Deneen holds a Ph.D. from Rutgers University and is now employed at the U.S. Information Agency. His dissertation on the *Odyssey* won the Leo Strauss Award in political philosophy in 1995.

In Ha Jang is a research fellow in the Department of Political Science at the University of Toronto and holds a Ph.D. from Boston College.

Nick Janszen is a graduate of Berry College and earned a Ph.D. in politics at the University of Dallas. He is currently employed by the U.S. Department of State, and has taught at Felician College, Adams State College, and Arkansas State University.

Fred D. Miller, Jr., is Professor of Philosophy and Executive Director of the Social Philosophy and Policy Center at Bowling Green State University. In addition to publishing many articles on Greek philosophy, he is the author of *Nature, Justice, and Rights in Aristotle's "Politics"* and co-editor with David Keyt of *A Companion to Aristotle's "Politics."*

Joshua Parens is an NEH Postdoctoral Fellow in the Core Curriculum of Boston University. He is the author of *Metaphysics as Rhetoric: Alfarabi's "Summary of Plato's 'Laws'"* and of articles published in the *American Political Science Review*, *Polity* and *PS*.

Katherine Philippakis is a J.D./Ph.D. candidate at Arizona State University. She has an M.Litt. in politics from Oxford University, an M.Phil. in philosophy from the University of St. Andrews.

Leslie G. Rubin is Associate Director of the Society for Greek Political Thought, North American Chapter, and has taught political science at Kenyon College, the University of Houston, and Duquesne University.

John T. Scott received his Ph.D. in political science from the University of Chicago and is currently teaching in the Department of Political Science and the Honors College at the University of Houston. He has previously written on Machiavelli, Hobbes, and Rousseau.

Judith A. Swanson teaches political science at Boston University and is the author of *The Public and the Private in Aristotle's Political Philosophy*.